DRAMATIST IN AMERICA

DRAMATIST IN AMERICA

LETTERS OF
Maxwell Anderson, *1912–1958*

EDITED BY LAURENCE G. AVERY

The University of North Carolina Press, Chapel Hill

Frontispiece by Paul Radkai; courtesy of Mrs. Maxwell Anderson

Copyright © 1977 by
The University of North Carolina Press
All rights reserved
Manufactured in the United States of America
ISBN 0-8078-1309-5
Library of Congress Catalog Card Number 77-4491

Library of Congress Cataloging in Publication Data

Anderson, Maxwell, 1888–1959.
  Dramatist in America.

  Includes index.
  1. Anderson, Maxwell, 1888–1959—Correspondence.
2. Dramatists, American—20th century—Correspondence.
I. Avery, Laurence G. II. Title.
PS3501.N256Z53 1977   812'.5'2 [B]   77-4491
ISBN 0-8078-1309-5

FOR RACHEL, JONATHAN, AND LAURA

CONTENTS

ACKNOWLEDGMENTS

This edition of her husband's letters gives me another opportunity to express my appreciation of Mrs. Maxwell Anderson. Her contribution to the edition went much beyond permission to publish the letters and documents. In the large job of gathering the letters she was extremely helpful. And the multitude of matters that work on the edition brought before her she handled in a spirit of gracious cooperation. For all of her efforts on behalf of the edition, and her understanding and encouragement throughout, I am grateful.

I am also grateful to Lela Anderson Chambers, who made available to this edition her carefully assembled collection of her brother's letters and enriched the edition with her knowledge of the Anderson family's history. John F. Wharton, a founder of the Playwright's Company and now its chronicler, likewise put me in his debt by supplying the large number of Anderson letters in his possession and generously answering questions about them.

To the other individuals and the institutions that made available the Anderson letters and documents in their possession I also wish to express my thanks. They are Harold Anderson; Hesper Anderson; Quentin Anderson; Enid Bagnold; Mabel Driscoll Bailey; Mrs. S. N. Behrman; Bancroft Library, University of California at Berkeley; Avery Chambers; Oral History Collection, Columbia University; Manuscript Division, Library of Congress; Houghton Library, Harvard University; Lilly Library, Indiana University; Lotte Lenya; Middlebury College Library; Newberry Library; Theatre Collection, Library & Museum of the Performing Arts, New York Public Library at Lincoln Center; Southern Historical Collection, Louis Round Wilson Library, University of North Carolina at Chapel Hill; Chester Fritz Library, University of North Dakota; Charles Patterson Van Pelt Library, University of Pennsylvania; Princeton University Library; Alfred S. Shivers; University Library, Stanford University; George Arents Research Library, Syracuse University; Humanities Research Center, University of Texas at Austin; Clifton Waller Barrett Library, University of Virginia; Wellesley College Library; Wisconsin Center for Film and Theater Research, University of Wisconsin; Beinecke Rare Book and Manuscript Library, Yale University.

For permission to quote from unpublished letters and documents that they control, I wish to thank Robert Anderson, Lela Anderson Chambers, Allardyce Nicoll, Mrs. Robert E. Sherwood, and John F. Wharton. After repeated unsuccessful attempts to locate holders of the rights to a few other documents, I have retained quotations from them on the assumption that permission to do so would not have been withheld.

In tracing letters, answering questions about them, or obtaining information about Anderson's books, I received valuable assistance from the following, to whom I am grateful: Robert Anderson; Celeste Ashley, Theatre Librarian, Stanford University; Roy P. Basler, former Chief of the Manuscript Division, Library of Congress, and the present Chief of the Division, John C. Broderick; Irene Burns; Jerome Chodorov; George Cukor; George E. Delury, Editor, *World Almanac*; Rodney G. Dennis, Curator of Manuscripts, Houghton Library, Harvard University; Ann Farr, Princeton University Library; Nancy R. Frazier, Humanities Division, Louis Round Wilson Library, University of North Carolina at Chapel Hill; Donald Gallup, Curator of the Collection of American Literature, Beinecke Library, Yale University; Patricia Grace of Doubleday & Company; Milton Gross, School of Journalism, University of Missouri; Anne Grossman; Beth Halsall, Middlebury College Library; Diana Haskell, Special Collections, Newberry Library; Mary M. Hirth, former Librarian, Humanities Research Center, University of Texas at Austin, Lord Horder of Gerald Duckworth and Company Limited; Gregory A. Johnson, Manuscripts Department, Alderman Library, University of Virginia; Kay I. Johnson, formerly of the Wisconsin Center for Film and Theater Research, University of Wisconsin; Barbara Kenealy of William Morrow & Company; William Koppelman of Harold Freedman Brandt & Brandt Dramatic Department; Elfrieda Lang, Curator of Manuscripts, Lilly Library, Indiana University; Maureen C. Marry of Simon & Schuster, Inc.; Michael G. Martin, Jr., Southern Historical Collection, Louis Round Wilson Library, University of North Carolina at Chapel Hill; Mrs. Fred B. McCall; Jim Mendell of Viking Press; June Moll, former Librarian, Humanities Research Center, University of Texas at Austin; Philip F. Mooney, Assistant Director, George Arents Research Library, Syracuse University; Paul

Myers, Curator of the Theatre Collection, New York Public Library at Lincoln Center; Robert Newman; Valerie Norwood of Longman Group Limited; M. Abbott Van Nostrand of Samuel French, Inc.; Martine Préd'Homme of the *International Herald Tribune*; Estelle Rebec, Manuscript Division, Bancroft Library, University of California at Berkeley; V. Cullum Rogers, Drama Department, University of North Carolina at Chapel Hill; Susan R. Rosenberg, Archivist, University Library, Stanford University; Samuel Selden, Drama Department, University of North Carolina at Chapel Hill; Gail Sloan of David McKay Company; Katherine Staples, English Department, University of Texas at Austin; Louis M. Starr, Director, Oral History Collection, Columbia University; Mrs. F. Durand Taylor; Carolyn A. Wallace, Director, Southern Historical Collection, Louis Round Wilson Library, University of North Carolina at Chapel Hill; Neda M. Westlake, Curator of the Rare Book Collection, Van Pelt Library, University of Pennsylvania; Robert P. Wilkins, Editor, *North Dakota Quarterly*; Ronald S. Wilkinson, Manuscript Division, Library of Congress.

My interest in Anderson's letters originated at the University of Texas, and this edition would have been impossible in its present form without the sustained support of a host of people there. The Humanities Research Center at the university houses the largest collection of Anderson's papers, including both sides of much of his correspondence. At an early stage of the work on this edition Professors C. L. Cline and Gordon Mills, for whom my respect and affection are long-standing, simplified my access to the papers and thereby eased all later stages of the work. Professor F. Warren Roberts, Director of the center, made it the ideal facility for conducting research on the letters by his unfailing responsiveness to the needs of the work. And the efficient and congenial assistance of the staff at the center put me deeply in their debt. Assistant Director David Farmer kept me informed of developments in the collection and assisted me in numerous other ways. And Associate Librarian John R. Payne and his staff, by repeated investigation of the papers on my behalf, became partners in the research that underpins this edition. To each person there who participated in the work I am grateful.

It is a special pleasure to acknowledge the support of this edition by my own university. The University Research Council provided a grant for travel and other expenses connected with the edition, then provided a publication subsidy, and Dean George R. Holcomb, chairman of the council, administered the grants considerately. The Wilson Library reference staff, headed by Louise Hall, was indis-

pensable to the research entailed by the edition, and Pattie B.
McIntyre and Mary R. Ishaq made a special effort to see that none of
my questions went unanswered. My department through its successive
chairmen, C. Carroll Hollis, James R. Gaskin, and William R.
Harmon, provided much timely aid. My assistants while preparing the
edition were Rheumell Griffis, Deborah S. Kolb, Barbara Werner,
Wayne Sherrill, Kenneth Gelburd, Richard Schramm, and Arthur
Benjamin Chitty. They bestowed on the edition much ability,
perseverance, and good will, and their performance in this holds great
promise for the future work they undertake.

While preparing the edition, I was fortunate in the colleagues
who counseled me about it. Professors O. M. Brack, Jr., C. Carroll
Hollis, and Lewis Leary considered the edition at an early stage and
advised me concerning editorial principles and practice. Professors
Dennis G. Donovan and Harold I. Shapiro read the edition at a later
stage and saved it from several mistakes. And Professors Christopher
M. Armitage and C. Hugh Holman assisted me with particular
matters of editorial procedure as they arose. This edition has gained
much by the cooperation of these colleagues and friends, and to each
of them I am grateful.

My family encouraged and assisted me from the beginning of the
work on the edition, and at the end, along with two friends, were
indispensable to its completion. Preparation of the index could not
have gone as smoothly as it did without the efforts of Ruby V. Reid;
Rachel, Jonathan, and Laura Avery; and Julius and Martha Avery. On
the other hand the task of proofreading the book a final time was
made considerably lighter by Ben and Mary Glen Chitty. I am happy
for this opportunity to express publicly my thanks to all of them.

Finally, as with any project of this nature the search for
Anderson's letters is an ongoing process, and I should be most grateful
for directions to letters not accounted for in this edition.

Department of English
University of North Carolina at Chapel Hill
June, 1976

INTRODUCTION

Maxwell Anderson wrote at least several thousand letters over a long and active career. Before the middle twenties, as he moved from North Dakota to California and then to New York, he corresponded with a small group of friends and with people who began to hear about him as a poet. From the middle twenties onward, following the phenomenal success of *What Price Glory* in 1924, he was among the most prominent playwrights in America and received hundreds of letters from people all over the country, then from all over the world. Practically all of those letters he at least acknowledged, and many he answered in detail. After 1938, when he joined in forming the Playwrights' Company and thus became his own producer, Anderson's correspondence took on the additional tasks of arranging for actors, directors, and theaters for his own plays, of criticizing the scripts of his colleagues, Elmer Rice, Sidney Howard, S. N. Behrman, and Robert Sherwood, and of conducting company business. With a few friends outside the theater and with members of his large family, he also corresponded extensively.

Although his letters ran into the thousands, their rate of survival is not great. Many went the way of the dustbin, including some the loss of which is especially regrettable. Despite the fact that he was their neighbor, Anderson had occasions to correspond with Kurt Weill and Burgess Meredith, both of whom were involved with several of his plays, but they lacked the letter-collecting habit altogether. And the same is true of another neighbor, the poet Frank E. Hill, a lifelong friend who frequently read and criticized early drafts of Anderson's plays. Still other letters, which were thought preserved, cannot be located now. Enid Bagnold typifies numerous recipients who found a few Anderson letters where they remembered many; other recipients, remembering many, usually in boxes in the attic, found none. Nor have attics been the only dangerous repositories, for publishers' files have proved just as risky. Anderson's first book helped to launch Simon & Schuster, but the company's early files no longer exist. And William Sloane Associates, Anderson's last publisher, has since merged with William Morrow & Company and transferred its files incompletely.

Among the letters known to survive, four groups were not available to this edition: the letters held by the heirs of Anderson's sister Ethel, those held by his brother Kenneth, the letters to Josephine Herbst in the Beinecke Library at Yale University, and the letters deposited in the Humanities Research Center at the University of Texas by Anderson's estate in 1973. The letters in his sister's estate, most of them written to her, deal largely with family matters. The letters to Kenneth, while they cover much family ground, pertain as well to the formation and operation of Anderson House, the publishing company organized by the two brothers in 1933 for the publication of Maxwell's work. For reasons best known to themselves, Kenneth Anderson and Ethel's son Ralph Chambers have not permitted a consideration of their letters for the present edition, though the nature of their holdings can be gauged by the other side of the correspondence, Ethel's and Kenneth's letters to Maxwell, which resides among the Anderson papers at the University of Texas. The letters to Josephine Herbst record their friendship in the early twenties and were restricted by the Herbst estate in its terms of deposit at Yale. The final group of letters, deposited at Texas in 1973, resulted from an unusually painful event, the suicide of Anderson's second wife in 1953, and several people caught up in that situation are still alive. I have agreed with Anderson's estate not to make use of those letters in this edition.

Except for those referred to above, the edition accounts for all Anderson letters that came to light during the eight years of its preparation. "Letters," for the purposes of the edition, is a generic term covering every kind of letterlike communication—telegrams, postcards, assorted notes, and drafts as well as letters in the usual sense—and a number of the letters are of limited interest. Anderson handled most of his business by mail, and the practice resulted in many hasty notes on routine matters such as granting permission to produce or quote from his work, thanking well-wishers, and conducting incidental Playwrights' Company business. Many other letters are substantial repetitions of one another, and a remaining few have no recoverable context. To include more than a representative sample of such letters would increase the size of the book without adding to the picture of Anderson that emerges from his correspondence. But, since the letters are widely scattered and no previous attempt has been made to locate them, a record of all the known letters is needed. For the purposes a comprehensive record can serve, among them assistance in the recovery of other letters, those not reproduced in this edition are listed with their location in Appendix IV.

After his start in the theater in the early twenties, Anderson devoted his energies almost wholly to the writing of plays, frequently leaving the first rehearsals of one play to begin planning the next. In a theater that has not encouraged sustained careers, the result of his application is impressive, even in numerical terms. During virtually every season from 1923 to 1954, Anderson had at least one new play in production. Several seasons saw two, and in 1936–37 he seemed to monopolize New York theaters and audiences with three successful plays opening within two months of one another, *The Wingless Victory*, *High Tor*, and *The Masque of Kings*. In all, during a career of just over three decades, Anderson produced thirty-three plays, twenty-nine of which he also published, and several of them are now among the monuments of American drama, including *What Price Glory*, *Elizabeth the Queen*, *Winterset*, *High Tor*, *Joan of Lorraine*, and *Lost in the Stars*. His letters reveal Anderson's immersion in his work, for most of them pertain to his playwriting career. What they show, of course, is the man behind the plays, the life in which the plays were written and produced. His life as a dramatist thus emerges as the focus of Anderson's letters. And such a view as they offer, presented with the immediacy of letters, has not been available before because this is the first edition of letters by a major American playwright.

The letters begin in 1912, shortly after Anderson graduated from the University of North Dakota, and run until 1958, only a few months before he died, thus documenting the beginning, middle, and end of his career. Anderson came to the writing of plays accidentally. Until 1924 he supported himself with teaching and newspaper jobs in North Dakota, California, and, after 1918, New York. During those years his essential energy went into poetry, and he began to win recognition as a promising young poet. As far away as London the editor and poet Harold Monro discovered and admired his "truthful poems" (no. 13, n. 1). But Anderson wanted to support himself with his writing as well as derive inner satisfaction from it, and by 1922 he had come to the practical realization that in the current age no one was likely to support himself as a poet. A neighbor, John Howard Lawson, had received a substantial advance for his play *Roger Bloomer*, and Anderson, after hearing it read, told himself, "If that's a play I can write one" (Chronology, October, 1922). His first play was hastily drawn from a biography of Benvenuto Cellini, but it led Anderson to write another. With the second play, *White Desert*, a simply structured and moving poetic tragedy, Anderson discovered that he could realize his artistic aspirations in the drama, and the play's short run in 1923 introduced him to the theater. The next year *What Price Glory* enabled him to announce to one of his sisters, with a great sense of relief, that "we've had financial luck this year with the play, and I've quit work on the papers" (no. 19). When *What Price Glory* opened in the fall of 1924, Anderson was three months short of his thirty-sixth birthday. Thereafter, though no future play had a continuous run as long as *What Price Glory*, he never supported himself again except as a playwright.

Between 1925 and 1940 Anderson became one of the most eminent and exciting playwrights in America. They were the most prolific years of his career, with nineteen original productions. *Both Your Houses* won the Pulitzer Prize in 1933. In 1936 and 1937 *Winterset* and *High Tor* received the first two Drama Critics' Circle Awards. And in 1939, when the Pasadena Playhouse sought a contemporary to whom it could appropriately devote a summer following summers devoted to Shakespeare and Shaw, it turned naturally to Anderson and staged eight of his plays. Anderson was not undone by such success because a high sense of purpose made him skeptical of contemporary acclaim. He wished to write plays with the power to move audiences over the ages—an aspiration for the fame that depends on work of fundamental worth performed in an excellent manner. Aiming at that kind of work, he invariably took a qualified view, and often a harsh view, of the work he accomplished. "I've sometimes pleased the public; I've sometimes pleased the critics. I've sometimes pleased both," he told John Mason Brown in 1937, "but I've not yet written [a play] that I think will endure the test of time—and that's what I want to do" (no. 56). During the same years, however, he astonished his contemporaries, first by his productivity and versatility (his nineteen plays of the era included comedies and tragedies, plays in verse and in prose, satires, fantasies, and musicals), and even more by his success in meeting the major challenge envisioned for dramatists of the era, the creation of poetic tragedy in the contemporary theater.

For those who cared greatly about the drama at the time, the excitement mounted as they watched Anderson, with *Elizabeth the Queen*, begin the series of experiments leading up to *Winterset*. The recent theater had been dominated by realistic norms that had lost an earlier vitality and now seemed to be trivializing the drama. To Allardyce Nicoll and Margery Bailey, Lee Simonson and Walter Prichard Eaton, and hosts of others throughout the country, Anderson's poetic tragedies were experiments that were exhilarating because, at a dismal time for the theater, they offered much hope. By putting "poetry back on the stage" (no. 41, n. 1), Eaton wrote in 1934 after seeing *Mary of Scotland*, Anderson had provided a liberating example of how the drama once again could achieve the impact and significance of poetic tragedy. If the Tudor plays lacked anything, Eaton added, it was indicated by their historical setting, for the final challenge was "a poetic drama of modern life." *Winterset* the next year met that challenge. Allardyce Nicoll, voicing the majority reaction, literally could not rest after seeing the play until he wrote to Anderson about it. It was "the play of which I have dreamed," he began. In recent years he had begun to despair, thinking the theater "fated to perish" unless it "reachieved the spirit of poetry." But now *Winterset* had rekindled his faith. "It does what the poetic drama should do—present under the terms of current life the lineaments of universal humanity. May I offer you my congratulations on thus heralding in the theatre of tomorrow? The experience of tonight's performance is one of those—alas, too rare—experiences when one realises that the theatre truly is worth the striving and the living for."*

During the twenties and thirties a number of people had dreamed about a "theater of tomorrow," a theater that did not materialize during the following years in part because of World War II and its

*Undated letter, Nicoll to Anderson, in the Anderson Papers, Humanities Research Center, University of Texas. Quoted by permission of Allardyce Nicoll.

aftermath. For Anderson the era through the war into the early fifties was very different from the triumphant earlier period. By 1953 his life and career were almost shattered.

✓ He had always thought of the theater in terms of its function in society, and that function, he felt, "above and beyond entertainment," was "to point out and celebrate whatever is good and worth saving in our confused and often desperate generations" (no. 151). His own plays during the period continued to serve that broadly moral purpose. *The Eve of St. Mark*, with its lively support of freedom, was one of the rare plays from World War II that had power and distinction. *Joan of Lorraine* movingly depicted the postwar crisis of faith. And *Lost in the Stars* celebrated brotherhood as the hope of divided races and nations. But during those years it became increasingly difficult for Anderson to think that the postwar theater could serve its purpose of upholding human values. Inflation caused a sudden change in the economy of the theater, and skyrocketing production costs dictated that a play be an instantaneous hit or close. Anderson's response to those new and perplexing conditions, voiced several times by himself (e.g., nos. 151 and 160), was widely shared in the theater. Instantaneous success for a play depended on rave reviews by newspaper drama critics, who seemed blind to the profounder concerns of the population and enthusiastic only about plays "with plenty of shock or sex, and vapid musicals" (no. 179). Seeing unrepresentative drama critics as the arbiters of the stage life of plays, Anderson felt more and more cut off from his proper audience, the society at large, and less and less able to function as a playwright. In the fall of 1951 *Barefoot in Athens* received tepid reviews and closed after a few performances, losing $70,000. In the play, through the story of Socrates, Anderson had dramatized the modern conflict between communist tyranny and democratic freedom, and the play's failure left him in despair. "The kind of theatre I have always written my plays for is gone or going," he told Robert Sherwood, and "I have no hope that it will be resuscitated" (no. 179). He seriously considered resigning from the Playwrights' Company and retiring from the theater.

✓ Anderson's personal life followed the course of his career into the early fifties. *Barefoot in Athens*, with its commitment to individual freedom, rested on the foundation of his social philosophy. Deploring the hearings on communist affiliation conducted by House and Senate

committees at the time, he nonetheless opposed communism un-
alterably. The spread of Russian dominance in Europe after the war
alarmed him. Following a trip to Greece in 1947, when that country
was doing battle with communist guerrillas, he became outspoken in
his attacks on Russia, and these public remarks in turn involved him in
newspaper and radio controversies at home. Then in the early fifties he
became convinced for a time that internal communists posed a threat
to the United States, and disagreement about the seriousness of the
threat strained his relationship with several close friends, most
painfully with Elmer Rice (see nos. 183 and 185). The turmoil of the
era left Anderson with a sense of personal isolation and bitter
disappointment at contemporary America. Then as his despair over
the theater and bitterness at the political situation reached a climax
between 1951 and 1953, the final blow fell. His wife, herself under
severe emotional stress for several years, became involved with
another man in 1952 and in March of the next year committed
suicide. Later in 1953, to his closest sister, Anderson revealed how life
looked to him then by calling it a time "when our years are broken
clean in two" (no. 188).

Anderson died at the age of seventy on February 28, 1959,
following a stroke suffered a few days earlier. If the years after the war
had been marked by conflicts that left him in despair, the last years
were calm and productive. It was the calm that comes with a
realization he used to describe one of Elmer Rice's plays, "that all men
must bear torture and loss and yet keep on—and that they can do it,
too, now that they must" (no. 196). Except for a tendency to speak
harshly of his earlier work, however, little remained of his personal
despondency. In the same letter to his sister that spoke of his broken
years, he added that "I am loved, and it's something not to be lonely. I
won't try to explain it, but there is a woman of great beauty and
sweetness who finds me worthwhile still and that has pulled me
through" (no. 188). In 1954 he married Gilda Oakleaf in Los Angeles,
and the next year they bought a home in Stamford, Connecticut,
overlooking Long Island Sound. Anderson's produced plays of the
final years were adaptations, *The Bad Seed* and *The Day the Money
Stopped*, which he called potboilers because they were done to reduce
a large tax debt that had accumulated from the sale of his plays to
motion picture companies in the forties. He did not push for
production of the plays that interested him in the final years. But

among them are two fine achievements, *The Masque of Queens*, a
moving verse tragedy written as a sequel to *Elizabeth the Queen*, and
Madonna and Child, a rollicking contemporary comedy imbued with
a feeling that even after great loss "life still tastes sweet and is worth
living" (no. 196).

Such are the contours of Anderson's career as reflected by his
letters. Throughout his career he shielded his life from public view
almost completely. Temperamentally he was shy, and on principle he
opposed biographical publicity in connection with his plays. Only
once did he give any substantial account of his career, and that was at
the end of his life for an archival collection (for its first publication see
Appendix I, no. 5). But in his private correspondence Anderson
showed no such reticence. Although he did not look on letter writing
as a confessional exercise, in the letters he was open about his
activities, full and frank in the expression of his ideas, attitudes, and
beliefs, and altogether unpretentious about himself and his work. The
letters are typically relaxed and informal but are suited to their
recipients.

Many people wrote to Anderson without previous acquaintance
because of his prominence as a playwright, and his replies quite
naturally confined themselves to matters raised by the correspondent.
But he treated their letters with respect, and a letter of substance never
brought a hasty or flippant response. A number of those who wrote to
him were actively engaged with the drama, frequently as students or
young playwrights. If they raised questions about his plays, he
invariably gave straightforward answers, as when he explained at
length that he used iambic pentameter for his dialogue because
experience had taught him that it was the verse form best adapted for
speaking from the stage (no. 55). By the mid-thirties Anderson had
become something of a patron to aspiring verse dramatists of the
country, and he took a special interest in them. What he hoped to find,
he told a friend, were "youngsters who have an instinctive grasp of the
problems it took me decades to approach solving and who can write
plays that will put the modern drama on a par, at least in attempt,
with the best there's been" (no. 52). As busy with his own work as he
was, he read the scripts they sent him, attempted to arrange
productions or find other means of encouraging their development,
and sent them hardheaded but sympathetic critiques of their work

(e.g., nos. 70, 71, 85, 92). The critiques focus on the verse and structure of a play, aspects he could consider without intruding on the playwright's vision—"*what* the writer is trying to say," he felt, "must be left always to the insight and intuition of the writer" (no. 94). Consequently they reveal some of Anderson's practical conclusions about dramatic art and some of the habits of mind that guided the writing of his own plays.

The largest group of Anderson's correspondents consists of professional associates, people whose career brought them into contact with him. To Alan Paton, whose *Cry, the Beloved Country* he would dramatize, Anderson explained the origin of his interest in the novel: "For years I've wanted to write something which would state the position and perhaps illuminate the tragedy of our own negroes. Now that I've read your story I think you have said as much as can be said both for your country and ours" (no. 158). To a colleague in the Playwrights' Company whose suggestions made him rethink the early draft of a play, he sent "thanks for your letter, which pretty closely parallels my second thoughts on *Key Largo* and clarifies what I have left to do, or a beginning on it. Just to indicate what I've been thinking I list the changes I have in mind" (no. 79). Paul Robeson wanted to return to the stage, and Anderson outlined a play for him, a play that was rejected by the actor and became one of numerous unproduced plays discussed in the letters (no. 76). To the Theatre Guild, which had produced several of his plays, Anderson explained his dissatisfaction with the productions and his intention of directing the next one himself: "There's no getting away from the fact that I know better what I planned to put on the stage than any director" (no. 49). Dorothy Thompson, enthusiastic about establishing a professional repertory theater in New York, got a cool reception from Anderson; he pointed out that such a theater could not sustain itself financially and added pragmatically that "I have my doubts of the soundness of any scheme that doesn't at least promise a return" (no. 91). And to the president of Stanford University, who had just built an outdoor theater on campus, Anderson outlined a national play competition and drama festival on the Athenian model, emphasizing with enthusiasm of his own that "this country has spent huge sums on theatres and theatre equipment . . . but has neglected almost completely to provide an incentive for the writing of plays which should fill such theatres. Without the plays the theatres become a dead

weight" (no. 58). In addition to fellow writers, actors, producers, and
interested persons outside the theater, Anderson's correspondents
include editors, literary agents, and legal advisers; critics and scholars
of the drama; people in the theater outside New York City; and those
in all phases of motion picture production. Taken together Anderson's
letters to the people he worked with provide an enlightening view of
his own career in all its facets and also of the productive world of the
theater in America while he was at its center.

They also convey a sense of Anderson the person in the midst of
his career. The feelings of the moment are there. Embarrassed by
praise, he playfully ridiculed Alexander Woollcott, who had praised
What Price Glory extravagantly (no. 18). Later, as an experiment like
Winterset beckoned, he clearly longed for Walter Prichard Eaton to
argue him out of the idea that a contemporary poetic tragedy was
impossible (nos. 41, 44, and 45). Following Sidney Howard's death,
sympathy for his widow and the demands of producing Howard's last
play created a frustrating dilemma for Anderson when Mrs. Howard
refused to allow revisions in the unfinished script (nos. 82 and 86).
And Ingrid Bergman's box-office appeal made Anderson keep her as
the star of *Joan of Lorraine*, though her lack of respect for the theater
and his play brought his resentment to a boil (nos. 139, 140, 143, and
165).

Also present in the letters to his associates are those permanent
views and convictions that shaped Anderson's personality and career.
Once even an invitation to dinner, since it was rejected as coming from
a drama critic, pried loose a lengthy and amusing but wholly serious
explanation of his aspirations as a dramatist (no. 56). The topic comes
up frequently, as one situation after another forced Anderson to
elaborate his conception of the theater, and the letters document more
fully than any other source the complex development of views that led
Anderson finally to think of the theater as the temple of democracy
(e.g., nos. 56, 57, 58, 91, 110, 111, 145, 151, 152, 158, 160). That
label indicates the link between his plays and his social philosophy, the
other major strand in Anderson's thought. And again the letters
document the development of his ideas, as he began with a
commitment to the individual (no. 4), became an advocate of freedom
(nos. 81 and 88), governmental openness (no. 108), preservation of
the natural environment (no. 112), and social justice for minorities
(no. 158), and then remained consistent with his values in opposing

communism (e.g., nos. 183 and 184). Finally, the letters to those he worked with betray the basic traits of character that made Anderson admired by his contemporaries even in the midst of disagreement—his independence of mind, his forthrightness in stating his beliefs, and his integrity in living by them.

While the letters to associates and to people he did not know tend to be guided by a particular purpose, the remaining letters, to close friends and members of his family, are more intimate and expansive. Anderson's sense of humor, which did not have a free rein in correspondence, slipped out most often in letters to his friends in the Playwrights' Company. Characteristically the humor was casual and self-effacing, as when he mentioned that the dullness of its source was the only thing that carried over to one of his plays (no. 209). But he also sent the group a rollicking burlesque, a tongue-in-cheek attack on S. N. Behrman as president of the company, written to rally their spirits when all the playwrights were despondent about their work (no. 128). In a different vein, to Margery Bailey, a friend since their student days at Stanford who provided strong encouragement for his effort at poetic drama, he unfolded some of his basic hopes for the drama (e.g., nos. 52 and 54) and, when she led him to wonder what posterity might think of his work, some of his fears as well: "I naturally remember that posterity may not think of it at all" (no. 89). And the anguish involved in Anderson's commitment to World War II is nowhere revealed except in letters to his sister Lela, where he shared her suffering at the loss of two sons in the war and gave his view of the war as a necessary tragedy (e.g., nos. 103, 105, 109, 133).

In addition to exhibiting states of mind not prevalent in other letters, the letters to family and friends also provide fascinating glimpses of Anderson in the midst of his activities. Especially to Mab, his wife during the major decades of his career, he recounted his experience when traveling. An early letter to her describes a hectic time in Hollywood when he performed the unlikely feat of writing film scripts during the day and *Mary of Scotland* at night and on weekends (no. 37). And among the most engrossing of all the letters are the ones he wrote to her during a trip to London and North Africa in 1943 (nos. 115–125). The trip had the trials and fascination of an adventure. German submarines still sank Allied shipping in the Atlantic as he crossed, bombs fell nightly on London while he was there, fighting continued in North Africa after he arrived, and the ship he took home from Casablanca was filled with German and Italian prisoners of war. He was gone three months, March through June, and the letters, written in part to stir his memory later on, are a vivid record of his contact with people caught up in the war. His reason for making the trip reveals the seriousness of purpose that characterized Anderson throughout his career. The war was the central fact of the time, affecting America's and the world's population both spiritually and physically. Since that was the case, he felt compelled as a writer to experience life in the midst of the war, to touch the core of things himself. To do otherwise would have amounted to an enervating evasion. Given "the present state of the world," he wrote in the first letter, explaining the impulse behind his going, "I must get a breath of its desperation before I can write again."

On March 3, 1959, a few days after he died, a memorial service was held for Anderson at St. Paul's Chapel, Columbia University, and he was widely eulogized in newspapers and journals. Throughout his career Anderson had been unpretentious about himself, and his aspirations led him always to take a qualified view of his work. But the memorial service and printed tributes presented a more prevalent estimate. William Fields, an associate in the Playwrights' Company for twenty years, summarized his impression of Anderson as a person by calling him "a hardy man, a humble man and, dear God, what a good one." And Robert Anderson remembered his plays for their "excitement and splendor and sweep of words and poetry." These and other friends such as Mark Van Doren and Marc Connelly, as well as people who had known him only through his work, emphasized the lasting importance of a number of Anderson's plays, the significance of his creation of successful plays in verse, and the stature his career gave to the American theater.

PLAN OF THE EDITION

Preceding the letters is a chronology of Maxwell Anderson's life. The chronology focuses on Anderson's career as a playwright and traces each of his plays from inception to final disposition. At the opening date of produced plays it gives the number of performances in the original production. At the publication day of books it notes the price per copy and publishing history of the work (gaps in printing and sales figures reflect gaps in publishers' records and the inaccessibility of Anderson House files). In less detail it also lists his poems, essays, film scripts, and speeches in order to provide a complete record of Anderson's writing and publication. While the chronology emphasizes his writing, it places the writing within the framework of Anderson's life by including much of his other activity as well. Within limits it provides a yearly and monthly (and sometimes daily) account of the various jobs he held, his travels, something of his reading and playgoing, major occurrences in his personal life, his response to people and events in the theatrical and social worlds, and his participation in the Playwrights' Company and other enterprises. An edition of letters needs the context of the writer's life for its largest coherence. No biography of Anderson exists, and his life has been known only in the scantiest outline. The chronology is designed to provide the biographical context for Anderson's letters that would otherwise be lacking.

The letters in the edition are arranged in chronological order, and each letter is presented in three parts: heading, text, and annotation.

Headings provide the number of each letter in the chronological sequence, the usual full name of the person to whom the letter was written, and the place and date of the letter's composition. For the place and date of composition the edition uses a standard form. Anderson sometimes gave the place and date at the end of a letter but usually put that information at the upper right-hand margin. And he had little preference for a single form for dates, using with about equal frequency the forms represented by 2/1/47, Feb. 1, '47, and February 1, 1947. The edition adopts the last form and gives the place and date in the heading in order to reduce the possibility of its being misread or missed. The place of composition is stated as precisely as possible, but information from printed letterheads has been used with care. Company letterheads (*New Republic*, *Globe*, *World*, and Playwrights' Company) tend to support only the city of composition, since Anderson used them at home and at the office, and sometimes he carried Playwrights' Company stationery on trips. Hotel stationery, on the other hand, indicates the place more exactly. No instance has come to light of his using it at a place other than the hotel in question.

When the date or place of composition does not appear on the original but can be established, it is given within square brackets, followed by a question mark in the few cases of conjectural information. Partially dated letters (there are no undated ones) are placed in the chronological sequence at the point where internal and external evidence show they were written.

Except for four that come from published sources, texts in the edition derive from the original letters or photocopies of them. Originals (including photocopies) are either the mailed letter itself, a copy of it preserved in Anderson's files or those of the Playwrights' Company, or a preliminary draft. The list of letters in the edition, a list preceding the body of the work, states the nature of each original along with its location when it became available to the editor.

The aim of the texts in the edition is to represent the language of the originals exactly, and a need to prevent confusion required only a few departures from that aim. The departures do not detract from the definitive nature of the texts.

In mailed letters and their copies a few proper names are inadvertently misspelled, and those are corrected in the edition in order to forestall questions of identity. Obvious typographical errors and, in handwritten originals, slips of the pen (such as the writing of "to in" for "into") have also been removed. Where a small word clearly needed for the sense has been accidentally omitted in the originals (as might occur when pen or typewriter failed to move as fast as the mind), the edition supplies the missing word within square brackets. And the few words that remained indecipherable are indicated by the insertion [illegible]. But in spelling, capitalization, and punctuation Anderson had only one eccentricity, a fondness for the dash. Dashes appear frequently in the originals in place of any kind of punctuation, and sometimes where a paragraph division would otherwise occur. Though they may appear unorthodox, especially in their abundance, dashes represent Anderson's instinctive response to the need for punctuation, and they do not interfere with the clarity of the letters. In line with the policy of altering only mechanical obstacles in the way of clarity, the edition retains Anderson's dashes as he wrote them.

In the case of texts derived from a preliminary draft, the edition presents a fair copy reading of the letter. All words deleted in the drafts are omitted in the texts, and all additions are included in their proper places. Deletions having some interest are pointed out in the notes. Texts are based on a preliminary draft only when no final copy was available. To have excluded letters derived from preliminary drafts would have deprived the edition of some of its more valuable letters (for instance no. 166, which recounts at length the origin and development of *Anne of the Thousand Days*). But to have provided complete evidence of revision would have required complicated and obstructive typographical arrangements, which are not justified. Revisions tend to cancel false starts and slips of the pen or to clarify discussions rather than change their direction. A fair copy reading thus represents the intended letter in its fullest available form.

Footnotes supply the factual context of individual letters. Notes identify recipients the first time they appear, and people and works referred to in the letters. Events or circumstances assumed but not specified in the letters are also noted, frequently with reliance on letters from Anderson's correspondents or other unpublished material. Usually the first note to a letter provides necessary background, briefer notes supply details needed in the body of the letter, and the final note indicates the outcome of the letter's concern. That way of leading into, through, and out of each letter should make the reader a party to the correspondence without undue postponement or interruption of attention.

Some information could not be accommodated in footnotes, however. Facts about Anderson's unpublished plays needed by the context of a letter appear in the notes, but each unpublished play is also identified by a reference to the appropriate pages in a work called the *Catalogue*. The work in question is Laurence G. Avery, *A Catalogue of the Maxwell Anderson Collection* (Austin: Humanities Research Center, University of Texas, 1968). Anderson wrote a number of plays that he did not publish (twenty-two, plus several that he left unfinished), and references to them abound in the letters. The *Catalogue* locates the drafts and summarizes the plot of each one, and thus describes these generally unavailable plays more fully than they could be described in the edition.

Following the letters, in Appendix I, are five Anderson documents related to his playwriting career that have not been published before. Three of them are acceptance speeches for awards to his plays. The first two accept Drama Critics' Circle awards to *Winterset* and *High Tor* in 1936 and 1937 and reveal important stages in the development of Anderson's conception of the theater. The third speech, delivered on the occasion of the Brotherhood Award to *Lost in the Stars* in 1950, discusses the circumstances behind the writing of the play and Anderson's intention in it. Another document is a scene written for the London production of *The Eve of St. Mark* in 1943. Though it does not alter the play significantly, Anderson thought well enough of the new scene to want it inserted in the New York production and would have published it if a later edition of the play had appeared. The remaining document has been mentioned already. It is the "Anderson Memoir," the only account of his life and career that Anderson gave.

Appendix II supplements the biographical information in the footnotes. Several members of Anderson's extended family appear in the letters, some of them frequently, and the family relationships are outlined in Appendix II by a genealogical tree that covers three generations beginning with Anderson's parents. Much of the information in the tree has not been available before. Some of it derives from the letters and related sources, but most of it comes from notes by one of Anderson's sisters, Lela Anderson Chambers. Mrs. Chambers made the notes for her personal history of the Anderson family and graciously provided them for this edition.

Appendix III includes biographical sketches of several people whose association with Anderson was especially close and extended. They include members of the Playwrights' Company and a few other friends and family members. Those whose biographical sketches appear in Appendix III have an asterisk by the name in the heading of the earliest letter to each one.

The final appendix, mentioned already, lists the letters not printed in this edition. The list is chronological and gives for each letter its date, recipient, place of composition, type, and location. If the date or place of composition does not appear on a letter, the list indicates the fact by giving that information within square brackets. And it indicates the length of each letter by stating its number of pages when greater than one. These details in the descriptions in Appendix IV are designed to identify the omitted letters precisely and to make them easily accessible.

MAXWELL ANDERSON:
A CHRONOLOGY

SHORT FORMS OF CITATION

Abbott	George Abbott. "*Mister Abbott.*" New York: Random House, 1963.
Am. Lit.	Laurence G. Avery. "The Conclusion of *Night Over Taos.*" *American Literature* 38 (November 1965): 318–21.
Behrman	S. N. Behrman. *Tribulations and Laughter: A Memoir.* London: Hamish Hamilton, 1972.
Bliven	Bruce Bliven. *Five Million Words Later: An Autobiography.* New York: John Day, 1970.
Catalogue	Laurence G. Avery. *A Catalogue of the Maxwell Anderson Collection at the University of Texas.* Austin: Humanities Research Center, University of Texas, 1968.
Clark	Barret H. Clark. *Maxwell Anderson: The Man And His Plays.* New York: Samuel French, 1933.
Clurman	Harold Clurman. *The Fervent Years: The Story of the Group Theatre and the Thirties.* 2d ed. New York: Hill & Wang, 1957.
"Confession"	Maxwell Anderson. "A Confession." *New York Times*, December 5, 1954, sec. 2, p. 7, cols. 1–3.
Deutsch	Helen Deutsch. "A Playwright and Poet." *New York Herald Tribune*, September 22, 1935, p. 1, cols. 5–6, p. 5, cols. 1–4.
Diaries	(Except as noted, diaries are in the Anderson Collection, Humanities Research Center, University of Texas.)

1945: 190 pp., 20.4 x 12.8 cm., in black vinyl ring binder.

1946: 368 pp., 19.2 x 12.9 cm., in black leather covers.

1947 (except November 1 through December 15): 384 pp., 22.3 x 14.4 cm., in red leather covers.

1947 (November 1 through December 15): 158 pp., 16.4 x 9.9 cm., in green vinyl binder.

1948: 400 pp., 22.1 x 14.4 cm., in red leather covers, Anderson Collection, Chester Fritz Library, University of North Dakota.

1949: 440 pp., 22.2 x 14.5 cm., in red leather covers.

1950: 400 pp., 22.3 x 14.6 cm., in red leather covers.

1951: 192 pp., 19.9 x 12.8 cm., in black vinyl ring binder.

Duffus — Robert L. Duffus. *The Tower of Jewels: Memories of San Francisco*. New York: W. W. Norton, 1960.

Goldstein — Malcolm Goldstein. *The Political Stage: American Drama and Theater of the Great Depression*. New York: Oxford University Press, 1974.

Hagan — John P. Hagan. "Frederick H. Koch and North Dakota: Theatre in the Wilderness." *North Dakota Quarterly* 38 (Winter 1970): 75–87.

Hill — Frank Ernest Hill. Memoir, TS. Oral History Collection, Columbia University.

Himelstein — Morgan Y. Himelstein. *Drama Was a Weapon: The Left Wing Theatre in New York, 1929–1941*. New Brunswick: Rutgers University Press, 1963.

Houseman — John Houseman. *Run-Through*. New York: Simon & Schuster, 1972.

A. Johnson — Alvin Johnson. *Pioneer's Progress: An Autobiography*. New York: Viking Press, 1952.

Johnson — Kay Irene Johnson. *Playwrights as Patriots: A History of the Playwrights' Producing Company*. Ph.D. dissertation, University of Wisconsin, 1974.

W. Johnson — Walter Johnson. *The Battle against Isolation*. Chicago: University of Chicago Press, 1944.

Mantle — Burns Mantle. *American Playwrights Today*. New York: Dodd, Mead & Co., 1929.

NDQ   Laurence G. Avery. "Maxwell Anderson and *Both Your Houses*." *North Dakota Quarterly* 38 (Winter 1970): 5–24.

Notes   Maxwell Anderson. *Notes on a Dream*. Austin: Humanities Research Center, University of Texas, 1971.

PSBA 1 Laurence G. Avery. "Addenda to the Maxwell Anderson Bibliography: *The Measure*." *Papers of the Bibliographical Society of America* 63 (First Quarter 1969): 31–36.

PSBA 2 ———. "Addenda to the Maxwell Anderson Bibliography: Monro's *Chapbook*." *Papers of the Bibliographical Society of America* 65 (Fourth Quarter 1971) 408–11.

Quaker "Many New Faculty Members Are Appointed This Year." *The Quaker Campus* (Whittier College student newspaper), September 20, 1917, p. 1, col. 1.

Rice   Elmer Rice. *Minority Report: An Autobiography*. New York: Simon & Schuster, 1963.

R. Rice Robert Rice. "Maxwell Anderson: A Character Study of the Most Talked of Playwright in America Based on the First Interview He Has Granted since 1937." *PM's Sunday Picture News* 3 (November 29, 1942): 23–27.

Sedgwick   Ruth Woodbury Sedgwick. "Maxwell Anderson, Playwright and Poet." *Stage* 14 (October 1936): 54–56.

Sherwood   Robert E. Sherwood. " 'White Desert' to 'Bad Seed.' " *Theatre Arts* 39 (March 1955): 28–29, 93.

Tanselle G. Thomas Tanselle. "Additions to the Bibliography of Maxwell Anderson." *Papers of the Bibliographical Society of America* 57 (First Quarter 1963): 90–91.

Tietjens Eunice Tietjens. *The World at My Shoulder*. New York: Macmillan, 1938.

Wharton John F. Wharton. *Life among the Playwrights, Being Mostly the Story of the Playwrights' Producing Company, Inc*. New York: Quadrangle/New York Times Book Company, 1974.

World   Who's Who on the [New York] World. n.p., [c. 1922].

THE CHRONOLOGY

1888

December 15 Born as second child to William Lincoln Anderson
and Charlotta Perrimela Stephenson Anderson on
farm of maternal grandmother near Atlantic,
Pennsylvania (sister, Ethel May, born January
3, 1887).
Father tends farm, maternal grandfather having
died sometime earlier (Appendix I, no. 5).

1890

Family moves to Andover, Ohio. Father, now a
railroad fireman, studies at night for the ministry (Appendix I, no. 5).

1891

February 19 Lela Blanch, second sister, born.
Father begins to preach in Andover Baptist Church.

1892

Family moves to Richmond Center, Ohio, where
father is pastor of a Baptist church for $250 per
year, donated food, and parsonage (Appendix I,
no. 5).

1893

Family moves to Townville, Pennsylvania, where
father is pastor of a Baptist church.

1895

August 9 Harold Alfred, first brother, born.
Family moves to Edinboro, Pennsylvania, where
father is pastor and Maxwell begins schooling in
the local public school.

1896

Family moves to McKeesport, Pennsylvania,
where father is pastor.

1897

Family moves to New Brighton, Pennsylvania,
where father is pastor.

1898
April 14   Ruth Virginia, third sister, born.
Family moves to Harrisburg, Pennsylvania,
where father is pastor. Because "the pickings
were rather thin" (Appendix I, no. 5),
Maxwell spends winter and spring with maternal
grandmother on farm near Atlantic, Pennsylvania.

1901
Family moves to Jefferson, Ohio, where father
is pastor.

1902
July 29   John Kenneth and Dorothy Elizabeth, twins,
second brother and fourth sister, born.

1903
Family moves to Algona, Iowa, where father is
pastor.
Summer   Maxwell works on a farm and continues to do so in
the summers until about 1910, for "$25 or $30 a
month" (Appendix I, no. 5).

1904
Family moves to New Hampton, Iowa, where
father is pastor.
September   Maxwell begins high school (Appendix I, no. 5).
Also works as printer's devil and prints card for
himself: "Cymbeline, Blackfriar's Theatre.
Admit One" (Deutsch). By this time, had "read
most of the well-known novelists, Dickens,
Stevenson, Scott, Dumas, Cooper, and a vast
sampling of others" (no. 212). Father's
favorite was Dickens; own favorites were
Treasure Island, *Kidnapped*, *The Adventures of
Sherlock Holmes*. Both parents encouraged reading,
which "went on . . . constantly" (Appendix
I, no. 5).

1907
Family moves to Jamestown, North Dakota.
Fall   Maxwell begins last year of high school. Also
works at night as fire-up man in local train
yard (R. Rice).

1908

Spring   Maxwell graduates from Jamestown High School.
            By this time, primary literary interest is poetry.
            In high school, had discovered "first Keats,
            then Shelley and Shakespeare—these in drugstore
            shelves and in libraries—and then all the major
            names from Tennyson, Browning and Swinburne on
            into the past." Also had begun to write poetry,
            in secret, for fear of ridicule (no. 212).

September   With encouragement of high school classmate Garth
            Howland, enters University of North Dakota,
            at Grand Forks.

1908–1909

Fall–Spring   Earns first year's school expenses "doing odd
              jobs and waiting on tables" (Appendix I, no.
              5). Finds for the first time a public sanction for
              his interest in poetry (no. 212).

1909–1911

Earns school expenses as copy editor for *Grand
Forks Herald* (Appendix I, no. 5). Plays varsity
football (*Quaker*). Introduced to Greek philosophy
by Professor Gottfried Hult and to populist so-
cialism by Professor John M. Gillette.

1910

January 3   Charter member of Sock and Buskin Society, the-
            atrical group organized at university by Professor
            Frederick H. Koch (Hagan).

1910–1911

Fall–Spring   Edits school yearbook, *The Dacotah*, and publishes in
              it a short story, "The End of the Furrow," and two
              poems, "The Grail" and "The Mirage." Writes class
              play, "The Masque of Pedagogues," a satire on
              university life.

May   Graduates after three years, having earned credit
            for several English courses through examinations
            (Appendix I, no. 5).

July   Marries Margaret Haskett, classmate from
            Bottineau, North Dakota.

Fall   Becomes principal of high school in Minnewaukan,
            North Dakota; also teaches English.

1912
Meets sister-in-law of Thorstein Veblen, on whose
Theory of the Leisure Class he had reported in college
(no. 1).

July 21 First son, Quentin, born.

1913
Summer Moves to Palo Alto, California.
November Third brother, Lawrence, born in Wolf Point,
Montana.

1913–1914
Fall Enters graduate program in English at Stanford
University.
Fall–Spring Earns expenses as janitor in country school and as
instructor in Stanford English Department until
December, when he gives up job as janitor (no. 2).
Becomes friends with fellow student Margery Bailey
and young instructor Frank Ernest Hill. By Hill,
introduced into a group "who were writing poetry
and . . . other things" where he meets and becomes
friends with Robert L. Duffus, editorial writer on
Fremont Older's *San Francisco Evening Bulletin* (Appendix I, no. 5). Group meets once a month at home
of English professor and aspiring playwright Henry
David Gray, where they read aloud and discuss their
writing (Bliven, p. 48). Anderson writes three one-act
plays under Gray (no. 25), one laid in North Dakota
(Hill, p. 164).
May Receives M.A. in English from Stanford, thesis
entitled "Immortality in the Plays and Sonnets of
Shakespeare."

1914
September Lives in Palo Alto and begins teaching English at San
Francisco Polytechnic High School (Appendix I,
no. 5)

1916
Has six poems in a Stanford English Club publication
A Stanford Book of Verse, 1912–1916: "Youth's
Song," p. 1; "The Instrument," p. 4; "End-All,"
p. 17; "Shakespeare Went to Italy," pp. 65–67;
"Kings," p. 75; and "Youth," p. 84.

Summer   Duffus and Anderson families often picnic at Sears-
          ville Lake above Stanford (Duffus, p. 147).

          1917
Summer   With Duffus takes two-day bicycle trip from Palo
          Alto over the Coast Range to Half Moon Bay; at road
          house plays music he had written for an operetta,
          then during discussion of the war says he thinks no
          war is "as good as a good poem" (Duffus, p. 206).
          Later in summer walks with Duffus from Mission San
          Juan Batista to coast south of Santa Cruz (Duffus,
          p. 206).

Fall   Leaves job at Polytechnic High School and becomes
          chairman of the English Department at Whittier
          College.

September 8   Has poem, "Sic Semper," in *New Republic*
               12:159.

December 9   Second son, Alan, born.

22   Has two poems, "Flame from Ashes" and "Earth
      Evanescent," in *New Republic* 13:217.

          1918
May 25   Has poem, "The Spirit Legion," in *Nation*
          106:623.

Spring   Dismissed by Whittier "because I didn't want to sit
          on the platform during chapel. I didn't enjoy prayers"
          (Appendix I, no. 5). Also because of his pacifist views.

Late July   Joins Duffus as editorial writer on *San Francisco
             Evening Bulletin* after Fremont Older resigns (Duffus,
             pp. 246–47).

October 24   Writes to Older urging him to publish newspaper
              series, "My Own Story," as book (no. 5).

November   Loses job on *Bulletin* through sickness and goes to
            copydesk at *San Francisco Chronicle* (Appendix I,
            no. 5).

2   Has letter ("Incommunicable Literature") in *Dial*
     65:370 (no. 6).

December   Has poem, "Star-Adventurer," in *Upton Sinclair's:
            For a Clear Peace and the Internation*, 1, no. 8:15
            (no. 4).
            Receives letter from Alvin Johnson, on editorial
            board of *New Republic*, inviting him to join *New
            Republic* staff. Johnson and Herbert Croly, editor of

New Republic, impressed with poems and essay he had submitted, hire him on strength of that work (A. Johnson, p. 272; Bliven, p. 120). Borrows $1,500 from friends and moves to New York.

14　Has essay, "The Blue Pencil," in *New Republic* 17:192–94.

1919

March 29　Has review of Barrett H. Clark's *European Theories of the Drama* in *New Republic* 18:283–84.

May　Leaves *New Republic* to join Duffus, Frank Hill, and Bruce Bliven as editorial writer on the daily *Globe and Commercial Advertiser*, where Bliven considers him "a philosophical anarchist, with the utter pessimism about reform and reformers appropriate to that attitude" (Bliven, p. 120).

31　Has letter ("One Future for American Poetry") in *Dial* 116:568–69 (no. 8).

June 10　Has unsigned editorial, "Gompers as a 'Direct Actionist,'" in the *Globe*, p. 14, col. 1.

September 20　Has essay, "The Scholar Too Late," in *Dial* 117:239–41, a satire probably on Professor Henry David Gray at Stanford (see Bliven, pp. 48–49.)

1920

March 17　Has letter ("Friendly Advice") in *Freeman* 1:11 (no. 11).

June 23　Has poem, "Full-Circle," in *New Republic* 23:110.

July 14　Has essay, "The Revolution and the Drama," in *Freeman* 1:425–26.

August 11　Has review of Charles C. Dobie's novel, *The Blood Red Dawn*, in *Freeman* 1:525–26.

14　Has poem, "Prometheus Bound," in *Nation* 111:187.

25　Has essay, "Modern Casuists," in *Freeman* 1:565.

September 15　Has essay, "How Will It Be Done Again?," in *Freeman* 2:9–10.

22　Has unsigned essay, "An Age of Hired Men," in *Freeman* 2:31–32 (Tanselle).

October 6　Has poem, "Telemachus Muses," in *Freeman* 2:88.

November　With eight others, begins to plan a monthly poetry magazine, *Measure* (no. 14 and *PSBA* 1).

December 8　Has poem, "Sea-Challenge," in *New Republic* 25:48.

15　Has eleven prose epigrams in *Nation* 111:689.

1921

January   Has poem, "Dark Oracles," in Harold Monro's *Chapbook* (London), no. 19, pp. 5–8; also "Epigrams" (previously in *Nation*), pp. 9–11 (*PSBA* 2).

19   Has poem, "Emptying Ashes," in *New Republic* 25:231.

February   His *Globe* editorials attract Herbert Bayard Swope of *New York World*, and he leaves *Globe* to become editorial writer on *New York World* (*World*, p. 13).

March   Elected editor of the *Measure* for the first quarter (March, April, and May) and has editorial, "Thunder in the Index," in *Measure*, no. 1, pp. 23–25.

16   Has poem, "St. Agnes' Morning," in *New Republic* 26:74.

April   Has editorial, "An Open Letter to Writers of Verse," in *Measure*, no. 2, pp. 17–19.

May   Has review essay, "Conrad Aiken and the Minor Mode," in *Measure*, no. 3, pp. 25–26.

June   Retires as editor of the *Measure* and begins to serve on its editorial board.
Has essay, "Looking Back at Synge," in *Measure*, no. 4, pp. 20–21.

August   Has review essay, "A Prejudiced Word on Amy Lowell," in *Measure*, no. 6, pp. 17–18.

September   Has poem, "Judith of Minnewaukan," in *Measure*, no. 7, pp. 7–11; also review essay, "Second April," p. 17.

October   Has review essay, "Further Prejudiced Words on Amy Lowell," in *Measure*, no., 8, p. 18.

November   Has poem, "Bald The' at the Play," in *Measure*, no. 9, pp. 12–13.

December   Has poem, "The Beggar God," in *Measure*, no. 10, pp. 3–5; also review essay, "Treacle Tears for Keats," p. 17.

1922

January   Has poem, "Lucifer," in *Measure*, no. 11, p. 7; also review essay, "Nets to Catch the Wind," p. 18.

April   Has review essay, " 'Temple Music,' " in *Measure*, no. 14, p. 18. With Frank Ernest Hill has paid operating expenses of *Measure* during its first year (Hill, pp. 213–14).

May Has poem, "Noon in a Wood," in *Measure*, no. 15, p. 12; also review essay, "Irish History in Little," pp. 17–18.

Summer (?) Buys three acres for $3,000 (later buys larger acreage) on South Mountain Road at New City in Rockland County, west of Hudson River from New York City; begins to move household there ("Confession").

June 21 Has poem, "The Time When I Was Plowing," in *New Republic* 31:104.

July 5 Has poem, "She Said, Though You Should Weave," in *New Republic* 31:161.
Has review, "Sandburg Over-Does It a Little," in *Measure*, no. 17, pp. 15–16.

August 9 Has poem, "Epitaphs: For All Who Have Died in Wars," in *Freeman* 5:519.
Has review, "Word-Craft," in *Measure*, no. 18, p. 16.

September Has poem, "Her Heart Was Curiously Wrought," in *Smart Set* 69:97.
Has poem, "'Who Has Burned His Wings,'" in *Measure*, no. 19, p. 5.

October Leaves editorial board of the *Measure* "because of too great stress of other work" (*Measure*, no. 20 [October 1922], p. 19). "Other work" probably his first full length play, *Benvenuto*, which he writes during this time (*Catalogue*, pp. 64–65), after listening to reading of John Howard Lawson's *Roger Bloomer* and thinking, "If that's a play I can write one" ("Confession").
Has poem, "Mazurka (To Anna)," in *Chapbook*, no. 30, pp. 23–24.

December Has review, "The Going of the Old Ireland," in *Measure*, no. 22, pp. 17–18.

1923
Writes *White Desert*, second full-length play and first one in verse (*Catalogue*, pp. 80–82). Laurence Stallings, literary editor of the *World*, shows it to paper's music critic, Deems Taylor, who contacts friend, the producer Brock Pemberton, who schedules it for production (Appendix I, no. 5). Pemberton has

script retyped as prose so as not to frighten the actors (Sedgwick).

June With Laurence Stallings hears Frank Cobb, editor of the *World*, tell about his meeting with President Wilson early in the morning of the day Wilson delivered the War Message to Congress, April 2, 1917.

September 18 Third son, Terence, born.

October 18 *White Desert* opens in New York, to run for twelve performances.

23 Has letter in *World* defending play against attack of paper's drama critic, Heywood Broun (no. 17).

November (?) With George Abbott, who played lead in *White Desert*, writes *The Feud* "in four days" in Boone, North Carolina (Appendix I, no. 5; Abbott, p. 104).

December Has editorial, "New York's Theatre," in *Measure*, no. 34, pp. 17–19.

At work on *Sea-Wife*, verse tragedy based on Matthew Arnold's *Forsaken Merman* (*Catalogue*, pp. 76–77.

1924

Writes *What Price Glory* from war stories told by Stallings at lunch, doing much of the writing in the evenings in New York Public Library and modeling play on Henry IV, Part I (Hill, p. 291). Play reflects romantic pacifism of San Francisco days (see Duffus, passim, esp. pp. 212–13).

March 9 Has article critical of critics, "Critical Mr. Anderson," in *World*, sec. E, p. 6, cols. 1–2.

26 Has poem, "You Who Have Dreams Born in the Bone," in *New Republic* 38:124.

May 21 Has poem, "Whether the Dark Had Ushered in the Rain," in *New Republic* 38:331.

Spring With Stallings writes account of Cobb's interview with President Wilson, the account written for inclusion in John L. Heaton (associate on *World*), *Cobb of THE WORLD*.

July Heaton's *Cobb of THE WORLD* published, by E. P. Dutton, the Anderson/Stallings contribution entitled "On the Eve of War: A Recollection," pp. 267–70.

September 3   *What Price Glory* opens in New York, to run for 299 performances. Robert Sherwood, seeing audience "stand up and cheer," decides to become a playwright because "no writer could hope for a reward more thrilling and more immediate than this" (Sherwood, p. 28).

4(?)   Knowing from reviews that play is success, resigns from *World* (Appendix I, no. 5).

Repays last of $1,500 borrowed from friends in 1918 when he left San Francisco for New York.

Begins remodeling old house on farm in Rockland County.

November   Interviewed with Stallings, "How a Great Play Is Written," in *Current Opinion* 77:617–18.

Has poem, "Epilogue," in *Measure*, no. 45, p. 14.

December   Buys two farms in western New York, near Richburg, and moves parents to one of them (Appendix I, no. 5).

3   Has poem, "Prayer After Youth," in *New Republic* 41:39.

1925

Early   Probably completes *Outside Looking In*, based on Jim Tully's *Beggars of Life*. With Stallings writes *First Flight*, then *The Buccaneer*.

June 24   Has poem, "When We Have Heard That Time Is Only Seeming," in *New Republic* 43:126.

September 7   *Outside Looking In* opens in New York, to run for 113 performances.

15   Publishes poems *You Who Have Dreams* with Simon & Schuster (one of their first books) in limited edition of 1,000 copies at $2.00.

17   *First Flight* opens in New York, to run for twelve performances.

October 2   *The Buccaneer* opens in New York, to run for twenty performances.

20   With neighbor Eunice Tietjens attends opening of her play *Arabesque* and tries to assuage her disappointment at Norman Bel Geddes's staging (Tietjens, pp. 257–58).

1926

Writes *Chicot the King* (*Catalogue*, pp. 66–67); probably also at this time writes *Hell on Wheels*, a musical (*Catalogue*, p. 71).

September 30   With Stallings publishes *Three American Plays* (*What Price Glory*, *First Flight*, and *The Buccaneer*) with Harcourt, Brace at $2.50.

Writes *Saturday's Children*, theme perhaps suggested by Ibsen's *Love's Comedy* (Appendix I, no. 5).

1927

January 26   *Saturday's Children* opens in New York, to run for 167 performances, then to be revived.

Winter–   Writes *Gypsy* (*Catalogue*, p. 70).
Spring

May 4   Writes to Arthur Hobson Quinn, at work on history of American drama, that "what I want more than anything else is to successfully put poetry into plays" (no. 25).

28   Has essay, "Stage Money," in *Colliers'* 79:24, 30. Works at play involving a love triangle, but does not finish it or give it a title (*Catalogue*, p. 79).

September   Publishes *Saturday's Children* with Longmans, Green at $2.00.

1928

Winter–   With Harold Hickerson writes *Gods of the Lightning*,
Spring   based on trial of Sacco and Vanzetti and their execution in previous year.

Responds to Burns Mantle's request for biographical information: "when a man starts peddling personal stuff about himself they should send a squad of strong-arm worms after him, because he is dead" (Mantle, facing p. 68).

May 23   Has poem, "Your Love Is Like Quicksand Where Men Build," in *New Republic* 55:19; poem associated with *Gypsy* (*Catalogue*, p. 58).

June 13   Has poem, "Now Could I Trace the Passages Through Air," in *New Republic* 55:89.

October 24   *Gods of the Lightning* opens in New York, to run for twenty-nine performances.

1929

January   Publishes *Gods of the Lightning* and *Outside Looking In* together, with Longmans, Green at $2.50.

14   *Gypsy* opens in New York, to run for sixty-four
performances.

Winter or   In need of money, goes to Hollywood to write motion
Spring   picture scripts. Rents house on beach and writes script
for *All Quiet on the Western Front*, directed by Lewis
Milestone and released the next year by Universal
Pictures. Later works on several scripts for Metro-
Goldwyn-Mayer, including *Trader Horn* and *The
Phantom of Paris* (no. 29).

While at work on motion picture scripts, writes
Elizabeth the Queen, "inspired" by Lytton Strachey's
Elizabeth and Essex: A Tragic History (Appendix I,
no. 5).

1930

Probably at this time writes motion picture script
Rain, directed by Lewis Milestone and based on
Somerset Maugham's "Miss Thompson" and drama-
tization, *Rain*, by John Colton and Clemence
Randolph.

May 10   Has historical story, "The Battle of Gibraltar," in
Colliers' 85:26, 31, 36, 38.

By June   Back in New York.

When Hill criticizes verse in *Elizabeth the Queen* for
lack of elevation, replies that he does not want "the
verse to get in the way of the play" (Hill, p. 400).

November 3   *Elizabeth the Queen* opens in New York, to run for
147 performances.

19   Publishes *Elizabeth the Queen* with Longmans, Green
at $2.00.

Writes *The Princess Renegade* (*Catalogue*, p. 74;
Clurman, p. 34).

1931

February 26   First wife, Margaret, dies suddenly from a blood clot.

April 1   After attending discussions among those who would
form Group Theatre, gives them $1,500, then several
hundred dollars more, toward support during summer's rehearsal (Clurman, p. 34).

Summer   At Brookfield, Connecticut, with Group Theatre, writes, and conducts "friendly arguments . . . about contemporary drama" with Harold Clurman and others (Clurman, p. 44).

October   Begins *Night Over Taos* after finishing Harvey Fergusson's series on Rio Grande Valley in *American Mercury* (six installments, May to October), the last installment being "The Strange History of Padre Martinez of Taos," 24:230–42.

28   Named to Advisory Board of Group Theatre (Goldstein, p. 80).

1932

Early   Gives *Night Over Taos* to Group Theatre because a " 'playwright who gets a chance to write for actors he knows . . . has a better chance for permanence in the theater—where permanence is so badly needed.' " Adds that " 'all great plays I can remember were in verse. If we are going to have a great theater in this country somebody has to write verse, even if it is written badly. It is at least a beginning' " (Clark, p. 4).

March 9   *Night Over Taos*, the script drastically cut and the production financed largely by himself, opens in New York to run for thirteen performances as third production of Group Theatre and their first as a producing company independent of Theatre Guild (Clark, p. 25; Clurman, p. 74; Himelstein, p. 159).

Spring–   In Hollywood works on motion picture *Washington*
Summer   *Merry-Go-Round* and writes *Both Your Houses*. Tells Barrett Clark, " 'this modern craze for biographical information leaves me cold. . . . For one thing it's always inaccurate, for another it's so bound up with publicity and other varieties of idiocy that it gags a person of any sensibility' " (Clark, p. 4; no. 26).

May 2   Publishes *Night Over Taos* with Samuel French in printing of 1,034 copies at $2.00; second printing of 1,466 copies not called for until February, 1947; ending accidentally omitted in both printings (*Am. Lit.*).

Fall   Retains Harold Freedman, of Brandt & Brandt Associates, as theatrical agent because of difficulties with producer Jed Harris over *Both Your Houses*.

November 30	Has poem, "The Tragedy of Humphrey: And the Three-State (Tin and Chromium) Discount Company," in *New Republic* 73:65–66.
December 6	*Sea-Wife*, the script shown them by Barrett Clark (Clark, p. 30), produced at University of Minnesota, to run for five performances.

1933

March 6	*Both Your Houses* opens in New York, to run for seventy-two performances, then to be revived.
April 8	Publishes *Both Your Houses* with Samuel French in printing of 1,000 copies at $2.00; within the year four additional printings needed totaling another 6,000 copies.
May 4	Announcement of Pulitzer Prize for *Both Your Houses*.
May–August	In Santa Monica, California. Writes motion picture scripts for *Death Takes A Holiday*, based on Alberto Casella play, and *We Live Again*, based on Tolstoy's *Resurrection*.
July 14	Finishes first draft of *Mary of Scotland* (*Catalogue*, pp. 21–22), having written it "nights and Sundays" (no. 37).
August 16	Has review of Harvey Fergusson, *Rio Grande*, in *Nation* 127:190–91.
September–October	Has returned to New City. Marries Gertrude Anthony. With brother, Kenneth, forms Anderson House Publishing Company for publication of own plays.
November 27	*Mary of Scotland* opens in New York, to run for 248 performances. Publishes *Mary of Scotland* in limited edition of 550 copies in calf as first book by Anderson House, the book ready by opening of play.

1934

During the year completes home on South Mountain Road at New City designed by neighbor Henry Varnum Poor.

January 10	Publishes *Mary of Scotland* with Doubleday, Doran in printing of 6,436 copies at $2.00; by last printing in February, 1941, additional 6,054 copies printed.
February 1	Writes to George Middleton refusing use of remarks about a Middleton play: "I have made it a fast

principle never to say anything for publication or direct quotation" (no. 42).

9   Writes to Walter Prichard Eaton that "I don't believe great verse can be written in a play on a contemporary theme," but is interested in pursuing the question of a contemporary poetic tragedy with Eaton (no. 44).

Winter–   At work on *Valley Forge*.
Spring

March   From its editor, John C. Fitzpatrick at the Library of Congress, receives first nine volumes of Bicentennial Edition of *The Writings of George Washington from the Original Manuscript Sources*; also volumes 10 through 12 (covering Valley Forge period) in page and galley proof (nos. 46 and 47).

20   Writes that bicentennial volumes have "given me a new insight [unspecified] into [Washington's] situation" (Appendix IV, Slade).

April 21   Turns down offer of research assistance because "I always have done this work myself, inasmuch as the facts surrounding the characters in my plays seem to stick more clearly when I do the reading myself" (no. 48).

Summer   Plans production of *Valley Forge* with Theatre Guild, wishing to direct play himself (no. 49); Guild consents (Houseman, p. 136).

August   Persuaded by Theatre Guild to get another director for *Valley Forge*; chooses John Houseman (Houseman, p. 137).

10   Daughter, Hesper, born.

September 19   Outlines plot he will use in writing motion picture *So Red the Rose*, based on Stark Young's novel (no. 50).

December 10   *Valley Forge* opens in New York, to run for fifty-eight performances. Publishes *Valley Forge* with Anderson House in limited edition at $7.50 and trade edition at $2.50.

1935

Early   Hears from Boston lawyer, friend from UND days, that judge who passed sentence on Sacco and Vanzetti is "about out of his mind" from conflict between guilty conscience and sense of integrity. "That really gave me the idea for the judge [in *Winterset*], and then for the rest of [the play]" (Appendix I, no. 5).

March 21   Begins first draft of *Winterset*.

June 1   Finishes first draft of *Winterset* (*Catalogue*, p. 24).

August 7   Begins first draft of *The Wingless Victory*.

September   Has poem, "1908–1935 (For F. H. Koch)," in *The Carolina Playbook* 8:85–86.

25   *Winterset* opens in New York, to run for 179 performances, then to be revived.

28   Writes preface for *Winterset*, "A Prelude to Poetry in the Theatre."

October 11   Finishes first draft of *The Wingless Victory* (*Catalogue*, p. 25).

November   Publishes *Winterset* with Anderson House at $2.50.

1936

Late January   Probably in Hollywood working on motion picture

–February   scripts of *Mary of Scotland* and *Winterset*.

March–April   At home, writes *The Masque of Kings*.

April 5   Accepts Drama Critics' Circle Award for *Winterset*, acceptance speech broadcast nationally (Appendix I, no. 1).

9   Encourages verse play contest at Stanford, sponsored by Margery Bailey, classmate at Stanford, because "if anything can be done to steer our theatre away from realism and toward poetry I'm for it" (no. 52).

May 31   Begins writing *High Tor*.

July 2   Finishes first draft of *High Tor* (*Catalogue*, p. 27).

Fall   Involved in casting of *The Wingless Victory*, *The Masque of Kings*, and *High Tor*.

November 25   Sends "admonitions" for contestants in verse play competition at Stanford, such as: "Play structure is much more important than playwriting, even in a poetic play. . . . Read Aristotle on the 'recognition scene'. . . . Spend three times the effort planning your play which you will require to write it" (no. 54).

December 23   *The Wingless Victory* opens in New York, to run for 110 performances.

Publishes *The Wingless Victory* with Anderson House, distributed by Dodd, Mead at $2.50.

Publishes *The Masque of Kings* with Anderson House

in printing of 2,000 copies, distributed by Dodd, Mead at $2.50.

1937

January 6   Publishes *High Tor* with Anderson House, drawings by neighbor Henry Varnum Poor, distributed by Dodd, Mead at $2.50.

9   *High Tor* opens in New York, to run for 171 performances.

February 8   *The Masque of Kings* opens in New York, to run for eighty-nine performances.

23   Withdraws first edition of *The Masque of Kings* because of libel suit by Austrian Countess Larisch for his use of her as character in the play.

April 1   Accepts Drama Critics' Circle Award for *High Tor* (Appendix I, no. 2).

May   Has essay, "Yes, By the Eternal," in *Stage* 14:51, a response to Max Eastman, "By the Eternal," *Stage* 14 (April, 1937), p. 51.

June 8   Begins first draft of *The Star-Wagon*.

July 2   Completes draft of *The Star-Wagon* (*Catalogue*, p. 29).

Later in month publishes revised edition of *The Masque of Kings* in printing of 1,000 copies, substituting Baron and Baronin Neustadt for Count and Countess Larisch, and countess drops libel suit.

September 2   Explains to a graduate student that he uses iambic pentameter in plays because it combines "the maximum of intensity and elevation with a minimum of artificiality in the theatre" (no. 55).

29   *The Star-Wagon* opens in New York, to run for 223 performances.

October   Refuses invitation to lunch with critic John Mason Brown "because I want and need honest criticism, and no man can be strictly honest about the work of his friends" (no. 56).

Probably at this time buys farm near Hudson, Maine, for vacations.

7   Publishes *The Star-Wagon* with Anderson House, distributed by Dodd, Mead at $2.50; by June, 1940, sold about 3,000 copies.

14   Delivers "The Arts as Motive Power" as Founder's Day Address at Carnegie Institute, Pittsburgh.

17 Has essay, "The Arts as Motive Power," in *New York Times*, sec. 11, p. 1, cols. 6–8, p. 2, cols. 1–5.

November 6 Has poem, "Words for Sir Basil Zaharoff," in *Scholastic* 31:23.

17 Explains to John Mason Brown, who wants to discuss a play subject, that "it's the business of the playwright to please both himself and his audience and I have looked long and hard at that Broadway audience and found only a narrow margin of over-lapping between me and it" (no. 57).

Begins discussions with Robert Sherwood and Elmer Rice about forming a company to produce their own plays. Sidney Howard and S. N. Behrman are brought in, then the attorney John F. Wharton, and in the next year the group forms the Playwrights' Company, name suggested by Anderson "in emulation of the medieval guilds of artisans" (Rice, p. 375).

December 9 Outlines a national drama festival based on Greek model, with competition focused on poetic tragedy because "poetic tragedy has always been the highest aim of the theatre" (no. 58).

1938

January Has one-act play, "Feast of Ortolans," in *Stage* 15: 71–78.

January– Probably at work on *The Duquesnes*, an unfinished
February play (*Catalogue*, p. 68).

February 18 Makes suggestions to John Wharton about charter of Playwrights' Company (no. 59).

To Donald Ogden Stewart, president of the League of American Writers, indicates that he opposes Franco and fascism and supports Loyalist Republicans in Spanish Civil War (Goldstein, p. 175).

March Has one-act play, "Second Overture," in *Stage* 15: 41–45.

8 Suggests revisions to Robert Sherwood for *Abe Lincoln in Illinois* (no. 62). Formation of Playwrights' Company announced in New York papers. Learns the same day that David Selznick, who had promised to buy film rights to *The Star-Wagon*, has reneged on the deal (Wharton, p. 25); consequently does not have $10,000 to invest in Playwrights' Company until the

production of *Knickerbocker Holiday* (Behrman, p. 217).

April–May　At work on *Knickerbocker Holiday*, with Kurt Weill composing the music.

May 28　Has one-act play, "The Bastion Saint-Gervais," broadcast on radio (*Catalogue*, p. 64).

June　Revises *Knickerbocker Holiday*.

26　Suggests revisions to Elmer Rice for *This House* (later, *American Landscape*) (no. 66).

October 19　*Knickerbocker Holiday* opens in New York, to run for 168 performances. Other members of Playwrights' Company have persuaded him, "by cajolery," to tone down play's satire on New Deal (Rice, p. 380).

November 7　Writes "A Preface to the Politics of *Knickerbocker Holiday*."

10　Suggests "The Bastion Saint-Gervais" to Gilmor Brown for forthcoming Midsummer Drama Festival at Pasadena Playhouse (no. 68).

20　During intermission in *Knickerbocker Holiday* makes speech to raise money for relief of Europeans oppressed by Nazis (*NDQ*).

December　Has article, "About the Playwrights' Company," in *Stage* 16:17.

Publishes *Knickerbocker Holiday* with Anderson House, distributed by Dodd, Mead at $2.50; by June, 1940, sold 3,473 copies.

30　Reads paper, "The Essence of Tragedy," to American Literature Group of Modern Language Association of America meeting in New York City.

1939

March 3　Outlines musical, *Ulysses Africanus*, about "a man in a chaotic world in search of his own manhood," to Paul Robeson (no. 76).

Spring　Begins *Key Largo*.

April　Publishes collection of essays, *The Essence of Tragedy and Other Footnotes and Papers*, with Anderson House at $1.25; by June, 1940, sold 862 copies.

Late May–　In Hollywood, revising *Key Largo* and casting it,
Early August　perhaps working on motion picture scripts.

May 31　Thinks production of Elmer Rice play, *Siege of Berlin*, unwise (no. 78).

June 7   To Sidney Howard, outlines revisions in *Key Largo*
and suggests revisions for Howard's *Madam, Will
You Walk?* (no. 79).

23   Signs Paul Muni to play lead in *Key Largo* (no. 80).

30   Balks at filling out Social Security form because it is
"an application blank and I'm not applying for
anything" (Appendix IV, Young).

Mid-July   Revises *Both Your Houses* for production in Midsummer Drama Festival at Pasadena Playhouse.
Festival runs from June 26 to August 19 and consists
of eight Anderson plays (*NDQ*).

August 21   Writes to Brooks Atkinson that he opposes New Deal
because "a poet or artist is able to function only in a
free society" (no. 81).

23   Sidney Howard killed in tractor accident on his farm
at Tryingham, Massachusetts.

28   With other members of Playwrights' Company, goes
to Tryingham for Howard's funeral and serves as
pallbearer (Wharton, p. 71; Behrman, p. 219).

September 13   Portion of *Valley Forge* broadcast to rally public
opinion to defense of freedom (*Catalogue*, p. 23).

Fall   Begins financial support of nephews, Keith and Avery
Chambers, as they attend Drake University.

November 27   *Key Largo* opens in New York, to run for 105
performances.

28   Publishes *Key Largo* with Anderson House, distributed by Dodd, Mead at $2.50; by June, 1940,
sold 3,494 copies.

1940

January–   At work on *Journey to Jerusalem*. John Wharton tells
February   him of a New York state law prohibiting the
representation of deity on stage, and Anderson
changes name of central character from Jesus to
Jeshua (*Catalogue*, p. 35–36).

February 4   Has cantata, "The Ballad of Magna Carta," music by
Kurt Weill, on CBS radio, narrated by Burgess
Meredith.
Publishes "The Ballad of Magna Carta" with
Chappell & Co.

March   Writes preface for neighbor Amy Murray's book of

poems, *November Hereabout*, to be published in the fall by Henry Holt & Co., pp. xiii–xv.

21   Finishes draft of *Journey to Jerusalem* (*Catalogue*, p. 35).

May 5   Revising *Journey to Jerusalem*, writes to Harold, brother living in Iowa, that his yearly writing schedule "is much like farming. I plant an idea in the fall—it comes up, sometimes, in the spring—and by autumn again I hope for something out of it" (Appendix III).

18   To Margery Bailey, writes that he has begun to feel "that I am trying to do something which neither the critics nor the public is likely to understand—something . . . which will have to wait for a decision later on" (no. 89).

Summer   Asks Elmer Rice to direct *Journey to Jerusalem*; Rice spends summer at New City to discuss play and production (Rice, p. 391).

June 4   Playwrights' Company meets at Anderson's home to help Robert Sherwood prepare the "Stop Hitler Now" newspaper ad (Johnson, p. 170), an ad to be run in six national newspapers on June 10 at cost of $25,000, to which Anderson contributes (W. Johnson, pp. 85–87, 153).

September 8   Disagrees with Dorothy Thompson's view that a playwright cannot do his best work in the professional theater. "The theatre is always part of a civilization, and that limits its scope. But within the limits of what our civilization calls for we are free to do the best we can" (no. 91).

29   Has article, "Journey to Jerusalem," in *New York Times*, sec. 9, p. 1, col. 8, p. 2, cols. 4–5.

Publishes *Eleven Verse Plays* with Harcourt, Brace at $3.75.

October 5   *Journey to Jerusalem* opens in New York to run for seventeen performances.

30   Outlines *Candle in the Wind* to agent, Harold Freedman (no. 93).

November 1   Announces support of Wendell Willkie for president (*New York Times*, November 2, 1940, p. 12, col. 1). Believes Willkie is " 'the first unbossed and completely honest man to be nominated for the presidency since Wilson' " (R. Rice).

December 6   Urges S. N. Behrman not to alter the theme of *The Talley Method*. "There should be no rules in literature except those concerned with effectiveness. *What* the writer is trying to say must be left always to the insight and intuition of the writer" (no. 94).
Publishes *Journey to Jerusalem* with Anderson House, distributed by Dodd, Mead at $2.50.

1941

Early   Completes *Candle in the Wind*.
April 7   Has thirty-minute radio play, "John Keats and America," broadcast on NBC.
27   Has one-act play, "The Miracle of the Danube," broadcast on CBS radio.
Summer   Has "The Miracle of the Danube" in *The Free Company Presents: A Collection of Plays about the Meaning of America* (published by Dodd, Mead), pp. 239–67.
June   With Van Wyck Brooks, Lewis Mumford, and Louis Finkelstein helps plan Conference on Science, Philosophy and Religion at Columbia University (nos. 99 and 101).
By this time is planning *The Eve of St. Mark*.
October 10   Has paper, "The Basis of Artistic Creation in Literature," read by son Quentin at Rutgers University symposium on the arts.
22   *Candle in the Wind* opens in New York, to run for ninety-five performances.
26   Rutgers paper in *New York Times*, as "By Way of Preface: The Theatre As Religion," sec. 9, p. 1, cols. 5–8, p. 3, cols. 1–5.
December   Publishes *Candle in the Wind*, Rutgers paper as preface (for history of preface, see *Catalogue*, pp. 47–48), with Anderson House, distributed by Dodd, Mead at $2.50.

1942

February   Visits Camp Butner and Fort Bragg, North Carolina, gathering background material for *The Eve of St. Mark*.

11	Has one-act play, "Your Navy," broadcast on four major radio networks.
22	Has essay, "A Summons from Valley Forge," in *New York Times Magazine*, p. 8.
March	Writes humorous skit, "From Reveille to Breakfast," for production at Fort Bragg and other military camps.
14	By now, has granted amateur rights to *The Eve of St. Mark* to the National Theatre Conference (Appendix IV, Norvelle).
29	Will not support censorship even as part of war effort, not trusting "any man or board to decide what should be said aloud in the United States during the next few years" (no. 108).
June 1	To sister, Lela Chambers, indicates intention of dedicating *The Eve of St. Mark* to her son, Lee, killed in military accident (no. 109).
15	Finishes draft of *The Eve of St. Mark* (*Catalogue*, p. 38).
Summer	Helps organize Rockland County Committee To Save High Tor (no. 112).
October 7	*The Eve of St. Mark* opens in New York, to run for 291 performances. At opening publishes *The Eve of St. Mark*, dedicated to Lee Chambers, with Anderson House, distributed by Dodd, Mead at $2.50. Writes preface for Francis Marion Hargrove, *See Here, Private Hargrove*, having met Hargrove at Fort Bragg in February and had his help on "From Reveille to Breakfast" (*Catalogue*, pp. 39–40).
November	To Twentieth Century-Fox sells film rights to *The Eve of St. Mark* for $300,000, but major result, because he follows poor legal advice about paying taxes on the amount, is staggering tax debt for remainder of life (Wharton, pp. 124–25). Has "Your Navy" in *This is War!: A Collection of Plays about America on the March* (published by Dodd, Mead), pp. 45–68.

1943

January 12	On program with Wendell Willkie, speaks at Astor Hotel to oppose censorship and uphold freedom (*New York Herald Tribune*, January 13, 1943, p. 1, col. 4).
13	Leaves for Washington to arrange trip to England and North Africa.

24   In Washington attends *The Eve of St. Mark* in
command performance for the President at National
Theatre.

February   Tours military camps in Virginia, North Carolina
(Fort Eustis, Fort Monroe, Camp Butner) to collect
material for play on Negroes in the services (not
written).
Publishes revised edition of *The Eve of St. Mark*.

March 23   Sails from New York on Portuguese ship, *Pinto*. Trip
takes him to London for production of *The Eve of St.
Mark* and to North Africa where he collects material
for next play, *Storm Operation* (for daily account, see
nos. 115–125).

April 1   *Pinto* arrives in Azores.

10   Docks at Lisbon.

13   Flies to Bristol and takes train to London.
In London arranges for production of *The Eve of St.
Mark* and writes a new scene (Appendix I, no. 3);
revises *The Wingless Victory* for fall production in
London; writes scripts for several short war films.
Sees several plays; reads Jung's *Modern Man in
Search of a Soul*.

May 25   Takes overnight train to Alloway, Scotland; to avoid
censorship, identifies the town simply as the one with
"the bridge that Tam o'Shanter rode across" (no. 124).

26   Takes military flight to Algiers.
Travels much, interviews Dwight D. Eisenhower,
makes wide acquaintance among American troops,
collects addresses of their families in America to be
contacted on his return.

June 17   Sails from Casablanca.

26   Docks in Boston at noon and takes train for New
City.

July   Begins to plan *Storm Operation*.

September 19 Has report on trip to North Africa and *Storm
Operation*, "A Dramatist's Playbill," in *New York
Herald Tribune*, sec. 5, p. 1, cols. 7–8, p. 4, cols. 1–2.

October 21 Humorously attacks Behrman's campaign for presidency of Playwrights' Company (no. 128; Wharton,
pp. 102–5).

November   Finishes draft of *Storm Operation*.

December 6 Receives telegram indicating disapproval of play by

War Department (no. 131 and *Catalogue*. p. 42).
Revises *Storm Operation*.

1944

January   Has essay, "How *Storm Operation* Grew," in
          National Theatre Conference Quarterly Bulletin
          6:21–26.

9   Has essay, "Notes for a New Play," in *PM*.

11   *Storm Operation* opens in New York, to run for
          twenty-three performances.

Late February   Writes first draft of poem, "Mr. Fish Crosses the
                River."

March   Writes one-act play celebrating Greek Independence
          Day (Johnson, pp. 336–37).
          Revises "Mr. Fish" at suggestion of Katherine White
          (no. 132).

May   Begins *Warrior's Return*, first version of *Joan of
          Lorraine*.

13   "Mr. Fish Crosses the River," in *New Yorker* 20:28.

Early   Organizes Committee to Defeat Hamilton Fish in
Summer   congressional election; committee is active through
          election day, November 7, when Fish is defeated.
          Has "Letter to Jackie" in *The Best One-Act Plays of
          1943* (ed. Margaret Mayorga, published by Dodd,
          Mead), pp. 1–7.

July 8   Has poem, "Parallax," in *New Yorker* 20:24.

August   Publishes *Storm Operation* with Anderson House,
          distributed by Dodd, Mead at $2.50. Sends copy to
          General Eisenhower (no. 134).

November 22   Finishes *Warrior's Return* (for the play and its
              relation to *Joan of Lorraine*, see *Catalogue*, pp. 43–
              46).

December Reads Joseph Wood Krutch's *Samuel Johnson*
          (no. 137).

26   Outlines need within Playwrights' Company for
          someone to assume duties of producer (no. 136).

1945

January   Rewrites Joan of Arc play, now entitling it *A Girl
          from Lorraine*.

Mid-February   In Hollywood, revises *A Girl from Lorraine* and
to Mid-June   negotiates with Ingrid Bergman to take the lead on
               stage and in motion picture adaptation; negotiations

are complicated and inconclusive. Also begins *Fortune, Turn Thy Wheel*, unfinished play (*Catalogue*, pp. 68–69).

April 12   At studio with Ingrid Bergman, hears of President Roosevelt's death; all work stops (diary).

May 8   Hears President Truman's proclamation of victory in Europe and writes to sister who lost two sons in the war (Appendix IV, Chambers).

June 18   Takes train for New City, reading *King Lear* on the way (diary).
Ingrid Bergman presents selections from *A Girl from Lorraine* on tour of Allied army camps in Germany (*New York Times*, June 23, 1945, p. 9, col. 4).

July 6   Reads Joseph Jefferson's *Autobiography* and considers writing a play about him (diary).

18   Rereads *Winterset* for first time since production (diary).

24   Begins to write *Truckline Cafe* (diary).

August 6   Hears news of atomic bomb dropped on Japan (diary).

14   Hears news of Japanese surrender; in evening, a spontaneous neighborhood party at his house (diary).

29   Reads in John Keats's letters (diary).

September 1   Listens to ceremony of Japanese surrender (diary).

30   Finishes draft of *Truckline Cafe* (diary).

October–
December   Revises *Truckline Cafe* and arranges for its production.

October 28   Reads in *David Copperfield* (diary).

November 21   Writes to Louis Kronenberger, maintaining that present impotence of theater results from "a crippling lack of faith" in the population (no. 145).

1946

January–
February   Revises *Truckline Cafe* and arranges production.

February 27   *Truckline Cafe* opens in New York, to run for thirteen performances.

28   All reviews "according to report are malevolent and vindictive" (diary).

March 3   Writes statement about inadequacies of drama critics (diary).

4   The statement, "To the Theatre Public," in *New York Herald Tribune*, p. 10, cols. 1–2.

8   Sees production of *Antigone* (diary).

9   *Truckline Cafe* closes for lack of business.

18   Returns to statement on critics, expanding it as preface for *Truckline Cafe* (but play is not published; see *Catalogue*, pp. 77–78). Works on statement intermittently into September.

April 5   Arrives in Hollywood for further negotiations with Ingrid Bergman to do Joan play on stage and as motion picture (diary).

18   Leaves for New City, arrangement with Ingrid Bergman still unsettled (diary).

24   Revising Joan play, changes title to *Joan of Lorraine* (diary). Revision continues until opening of play.

May 17   Reads *King Lear* (diary).

18   Reads *Macbeth* (diary).

19   Reads *Antony and Cleopatra* (diary).

22   Sees Old Vic production of *Oedipus the King*, "the finest experience I have ever had in the theatre" (diary).

27   Reads in *Tom Jones* (diary).

June 4   Sees *Henry IV*, I (diary).

5   Sees *Henry IV*, II (diary).

10   Goes again to see *Oedipus* (diary).

14   S. N. Behrman resigns from the Playwrights' Company (Johnson, p. 373).

26   Reads Edmund Wilson, *The Shock of Recognition* (diary).

Early July   Reads several Shaw plays (diary).

9   Begins attempt to arrange for motion-picture production of Playwrights' Company plays, and "the most important item in the arrangement would be the control we kept over the making of the pictures" (no. 147).

20   Writes essay, "St. Bernard" (diary).

25   Reads essay as part of celebration of Shaw's ninetieth birthday at dinner at Waldorf-Astoria Hotel (diary).

August 1   Begins to consider play on Marlowe, with much reading on Marlowe and Elizabethan era in following months (diary).

September 15   Finishes draft of statement (now letter) on critics (no. 151).

October 12   Sees *The Iceman Cometh*, which is "long, trenchant, despairing, not moving" (diary).

26   Sees Synge's *The Playboy of the Western World* (diary).

November 18   *Joan of Lorraine* opens in New York, to run for 199 performances, Ingrid Bergman in the lead.

December 1   Has article "Playwright Tells Why He Wrote *Joan* and How He Signed His Star," in *New York Times*, sec. 2, p. 3, cols. 1–2.

3   Reads Douglas Bush, *English Literature in the Earlier Seventeenth Century, 1600–1660* (diary).

1947

January   Plans collection of essays, revising several earlier ones (diary).

Publishes *Joan of Lorraine* with Anderson House, distributed by Dodd, Mead at $2.50.

31   Begins revisions of script for motion-picture version of *Joan of Lorraine* (diary).

February   Has article, "The Temple of Democracy," in *Ladies Home Journal* 64:34–35.

16   Has article, "The Mighty Critics," in *New York Times*, sec. 2, p. 1, cols. 1–2, p. 2, cols. 1–2.

March 6   Writes poem, "Bird and the Thunderstorm" (diary).

10   Begins essay, "Compromise and Keeping the Faith" for forthcoming collection (diary).

12   Finishes "Compromise and Keeping the Faith" and revises "Cut Is the Branch that Might Have Grown Full Straight" (diary).

13   Revises "The Politics of *Knickerbocker Holiday* (diary).

April 23   Goes to Los Angeles for work on the *Joan* script with director Victor Fleming and producer Walter Wanger (diary).

26   Has poem, "Bird and the Thunderstorm," in *New Yorker* 23:34.

May 8   Buys first three volumes of Arnold Toynbee's *A Study of History*; reads into September (diary).

Greek publisher Theodore Kritas, founder of Arts, Inc., for publication and production of American books and plays in Near East, schedules *Joan of Lorraine* for his first production (in Athens during fall of 1947), and Basil Vlavianos, publisher of Greek daily *National Herald*, invites Anderson to be his guest during the production.

June 3 Visits Whittier College, first time since leaving it in 1918 (diary).

4 Writes to Upton Sinclair, criticizing his play *A Giant's Strength*, which offers solution to problems posed by atomic bomb, as unconvincing (no. 155).

23 Publishes *Off Broadway* with William Sloane Associates at $2.50; by 1950 about 3,000 copies sold.

July 26 Writes to Robert Sherwood, criticizing his play *The Twilight* for lack of thematic focus (no. 156).

August 2 Sees Bertolt Brecht's *Galileo* and finds it uninteresting (diary).

9 Leaves Los Angeles by car.
Visits brother, Harold, in Hayward, California; visits Minnewaukan and Grand Forks, North Dakota, first return since leaving in 1913; arrives in New City about the 19th (diary).

September 3 Begins to consider a collected edition of his plays and works at a preface for *White Desert* (diary).

4 Begins short story, "West Coast, Night" (diary).

6 Finishes "West Coast, Night" (*Catalogue*, pp. 98–99).

14 Learns that producer intends to change name of motion picture *Joan of Lorraine* to *Joan of Arc*; "saw red at once" (diary).

October 8 From reading in sixteenth century for play about Marlowe, begins to consider a play on Anne Boleyn (diary).

21 Finishes revisions of *Joan* script (diary).

November 1 Leaves New York on SS *Queen Elizabeth* for trip via London to Athens for Theodore Kritas's production of *Joan of Lorraine* (diary).
In Greece (from November 10), tours the country and writes five articles for *New York Herald Tribune*, only two of which are published (see no. 157, n. 1).

28 First article, "An American Observer in Greece," in *New York Herald Tribune*, p. 26, cols. 5–7.

December 1 Takes plane from Athens to London (diary); also second article, "The Plight of the Greek People," in *New York Herald Tribune*, p. 22, cols. 5–7.

9 Boards SS *Mauretania* for New York (diary).

During crossing receives enthusiastic accounts from Dorothy Hammerstein of Alan Paton's forthcoming novel, *Cry, the Beloved Country*, and decides to dramatize it (diary; *NDQ*, p. 18, n. 8).

15   Arrives in New City (diary).
        With Kurt Weill, discusses possibility of musical based on *Cry, the Beloved Country* (diary).

1948

January 3   Considering play on Anne Boleyn, gets idea "that the whole play takes place in her reverie, looking back. . . . Henry as the sexual Everyman" (diary).

6   Sees *Antony and Cleopatra* (diary).

15   Begins writing *Anne of the Thousand Days* (*Catalogue*, p. 48).

18   Responds to attacks on his view of Greek situation in letter, "An American Playwright Looks at Greece," in *New York Herald Tribune*, sec. 2, p. 7, cols. 3–6 (no. 157).

20   On St. Agnes' Eve, holds family reading of Keats's poem (diary).

22   Sees Tennessee Williams's *A Streetcar Named Desire*; while others in family liked it, "I wasn't much taken" (diary).

February 12   Signs letter from National Institute of Arts and Letters protesting investigations by House Committee on Un-American Activities under chairman J. Parnell Thomas, letter sent to Speaker of the House Joseph Martin.

March 1   Dorothy Hammerstein brings him copy of just-published *Cry, the Beloved Country* (diary).

3   With Kurt Weill, begins to plan musical adaptation of *Cry, the Beloved Country* (diary).

8   Has letter to editor on Russian danger in *New York Times*, p. 22, cols. 6–7 (disputed, March 18, p. 26, col. 6).

15   Writes to Alan Paton explaining why and how he wishes to dramatize *Cry, the Beloved Country* (no. 158).

May 1   Has poem, "Hi-Yo, Hi-Yo, Discernible Day (A Song After Reading Toynbee)," in *New Yorker* 24:26.

15   Finishes draft of *Anne of the Thousand Days*; continues to revise until opening (diary).

June 4   Takes train for Los Angeles to write motion picture
           script for Lloyd Douglas novel *The Robe*; reads
           Renan's *Life of Christ* on the way (diary).

July 31   Begins to consider play on Socrates, with theme, is it
           true that "knowledge is virtue"? (diary).

August   Returns to New City.

October 10 Has article on Playwrights' Company, "The Play-
           wrights' Birthday," in *New York Times*, sec. 2,
           p. 3, cols. 1–3; has article, "More Thoughts about
           Dramatic Critics," in *New York Herald Tribune*, sec.
           5, p. 1, cols. 3–5.

November   Has letter defending position on Greece in *Atlantic
           Monthly* 182:18 (no. 159).

4   Publishes motion picture script *Joan of Arc* with
           William Sloane Associates at $2.95.

5   Publishes *Anne of the Thousand Days* with William
           Sloane Associates in printing of 3,000 copies at $2.75;
           in December second printing of 2,000 copies; later
           printings bring total to 7,000 copies.

December 8 *Anne of the Thousand Days* opens in New York, to
           run for 198 performances; reads Edmund Blunden,
           Shelley: A Life Story (diary).

22   Begins writing *Lost in the Stars*, dramatization of *Cry,
           the Beloved Country* (Catalogue p. 50).

31   With Kurt Weill, who composes score for *Lost in the
           Stars*, listens to recordings of African songs (diary).

1949

January 21 Criticizes Garson Kanin's play *The Sky Is Falling* for
           lack of focus and contemporary interest (no. 162).

February 14 Finishes draft of *Lost in the Stars* (Catalogue, p. 50);
           continues to revise into September (diary).

24   Sees Arthur Miller's *Death of a Salesman*; likes it, but
           is disappointed that it has same story as Miller's
           earlier *All My Sons* (diary).

Early March Considers musical version of *High Tor* for television
           (diary).

March–April Works on prefaces for collected edition of his plays
           (diary).

April 13   Responds to attack by drama critic John Crosby
           (no. 164).

May 3   Learns that Francis Hackett plans plagiarism suit in connection with *Anne of the Thousand Days*; begins writing a refutation of the charges (no. 166).

August 6   Has article, "Democracy's Temple," in *Saturday Review* 32:135.

21   Has article based on refutation of Hackett's plagiarism charge, "How a Play Gets Written: Diary Retraces the Steps," in *New York Herald Tribune*, sec. 5, p. 1, cols. 1–2, p. 2, cols. 3–6.

October 2 Has memorial, "Mary MacArthur," at death of daughter of Helen Hayes and Charles MacArthur, in *New York Herald Tribune*, sec. 5, p. 2, col. 3.

11   At Idlewild airport meets Alan Paton, coming for production of *Lost in the Stars*. Because of South African displeasure with *Cry, the Beloved Country* Paton has had difficulty in leaving the country and has "arrived with 3 sixpenny pieces. Nothing else" (diary). Takes Paton home with him and arranges for advance on royalties.

30   *Lost in the Stars* opens in New York, to run for 250 performances. Has article concerning production of *Lost in the Stars*, "Assembling the Parts for a Musical Play," in *New York Herald Tribune*, sec. 5, p. 1, cols. 1–3, p. 2, cols. 1–3.

November 5 Begins to read *The Adventures of Huckleberry Finn* as source for musical with Kurt Weill (diary). Also reads *The Adventures of Tom Sawyer* and *Life on the Mississippi* (diary).

18   With Weill, begins to plan muscial based on *Huck Finn* (diary).

29   In secret begins novel that will become *Morning, Winter and Night* (diary).

December 7 Learns that four other musical adaptations of *Huck Finn* are in preparation; with Weill, wonders if they should continue their own (diary).

1950

January 6 Finishes chapter XI of *Morning, Winter and Night* and thinks "this novel of mine is so shocking . . . it would have to be issued under a pen name. . . . John Nairne Michaelson" (diary).

25   Begins writing the Huck Finn musical, entitling it *Raft on the River* (diary).

26   Learns that National Conference of Christians and Jews will present him the Brotherhood Award for *Lost in the Stars* and writes acceptance speech (diary).

February 2   Reads speech at presentation of Brotherhood Award (Appendix I, no. 4).

26   Excerpts from *Lost in the Stars* shown on CBS television for National Brotherhood Week.

March 12   Finishes draft of *Raft on the River* (diary).

13   Publishes *Lost in the Stars* with William Sloane Associates at $2.75; by end of year sold 6,328 copies.

14   Expresses hope that *Raft on the River* is not "a desecration of the original. It's happy stuff to work with" (no. 169).

19   Kurt Weill, at work on music for *Raft on the River*, has heart attack and is taken to the hospital (diary).

31   Finishes revisions on *Raft on the River*. Weill seems better; takes script to him in the hospital (diary).

April 3   Weill dies (diary).

4   Writes eulogy of Weill (diary).

5   Reads Weill eulogy at graveside service (diary).

8   "A sad sad day—over broken plans and lives" (diary).

19   The Francis Hackett plagiarism suit in connection with *Anne of the Thousand Days* is dropped (diary).

May 2   Finishes first draft of *Morning, Winter and Night* (diary); will be revising it through 1951.
Begins search for new musical collaborator on *Raft on the River* (diary).

29   With Burgess Meredith discusses possibility of a play on the life of T. E. Lawrence (diary).
Reads Lawrence's *Seven Pillars of Wisdom* and *The Mint* (diary).

June 12   Returns to earlier interest in play on Socrates; begins to read in Plato and Xenophon (diary).

21   Begins writing play on Socrates, *Barefoot in Athens* (diary).

25   Depressed by news of North Korean invasion of South; seems we will have "war for the rest of our lives" (diary).

July 12   Reads eulogy of Weill at memorial concert for him in New York (diary).

13   "News from Korea so bad it's hard to think about Socrates" (diary).

August 10   Has full-page ad in *New York Times*, p. 19, written by himself and signed with twenty-six others, urging public support of American action in Korea.

September 3   Finishes draft of *Barefoot in Athens* (diary).

October 5   Cancels production of *Lost in the Stars* in Baltimore because theater there is segregated (Johnson, pp. 437–38).

30   Outlines play *Art of Love*, modernization of Ovid's *Art of Love* (diary).

November 3   Begins writing *Art of Love* (diary).

16   Drops *Art of Love* (*Catalogue*, pp. 63–64) and returns to *Raft on the River* (diary).

December   Has article, "Kurt Weill," in *Theatre Arts* 34:58.

30   Finishes revision of *Raft on the River*; thinks it is set for production (diary).

1951

January–   Revises *Raft on the River* with suggestions from
February   prospective director, Joshua Logan; has secured Irving Berlin to compose music (diary).

January 27   Has poem, "View South from 50th St," in *New Yorker* 26:33.

March 3   Loses patience with Logan's suggestions for *Raft on the River*; Berlin withdraws from the collaboration; "I quit writing" (diary) (*Catalogue*, p. 75).

April 4   Begins revising *Barefoot in Athens* with new idea, that search for truth kills belief (diary).

11   Hears President Truman's defense of dismissal of General Douglas MacArthur as commander in Korea (diary).

15   Is reading K. R. Popper, *The Open Society and Its Enemies*, and finds that it encourages his point of view in *Barefoot in Athens* (diary).

23   Begins to plan a new play, *Adam, Lilith and Eve* (diary).

24   Criticizes Robert Sherwood's new play, *Girls With Dogs*, for lack of thematic focus (no. 175).

May 1   Begins writing *Adam, Lilith and Eve* (diary).

3   Pays $25,000 on bill for back income tax that amounts to $80,000 (diary).

6 Under pressure of tax problems wife's emotional health is deteriorating, and she "says life is hopeless" (diary).

July 28 Finishes *Adam, Lilith and Eve* (diary) (*Catalogue*, pp. 62–63).

August 2 Begins preface for *Barefoot in Athens* (diary).

September 1 Publishes *Barefoot in Athens* with William Sloane Associates at $2.75; by 1952 sold 5,447 copies.

October 28 Has article based on preface, "Notes on Socrates," in *New York Times*, sec. 2, p. 1, cols. 6–7, p. 3, cols. 4–6.

31 *Barefoot in Athens* opens in New York, to run for thirty performances. Anderson's son Alan directs; and Weill's widow, Lotte Lenya, is Xantippi. Celanese Theater presents *Winterset* on ABC television.

1952

Early In Los Angeles to work on motion picture scripts, begins *Cavalier King*, play based on Arthur Bryant's *King Charles II*, book given to him by Rex Harrison.

February 13 Differs with Elmer Rice and John Wharton about appropriate status under American law of Americans active in Communist party. Rice and Wharton "believe our local Communists to be acceptable citizens, while I believe them to be enemy agents, engaged in wrecking us from within" (no. 183).

April 3 Publishes *Morning, Winter and Night* with William Sloane Associates at $3.00. Uses pen name John Nairne Michaelson, and no one except family and Sloane knows he is author.

July Has returned to New City, but leaves home on discovering wife's infidelity and takes up residence in New York City (no. 186).

Fall Completes *Cavalier King* (*Catalogue*, pp. 65–66). Makes acquaintance of Gilda Oakleaf and writes poems "For Gilda," "Triton," and "Evadne" (*Notes*, pp. 13, 15, and 17).

October Writes poem "For Gilda" (*Notes*, pp. 21–22).

November Decides to obtain a divorce. Writes poems "Written, as You Will Notice, on a Day When There Was to Be No Phone Call," "Here in the

East," "For Gilda," and "Dear Gilda," (*Notes*, pp. 19, 23, 25, 27).

Goes to Los Angeles and works on various motion picture scripts.

1953

January	Has poem "Yellow-Breasted Chat" in *Ladies Home Journal* 70:160.
18	Attacks Authors' League for defending those listed in *Red Channels*, *New York Times*, sec. 2, p. 13, cols. 2–5.
February 8	Reiterates attack on Authors' League, *New York Times*, sec. 2, p. 13, col. 1 (following defense of league by its president, *New York Times*, January 25, 1953, sec. 2, p. 13, cols. 3–4).
Early	Buys home in Agoura, California. Begins musical, *Devil's Hornpipe*, with Rouben Mamoulian collaborating on script and Allie Wrubel composing music. Writes poem "Night-Thought" (*Notes*, p. 29).
March 21	Wife dies in New City, an apparent suicide.
22	Flies to New City for wife's funeral.
Early April	Returns to Agora, California.
Mid-June	Finishes draft of *Devil's Hornpipe* and begins revising.
July	Sells New City home and most of property there to artist Sidney Simon.
August	Finishes *Devil's Hornpipe* and sends script to Playwrights' Company for consideration.
Late August	Hears from Robert Sherwood that Playwrights' Company rejects *Devil's Hornpipe*. Begins extensive revision (no. 187).
December 16	Leaves for New York with script of *Devil's Hornpipe* for second consideration by Playwrights' Company (no. 188). Playwrights' Company rejects play again and he drops it. Writes poem "Sometimes I See You" (*Notes*, p. 31).

1954

Early February	Returns to Los Angeles and begins writing *The Masque of Queens*. Writes poem "For Gilda" (*Notes*, p. 33).

May 6	Marries Gilda Oakleaf in Los Angeles.
23	Hospitalized in Cedars of Lebanon by acute diaphragmatic hernia.
26	In absentia is presented Gold Medal for Drama by American Academy and National Institute of Arts and Letters in New York.
July	Finishes *The Masque of Queens* (*Catalogue*, pp. 73–74).
	Has prostate operation at Cedars of Lebanon.
	Begins dramatization of William March novel *The Bad Seed*.
Late August	Finishes draft of *The Bad Seed*.
Late September	After revising *The Bad Seed*, goes to New York to arrange its production.
	Writes poems "Emotion Recollected in Tranquility," "Darling," and "In Dream" (*Notes*, pp. 35, 37, 39).
December 5	Has article on his plays, "A Confession," in *New York Times*, sec. 2, p. 7, cols. 1–3.
8	*The Bad Seed* opens in New York, to run for 200 performances.
23	Has "The Christmas Carol," one-act adaptation of Dickens's "A Christmas Carol," on CBS television (*Catalogue*, p. 67).

1955

January	Begins writing *Richard and Anne*, suggested by Josephine Tey [pseud. of Elizabeth Mackintosh], *The Daughter of Time* (1951).
February	Has operation for diaphragmatic hernia at Lenox Hill Hospital in New York.
March 28	Publishes *The Bad Seed* with Dodd, Mead at $3.00.
	Buys home in Stamford, Connecticut, and moves there.
	Revises *Richard and Anne* (*Catalogue*, pp. 76–76).
	Makes musical adaptation for *High Tor* for television production.
November 14	Sherwood dies.
17	Has eulogy, "Robert E. Sherwood," in *New York Times*, p. 35, cols. 1–2.
28	Has "Robert E. Sherwood: A Colleague's Eulogy," in *Time* 66:26.

| December 9 | Elected to membership in American Academy of Arts and Letters. |

1956

Early	Writes script for *The Wrong Man*, motion picture directed by Alfred Hitchcock.
February	Writes poem "For Gilda" (*Notes*, p.41); has article, "Robert E. Sherwood," in *Theatre Arts* 40:26–27, 87.
March 10	His musical adaptation of *High Tor* on CBS television.
26	Explains to sister that he hesitates to work on family history because "I have always fought shy of writing down anything about myself. Not from reluctance to reveal what happened, but because autobiography is not the kind of work that interests me, yet it does take time" (no. 199).
April	Considers selling his stock in Playwrights' Company and resigning in order to finish paying income tax that had begun to accumulate in 1946 and by 1951 had amounted to $80,000 (no. 200).
May 10	Interviewed at his home by Louis M. Starr of the Oral History Collection at Columbia University; the interview taped and deposited in the Oral History Collection (Appendix I, no. 5).
23	Inducted into American Academy of Arts and Letters, reads memorial poem "Robert E. Sherwood." Plans and begins to write *Madonna and Child*.
December 22	Has poem "The World of Mathematics" in *New Yorker* 32:70.

1957

February (?)	Writes poem "Notes on a Dream" (*Notes*, pp. 43–44).
Spring	His class play at the University of North Dakota in 1911, "The Masque of Pedagogues," is published in *North Dakota Quarterly* 25:33–48. Writes *The Golden Six* (*Catalogue*, pp. 69–70).
Summer	At suggestion of Guthrie McClintic, dramatizes Brendan Gill novel *The Day the Money Stopped* (*Catalogue*, p. 68; Wharton, p. 255).
Fall	Arranges production of *The Day the Money Stopped*.

1958

| February | Writes poem "For Gilda" (*Notes*, p. 45). |

16 Has article on theater as reflection of national culture, "Curtains—Iron and Asbestos," in *New York Times*, sec. 2, p. 3, cols. 4–6.

20 *The Day the Money Stopped* opens in New York, to run for four performances.

May *The Golden Six* produced at Brown University.

Summer Returns to *Madonna and Child* and begins writing it.

October 26 *The Golden Six* opens in New York, to run for fifteen performances.

November Finishes *Madonna and Child* (*Catalogue*, pp. 71–73).

6 Flu prevents him from going to University of North Dakota for presentation of honorary doctorate; sends "Love Letter to a University" (no. 212).
Attempts to cast *Madonna and Child*.
Writes preface for *Four Verse Plays*, to be published by Harcourt, Brace & World on March 25, 1959, at $2.25.

1959

January 18 Interview with him reported in *New York Times*, sec. 2, p. 5, cols. 1–4.

February Writes poem "Valentine for Gilda" (*Notes*, pp. 47–48).

25 Buys first folio of Shakespeare and reads in it until one in the morning.

26 Suffers stroke and is taken to Stamford Hospital.

28 Dies.

March 3 Memorial service for him in St. Paul's Chapel, Columbia University.

CODE TO DESCRIPTION
OF LETTERS

AL   Autograph letter unsigned; preliminary draft with revisions.

ALi   Autograph letter initialed; preliminary draft with revisions.

ALs*   Autograph letter signed; preliminary draft with revisions.

ALs   Autograph letter signed; mailed letter.

C   Unsigned carbon of mailed letter.

Cs   Signed carbon of mailed letter.

P   Postcard.

TC   Typed copy of mailed letter made for Playwrights' Company files.

Tel   Telegram.

TL   Typed letter unsigned; fair copy of mailed letter.

TLs   Typed letter signed; mailed letter.

CODE TO LOCATION
OF LETTERS

PTA   Theatrical Autograph Collection, Princeton University Library

QA   Quentin Anderson

S   Margery Bailey Papers, Archives, University Library, Stanford University

SNB   S. N. Behrman Literary Estate

SY   Archer Milton Huntington Collection, George Arents Research Library, Syracuse University

T   Maxwell Anderson Collection, Humanities Research Center, University of Texas at Austin

TR   Elmer Rice Collection, Humanities Research Center, University of Texas at Austin

V   Maxwell Anderson Collection, Clifton Waller Barrett Library, University of Virginia

VE   Walter Prichard Eaton Collection, Clifton Waller Barrett Library, University of Virginia

W   Playwrights' Company Collection, Wisconsin Center for Film and Theater Research, University of Wisconsin

WC   Wellesley College Library

Y   Collection of correspondent, Beinecke Rare Book and Manuscript Library, Yale University

LIST OF LETTERS

No.	Date	Recipient	Place of Composition	Type and Location of Original
1912				
1	September 15	John M. Gillette	Minnewaukan	TLs; NDG
1913				
2	December 22	Henry Cowell	Stanford	P; QA
1917				
3	April 29	Marguerite Wilkinson	Stanford	ALs; MC
1918				
4	June 21	Upton Sinclair	Stanford	TLs; I
5	October 24	Fremont Older	Menlo Park	ALs; B
6	October	Editor, *Dial*	Whittier	*Dial* 65 (Nov. 2, 1918): 370
1919				
7	February 17	Upton Sinclair	New York City	ALs; I
8	May	Editor, *Dial*	New York City	*Dial* 66 (May 31, 1919): 568–69
9	June	Upton Sinclair	New York City	ALs; I
10	September 24	Upton Sinclair	New York City	ALs; I
1920				
11	March	Editor, *Freeman*		*Freeman* 1 (March 17, 1920): 11
12	July 6	Van Wyck Brooks	New York City	ALs; P
13	July 26	Harold Monro	New York City	ALs; LC
14	November 29	Harold Monro	New York City	ALs; LC

No.	Date	Recipient	Place of Composition	Type and Location of Original
1921				
15	January 24	Ridgely Torrence	New York City	ALs; PT
1922				
16	Summer	William Stanley Braithwaite	New York City	ALs; H
1923				
17	October	Heywood Broun	New York City	*World*, Oct. 23, 1923, 11:3
1924				
18	September	Alexander Woollcott	New York City	ALs; H
1925				
19	January 21	Lela and Dan Chambers	New York City	ALs; LAC
20		Alexander Woollcott	New York City	ALs; H
21	October 4	Lela Chambers	New City	ALs; LAC
22	October 26	Barrett H. Clark	New York City	ALs; Y
23	November 8	Sidney Howard	New City	ALs; B
24	November 18	Sidney Howard	New City	ALs; B
1927				
25	May 4	Arthur Hobson Quinn	New City	TLs; P
1929				
26	April 5	Barrett H. Clark	New City	ALs; Y
27	October 16	Theresa Helburn	Hollywood	TLs; Y
1930				
28	June 16	Barrett H. Clark	New York City	TLs; Y
29	June 16	A. George Volck	New York City	C; T
30	June 30	Dale Van Every	New City	C; T
31	August 23	Barrett H. Clark	New City	TLs; Y
1931				
32	Early March	Theresa Helburn	New York City	ALs; Y

No.	Date	Recipient	Place of Composition	Type and Location of Original
1932				
33	March 25	Barrett H. Clark	New City	ALs; Y
34	Summer	Gertrude Anthony (Anderson)	New City	ALs; T
1933				
35	June 3	Barrett H. Clark	Santa Monica	ALs; Y
36	July 11	Lela Chambers	Santa Monica	ALs; LAC
37	Late July —	Gertrude Anthony (Anderson)	Santa Monica	ALs; T
38	Fall	Paul Green	New City	ALs; NC
39	December 6	George Middleton		ALs; C
1934				
40	January 24	George Middleton	New York City	TLs; LC
41	January 29	Walter Prichard Eaton	New York City	ALs; VE
42	February 1	George Middleton	New York City	ALs; LC
43	February 9	George Middleton	New York City	TLs; LC
44	February 9	Walter Prichard Eaton	New York City	TLS; VE
45	March 7	Walter Prichard Eaton	New York City	TLs; VE
46	March 12	John C. Fitzpatrick	New York City	ALs; LC
47	March 16	John C. Fitzpatrick	New City	ALs; LC
48	April 21	Harriet Keehn		C; T
49	Summer	Lawrence Langner		ALi; T
50	September 19	Russell Holman	New City	TLs; V
1935				
51	October 14	S. N. Behrman	New City	ALs; SNB

No.	Date	Recipient	Place of Composition	Type and Location of Original
1936				
52	April 9	Margery Bailey	New City	ALs; S
53	October/ November	Margery Bailey	New City	ALs; S
54	November 25	Margery Bailey	Washington	ALs; S
1937				
55	September 2	Hazel A. Reynolds	New City	C; T
56	October	John Mason Brown		ALi; T
57	November 17	John Mason Brown	New City	C; T
58	December 9	Ray Lyman Wilbur	New City	C; T
1938				
59	February 18	John F. Wharton	New City	C; T
60	March 5	Margery Bailey	New City	TLs; S
61	March 5	Guthrie McClintic	New City	C; T
62	March 8	Robert Sherwood	New City	ALs*; T
63	April 5	Mrs. F. Durand Taylor	New City	C; T
64	April 22	John F. Wharton	New City	TLs; JFW
65	May 18	John F. Wharton	New City	TLs; JFW
66	June 26	Elmer Rice	New City	C; T
67	November 10	Mrs. F. Durand Taylor	New City	C; T
68	November 10	Gilmor Brown	New City	C; T
69	November 12	Mrs. Florence B. Hult	New City	C; T
70	November 25	Helen Deutsch	New City	C; T
71	December 5	Laurence Moore	New City	C; T
72	December 5	Albert H. Gross	New City	C; T
73	December	Paul Muni	New City	ALi; T
74	December 31	Paul Muni	New City	C; T
1939				
75	February 18	Marston Balch	New City	C; T

No.	Date	Recipient	Place of Composition	Type and Location of Original
76	March 3	Paul Robeson	New City	C; T
77	Spring	Sidney Howard		Tel; T
78	May 31	Victor Samrock	Hollywood	Tel; W
79	June 7	Sidney Howard	Malibu	TC; W
80	June 24	Paul Muni	Malibu	TLs; NYP
81	August 21	Brooks Atkinson	New City	C; T
82	September/ October	Polly Howard	New York City	AL; T
83	October 3	Archer Milton Huntington	New York City	ALs; SY
84	October 8	Lela Chambers	New York City	ALs; LAC
85	October 20	Wallace A. Bacon	New City	C; T
86	Early November	Polly Howard	Indianapolis	ALs*; T
87	November 7	Victor Samrock	Cleveland	ALs; W
88		Quentin Anderson		ALs; QA
1940				
89	May 18	Margery Bailey		ALs; S
90	July 10	Paul Muni	New City	TLs; NYP
91	September 8	Dorothy Thompson	New City	C; T
92	October 12	Reginald Gaimster	New City	C; T
93	October 30	Harold Freedman	New City	C; T
94	December 6	S. N. Behrman		C; T
1941				
95	March 3	Helen Hayes	New City	C; T
96	March 11	Donald Ogden Stewart	New City	C; T
97	April 21	George Middleton	New City	TLs; LC
98	April 21	Gordon K. Chalmers	New City	C; T
99	April 21	Van Wyck Brooks	New City	TLs; P
100	May 26	Playwrights' Company	New City	C; T

No.	Date	Recipient	Place of Composition	Type and Location of Original
101	July 17	Louis Finkelstein	New City	ALi; T
102	October 12	Brooks Atkinson	Washington	ALs; NYP
103	November 2	Lela and Dan Chambers	New City	ALs; LAC
104	November 2	Brooks Atkinson	New City	ALs; NYP
105	December 15	Lela Chambers	New City	ALs; LAC
1942				
106	February 5	Avery Chambers	New City	ALs; AC
107	March 11	Gen. Edwin P. Parker		C; W
108	March 29	Russel Crouse and Clifton Fadiman	New City	C; T
109	June 1	Lela and Dan Chambers	New City	ALs; LAC
110	June 2	Lee Norvelle	New York City	C; W
111	June 16	Lee Norvelle		C; T
112	August 10	Archer Milton Huntington		ALi; T
113	August 17	Lela and Dan Chambers	New City	ALs; LAC
114	December 19	Gen. Edwin P. Parker		C; W
1943				
115	March 23	Gertrude Anderson	At Sea	ALs; T
116	April 1	Gertrude Anderson	At Sea	ALs; T
117	April 6	Gertrude Anderson	Ponta del Gado	ALs; T
118	April 26	Gertrude Anderson	London	ALs; T
119	May 2	Gertrude Anderson	London	ALs; T
120	May 6	Gertrude Anderson	London	ALs; T

No.	Date	Recipient	Place of Composition	Type and Location of Original
121	May 11	Gertrude Anderson	London	ALs; T
122	May 11	Hesper Anderson	London	ALs; T
123	May 18	Gertrude Anderson	London	ALs; T
124	May 30	Gertrude Anderson	Algiers	ALs; T
125	June 13	Gertrude Anderson	Casablanca	ALs; T
126	July 1	Gen. Dwight D. Eisenhower		C; T
127	July 27	Harold Anderson	New City	ALs; HA
128	October 21	Playwrights' Company		C; T
129	November	Gen. Dwight D. Eisenhower		ALi; T
130	November 22	Gen. Alexander D. Surles	New York City	C; W
131	December 7	Gen. Alexander D. Surles	Baltimore	Tel; W
1944				
132	March 17	Katharine White	New City	C; T
133	June 9	Lela and Dan Chambers	New City	ALs; LAC
134	August	Gen. Dwight D. Eisenhower		C; T
135	Early November	The Editor		TLs; W
136	December 26	Playwrights' Company		TLs; W
137	December 27	Joseph Wood Krutch		C; W
1945				
138	March 18	John F. Wharton	Hollywood	ALs; JFW
139	April 23	Ingrid Bergman	Los Angeles	ALs*; T
140	April 25	Ingrid Bergman	Los Angeles	ALi; T
141	May 24	Playwrights' Company	Los Angeles	ALs; W

No.	Date	Recipient	Place of Composition	Type and Location of Original
142	Fall	George [Cukor?]	New City	ALi; T
143	October 20	Ingrid Bergman	New York City	ALs*; T
144	October 26	S. N. Behrman	New York City	ALs; SNB
145	November 21	Louis Kronen-berger	New City	ALi; T
1946				
146	March 8	Frank D. Fackenthal		C; W
147	July 9	Arthur S. Lyons	New City	C; W
148	August 1	S. N. Behrman		ALs; SNB
149	August 2	Arthur S. Lyons		C; W
150	August 29	S. N. Behrman	New City	ALs; SNB
151	September 15	New York Theater Critics	New City	C; T
1947				
152	March 1	E. B. White		ALs*; T
153	March 10	E. B. White		C; T
154	April 27	Archer Milton Huntington	Los Angeles	ALs; SY
155	June 4	Upton Sinclair	Los Angeles	ALs; I
156	July 26	Robert Sherwood	Culver City	C; T
1948				
157	January 9	*New York Herald-Tribune*	New City	C; T
158	March 15	Alan Paton	New City	C; T
159	August 30	Editor, *Atlantic Monthly*	New City	C; T
160	September	New York Theater Critics	New City	C; T
161	December 29	Brooks Atkinson	New City	TLs; NYP
1949				
162	January 21	John F. Wharton	New City	Cs; W
163	March 17	Alan Paton	New York City	Tel; W
164	April 13	John Crosby	New City	C; T
165	May 18	John Mason Brown		C; T
166	May	John F. Wharton	New City	AL; T

No.	Date	Recipient	Place of Composition	Type and Location of Original
167	June 9	Samuel J. Silverman	New City	C; T
168	September	John Chapman		ALs*; T
1950				
169	March 14	Archer Milton Huntington	New City	ALs; SY
170	July 1	Archer Milton Huntington	New City	TLs; SY
171	August 8	Brooks Atkinson	New York City	TLs; NYP
172	August 18	Brooks Atkinson	New City	ALs; NYP
173	August 30	John F. Wharton	New City	ALs; JFW
174	September 5	Playwrights' Company	New City	TLs; W
1951				
175	April 24	Robert Sherwood	New City	C; W
176	July 5	John F. Wharton	New City	ALs; JFW
177	November 3	Brooks Atkinson	New City	ALs; NYP
178	November 20	Victor Samrock	New City	TLs; JFW
179	November 29	Robert Sherwood	New City	C; TR
180	November 30	Jackson Toby	New City	C; W
181	November 30	Stephen Sondheim	New City	C; W
182	December 5	John F. Wharton	New City	ALs; JFW
1952				
183	February 13	Elmer Rice	Beverly Hills	TLs; TR
184	February 20	John F. Wharton	Beverly Hills	C; TR
185	February 27	Elmer Rice	Beverly Hills	ALs; TR
1953				
186	March 29	Archer Milton Huntington	New York City	ALs; SY
187	October 19	Robert Sherwood	Los Angeles	TC; W
188	December 14	Lela Chambers	Los Angeles	ALs; LAC
1954				
189	February 7	Robert Sherwood	Los Angeles	TLs; JFW
190	February 27	John F. Wharton	Los Angeles	ALs; JFW

No.	Date	Recipient	Place of Composition	Type and Location of Original
191	April 14	Lela Chambers	Los Angeles	ALs; LAC
192	July 13	Lotte Lenya Weill	Los Angeles	ALs; LW
193	July 22	Victor Samrock	Los Angeles	ALs; W
194	August 23	Victor Samrock	Los Angeles	ALs; W
1955				
195	January 22	John F. Wharton		ALs; JFW
196	March 8	Elmer Rice		TLs; TR
1956				
197	January 8	Van Wyck Brooks	Stamford	ALs; P
198	February 19	Van Wyck Brooks	Stamford	ALs; P
199	March 26	Lela Chambers	Stamford	ALs; LAC
200	April	Playwrights' Company		ALs*; T
201	April 18	John F. Wharton	Stamford	ALs; JFW
202	April 20	Elmer Rice	Stamford	ALs; TR
203	April 27	Enid Bagnold	Stamford	ALs; EB
204	May 14	Enid Bagnold	Stamford	ALs; EB
205	September 19	Elmer Rice		ALs; TR
206	October 9	Victor Samrock	Stamford	ALs; W
207	October 19	Editor, *New York Times*		C; T
1957				
208	April 21	John F. Wharton	Stamford	ALs; JFW
209	April 22	John F. Wharton	Stamford	ALs; JFW
210	October 7	Mabel Driscoll Bailey	Stamford	ALs; MDB
1958				
211	August 13	Paul Green	Stamford	ALs; NC
212	November 3	University of North Dakota	Stamford	TLs; ND

Part I

BECOMING A PLAYWRIGHT
1912–1925

We've had financial luck this year with the play, and I've quit work on the papers and gone to writing for the stage in the hope that I can repeat.
    —ANDERSON *to* LELA ANDERSON CHAMBERS,
     January 21, 1925

I. TO JOHN M. GILLETTE[1]

Minnewaukan, North Dakota
September 15, 1912

Dear Mr. Gillette:

Since I left the University the practical side of my nature has won a complete victory over the academic, and I have become a Socialist. For some time I have been pondering over this complete change of front, trying to trace the influences which brought it about; and it seems that so far as I am able to judge now it was your social psychology class which sowed the seeds of dissolution. Perhaps the result was not direct, but I simply learned to think in that half-year. At any rate I want to ask you whether or not my present position is sound from the point of view of one who has spent a life-time on the subject of social life? Is there any other way out?

Mrs. Anderson sends her regards—she is also a Socialist by the way, and we intend the boy to have liberal education along that line.[2] Do you remember that I gave a report on *The Leisure Class* by Veblen? A sister of Mrs. Veblen's, Mrs. Shellenberger, lives here, and we have come to know her very well. We hope to see you again.

Sincerely,
Maxwell Anderson

1. Gillette (1866–1949), who left the Presbyterian ministry to take a Ph.D. in sociology at the University of Chicago, joined the faculty at the University of North Dakota in 1907, and both Anderson and Margaret Haskett, who married following their graduation in 1911, were among his students. Gillette pioneered the study of rural sociology, his *Constructive Rural Sociology* (1913) going through numerous editions, and was an ardent pacifist. He was also a mid-western leader of the Socialist party, whose presidential nominee, the labor leader Eugene Debs, was to make his strongest showing in the 1912 elections, when he ran against Taft, Wilson, and Theodore Roosevelt.

2. Their first child, Quentin, born July 21, 1912.

2. TO HENRY COWELL [1]

Stanford, California
December 22, 1913

Dear Henry—

I wish to thank you very much for the music. No doubt you think it is good—so I shall learn to play it. I have no time for music these days, though. I resigned the janitor's position the other day—have been made a teaching assistant in the Eng. dept. at Stanford, and can't carry both. I hope you are getting along well. —Give my regards to your mother and Mrs. Veblen. [2]

Sincerely,
Maxwell Anderson

1. Cowell (1897–1965), experimental composer and pianist, lived at Carmel and was studying at the University of California at Berkeley, where he began *New Musical Resources* (1919), an explanation of the theories behind his nontraditional music. Anderson, whose interest in music was lifelong, got to know Cowell through the group of writers and artists that gathered at Palo Alto, and Cowell had sent Anderson one of his own compositions.
2. Ellen May Rolfe, estranged wife of Thorstein Veblen, remained in Carmel when Veblen left Stanford for the University of Missouri in 1911.

3. TO MRS. MARGUERITE WILKINSON [1]

Stanford University,
California
April 29, 1917

My dear Miss Wilkinson,

You have my permission to reprint anything of mine which you take a fancy to. I have never reached the ultimate glory of magazine publication, and the English Club at Stanford, which published the Stanford book, will make no trouble for you, I am sure.

You have my best wishes for success with your book. [2]

Sincerely,
Maxwell Anderson

P.S. Born in 1888, in Pennsylvania. If you do not know of him already, let me refer you to a much better poet than myself—F. E. Hill, now attending Columbia U., and born in San Jose.[3]

1. Mrs. Wilkinson (1883–1928), a poet living in New York City, also compiled several anthologies of poetry. Her next anthology was *New Voices: An Introduction to Contemporary Poetry* (1919), and she had asked Anderson for permission to include in it some of his poems from *A Stanford Book of Verse* (1916).

2. Mrs. Wilkinson used none of Anderson's poems in *New Voices*.

3. Frank Ernest Hill (1888–1969) was one of Anderson's closest friends throughout life, but none of Anderson's letters to him have survived. They met at Stanford, where Hill took a B.A. in 1911, then taught in the English department from 1913 to 1916. Following study at Columbia and war service, Hill joined Anderson as an editorial writer on the *Globe* in 1919. The two were the principal founders of the poetry magazine the *Measure* in 1920, and Hill moved to New City, in Rockland County, New York, soon after Anderson moved there in 1922. Thereafter Hill frequently read drafts of Anderson's poems and plays. Hill had several newspaper and publishing jobs until the mid-thirties, when he joined the American Association for Adult Education, thereafter publishing extensively in that area. He collected his own poems in *Stone Dust* (1928), published a modern English translation of selections from *The Canterbury Tales* (1930), did a fictionalized biography, *To Meet Will Shakespeare* (1949), and collaborated with Allan Nevins on a three-volume history of the Ford Motor Company (1954, 1957, 1963). His memoir in the Oral History Collection at Columbia University recounts his long association with Anderson. *A Stanford Book of Verse* included several of Hill's poems, but Mrs. Wilkinson used none of them in her anthology.

4. TO UPTON SINCLAIR[1]

Stanford University, California
June 21, 1918

My dear Upton Sinclair:

I never expect to get paid for poetry. You are very welcome to Star-Adventurer. Anyway your magazine is the only one in the country that would consider it. If it can be made into a poem by omissions leave out anything you like.[2]

I agree with you about religious and political conditions almost always, but you are more hopeful than I am about getting out of the mess. The individual seems to me the only hope, and nobody gives him a chance.

By the way, I am a subscriber, and my address is changed from

Whittier to the above. I shall be glad to have the magazine follow me, for we need independent voices these days.

Sincerely,
Maxwell Anderson

1. Sinclair (1878–1968), muckraking novelist and social reformer with strong socialist and pacifist commitments, published a magazine, *Upton Sinclair's: for a Clear Peace and the Internation*, from his home in Pasadena, California. For the magazine he had accepted an Anderson poem.

2. "Star-Adventurer," *Upton Sinclair's: for a Clear Peace and the Internation* 1, no. 8 (December, 1918): 15. No other text of the poem has been located, so it cannot be determined whether Sinclair altered it for publication. But line 10 contains a typographical error, printing "law-given" where the context calls for "law-giver."

5. TO FREMONT OLDER[1]

Menlo Park, California
October 24, 1918

My dear Mr. Older,

I have been following the chapters of your story with all the interest and delight that used to carry me through Cooper and Stevenson. There is a distinct feeling of regret at the end of every chapter. The material is a revelation, and would have held however expressed, but you have made it absolutely convincing to me, and added that artistic turn that gives work permanence. It ought to be put in book form.[2]

Sincerely,
Maxwell Anderson

1. Older (1856–1935), editor of the *San Francisco Evening Call-Post*, had made his name as a great reform journalist while editing the *San Francisco Evening Bulletin* (1895–July, 1918), whose editorial staff Anderson joined just after Older resigned. At the time of the present letter Older, in the *Call-Post*, was serializing an account of his newspaper crusades in the *Bulletin*. Begun with the intention of ridding San Francisco of crime and vice, the crusades ended with Older's development of a sympathetic understanding of criminals and a commitment to rehabilitative work with them.

2. Later expanded, the series was published as *My Own Story* (Oakland, Cal.: Post-Enquirer Publishing Co., 1925).

6. TO THE EDITOR, *Dial*[1]

Whittier, California
[October, 1918]

Sir:

Francis Bacon was given to tripartite analyses. If his subjects did not fall naturally into three sections he so treated them that they seemed to. "Studies serve for delight, for ornament, and for ability," he said judicially, looking about him at the revival of learning.[2] Having undertaken an examination of this statement lately, I am forced to the conclusion that we in modern America who study literature—especially English literature—do so for none of these reasons. Not for delight; the students find it drudgery. Not for ornament; it is a disgrace to seem, outside the classroom (and in it, too, for that matter) to know much of the great masters of prose or poetry, or to manifest a power of expression. Not for ability; wherein shall it result to the material profit of any of us, save the pale priests who pass along the lamp, to know there were two Wartons?

There is a friend of mine who would say that we have gone beyond the Baconian exposition, that we study literature for its effect of broadening and deepening the character. Let his students beware of him. Let them become more human, let their sympathies have wider scope, at their own peril. It will ruin them for business. They will be failures in this progressive civilization if they forget him not quickly, and all the dangerous nonsense he has taught them. Indeed, he does alarm them; we all do; and they take over-elaborate precautions lest they be softened and made gentle by the speculations of the great minds of the world. Instinctively self-protective, they steel themselves against all prophets of the humanities. Usually it is a needless defense. They are already isolated and immune. Only those who have ears can hear—and they have been hearing all along.

It is self-evident to the man who has corrected themes for many classes that the creative faculty in any one student remains practically static, and that there are no visible results from methods the most varied, the most drastic, the most conscientious. No student has ever learned under my instruction to spell, or punctuate, or build a sentence. Nobody can teach these things. The original cryptogram of letters is transferred to us in childhood, and afterwards we puzzle over it alone. He who can spell at the beginning remains able to spell at the end; he who could punctuate at first can punctuate still; he who early in life can narrate, describe, and analyze retains his power. Our students in composition grow, flourish, and die aloof from our aid, integral, sufficient to themselves, relying upon chance and whatever innate ability they possess. In the realm of literature the conditions are similar. The same lad who in high school precociously understood the sonnet on Westminster Bridge will in the university find subtle meanings and interplay of thought in the series to the River Duddon.[3] We do not broaden and deepen them. If they are broadened and deepened they do it themselves, by the force of hidden aspirations, by natural mental growth. Those who are stupid, except in extraordinary instances, will remain stupid; the man who was brilliant once is now unchanged. Knowledge can be imparted in limited quantities, a dead and useless, uninspired knowledge of the anatomy of certain poetry and prose. But whatever appreciation of the masters your student may show in your presence he has capacity for in your absence. You may amuse him and yourself by what you say; the time in class may pass pleasantly enough; but you cannot add a cubit to his understanding. George Bernard Shaw is always himself; so is William Cowper; so are Janet, and Fred, and Algernon. The boy who loves literature will read it in the library; the others suffer many purposeless and grilling hours. As well attempt to explain orthodox Christianity to a Buddhist, as the flower of literature to the uninterested. He cannot understand, and he does not wish to. We are tilting against a mill—a huge, bellyless, soulless organization, compact of dullness, custom, and immutable law. We may tear a flange, but there is no possibility of convincing.

It is evident that I am pessimistic this morning. I have overstated my case. Is there no hope for us? I once asked a friend if he had read The Theory of the Leisure Class. "Why, no," he retorted; "why should I? All of my friends have read it. It permeates the atmosphere in which I live." Perhaps professors are, in a vague way, makers of atmosphere —as has been so often less flatteringly hinted by sundry college journals. We read; we understand; we fulminate. Who knows by what devious and shadowy trails civilization and culture are advanced? There is little enough progression on the high road. Our recognized output is sugared stupidity; but the plant may be worth maintaining for its by-products.

Maxwell Anderson

1. Earlier in 1918 the *Dial* (1880–1929) had been moved from Chicago to New York, and its new board of editors, including Conrad Aiken, Van Wyck Brooks, Randolph Bourne, and Harold Stearns, made it for a time a leading journal of social and cultural reform.

2. Bacon's "On Studies" (*Essays*, 1597) opens with the quoted sentence, and his *Advancement of Learning* (1605) assumes the revival of learning.

3. Poems by Wordsworth.

7. TO UPTON SINCLAIR

[New York City]
February 17, 1919

Dear Upton Sinclair—[1]

I got your appreciative note in regard to the Blue Pencil—for which thanks. And I should have written you then, but neglected it.

The truth is I am no longer at Whittier, no longer at Stanford, in fact lost to you geographically and politically, serving as a sort of apprentice editor on The New Republic.[2] My tenure depends upon my ability to tone down to a judicial attitude—or to go over to the literary end and write book reviews or essays. A choice between dodging and evading. But this is not to the point.

I am glad you remembered me, and hope you will be in New York sometime that we may meet. The jolly good times are on, bedad; we live in the spring of centuries, and your magazine is thawing a good deal of ice. When the blue bonnets go over the border I hope to be along.

Sincerely
Maxwell Anderson

1. Sinclair had praised Anderson's satire on the cynicism of journalists, "The Blue Pencil," *New Republic* 17 (December 14, 1918): 192–94.

2. The *New Republic* under its founding editor Herbert Croly supported President Wilson and the Democratic party, while Sinclair, a socialist, was at the time urging the formation of a labor party.

8. TO THE EDITOR, *Dial*

New York City
[May, 1919]

Sir:[1]

It would be difficult to ascertain whether the discussion of an art is usually a sign of its birth or of its dissolution. A corpse is most convenient for dissection. But in the case of American poetry it is almost unnecessary to remark that there has been as yet no body of verse worthy the name; and since the awakening interest in such things, vouched for by their publication, cannot indicate postmortem curiosity, we can afford to assume that there is an immediate flowering in preparation for the submerged art in this country. Meanwhile, come what will, the discussions are stimulating and exhilarating, and especially so the clear-headed critical estimates of Mr. Conrad Aiken, who, though a member of the craft, retains a delightfully unpartisan attitude toward the members of every school, group, and chorus. Yet it is impossible to please anybody all the time, and Mr. Aiken's classification of American poetry leaves me convinced and unsatisfied. Convinced as to the state of our poetical product, unsatisfied with the remedy offered.

To Mr. Aiken there seems a middle dish between vulgar sentimental sugar-candy and recondite peacock's tongues; the ham and eggs—may I say—of verse, appetizing, nourishing, and generally available. He laments its absence from the American menu. In Browning's words, "the poets pour us wine,"[2] some so sweet that it sickens us, others of so condensed, complex, and occult a flavor that we take it puzzled, in tentative sips. The plea is for a medium grade, palatable but with body.

One classification suggests another; and when I came in the same hour upon Landor's tribute to Browning it occurred to me that in this poem lay the basis of another and truer division, applicable in almost every instance, and pointing to a possible poetical future in a country whose artists have shown a tendency toward clarity, conciseness, cleverness, and away from sentimentality:

> *Browning! Since Chaucer was alive and hale*
> *No man hath walked along our roads with step*
> *So active, so inquiring eye, or tongue*
> *So varied in discourse.*

The linking of these two names is impressive in itself. These are men
outside the great tradition of English poetry, who strive, not after
sensuous imagery, the purple patch, incense-breathing melody, but for
intellectually stimulating analysis and gleeful, ironical portraiture.
English poetry has been dominated, from Spenser down, by all that is
sweet and lovely in music, picture, and sentiment. Shakespeare, able to
do as he pleased, finally threw his great weight into the scale on
Spenser's side, donned for his tragedies gorgeous trailing robes, and
spoke in elegiac music. Milton is a high priest of harmony;
Wordsworth (at his best), Blake, Coleridge, Keats, Shelley, Tennyson,
Swinburne, Rossetti, utter the emotional and lyrical cry. But the
appeal of Chaucer and Browning, together with that of Byron and
Burns, at their highest, is based upon detached and philosophic
observation of the human comedy. The characteristic works of
these four men—such as the Prologue, Fra Lippo Lippi, Don Juan,
Tam o'Shanter—indicate their attitude immediately. Keen, critical,
humorous observers of human nature are they all, attempting other
manners only at the risk of becoming rhetorical—as witness Burns in
his love songs. The grand division is in attitude. Spenser leads a group
of poets who were in the main seekers after the beautiful preeminently
receptive and emotional. And Chaucer, no less English, heads a
smaller list of those who loved truth and its ironies, and an active
intellect, more than the singing robes.

Many of us are sick of that ubiquitous insipid sweetness which
results from a too absolute surrender to that main tradition of "the
light that never was on sea or land."[3] The past glories of English
poetry are largely due to the creation and re-creation of that light; but
the age and the land in which we live are too clear-eyed to appreciate
the beautiful illusion. Many of us also have a preference for Keats, but
his purple is foreign to our garish day; and an attempt to imitate him
now is as futile and shallow as the piano reveries of ten years ago.
Perhaps the future lies with those who are able to look at modern
things in modern daylight, and who are willing to report them without
throwing about them any glamour of age, distance, or exotic custom.
In this realistic age all the old paraphernalia of romance, once so
natural, spontaneous, and true, seems trashy and affected. The tinsel is
frayed; the tricks are stale. There must exist, on every hand, waiting
for the seeing eye, exquisite ironies comparable with To a Louse, The
Bishop Orders His Tomb, and The Vision of Judgment. Our own most

distinctively national verse has included lesser attempts in the
Chaucerian tradition. Some of the Biglow Papers, On Lending a Punch
Bowl, and The Last Leaf[4]—and a few of the etchings of Emerson—are
natural and forthright utterances in that vein.

Those who try to prettify modern life and adventure, in the
manner of Masefield and Noyes, receive an immediate and imperma-
nent reward. They have poured new wine into ancient and leaky
receptacles. And no great modern master in the other school has
arisen, though Edwin Arlington Robinson in this country has shown
the way, and with Robert Frost we turn with finality from Tennyson
and look freely about us. The future may be his. But America has not
yet been expressed. For the most part attempts at poetical utterance
have been limited, even in the hands of a man like George Sterling, to
endeavors to imitate the inimitable in sonnet and lyric.[5] We have
wished to reproduce beauty in mood and speech, but beauty is a
foreign element to our nation; there is no sincerity in our rhapsodies.
It is to Chaucer, and not to Milton, that we must turn for "freedom,
virtue, power."[6]

Maxwell Anderson.

1. Conrad Aiken (1889–1973), who had already published six volumes of poetry,
was poetry editor of *Dial*. In the *New Republic* of May 10, 1919 (19:58–60), he had
reviewed Louis Untermeyer's *The New Era in American Poetry* (1919) and had
attacked Untermeyer for his attachment to sentimental poetry. The attachment, Aiken
said, blinded Untermeyer to the other and more promising kind of contemporary
poetry, which was analytic and oblique.

2. "Epilogue," *Pacchiarotto and How He Worked in Distemper* (1876).

3. Wordsworth, "Elegiac Stanzas Suggested by a Picture of Peele Castle" (1805).

4. *The Biglow Papers*, two series (1848 and 1867) by James Russell Lowell; and
"On Lending a Punch-Bowl" (1848) and "The Last Leaf" (1833) by Oliver Wendell
Holmes.

5. Sterling (1869–1926), poet known by Anderson in San Francisco and probably
the model for Brissenden in Jack London's *Martin Eden* (1909), published several
volumes of poetry, the last one, *Thirty-five Sonnets* (1917), heavily influenced by Keats.

6. Variation on Wordsworth's expostulation to Milton in "London, 1802":
"Milton! thou shouldst be living at this hour. . . . And give us manners, virtue, freedom,
power."

9. TO UPTON SINCLAIR

[New York City]
[June, 1919?]

My dear Sinclair—

You will be interested to note that I grew too Bolshevistic for the N. R. and am writing editorials on the Globe. Liberal sheet, no pretence of telling the whole truth. More money.

And more, I hope.

But I've already got over a boost for the Labor Party and a knock for Gompers.[1]

If you want information about the radical weeklies I could say a few words—in confidence—[2]

Maxwell Anderson

1. Probably the unsigned editorial, "Gompers As A 'Direct Actionist,'" *Globe*, June 10, 1919, p. 4, col. 1, which attacked Samuel Gompers, president of the American Federation of Labor, for his opposition to an American labor party and his support of labor strikes. The editorial thought strikes undemocratic and a national labor party, which Sinclair also supported, the best avenue for labor's social aspirations.

2. Sinclair was at work on *The Brass Check* (1920), an attack on American journalism.

10. TO UPTON SINCLAIR

[New York City]
September 24, 1919

My dear Sinclair—[1]

I have been out of town for a long period, and your letters have accumulated with a great many other things. I am exceedingly sorry. I am leaving tomorrow for another week, and there after will be here at my desk, all too solidly planted.

In regard to the Blue Pencil. The proprietor was not de Young but R. A. Crothers of the Bulletin. The office described was the office of de Young's Chronicle. I knew Crothers and did not know de Young. I knew the Chronicle office but not the Bulletin—at least not so well. I only wrote editorials there. So it is Crothers superimposed on the

Chronicle. And because these facts are evident to those who know the "local situation" you will not need to quote me.

Your questions about New York papers I can't answer off hand because I haven't been here long. A few hasty inquiries only made the matters more dubious. It is certain, however, that Munsey owns both the morning and evening Sun.[2]

I shall be interested in your book, and wish I had time to contribute more to your background.[3]—It may interest you to know that Croly controls the New Republic because he has the purse strings between his teeth, but that Johnson, who sits next to him in council, is a far-seeing, alert and level-headed radical. His is the brain of the organization. Lippmann is usually misinformed and muddled.[4]

Sincerely

Maxwell Anderson

1. Sinclair, at work on *The Brass Check* (1920), an exposé of American newspapers, had asked Anderson about newspapers in San Francisco and New York. Anderson's "The Blue Pencil" was based on his experience with two San Francisco papers, the *Evening Bulletin*, owned by R. A. Crothers, and the *Chronicle*, owned and edited by Meichel Harry de Young. In "The Blue Pencil" Crothers is called De Smith.

2. Frank Andrew Munsey owned the *New York Sun* and numerous other magazines and newspapers, including the *Globe*, on which Anderson worked at the time.

3. *The Brass Check* uses "The Blue Pencil" and information from the present letter to indict San Francisco newspapers (pp. 250–51).

4. Willard Straight gave Herbert Croly the money to found the *New Republic* in 1914 and to operate it until Croly's death in 1930. Alvin Johnson, who had invited Anderson to join the *New Republic*, and Walter Lippmann were on the editorial board of the *New Republic*.

11. TO EDITORS, *Freeman* [1]

[March, 1920]

Sirs:

It seems to me that all our independent periodicals are basing their efforts on the theory that whatever is to be done must be the fruit of governmental action. They are shoving with their whole weight in the direction of a more nearly centralized nation and a more nearly socialized system of production. Now it seems obvious that unless we make certain fundamental changes in the State, the more power you give it the less power the people hold, and the less their wishes are considered. The aim of every reformer, if he knows what he is about, is to secure a larger life for the individual, and man does not live by bread alone. If the heaven of a certain one of your contemporaries is a mechanized existence (and in reading it one can discern no other paradise) I'm against it.[2] Personal liberty at all costs, rather than comfort under benevolent autocracy. Your contemporary recognizes that we have an autocracy and that it is bad. It says to us, "Come, let us make this autocracy benevolent, and it will thereafter serve us." Right here I object and exclaim, "Alas, there is no virtue in them!"

We have gained political liberty. What we want now is emancipation from industrial masters. Whatever political oppression still exists is only a reflection of capitalistic fear. To put more authority in the hands of the law-makers by depending on them to right our difficulties is to bolster this capitalistic authority. It controls the State. Its reforms, when they arrive, will be palliatives, and it will continue to exploit us as a nation of neat and nimble slaves. It was Thomas Jefferson who put into the Constitution whatever good it has, and he was a doubter and a near-bolshevik. He believed in the individual and he did not trust centralized political mechanism. Perhaps the best field open to a weekly is the advocacy of personal rights as opposed to public and controlled policies. Why should the mob or its leaders always have their way with a free man? A government is always on the side of the powers that be; and the citizen is always flattened by its processes. The hope for the man is in co-operative economic action, not in governmental regulation of corporations and prices. The hope for the child is in being taught at home instead of by the usual sausage-stuffing process of the school, whereby he is filled with a miscellaneous assortment of odds-and-ends, exploited by fads of all kinds, but never taught or encouraged to think for himself. I am, etc.,

M. A.

1. The *Freeman* (1920–24), a weekly magazine of liberal social opinion edited by Van Wyck Brooks and Albert Jay Nock.
2. Probably the *New Republic*, whose editorial staff Anderson left in May, 1919. Under its editor Herbert Croly, the *New Republic* urged social planning and control by the central government (see also Croly's *The Promise of American Life*, 1909).

12. TO VAN WYCK BROOKS [1]

[New York City]
July 6, 1920

Dear Van Wyck Brooks:

I have been out of town the last three weeks, and your note has lain on my desk the same length of time. But I should be glad to review The Blood Red Dawn, or anything else you may have, if the offer is not withdrawn. [2]

Sincerely
Maxwell Anderson

1. Brooks (1886–1963), who taught at Stanford the two years prior to Anderson's going there in the fall of 1913, was during the first half of the century an influential molder of opinion about American culture, and his early book *America's Coming-of-Age* (1915) had popularized a condemnatory view of the puritan and pioneering heritage. He exerted an influence also through the several magazines he edited, among them the *Dial* and the *Freeman*, in which Anderson had published several poems and essays. Because of Anderson's San Francisco background, Brooks had asked him to review *The Blood Red Dawn* (1920), first novel by San Francisco writer Charles Caldwell Dobie (1881–1943).

2. Anderson's unsympathetic review of *The Blood Red Dawn*, a love story of a San Francisco stenographer, appeared in *Freeman* 1 (August 11, 1920): 525–26.

13. TO HAROLD MONRO [1]

[New York City]
July 26, 1920

Dear Harold Monro—

Thank you very much for your word about Full Circle. I fear there is nothing in my portfolio which will greatly interest you, but I am sending—in another envelope—a number of poems and epigrams which may possibly have some appeal. —Now that I think of it I shall add another to my offering and send it with this note. Don't be overwhelmed. I realize you may not like any of 'em. Probably I shouldn't if I were at the other end of the correspondence. [2]

Sincerely
Maxwell Anderson

1. Monro (1879–1932), poet and sponsor of contemporary poetry through his Poetry Bookshop, founded in London in 1913, and the poetry magazines he edited, including the *Chapbook* (1919–1925). Soliciting for the *Chapbook*, he had written to Anderson saying he had seen "Full-Circle" in the *New Republic* and asking Anderson to send him any other poems "on, or connected with, the same subject. I like truthful poems" (July 3, 1920; T).
2. Monro's reply (November 12, 1920; LC) lists the poems sent and the payment for those accepted: eleven epigrams (2 guineas), "Dark Oracles" (3 guineas), "Mazurka" (1 guinea), and "Star-Adventurer."

14. TO HAROLD MONRO

[New York City]
November 29, 1920

Dear Harold Monro—[1]

I thought my manuscripts must have gone astray or been forgotten, and therefore criminally gave the New York Nation my Epigrams. They are to be published, I understand, toward the end of the year. Probably you can't use them, but if you can get them into the January number of the Chapbook the overlapping will be slight. Since I am to be paid for them on this side they are yours gratis. —The others have not been offered elsewhere, and will not be. I shall be glad to see them sometime in type, and your offers of pieces of eight, or whatever it was you mentioned, seem thoroughly respectable, even by American standards. My poetry brings me nothing, whereas editorial writing, which I detest, supports me in fair comfort. —Proofs will not be necessary. These things I leave on the knees of the gods. —I have some friends, Frank Hill, George O'Neil, and Genevieve Taggard, who will send you verses. They all write well. Hill—another editorial writer—and I are starting a daily column of reprinted poetry, for which the Chapbook would be welcome. We sometimes buy it, but not always.[2] We are thinking, also, of starting a poetry magazine which would *not* accept the works of Amy Lowell and Louis Untermeyer. We prefer Conrad Aiken.[3]

Sincerely
Maxwell Anderson

I shall send more of my own, when I have any.

1. Monro had not responded to no. 13 (July 26, 1920) until November 12. In the response he listed the Anderson poems he wanted to publish in the *Chapbook*, including the epigrams, and apologized for being "one of the very slow and deliberate people of this world" (for the response, see no. 13, n. 2).

2. The *Globe*, on which Anderson and Hill worked at the time, shows no poetry column through January, 1921, when Anderson left the paper.

3. *The Measure: A Journal of Poetry*, the first number of which appeared in March, 1921, was started by Anderson and Hill and several others, including Genevieve Taggard and George O'Neil. Anderson was the journal's first editor.

15. TO RIDGELY TORRENCE [1]

[New York City]
January 24, 1921

Dear Ridgely Torrence—

I'm enclosing a very slight little poem, hoping it will find favor for the New Republic. And hoping also you will be able to let the Measure have something soon.

Thank you for your interest, and the subscription. We are going to have a passing fair first number.[2] Would you mind telling me how you value Aiken? I like him immensely—but I fear I must be biased. Did you read the Portrait of One Dead?[3]

Maxwell Anderson

1. Torrence (1875–1950), poet and playwright, was long the poetry editor of the *New Republic* (1920–1934). He had taken a subscription to the *Measure*, and with the present letter Anderson sent him "St. Agnes' Morning," a poem Torrence ran in *New Republic* 26 (March 16, 1921): 74.

2. In the first number of the *Measure*, which appeared in March, 1921, Anderson had poems by Conrad Aiken, Robert Frost, and Wallace Stevens. Others represented were Padraic Colum, Frank E. Hill, Alfred Kreymborg, and Amy Murray.

3. In a review of Aiken's poetry Anderson called "The Portrait of One Dead," from *The House of Dust: A Symphony* (1920), "one of the most poignant lyrics ever written" ("Conrad Aiken and the Minor Mode," *Measure* 3 [May, 1921]: 25–26). Aiken was Anderson's favorite among modern poets, and the enthusiasm was lasting (see nos. 14 and 198). It is especially clear in the *Measure* during Anderson's editorship (March, April, and May, 1921). He included an Aiken poem in the first number ("The Milestone," pp. 5–6) and made the third an Aiken number by running a long portion of "The Pilgrimage of Festus" (pp. 8–16) and devoting the review essay to Aiken (cited above). It was Aiken's artistry that most impressed Anderson, and in a later review he said that "Conrad Aiken has gone more deliberately to work to make himself a poet than anybody else who has been published in the United States, not even excepting Poe" ("Word-Craft," *Measure* 18 [August, 1922]: 16).

16. TO WILLIAM STANLEY BRAITHWAITE [1]

[New York City]
[Summer, 1922]

Dear Mr. Braithwaite—

Your letter heartens me greatly, for I have written verse for a number of years without achieving much in the way of recognition. It seems to me that my work is better lately; if only I had more free time I might really break loose and do something. —Just at present I have no photograph by me, but I shall hunt one up and send it to you. The card is enclosed.[2]

I haven't always agreed with you—who does always agree with an anthologist?—but the more I contemplate your work the more valuable it seems to me. It gave me the first birds eye glimpse I had of modern poetry.

Sincerely
Maxwell Anderson

1. Braithwaite (1878–1962), poet and teacher in Boston, edited the *Anthology of Magazine Verse and Yearbook of American Poetry*, which appeared annually from 1913 to 1929. He had asked permission to reprint in the *Anthology* for 1922 Anderson's poem in the *New Republic*, "The Time When I Was Plowing."

2. Presumably the card gave permission to anthologize the poem. The purpose of the photograph has not been determined; photographs were not used in Braithwaite's anthologies.

17. TO HEYWOOD BROUN [1]

[New York City]
[October (19?), 1923]

I meant it to [.] There is no such thing as realism on the stage. The language of the stage, if it is to be worth listening to, does not follow the language of life, but sets the pace for it.

It was my intention, as you saw, to write a great play if I could—to write a play not only interesting but memorable. A great play cannot deal with ordinary people speaking commonplaces. It cannot deal with ordinary life. It has to concern itself with definitely unusual individuals in unusual situations, lifted by extraordinary emotions to extraordinary actions. And if it is to have the depth and reach of tragedy, it must pass before a setting that has in it something mysterious and titanic. It must rise above the usages of law, custom and religion into an elemental, spacious and timeless world, which we have all glimpsed but will never inhabit.

The people of such a world do not speak in the half-mumbled monosyllables of the average commuter hurrying with his toast in order to make a train. You cannot, of course, lift your dramatis personae off the ground in the first scene and make them playfellows of the gods, not if you draw your materials from the modern world as everybody knows it. But passion itself and the necessity for momentous decisions will lift them, if they have the courage to attempt a reshaping of their destinies without too much compromise with things as they are. Once they have broken the mould of formula that holds us so tightly, they can move free against a background of all that men and women have said and done since Helen burned Troy down.

1. Broun (1888–1939), columnist and drama critic on the *World*, for which Anderson wrote editorials. In his review of *White Desert* (unpublished play; see *Catalogue*, pp. 80–82), Broun said that the play was powerful but failed of greatness because of its departures from realism, particularly in its language, which "slips too often off the very edge of true talk" (*World*, October 19, 1923, p. 15, col. 4). Anderson replied to the criticism of his verse tragedy in the present letter, and Broun printed the letter in his column of October 23, 1923, p. 11, col. 3, introducing it as a reply to his charge that the dialogue deviated from "true talk." The letter as printed begins: "'I meant it to,' writes Mr. Anderson."

18. TO ALEXANDER WOOLLCOTT [1]

[New York City]
[September, 1924]

Dear Mr. Woollcott—

Marry, sir, as for my friends they praise me and make an ass of me; now my foes tell me plainly I am an ass; so that by my foes, sir, I profit in the knowledge of myself, and by my friends I am abused: so that—if your four negatives make your two affirmitives—why then, the worse for my friends and the better for my foes.

Sincerely
Maxwell Anderson

1. Woollcott (1887–1943), drama critic at the time on the *New York Evening Sun.* Anderson knew him very well, and Woollcott had helped *What Price Glory* into production by urging it on the producer Arthur Hopkins. The present letter, which parodies Woollcott's fanciful style, responds to Woollcott's effusive review of *What Price Glory*, in which he called it the best play of the last ten years and said he would see it on every spare night of the season (*Evening Sun*, September 6, 1924; collected in *The Portable Woollcott* [1946], pp. 441–43).

19. TO LELA AND DAN CHAMBERS *

> [171 West 12th Street
> New York City]
> [January 21, 1925]

Dear Lela and Dan—[1]

I may as well write you together because you'd read both letters anyway. I'm glad you're getting along well in the new place and hope you've fought through your share of sickness. We've had our troubled winters and they're hard to get through. Year before last was just about the limit.

We've had financial luck this year with the play,[2] and I've quit work on the papers and gone to writing for the stage in the hope that I can repeat. The show that's now running looks as if it would support us for a couple of years, and I have another finished and accepted which may go on in the spring—if not, then in the fall.[3]

We're having a sloppy winter so far as weather is concerned. It rains almost as much as it snows and the streets are mountains of half frozen slush which ten or twelve thousand men work steadily for weeks at a time to throw into the river. We're to have a total eclipse of the sun here Saturday morning and I'm going out to the farm, where it will last longer, to get a good look at it. Kenneth and Quentin[4] went out last night. Ken is getting ready for mid-year exams at Columbia but seems quite unworried.

Dad and Beth both write frequently, Beth from business school at Buffalo and Dad from Richburg.[5] He's got a new Franklin which Kenneth says is a beauty. Ken was out to Estherville at Christmas— that was his X-mas present from me. He still has the same girl and everything.

My book of poems is coming out in the spring.[6] I'll send it when it's printed.

Goodluck, and let me hear from you both—

Max

1. During the winter of 1924–25 Lela and Dan moved from Waukesha, Wisconsin, to Hinsdale, New York, where with Anderson's help they were buying a farm.

2. *What Price Glory.*

3. Probably *Outside Looking In.*

4. Anderson's brother and son.

5. Beth (Dorothy Elizabeth), Anderson's sister. Richburg, town in southwestern New York near which Anderson had bought a farm where his father and mother lived in retirement.

6. *You Who Have Dreams.*

20. TO ALEXANDER WOOLLCOTT

171 West 12
[New York City]
[1925][1]

Dear Woollcott—[2]

Speaking as one more heard of as speaking than heard speaking I wish to say that the worst of being quoted is that one is occasionally quoted correctly.[3] Broun was indeed wrong about Processional; you were indeed wrong about Bird. However I do not disown you. I cling to a faith, perhaps tenuous, that though you are sometimes mistaken about actors you are infallible in regard to plays.[4]

Maxwell Anderson

1. Probably earlier in 1925 than October, when Anderson stopped using the West 12th Street address.

2. In their reviews Broun and Woollcott had differed about John Howard Lawson's *Processional* and Richard Bird's portrayal of Marchbanks in Shaw's *Candida*. Broun thought that Bird's poor performance ruined the current production of Shaw's great play (*World*, December 13, 1924, p. 11, col. 3) and that *Processional*, though artistically rough, had the markings of the great American play (*World*, January 13, 1925, p. 9, col. 4). Woollcott, on the other hand, thought that Bird had perfectly realized his role (*Evening Sun*, December 13, 1924, p. 7, cols. 1–2) and that *Processional* was pretentious and boring (*Evening Sun*, January 13, 1925, p. 24, cols. 1–2). The controversy over the two matters enlivened their columns through the entire season.

3. Quotation not located.

4. A faith buttressed no doubt by Woollcott's opinion of *What Price Glory*.

21. TO LELA CHAMBERS

New City
[October 4, 1925]

Dear Lela—[1]

You've got it all wrong about the magnificence of our establishment. Our only retainer is a colored girl. We drag in our own logs to the fireplace. We haven't even any curtains on the windows. We're just camping out on a farm. —I saw both Ken's letter and Margaret's, you see.

Ken tells me you have a grand farm but there's more work than income on it at present. I'm taking a chance that you can use the enclosed check. First Flight failed. The Buccaneer has done something—I'm not sure what yet. The hobo play[2] is the best bet. It's running fine.

Good luck to you all, and much love—

Max

1. With money from *What Price Glory* Anderson had bought more land and remodeled his home at New City.

2. *Outside Looking In.*

22. TO BARRETT H. CLARK[1]

171 West 12th Street
[New York City]
October 26, 1925

Dear Mr. Clark—

I've been out of town a good deal and am late answering your query. I'll look forward with great interest to your discussion in the Drama. One of your volumes has been an almost constant companion of mine since it came out—European Theories. It's the most valuable book on the theatre I've ever found. I'd like very much to see you and talk with you. I am starting on a short holiday in a few days but will hope to find you when I get back.

I have no copy of First Flight. Stallings has one but he has gone south for a few weeks. You could perhaps locate one at the Hopkins office if you don't mind going round there. You could ask for Mr. Harris and tell him you have my permission to look over whatever manuscript of the play there is to be had.[2]

Sincerely

Maxwell Anderson

1. Clark (1890–1953), who was to write *Maxwell Anderson: The Man and His Plays* (1933), had a varied career in support of the drama, including the editing of *America's Lost Plays* (20 vols., 1940–41) and *European Theories of the Drama* (1918), to which Anderson devoted a lengthy and favorable review in 1919 (see Chronology). At present he was play reviewer for *Drama* and had asked Anderson for a script of *First Flight*, which had opened and closed during the previous month.
2. Jed Harris was then an assistant to Arthur Hopkins, who produced and directed *First Flight*. Clark did not get a script of the play. In "Some New American Plays and a Shaw Revival" [*Drama* 16 (November 1925): 52–53] he discussed *Outside Looking In* as "the best play I have seen so far" and added about *First Flight* that it "winged its way into the storehouse before the Hopkins office could inform me of the fact" (p. 52).

23. TO SIDNEY HOWARD *

New City

[November 8, 1925]

Dear Sidney Howard—[1]

In today's Tribune I happened on a perhaps over-generous note concerning What Price Glory and Outside Looking In and also on the bad news that Lucky Sam closes Saturday. Of course I would fain believe my stuff as good as you found it, though I don't quite, and I want to thank you for giving such a hearty cheer. I only hope that assiduous publicity woman at the Greenwich Village didn't hound you into it.[2] Even so it's very good for my (shall I say) soul.

I'm sorry about the demise of McCarver. I did wish you'd put more story into the later episodes, but other people have said that and you had your reasons. Perhaps it's better in the long run to fail with a character study than succeed with a melodrama. I expect more from you than from any other playwright I know. The world is all before you where to choose.[3]

Sincerely,
Maxwell Anderson

    1. In a letter to the drama editor Howard had called *What Price Glory* the finest play of the past season and *Outside Looking In* the finest of the present one, adding that it was "as salty and as real" as *What Price Glory* and "as poetic and profound" as Anderson's poetry (*New York Herald Tribune*, November 8, 1925, sec. 5, p. 1, col. 3). The same page noted the closing of Howard's play *Lucky Sam McCarver*.

    2. Stella Hanau was press representative for the Macgowan-O'Neill-Jones Experimental Theater, which produced *Outside Looking In* at the Greenwich Village Theater.

    3. *Paradise Lost*, XII, 646.

24. TO SIDNEY HOWARD

New City
November 18, 1925

Dear Sidney Howard—[1]

    I thought probably you'd been pumped a bit and I was sorry to have you bothered. It does me a world of good to know you like my stuff but I wish there were no such thing as publicity, or at least that I were the kind of person who never needed it. But even if you didn't need it they'd plaster it on you nowadays, I suppose.

    When I'm next in town I'll surely try to get hold of you.

Sincerely
Maxwell Anderson

    1. Responding to no. 23, Howard said that he had been asked to make a statement about *Outside Looking In* but that his remarks were sincere.

Part II

ACHIEVEMENT
AND
RECOGNITION
1926–1940

*So far I've sometimes pleased the public; I've sometimes
pleased the critics. I've sometimes pleased both, but I've
not yet written [a play] that I think will endure the test of
time—and that's what I want to do.*

> —ANDERSON *to* JOHN MASON BROWN,
> *October, 1937*

25. TO ARTHUR HOBSON QUINN [1]

New City
May 4, [1927]

Dear Mr. Quinn—

I have been in Vermont on an outing or I should have answered you earlier. White Desert has not been printed. I have had several opportunities to publish it and at least two to revive it on Broadway, but have felt that it was in such poor shape that it needed complete revision and have never had the inclination to go back to it. [2] Longmans Green are to print Saturday's Children as soon as I get it ready for the press. I am supposed to be preparing it now, but there is no work I hate more than revising and I keep putting it off. [3] When I was at the University of North Dakota I studied Shakespeare under Prof. Koch, who was then an instructor in the English Department and had not yet begun his classes in playwriting. [4] White Desert, written while I was an editorial writer on the N.Y. World, was my first play aside from three one-acters which I wrote in a play-construction course under H. D. Gray at Stanford U. [5] It was at Stanford in the same year and while taking an M.A. that I was an instructor in English. I was born Dec. 15, 1888, and am therefore no youngster. Before beginning to write plays I had been a teacher of English in North Dakota and California for seven years and had spent six years as editorial writer on the San Francisco Bulletin, the New Republic, the N.Y. Evening Globe and the Morning World. I quit teaching because I could make more money in journalism and I quit writing editorials because I could make more in the theatre. The only work of mine for which I have much respect is my one volume of verse. [6] What I want more than anything else is to successfully put poetry into plays. What the theatre needs more than anything else is poetry, and what poetry needs more than anything is an audience. Forgive my ex-cathedra utterance, and thanks for your interest.

Sincerely,
Maxwell Anderson

1. Quinn (1875–1960), in the English Department at the University of Pennsylvania from 1895 until retirement in 1945, was among the pioneering scholars in the field of American literature and published a number of historical studies, among them a survey of *American Fiction* (1936) and a biography of Poe (1941). But his main interest was in the drama and his most ambitious work *A History of the American Drama*, the first volume of which, coming to the Civil War, appeared in 1923. He devoted two volumes to the period from the Civil War to the present (1927) and, though the work must have been substantially complete before the present letter arrived, Quinn made use of its biographical information in his discussion of Anderson (2: 233–36).

2. *White Desert* was not produced again and has not been published.

3. The following September Longmans, Green published the acting script of *Saturday's Children*, unrevised.

4. Frederick H. Koch (1877–1944), a leader of the regional drama movement at the universities of North Dakota and (after 1918) North Carolina, was at North Dakota during Anderson's last two years there, 1909–1911. At North Dakota Koch, always an inspirational teacher, focused on acting and play production and developed his playwriting courses after moving to North Carolina, where Paul Green and Thomas Wolfe were among his students.

5. The one-act plays have not come to light, and Anderson omits his first full-length play, *Benvenuto* (1922; *Catalogue*, pp. 64–65). For Henry David Gray, see Appendix I, no. 5 and n. 3 there; and Chronology, 1913–14 and September 20, 1919.

6. *You Who Have Dreams* (1925). In the margin of the original Quinn marked this and the remaining sentences of the letter but did not use them when he discussed Anderson's verse plays in the second edition of his history (1936; 2:266–71).

26. TO BARRETT H. CLARK

New City
April 5, 1929

Dear Mr. Clark—[1]

I'll be in New City for a few weeks beginning next Monday. Our address in town is 323 W. 112th St. The telephone is Monument 3130.

I hope you won't think me discourteous if I am niggardly of information about myself. This modern craze for biographical information leaves me cold for many reasons. For one thing it's always inaccurate; for another it's never possible to be sure that it's relevant. For another it's so bound up with publicity and other varieties of idiocy that it gags a person of any sensibility. For another, to be heralded is to become a candidate for the newest list of "the busted geniuses of yesteryear" of whom I hope never to be one.

But I'd like to meet you and talk with you.

Sincerely
Maxwell Anderson

1. Clark, beginning to gather material for *Maxwell Anderson: The Man and His Plays*, had asked Anderson for an outline of his life.

27. TO THERESA HELBURN [1]

Knickerbocker Hotel
Hollywood, California
October 16, 1929

Dear Miss Helburn:

The Queen seems a very possible title. Perhaps *Elizabeth, The Queen* would do. Neither, however, is perfect and we are somewhat limited in our choice because of the necessity for referring definitely to our central figure. We'd better wait for an inspiration.

I see no reason for showing the manuscript to Harcourt, for even if it were possible to copyright historical incidents I have not used the incidents as Strachey related them, nor as they happened.

Since it appears improbable that I shall have a play on this year, I am likely to stay here through the winter.

Aside from cuts and slight alterations, in regard to which I shall be most amenable to suggestions from the director, I have only one revision in mind. I have thought that when Elizabeth and Essex are left alone in the second act,[2] there should be, instead of the rather rhetorical love scene, a really passionate abandonment in the relief they both feel at the discovery that they were separated by trickery rather than their own treachery.

The first act of *Campaspe*[3] is finished and excellent. The other two will perhaps never seem so good as they do in prospect.

I am now at this address.

Sincerely,
Maxwell Anderson

1. Helburn (c. 1888–1959) was a leading member of the Theatre Guild, which had accepted *Elizabeth the Queen* but postponed its production until the following season, when she would direct it. The play was suggested by Lytton Strachey's *Elizabeth and Essex: A Tragic History* (1928), published in America by Harcourt, Brace.

2. Act II, scene 3.

3. An unlocated play.

28. TO BARRETT H. CLARK

323 West 112th Street
New York City
June 16, 1930

Dear Mr. Clark:[1]

Thanks for your interest in *Sea Wife*. I fear you will find it, as others have, a difficult subject for representation. It is based on Arnold's *Forsaken Merman*, which is about the furthest south in something or other—but I'll try to get a copy to you within a few days.

I can locate only one copy and therefore ask you to take good care of this one.[2]

Sincerely,

1. Clark was attempting to arrange a production of the unpublished *Sea Wife* (*Catalogue*, pp. 76–77) and had asked Anderson for a script.

2. In *Maxwell Anderson: The Man and His Plays* (p. 30) Clark conflates this and letter no. 31.

29. TO A. GEORGE VOLCK [1]

323 West 112th Street
New York City
June 16, 1930

Dear Mr. Volck:

It looks now as if I would be free of picture work until Milly comes back from Europe as I don't seem to get together with Paramount.

In regard to the money still due me from Metro, I won't quarrel over the extra day. If they say I quit on Monday, let them have it their way. But as for the releases they want me to sign, I read those releases on the coast and refused to sign them because they were inaccurately stated. I'm willing to sign a general release of all work done for Metro, but I am not willing to put my signature to a series of papers which state that I am the sole author, among other things, of "Trader Horn", "Cheri-Bibi" and God knows what.

I wish you would transmit these sentiments of mine to Mr. Hendricks and tell him that when he draws up reasonable releases, I'll put my name to them—and not before.

I know that there are still commissions due you and will take care of that as soon as the final salary payment is adjusted.[2]

Sincerely,

1. Volck, vice-president of Myron Selznick, Inc., a talent agency in Hollywood, was Anderson's motion picture agent. During the winter of 1928–29 Anderson had gone to Hollywood to write his first motion picture script, the adaptation of Erich Maria Remarque's novel *All Quiet on the Western Front*. The picture was directed by Anderson's friend Lewis Mileston (Milly) and released by Paramount Pictures in 1929. Following *All Quiet*, Anderson stayed in Hollywood and worked on several pictures for Metro-Goldwyn-Mayer.

2. *Trader Horn* and *Cheri-Bibi* (as *The Phantom of Paris*) were released by MGM in 1931, without Anderson's name in the copyright notices.

30. TO DALE VAN EVERY [1]

New City
June 30, 1930

Dear Dale:

I can't answer your questions very satisfactorily because Milly is still in Europe and a lot of things are still unsettled. However, I received a cable from him Saturday saying that he will be back in about six weeks, agreeing to go to work immediately on his return on an original theme which we discussed before he left. My expectation is that we will do all the writing in New York and that I shall be in California only to go over dialogue on location.

Milly has a contract to do two more pictures for Universal. Under the contract he is in sole charge of all phases of the work and will hire his own writers and actors. I have no contract with him nor with the company but he has assured me many times that he is going to do his next picture with me, and when I mentioned you in connection with the enterprise he accepted the idea at once. He seems inclined to do whatever I ask him in regard to the theme and writing of the picture and I feel sure you would be part of the unit, and at an excellent salary, if you were free when Milly returned.

You can see, though, that I am not exactly in position to promise anything. I can only say that if you can manage to wait, we will both probably have a better chance to do our own stuff than we'd ever have anywhere else.

Your suggestion of a sea picture falls in with what Junior wanted to do for the next super-super but Milly would rather not go back to the war for his next picture. At the moment I am turning over in my mind the story of a young man who has been brought up to a life of crime by an uncle or guardian who has been almost maniacally embittered against the government by some past injustice. The youth rejects this mode of life and, in running away, falls in with tramps, among whom there are yegg-men.[2] By chance he is thrust into the commission of a crime—say a bank robbery—and is the one who is caught and held for murder. By chance, also, this same crime was directed by the aforesaid guardian, who discovers the plight of the boy and is obliged to choose between his own death and that of his ward. The love story might concern the daughter of the old man involved.

This is badly told but you see that it is a theme with a backbone and color.

I do hope you will be free and with us when we go to work—I'd feel safer and happier about the whole combination.[3]

Sincerely

---

1. Van Every (b. 1896), author of popular historical books, wrote film scripts in Hollywood during the thirties (*Lady, Be Careful*, 1936; *Souls at Sea*, 1937; and *Captains Courageous*, 1937). He had worked on the previous picture directed by Lewis Milestone (Milly) and written by Anderson, *All Quiet on the Western Front* in 1929, and had asked Anderson to include him on the next Milestone/Anderson film.

2. Burglars.

3. The motion picture contemplated in the present letter was not made, and Van Every was not involved with the next Milestone/Anderson picture, which was *Rain* (copyrighted October 1, 1932), adapted by Anderson from the play of the same title (1922) by John Colton and Clemence Randolph and from its source, Somerset Maugham's short story, "Miss Thompson," *The Smart Set* 64 (April, 1921): 3–26.

31. TO BARRETT H. CLARK

New City
August 23, 1930

Dear Mr. Clark:

After I had promised you a script of *Sea Wife* I looked around for a manuscript to send you and discovered that I didn't have any. Since then I have come upon traces of one in the neighborhood of Forty-fifth Street and will ship it to you as soon as it is recovered.

My enthusiasm for my plays cools very shortly after they are written and I don't care now whether *Sea Wife* is produced or not, but it contains some fairly good poetry and you may like to read it.[1]

Sincerely
Maxwell Anderson

1. Clark arranged a production of *Sea Wife* at the University of Minnesota in December, 1932, and in *Maxwell Anderson: The Man and His Plays* (p. 30) he conflated this letter and no. 28.

32. TO THERESA HELBURN

323 West 112th Street
[New York City]
[Early March, 1931]

Dear Miss Helburn—[1]

Forgive me for calling you two weeks ago with my bad news. I had just received your note and it seemed to me then that nothing could go on. My whole world had died—and not Margaret. —But now I know that she'd rather I didn't lose courage—and I am heartened by the fact that she thought this play on which I am working was likely to be by far the best I had done—and I shall go on with it within a few days.

The hardest work—the preparatory scenes—are finished, and the best and easiest of it is to come. It has a good theme and a good structure, though complicated, and I have great hopes for it. It should have a magnificent part for Alfred, and perhaps the woman's role is not too small for Lynn.[2] I am seldom over-sanguine as to how plays are coming out. This should be ready—and good—by the middle of April.[3]

Sincerely

Maxwell A.

1. Anderson's wife, Margaret, had died suddenly on February 26 from a blood clot. He was at work on *The Princess Renegade*, a play about an escaping Russian princess and her rescuer during the Russian Revolution, which the Theatre Guild wished to consider for its next season.

2. Alfred Lunt and Lynn Fontanne, currently starring in the Guild's production of *Elizabeth the Queen*.

3. The Guild rejected *The Princess Renegade*, and it was not produced or published (see *Catalogue*, p. 74).

33. TO BARRETT H. CLARK

[New City]

[March 25, 1932]

Dear Mr. Clark—[1]

The last page of that last act is missing, however, I've made a note of the cue and will supply the rest. Follow the 1st & 2nd Acts as given in this copy and the last act in the version which I return corrected.[2]

And all thanks

Maxwell A.

1. Clark, editor at Samuel French, was handling the publication of *Night Over Taos*, a script of which accompanied the present note.

2. With a note to Clark dated March 28, 1932 (see Omitted Letters) Anderson sent the last page of *Night Over Taos* and asked Clark to proofread the text for publication, saying he was leaving town and could not do it. The French text appeared in May, without the last page, and despite a later edition *Night Over Taos* has not been published with its proper ending. For details of its publication history, see Laurence G. Avery, "The Conclusion of *Night Over Taos*," *American Literature* 38 (November, 1965): 318–21.

34. TO GERTRUDE ANTHONY (ANDERSON)*

[New City]
[Summer, 1932]

Dear Mab—

As I planned I went to town today—got the MSS[1] and had lunch with Moses and Reinheimer[2]—giving them both copies. Then I took my copy away from Alec's office[3] and went to see Bickerton.[4] He said he could get money for production if I wanted to do it myself—the backers taking 50%, he taking 20% and I 30%. He's very nice, and was anxious to go ahead with it.— Hasn't read it yet, of course. Then he and I walked over to see Jed,[5] and to ask him whether he wanted to direct it. Jed said no, he wouldn't do that. He wanted to buy it. There's no competition between him and Bickerton really, because Bickerton is his lawyer. —Well, I decided nothing, left him the play, and came home. At dinner time he called up, said he'd read the 1st Act and it was magnificent—a sheer delight. After dinner he called to say he'd read the second act, and didn't need to read any more—it was just his dream come true, a real comedy and in almost perfect shape. He'd give me almost as large a share as Bickerton in the production, and also made promises of any other concession I wanted. I said couldn't decide yet, but am to see him tomorrow at eleven. Of course he would do it well—and his enthusiasm is heartening after Alec's lukewarm remarks. So I don't know—anyway, so it stands. Frank Hill read it tonight, and was delighted—also Waldy—[6]

So heigh to high fortune, darling—[7]

Max

1. Of *Both Your Houses*.
2. John Moses and Howard E. Reinheimer, lawyers specializing in matters related to the theater.
3. Possibly the director Alexander Dean.
4. Joseph P. Bickerton, Jr., lawyer involved with play production.
5. Jed Harris, prominent Broadway producer.
6. Waldemar Juers, a neighbor of Anderson on South Mountain Road.
7. Anderson gave Harris the rights to *Both Your Houses* for a production during the 1932–33 season, but because of casting problems Harris did not schedule it. In January, 1933, following difficult negotiations that persuaded Anderson to acquire a theatrical agent, Harold Freedman, Harris released the play to the Theatre Guild, and the Guild produced *Both Your Houses* on March 6, 1933.

35. TO BARRETT H. CLARK

16 Castle Rock Beach
Santa Monica, California
June 3, [1933]

Dear Barrett Clark—[1]

I opened your packet with misgivings, and was prepared to dislike the whole business, but you have done the job so nicely that I can't hold it against you. My horror is of having myself held in higher esteem than my work is worth—and though you may be slightly guilty in that direction I don't think the booklet can be considered a puff. —I should appreciate it if you would send a copy or two to my mother, Mrs. W. L. Anderson, % Maxwell Anderson, New City, N.Y. She'll get a thrill out of it.

As ever
Maxwell

1. Clark had sent his recently published *Maxwell Anderson: The Man and His Plays*.

36. TO LELA CHAMBERS

16 Castle Rock Beach
Santa Monica, California
July 11, [1933]

Dear Lela—[1]

I brought your letter to California with me, thinking I'd get a chance to answer it here, but things came on me so fast I haven't got to it yet. I'm working on my second picture out here, and will soon be finishing my new play, which I've been doing nights and Sundays. When I get out of this grind I'm going to write you, and meanwhile please remember me kindly if you can.—

I'm sending a small check as a present. I've no idea whether it's much needed or not, but unexpected money is always the most fun.

Love—
Max

1. In May, Anderson had gone to Hollywood to write two motion picture scripts, *Death Takes a Holiday* (based on Alberto Casella's play of the same title, which had opened in New York on December 12, 1929) and *We Live Again* (based on Tolstoy's *Resurrection*). Both pictures were released in 1934. On the trip Anderson also wrote *Mary of Scotland*.

37. TO GERTRUDE ANTHONY (ANDERSON)

[Santa Monica, California]
[Late July, 1933]

Dear—

I haven't written before because I've been in such a welter of finishing my picture,[1] seeing people in regard to the play[2] and entertaining the Lapworths, Alec, and so on.[3] As for the picture, I sat down last Saturday and wrote steadily till Tuesday—at the end of which time I had a hundred pages that looked pretty good. Tuesday I turned it in, and on Thursday they had read it and wanted some rewriting done. Now I had discovered that my contract called for five weeks and another free week if the picture was not entirely satisfactory, so I must stay till next Tuesday to finish. That means my time is so short before I want rehearsals to begin that I must take the train. I start Tuesday evening on the Chief. Charles[4] will follow with the car.

Marshall and Edna Best were at dinner with me at Tony's last night.[5] Marshall likes the play enormously and wants to play it but must be here till October 1st. Tony is not free till Oct. 15th. That's definitely too late. I talked to Helen H.[6] on the phone today, and she said she must know by August 7th what was going to happen, because she was turning down picture offers and she needs the money. As for Jock Whitney, he was at R.K.O. the other day when I went to see them about their possibly buying *Night Over Taos* for their first color film. I guess that's fallen through,[7] but Whitney had read Mary and is willing to finance it for me if I want to produce it. The Guild board is all over the place, but Terry and Langner are at Westport, and perhaps I can get an answer out of them.[8] I do think the rehearsals should start in September, because we'll need some time out of town, and the opening shouldn't be later than Nov. 1. I'm getting somewhat nervous over the way everybody seems to be entangled with other projects. I may be driven to taking Whitney's offer and doing the play with another director and someone else for Bothwell.

I haven't heard from you since you went to Warrensburg, so perhaps you're busy too.[9] No doubt there are a lot of things for you to catch up with. Or perhaps the part is not what you hoped. I won't have a car when I first get east, so can't drive out to see you at once. Also whatever I am to settle about the production will have to be done soon. No doubt the train is the best way to go to see you anyway if the distance amounts to six hours.

Your wire just came—giving your telephone number. I'll wire you tonight and make a date for a call tomorrow night. It's a relief to hear from you, darling—I was wondering if you'd forgotten me already. —Tomorrow I must settle down to rewriting the central part of the picture—quite a long and arduous job. Then on the train—I must do some work on that play of Alec's. But if I can get some money from him for it it will help, for I find I'll have little enough after paying income tax to get along on. Perhaps R.K.O. will buy Taos. But they were to call me yesterday if they wanted it, and they didn't call. Today I wrote the review of Harvey Fergusson's book—Rio Grande.[10]

I'm also worried about doing the play myself, but when you hear the ins and outs of the business it seems nobody cares much what happens to me or my play except myself. —It's nice you have a good part.

The Lapworths are waiting for me to go to Hollywood with them—we're to have supper at the Hofbräu and get some beer. It's been terribly hot here. Love to you, darling, and may I see you soon—the nights are long and wakeful without you.

Max

---

1. *We Live Again*.

2. *Mary of Scotland*, completed on July 14 (note on MS, T), the production of which Anderson was arranging.

3. Alec, not identified. Charles and Else Lapworth, friends from Anderson's San Francisco days.

4. Charles Lapworth?

5. Tony, interested in directing *Mary of Scotland* but not identified. Edna Best and Herbert Marshall, English husband-and-wife acting team. Marshall wished to play Bothwell in *Mary of Scotland*, a role eventually played by Philip Merivale.

6. Hayes, who played the lead in *Mary of Scotland*.

7. John Hay Whitney, financier, formed Pioneer Pictures earlier in the summer to make films in color, the first such motion pictures, using the Technicolor Process

developed by Walt Disney for his cartoons. Pioneer Pictures films were to be released through R.K.O., and their first color film was *Becky Sharp* in 1935.

8. Theresa Helburn (Terry) and Lawrence Langner, dominant voices in the Theatre Guild, which produced *Mary of Scotland* with Helburn directing it.

9. Gertrude was acting in a summer stock company at Warrensburg, in upstate New York.

10. *Rio Grande*, published by Knopf on July 21, 1933, through its magazine serialization had provided the basis for *Night Over Taos* (see Chronology, October, 1931). Anderson's review of the book, showing the interpretation of it used in the play, appeared in *Nation*, 137 (August 16, 1933): 190–91.

38. TO PAUL GREEN [1]

New City
[Fall 1933]

Dear Paul—

I'm writing to say that the houses across the road from mine are for sale, and I hope you'll come up to see me. How goes the writing? —Come with a play in your poke if you can for the theatre's crying for good ones.[2]

Mab is at Warrensburg and I've been up to watch rehearsals. It's green and luscious in the east—such a contrast with Paramount, et al. May we never have to return.

The Guild is to do Mary. It looks like the best of mine so far. Some good verse in it, and also, I think, a good play—

As ever—
Max

1. Green (b. 1894) met Anderson in 1931 when they spent the summer together in Connecticut with the Group Theatre, which had in rehearsal Green's *The House of Connelly* for its inaugural production. In 1932 Green went to Hollywood where he wrote a number of film scripts, among them three for Will Rogers (*State Fair*, *Dr. Bull*, and *David Harum*), and Anderson joined him there in the summer of 1933. Before returning to their homes in August Green told Anderson that with his motion picture money he hoped to buy a farm.

2. Green did not go to New City and, when he received the present letter, was in the process of buying a 200-acre tract adjacent to the town of Chapel Hill, N. C.

39. TO GEORGE MIDDLETON [1]

December 6, [1933]

Dear George—

I'm always hoping to deserve real tribute from the critics—and maybe sometime I will. At present I'm too close to this one to know. But one of the pleasant things about it is finding out who does appreciate it when you try for something above the dead level. —Thanks for your good words—and good luck to you—[2]

Maxwell A.

1. Middleton (1880–1968), playwright, had congratulated Anderson on the success of *Mary of Scotland*, which opened on November 27. He commented on the well-deserved praise of the critics and added his own praise of Anderson's ability to make audiences forget they were watching history (undated letter; T).
2. Middleton had also mentioned an upcoming production of his own play *Hiss! Boom!! Blah!!!*

40. TO GEORGE MIDDLETON

323 West 112th Street
New York City
January 24, 1934

Dear George: [1]

I certainly did get your play and found it full of blistering and pungent things, though perhaps more in your platform manner. It should clear the air a good deal if it gets a production soon and I hope it does.

Sincerely
Maxwell A.

1. Middleton had sent his play *Hiss! Boom!!! Blah!!* to Anderson. The play (published, 1933; not produced professionally) is a satiric panorama of succeeding national crises as they affect one American community from the days prior to World War I to the depression of the thirties.

41. TO WALTER PRICHARD EATON [1]

323 West 112 Street
New York City
[January 29, 1934]

Dear Mr. Eaton—

I want to thank you more than you'll be able to imagine for your sympathetic and amusing article in the Tribune. —Perhaps you give me a little more than I deserve, but I'll try to live up to it—in fact I've been intending to live up to praise like that for a long time.

In the same breath I'd like to tell Mr. Nicoll how much I was heartened by his article in the Times.[2] The air about your dramatic school must be stimulating, and I'll really have to treat myself to a little of it sometime soon—

Sincerely
Maxwell Anderson

1. Eaton (1875–1957), drama critic and student of American drama, had joined the Yale drama department in the fall of 1933, a position he held until retirement in 1947. In "He Put Poetry Back on the Stage" (*New York Herald Tribune*, January 28, 1934, sec. 8, pp. 12–13, 21), Eaton had praised *Mary of Scotland* for reaffirming the possibility of poetic tragedy in an age dominated by the conventions of realism.

2. Allardyce Nicoll had succeeded George Pierce Baker as head of the Yale drama department in 1933. In "The Decline of Realism in the Theatre" (*New York Times*, January 28, 1934, sec. 9, p. 1, col. 3, p. 3, cols. 1–3), Nicoll maintained that realism had lost its vitality as a dramatic mode and that such experiments in the contemporary theater as *Mary of Scotland* were portents of a more imaginative and greater theater of the future.

42. TO GEORGE MIDDLETON

323 West 112th Street
New York City
February 1, 1934

Dear George—[1]

I have made it a fast principle never to say anything for publication or direct quotation, and though it may seem unnecessary to cling to it in such instances I find that minor breaches lead easily to major ones—so I'd rather not be quoted. Besides, George, one shouldn't discourage the writing of personal letters in this fashion. —Only I don't like your play any the less.

Sincerely

Maxwell Anderson

1. Middleton had requested permission to quote no. 40 in advertisements of his play *Hiss! Boom!! Blah!!!*

43. TO GEORGE MIDDLETON

323 West 112th Street

New York City

February 9, 1934

Dear George:[1]

I don't know when I have known anybody to take a refusal so graciously. Personally I should have been very sorry if it had spoiled our friendship and your engaging reply comes as a great relief.

I have an idea Mabie will give your play an excellent production.[2] He was more or less cooperating with the people at Minnesota University last year when they put on SEA WIFE and I heard excellent reports of that production.[3] If I had only been able to see it I might have learned enough about the play so that I could re-write it for a New York audience. People do go west for their try-outs and Variety reviewed SEA WIFE in Minneapolis,[4] so you may find your way smoothed in New York. Good luck as ever.

Sincerely

Maxwell A.

1. Responding to no. 42, Middleton had said that he was more pleased to know Anderson liked *Hiss! Boom!! Blah!!!* than he would have been to have permission to use Anderson's remarks in publicity for the play (February 5, 1934; T).
2. Edward C. Mabie, director of the theater at the University of Iowa, had scheduled a production of *Hiss! Boom!! Blah!!!* for the spring of 1934 (later cancelled).
3. *Sea-Wife* was produced at the University of Minnesota by A. Dale Riley, director of dramatics at the school, December 6–10, 1932. Mabie acted as an adviser to Riley for the production.
4. *Variety*, December 20, 1932, p. 46.

44. TO WALTER PRICHARD EATON

323 West 112 Street
New York City
February 9, 1934

Dear Mr. Eaton:[1]

I am certainly coming up to see you and Yale and the dramatic school some time this year but I am so buried in things I·must do at present that I think it will have to be put off till spring.

Your remark about what the Tribune editor wanted reminds me that I didn't tell you how grateful I was for your avoidance of personality items and for a critical consideration of the work itself. Never before, I think, has anybody taken the trouble to try to place me or find out where I was going and why.

I still don't agree with you about modern plays in verse.[2] I don't believe great verse can be written in a play on a contemporary theme, but find me an instance if you can, ancient or modern.

Sincerely
Maxwell Anderson

1. In response to no. 41, which thanked Eaton for his article "He Put Poetry Back on the Stage" in the *Herald Tribune*, Eaton mentioned that the *Herald Tribune* editor was disappointed by the article because it did not focus on Anderson's personality. Eaton also invited Anderson to Yale to talk to the playwriting students (February 1, 1934; T).
2. In "He Put Poetry Back on the Stage" Eaton maintained that, following *Elizabeth the Queen* and *Mary of Scotland*, the next step for Anderson was poetic tragedy with a contemporary setting. He considered such a play a major goal and hoped Anderson would attempt it.

45. TO WALTER PRICHARD EATON

323 West 112 Street
New York City
March 7, 1934

Dear Mr. Eaton:[1]

There is a possibility that I will appear in New Haven tomorrow night in time for IN THE DAYS OF THE TURBINS.[2] I tell you this not to ask for hospitality but to warn you that I may drop in on the dramatic school the next day. It may be that I can't get away and will have to call the whole trip off but I have been hoping to see you and finish our conversation. I don't agree with you about COME OF AGE which I thought as bad in conception as in execution and doomed to disaster by what it attempted.

I must explain about Allen Scott. I had just met him and he was telling me what he hoped to do for the poetic theatre but I'm afraid he's too sure of himself.[3]

Sincerely
Maxwell Anderson

1. In his response to no. 44 Eaton continued to urge Anderson to undertake a verse play with a contemporary setting. Answering Anderson's request for instances of contemporary verse plays, Eaton said the absence of such plays would not prove the kind impossible, then cited several instances, including *Come of Age*, Clemence Dane's play that had opened in New York on January 12, 1934, and closed after a few performances. Eaton thought the play failed, not because it was in verse with a contemporary setting, but because the author was not poet enough to carry out her conception (February 12, [1934]; T).

2. Yale's production of *The Days of the Turbins*, which opened on March 6, attracted attention as the American premier of Mikhail Bulgakov's play about the Russian Revolution.

3. Scott, wealthy screenwriter, had a New York success with his prose play *Goodbye Again* in 1932, but what he hoped to do for the poetic theater has not come to light.

46. TO JOHN C. FITZPATRICK[1]

323 West 112
New York City
March 12, [1934]

Dear Mr. Fitzpatrick—

Thanks with all my heart for the 9 vols of Washington's writings. They're going to help immensely. What I need most of all is the next volume—the Valley Forge letters and orders—but if they're not printed, I guess I'll have to get along without them. —And the Library has been most munificent toward me—

Sincerely
Maxwell Anderson

1. Fitzpatrick (1876–1940), archivist at the Library of Congress from 1897, resigned in 1928 to edit the library's George Washington papers, the edition appearing as *The Writings of George Washington from the Original Manuscript Sources, 1745–1799*, 39 vols. (1931–1944). At the time of the present letter only the first nine volumes of the *Writings* had been published, and Fitzpatrick had sent them to Anderson for his work on *Valley Forge*. The nine volumes covered Washington's career through November 3, 1777, while the play dealt with the months from December, 1777, to June, 1778.

47. TO JOHN C. FITZPATRICK

New City
March 16, 1934

Dear Mr. Fitzpatrick—[1]

I have received the bundle of proof which you sent, and wish to thank you more than it's easy to put into words for your generosity. These volumes are exactly what I needed. I have had great difficulty in finding any accurate data over the winter I am treating, but with this help expect to do the best work I have ever done. —One question I'd like to ask you—did Washington have any regular military aide at Valley Forge—or were his associates mainly secretaries?[2]

And again many thanks—

Maxwell Anderson

You may be sure that I will read the proofs carefully and return them intact. I should like to keep them several weeks if possible. Address me, in case you write—323 West 112th St., N.Y. City.

1. In response to no. 46 Fitzpatrick had sent page proof of vols. 10 and 11 of *The Writings of George Washington* and vol. 12 in galley proof (Fitzpatrick to Anderson, March 13, 1934; LC). The three volumes contained Washington's writings from November 4, 1777, to September 30, 1778, thus covering the Valley Forge period (December, 1777, to June, 1778) during which *Valley Forge* was set.

2. Fitzpatrick's reply (March 19, 1934; LC) lists nine military aides to Washington at Valley Forge: Robert Hanson Harrison, John Fitzgerald, Richard Kidder Meade, Alexander Hamilton, Peter Presley Thornton, John Laurens, Tench Tilghman (who becomes a prominent character in the play), Caleb Gibbs, and George Lewis.

48. TO MRS. HARRIET KEEHN [1]

April 21, 1934

My dear Mrs. Keehn:—

In reply to your letter of April 3rd, I am gratified that you like "Mary of Scotland" so much.

As to doing the research work for me I am sorry but I always have done this work myself, inasmuch as the facts surrounding the characters in my plays seem to stick more clearly when I do the reading myself.

Thanking you.

Very truly yours,
Maxwell Anderson

1. Mrs. Keehn, on the staff of the Library of Congress, had asked Anderson if she could assist him in the research for *Valley Forge*.

49. TO LAWRENCE LANGNER [1]

[Summer, 1934]

Dear Lawrence—

As you will no doubt talk over the *Valley Forge* production before long it occurs to me that I might write you a letter to sum up my wishes regarding it and the plans I'd like to make so that you can lay them before the board.

Briefly, I want to direct the play myself with Lionel Berias as assistant, and I want Carroll French to set it and design costumes.[2]

For a number of years I've believed that the best director of a play was its author, at least when the author knew his way about the theatre and was equal to the occasion. I have avoided the job in the past because I'm well aware of its difficulties and had no wish to saddle myself with a month's work which is usually both thankless and ill-paid. But there's no getting away from the fact that I know better what I planned to put on the stage than any director, even the best, and I have no doubt that I've had enough experience now to get from the actors more nearly what the play needs than could be got by anyone else—even the most expert. Sometimes, it is true, a director adds something effective to a play which was not in the script. I may do that myself in the course of rehearsals. But what I add is certain to be in the spirit of the play—and what another director added might not be—in fact, would be pretty certain not to be. —In regard to the re-writing, the play will not need much. I have been working on a number of revisions, and will find other minor things to be patched, but as a whole the play must stand or fall as it is.

I would like Berias as assistant because he knows the technical end of the theatre exceedingly well, and I know I can work with him.

Mr. French has made sketches and plans for the sets that I like immensely and we've talked over the costumes and general atmosphere. He has not worked in the New York theatre before, and will have no other productions on his mind while he works on *Valley Forge*. He will have both time and enthusiasm to give the job. Last year I asked for Jo Mielziner, but the idea was vetoed by the board in favor of Bobby Jones. Bobby didn't care much for *Mary* and was sitting up nights with a Jed Harris production, with the result that he gave us an indifferent job—good-looking sets, and good-looking costumes but seldom what the play called for. This year I'd like to have a man who will work with me, who will give me what I want and who will be unsparing in his effort to get things right. Mr. French's experience has all been in Chicago and since he came to New York he has put his time on painting and architecture. But he has set many plays and taken many on the road—and is a very competent man in general. I understand that there are ways of getting around the fact that he's not a member of the scene-painters' union.

You will understand that I want a formal appointment as director and would want the business of the director left to me. The contract which Terry[3] had for *Mary* would be satisfactory. Hollywood is offering me three thousand a week just now, but I won't insist on that.[4]

Sincerely
Maxwell A.

1. Langner (1890–1962), patent lawyer who also wrote plays, was a guiding force on the board of directors of the Theatre Guild, which had produced three of Anderson's last four plays (the exception, *Night Over Taos*, was done by the Group Theatre, an outgrowth of the Guild). It was also to produce his next play, *Valley Forge*.

2. French, a neighbor of Anderson, was accepted as designer. Berias, unidentified, had no association with the play.

3. Theresa Helburn.

4. Grudgingly the Guild appointed Anderson director, then as rehearsals began in August accepted his suggestion that John Houseman be made director. Thinking the production unsatisfactory, however, Langner replaced Houseman with Herbert J. Biberman before *Valley Forge* opened. Difficulties with the Guild suggested by these changes and the letter itself led Anderson to switch producers after *Valley Forge*, and thereafter Guthrie McClintic was his main producer until the formation of the Playwrights' Company.

50. TO RUSSELL HOLMAN [1]

New City
September 19, 1934

Dear Mr. Holman:

I am writing this story outline of *So Red the Rose* in the form of a letter because I assume it's to be read only by those who have read the book and it saves a lot of explaining.

The only major change I would want in the story would be to make Edward the son of Sallie and Malcolm, Duncan the son of Hugh and Agnes, in order to give more coherence and importance to the character of Sallie Bedford. [2] This will necessitate some rearrangement in episodes and personal relations, but they are relatively easy, and this one shift throws the whole emphasis of the plot on Sallie.

With this change in mind the first sequence would revolve around the party at Montrose. Beginning with Malcolm's obituaries, I'd take Sallie, Malcolm, Mary Cherry and the children up to Montrose by the road, getting a good view of both estates, including the slave quarters, on the way. Edward, now Sallie's son, is home for a brief vacation from the academy, and rides to the party on horseback.

I'd like to retain as much as possible of the party, its songs, its discussion of Napoleon, its politics, especially the liberalism of Bedford and the McGehees—and their doubts about slavery and secession. Duncan, who has been away and been thrown out of school for a prank, reappears during the party and is seen by Edward, whom he asks the whereabouts of Valette. But Valette, though engaged to Duncan and in love with him, is unfortunately at the moment being wooed by George McGehee—and Duncan hears her as she tries to be kind to an unsuccessful suitor. He appears just long enough to quarrel with her—she takes off her ring—and he tries to get off his finger the birthday ring she has given him. It won't come off, so he goes to the slave quarters and has it filed off in his Mammy Tildy's room. Then he flings out of the place—and is seen no more till the war is over. When he goes he can't return to school, so he joins one of the Southern companies already forming. Valette is in agony over this, and comes down at night to talk to Sallie and Malcolm. Malcolm has a talk with Edward before he goes back to the academy, and Edward promises not to ride off to join the colors without first coming home. The party has been broken up, by the way, by old Henry Tate, walking up from the slave quarters to prophecy of the defeat of the South and to tell the company of the election of Lincoln, which news has come to him via the slaves' grapevine.

The second sequence begins with a time lapse. Secession is already a fact but Edward and Charles are still at the seminary. We see and hear the argument with Sherman over secession, then Edward and Charles leave school, Charles impatient of this going home business, but riding along. Edward visits Jeff Davis and while the visit is in progress, Lucy, visiting Valette, falls in love with Charles, who is at the moment taken up with the New Orleans Creole and doesn't notice her much. —Edward says goodbye to his father and mother and rides away with Charles, who keeps the tryst with the Creole at Natchez-under-the-Hill.

The third sequence again begins with a time lapse. Duncan, at the front, has spent his $4000 to arm his own company, but still does not write home. The war is now a drawn battle and feeling is higher. Mary Cherry damns the Yankees. Malcolm is away. Sallie tries to be open-minded about the conflict, but is cried down on every side. Lucy is Valette's confidant in regard to Duncan. Lucy has a couple of proposals and scorns them. The episode of the serenading of Mary Cherry comes in here. —Edward writes to Valette to ask her if she will see that a certain small amount of money is put into the hands of the Creole girl, explaining that this is not for himself. Valette lets this slip to Lucy—not knowing her interest in Charles—but Lucy guesses the situation and tells Valette what the message means.

The fourth sequence begins with Sallie's premonition concerning Edward's death, and her return from Shiloh with three coffins. The search of Shiloh field I would show only in part, holding the rest of it for the end of the picture. —Close on the funeral should come the Emancipation Proclamation, as it affects Sallie. The unrest of the Negroes—the beginning of the invasion of the South—then Malcolm's return ill, and

Sequence five, the siege of Vicksburg and the defeat of the South as seen through Malcolm's eyes as he fails under Sallie's nursing. Mary Cherry is running medicines through the blockade. Sallie's husband is dying. Slowly Sallie and Valette begin to hate the Yankees, as Lucy and Mary Cherry already hate them.

Section six is the pillage of the South, seen both as Sherman sees it, as a necessary military measure, and as the Southerners must see it, and as Sallie, Valette, Lucy and Hugh McGehee experience it when it rolls over them. This would include Sherman's visit to Sallie to apologize and condole with her over Edward, also the burning of the McGehee house, and Lucy's anger at Sherman. For the purposes of my thesis the whole South, including Sallie Bedford, is implacably angry toward the Northerners.

Sequence seven—A Northern soldier brings back the locket that was on Charles' neck. It holds not only his own child portrait, but the picture of the Creole. Now occurs the episode of the hanging, witnessed by Sallie, and the saving of the Northern soldier by Sallie and Valette—who take out of this a new attitude toward the whole war. They can no longer hold any part of the monstrous crime against the soldiers of either side—the boys of the North were victims as much as the boys of the South. —Sallie plows her garden with grape-vine harness. Both Montrose and Portobello are burned.

Sequence eight—The negroes have come back to work. The war is over but Duncan has not returned. The South is a waste. Northern prospectors roam over it looking for investments. Duncan returns. Lucy has gone to New Orleans to see the Creole. We witness this meeting—the nearest Lucy ever comes to reaching Charles' love— although the Creole never knows who Lucy is. Duncan and Valette are married. —Sallie goes to Shiloh with Middleton. They sit in the evening looking at the battlefield.

MIDDLETON: Edward isn't here, is he, mother?
SALLIE: No—he isn't here.
MIDDLETON: And he isn't where he's buried either?

SALLIE: No—he isn't there, either.
MIDDLETON: Do you know when I'm grown I'd like to go to war.
SALLIE: Would you, dear?
MIDDLETON: But you wouldn't want me to go, would you?
SALLIE: No—I wouldn't—
MIDDLETON: But I'd go anyway, wouldn't I?

In a vision Sallie sees herself coming to the battlefield long ago, stopped by the sentries and sending William Veal to search the ground. She sees him as he kneels hunting for Edward through the darkness. She sees him carrying Edward from the battlefield. She comes back to herself and looks down at Middleton, who looks up at her.

MIDDLETON: But I'd go anyway, wouldn't I?
SALLIE: Yes, son, you'd go anyway.

This is, of course, a very brief outline, and hardly touches the mass of material which the book contains. But it's as much of an outline as I'd need to work from. I'd like to leave myself free to build the episodes on this sketchy plot as I went along. I think I've suggested one that can be silhouetted clearly against a vast moving background. The more I study the book the more I respect it and the more convinced I am that the story is excellent for a picture and might become one of the most moving ever made.

Sincerely
Maxwell Anderson

1. Holman (c. 1894–), a journalist before World War I who later published novels based on motion pictures, in 1932 became head of Paramount Pictures's production staff in New York. In 1935 Paramount released the picture outlined in the present letter, *So Red the Rose*, written by Anderson and based on Stark Young's novel of the same title (1934). The novel focuses on two Mississippi families during the Civil War: the Bedfords, headed by Malcolm and his wife Sallie, whose plantation is Portobello; and the McGehees, headed by Hugh and his wife Agnes, whose plantation is Montrose.

2. In the novel Edward (eighteen) is the son of Hugh and Agnes McGehee, Duncan (twenty-one) the son of Malcolm and Sallie Bedford. Anderson's change reverses the families of the two boys.

51. TO S. N. BEHRMAN *

New City
October 14, 1935

Dear Sam—[1]

I don't know quite how to say this but I've always refused to set up my name where I'm not active behind it, and I'm not in fact one of the sponsors of the dinner. Also, although I have an aversion both to war and to fascism, they both seem to me hardy perennials, inherent in the race at its present stage of development, and not to be defeated by propaganda—even their own.

I hope this isn't a personal matter with you, for you're one of the few playwrights I sincerely admire and I regret continually that we don't live nearer together and see each other oftener—

Sincerely
Max

1. A popular front organization, the American League Against War and Fascism, had arranged a fund-raising dinner in New York City for its theater wing, the New Theatre, on October 23, 1935. A host of notables, including Archibald MacLeish and Clifford Odets, were to speak at the dinner on how the theater could be used for social action against war and fascism, and the league hoped to attract wide support in the professional theater. Behrman, not affiliated with the league, apparently supported the dinner and had asked Anderson if his name could be used as one of its sponsors.

52. TO MARGERY BAILEY *

New City
April 9, 1936

Dear Margery Bailey—[1]

I'm a little hurt that you should think I wouldn't remember and answer you, remember you if only as more fortunately endowed than myself for holding a university job in those days, and answer as to one who seems to be interested in the one thing that's held my interest constantly since I began to read for myself. If anything can be done to steer our theatre away from realism and toward poetry I'm for it.

Sometimes prizes help in initiating such changes—perhaps yours would help, and with luck much more than you'd dare hope.

But my advice would be to ask for plays in verse, saying nothing of the historical or biographical end. Verse drives you with unfortunate violence toward history—I know this by experience—and to apply verse to any other theme requires more stuff and experience than most of us are likely to have young. What I long for more than anything else is to see and welcome into the theatre some youngster or youngsters who have an instinctive grasp of the problems it took me decades to approach solving and who can write plays that will put the modern drama on a par, at least in attempt, with the best there's been. If you can offer fifty dollars I'll add another fifty to make it a hundred and give the boys and girls a bit more incentive.

As for the MS., I write in bound volumes, in long hand, these familiar record books they see for book-keeping in stationery stores, and would be loath to part with one. It pleases me to see them pile up, good bad and indifferent, but still my little pile of ambitions laboriously scrawled. I may have grandchildren soon, and they may ask me what I did during the great war and the quarrelsome peace that followed. I shall answer that very wisely I wrote verse, though not too well. —But you can quote anything I've said, if you can read it.

I drove through the Stanford grounds a year ago last winter, but didn't stop, not knowing who was there that I'd remember. Now that I know you do come east occasionally I hope you'll call me or let me know in advance when you're here. Frank Hill and I are still close friends, and perhaps we could have dinner together, we three. And if I'm near Stanford again I'll look for you.

Please let me know if the addition to the prize will be welcome.

As ever

Maxwell Anderson

1. Renewing an acquaintance from their student days at Stanford, Prof. Bailey had written to Anderson about her plan for inaugurating the Dramatists' Alliance of Stanford University, a national competition for plays in verse, with a cash prize and production offered for the winning script.

53. TO MARGERY BAILEY

New City
[October/November, 1936]

Dear Margery Bailey—[1]

Your letter and the MS of *Surrey* find me in the midst of
rehearsals of *The Wingless Victory* and the throes of casting *High Tor*
and *The Masque of Kings*—all three of them driving me mad, now
that I've learned that it's just as important to give plays good
productions as to write them well, and for me much more difficult—
hard as it is to write anything well. The upshot is that I've only looked
into *Surrey*, which arrived today, sufficiently to discover that it's
graciously written, and I'll have to let the reading go till I can put
what's left of my mind on it. Your letter, however, was both delightful
and astonishing. Delightful because you can be serious about plays in
verse and still keep your sense of humor—astonishing because I hadn't
dreamed you'd get such a response from the wide world for so modest
a prize in so modest a contest.

Burgess Meredith[2] has been here to dinner and we've been talking
over the implications. If there is so much interest as seems indicated by
the returns the prize should certainly be increased and given
importance. If you could secure Rockefeller backing part of the
problem would be solved, but if that doesn't materialize Burgess and I
will hope to be in a position—if certain plays succeed this year—to
contribute $500 toward a prize, and try to arrange backing for
bringing the three top plays in the contest within hailing distance of
Broadway. The plan we hit upon was to ask Guthrie McClintic,
Barrett Clark and perhaps one other, to look at the three plays with
us, with the hope of finding one that would warrant production here.
Promising nothing, of course, because nobody could be sure of what
would come of the competition, but assuring you that good plays,
even in verse, are producible, and that all concerned would wish to
find one that had poetic and dramatic quality. I rather assume, from
the subject, that *Surrey* is not for the New York stage, but there's no
telling when you'll get one that is, and we'll be pulling for just that
outcome. I realize that you've had an ocean of work over the contest,
and would be in for even more if these plans came to fruit, so if you've
had too much on your hands just tell me so—otherwise I'll count on
you to function as you did this year.

One more word—is it necessary to name the prize after me? I really and truly try to avoid publicity.

Sincerely—and gratefully
Maxwell Anderson

1. Prof. Bailey inaugurated her verse play competition at Stanford during the summer of 1936 and, with only six weeks between announcement and deadline and with a prize of only $50, received ninety-eight scripts. She had sent the winning play to Anderson, *Surrey* by Florette Henri, asking him to consider it for a Broadway production.

2. Neighbor, preparing for the lead in *High Tor*.

54. TO MARGERY BAILEY

Hotel Hay-Adams House
Washington, D.C.
[November 25, 1936]

Dear Margery Bailey—[1]

If ever a skeptic but hopeful middle-aged gentleman received during his life-time the comment on his work which he longed to receive while he still kept [going] but did not look for till after he was dead I got it in your last letter. A beautiful letter, my dear, and I shall treasure it not only for what it says but also as a sample of the art. And now you may certainly keep my name on the contest, and count on me to organize the New York committee for looking over three of the plays. Nobody shall be on it for name's sake only, though—they must actually be willing to consider the plays if they serve. Meredith will work, and so will Harold Freedman, with whom I discussed your earlier letter. Freedman is the one New York agent of real importance— and the one with the greatest integrity. I haven't yet spoken to McClintic or Cornell.[2] If they don't want to take the responsibility somebody on the Guild Board will do it. And Barrett Clark is certain to come in if we want him. If you want to announce the judges along with the conditions perhaps you should hold off until I've spoken to the others. But perhaps you would like to give out the conditions now, and release the names of the judges later. In any case you may count in the five hundred. Nick the Rockefellers if you wish, but I'll raise the money otherwise.[3]

May I suggest a few rules—well, not rules, but admonitions, for the contestants? —Play structure is much more important than playwriting, even in a poetic play. Look well to the emotional stress at the end of the second act, and take care that this stress emerges from the characters in the situation, not from the situation alone. Read Aristotle on the "recognition scene," the most important point in any dramatic structure. Avoid the imitation of verse mannerisms from another age, avoid archaisms, save rarely for historical color. Write the living language, even though in verse; try for limpidity, clarity of meaning and, above all, accuracy of metaphor. The accurate metaphor, instantly recognizable, is the test of good poetry for the stage. Use words carefully. Remember that every word you write is magnified by ten diameters when spoken on the stage. Never choose a soft or sentimental subject for poetic treatment. The more beauty and ornament your style carries the sturdier must be the skeleton of plot and thinking underneath. Spend three times the effort planning your play which you will require to write it.

Some few of these precepts are suggested to me by going through *Surrey*, which could have been improved by a more honestly woven diction. The girl has real dramatic talent, and builds scenes well, and your choice was probably the right one. But she occasionally tries to decorate her verse with borrowed ornament, and the result is a loss of interest.

I write this letter the day after our out of town opening of *The Wingless Victory*, which looks to be a hit here, and will come [into] New York the 23rd of December. Day after tomorrow I go to New York to start casting for *High Tor*. I'm still trying to get three plays on this season,[4] so if you hear little from me you'll know the reason. But if you're in the east call me at New City 202 in the evening sometime, and we'll arrange to meet.

As ever

Maxwell A.

Please don't quote the rules as mine—

1. Prof. Bailey's response to no. 53 is lost, unfortunately, but in it she insisted on naming first prize in her verse play competition the Maxwell Anderson Award.

2. At the time Guthrie McClintic was producer and director of *High Tor*, and his wife Katharine Cornell was producer and star of *The Wingless Victory*.

3. Unable to get money from the Rockefeller Foundation, Prof. Bailey set the cash prize for the Anderson Award at $100, half contributed by Stanford and half by Anderson.

4. *The Masque of Kings* was the other play.

55. TO HAZEL A. REYNOLDS [1]

New City
September 2, 1937

Dear Miss Reynolds:

If your questions were not so definite and intelligent, it would be easier to answer them briefly. I'll do my best, however, following your own outline.

I–a.

The stage-manager's copy is somewhat shorter and contains additional stage directions and notes for the practical conduct of the play.

I–b.

The prompter's copy is usually some pages shorter due to cuts of entire speeches or parts of speeches found unnecessary during rehearsal. In case the play is in verse this leads to inevitable dislocation of metrical scheme. Additional speeches or phrases found necessary during rehearsal add somewhat to the rhythmic confusion, though these additions are never sufficient to make up for the cutting in the matter of length.

I–c.

In my own case the original version is used for publication with occasional slight changes which have been found of immense value to the general scheme, even for reading purposes. This is not the general practice, which is to publish the stage version minus the prompter's notes.

II–a.

The use of iambic pentameter for the stage is certainly no accident. It has been found by trial and error to combine the maximum of intensity and elevation with a minimum of artificiality in the theatre. Verse which calls attention to itself detracts from actuality in representation. It might be assumed off-

hand that modern free or "sprung" verse would avoid this
difficulty, but in practice this form is the most artificial of all on
the stage. Since it is impossible to decide where a line begins or
ends without reference to the manuscript, free verse gives an
impression from the stage of involved and high-flown prose.
When the actor tries to avoid this effect by emphasis or pause he
defeats all reality by obvious and artificial mannerism. Pentameter,
when not stiltedly written, may be spoken with the effect of
complete reality and still retain its poetic character. I leave it to
the students of metrics to discover why this is, but of the fact I
have no doubt. I have searched high and low for another verse
form not so worn by use but I have discovered nothing suitable to
the stage unless for special use in stylized comedy or burlesque.

I wish you luck with your thesis which may perhaps answer some
questions for me. Give my regards to Professor Bassett who was a
member of the department when I was at Stanford.[2]

Sincerely

1. Miss Reynolds, candidate for the M.A. in English at Stanford, was writing a
thesis on Anderson and had sent him a questionnaire.

2. Lee Emerson Bassett, professor of English at Stanford from 1905 until
retirement in 1938, directed Miss Reynolds's thesis, but she did not complete it or take
her degree.

56. TO JOHN MASON BROWN [1]

[October, 1937]

Dear Mr. Brown—

I am in receipt, via the Guild offices, of an invitation to take lunch
with you and smoke a pipe of peace over a possible play subject, and I
must say definitely that I will not smoke a peace pipe with you or any
other critic because I have never quarrelled [with] a critic and never
will. By the time I get a play written and on I dislike my work so much
(though I usually have a tremendous admiration for the actress!) that I
agree with the most implacable censor before he can get the words out
of his typewriter. The morning after nearly every opening finds me
trussed in a sack in the corner of some hotel room, a dozen knives

buried in my vital organs, my nose slit and my ears cut off, but still breathing; and willing to state with my last breath that I deserved what my assailants did to me because of what I did to them. I once tried to tell the critics that it wasn't necessary to assassinate a sensitive man in order to indicate displeasure,[2] but I was probably wrong. The critics don't write for the playwrights; they write for the papers, and their readers enjoy nothing so much as a good drawing and quartering.

And so, the morning after every opening I walk, unarmed, into an ambush, expecting to be blown to pieces, and usually getting what I expect. And I don't want to turn one knife or spike one gun, because I believe the critics have a high and hierophantic duty to perform in the theatre, and that, under the journalistic circumstances, they do their best to perform it. It's their duty to keep the standards high and to shoot hell out of shoddy work. They sometimes attend to this function with a joyous abandon which attests a disproportionate love of fireworks on their part or their readers', but they put the fear of death into playwrights, and the playwright who can't get by the barrage simply has to move out or quit. So far I've lived through each assault, though there have been times when I thought no surgeon, no miraculous balsam, no stitching and nursing, would be able to put me together again. And I've learned a good deal by noting that when the critics really like what you do they will shoot you only in the periphery or the running gear, and some will withhold their fire altogether. In other words, they use a discernible discretion, and if I can stand the gaff long enough I may learn how to write a play that will please even me. So far I've sometimes pleased the public; I've sometimes pleased the critics. I've sometimes pleased both, but I've not yet written one that I think will endure the test of time—and that's what I want to do.

By these steps I come to the invitation to lunch. I'm by nature an amicable and gregarious person, susceptible to the blandishments and not without friends. But I have felt myself cut off from one section of the human race, the critical firing squad, because I want and need honest criticism, and no man can be strictly honest about the work of his friends—or even his acquaintances. Some of the critics told me at the time of the first award[3] that this isn't true, but I don't believe them. When a friend of yours writes a play you either remove the dum-dum bullets from your armory, or you lean over backward in your effort to be just and pump him full of lead. In either case you probably know what he was trying to do, which colors your whole attitude, or you know that he's in debt and the income tax people are taking his house. I flatter myself that if we had lunch together we'd be friends, but suppose we became enemies? The notion for a play which you have in mind might appeal to me; then if I wrote it we'd differ over the results. But the chances are I wouldn't like it, since I'm captious in such matters, and the rejected proffer would rankle.

This is a long letter and I hate writing letters, but I respect your work (and your target eye) too much just to say yes or no and let matters slide.

Sincerely

Not for publication, of course.

1. Brown (1900–1969) published and lectured extensively on the drama, and at the end of his life was immersed in a biography of Anderson's close friend Robert Sherwood. Formerly associate editor of *Theatre Arts Monthly* and later drama critic for *Saturday Review of Literature*, he was from 1929 to 1941 drama critic for the *New York Evening Post*, and Helen Deutsch of the Theatre Guild had reported to Anderson that Brown wished to propose a play subject to him.
2. Acceptance speech for the Drama Critics' Circle Award to *High Tor*, April 1, 1937 (Appendix I, no. 2).
3. Drama Critics' Circle Award to *Winterset*, April 5, 1936.

57. TO JOHN MASON BROWN

New City
November 17, 1937

Dear Mr. Brown:[1]

Your letter followed me to Maine where I was exploring a little wilderness on my own account. Your description of the St. Lawrence in conjunction with Parkman leads me to believe that I shall look into Canada some time, at least along the edges.

Also my first act on returning to the vicinity of a book store was to purchase Parkman complete and begin to find out how much I had missed by not reading him. I wish I had the volumes you read with the under-scorings and perhaps I shall be driven before I am through to beg for a personal consultation with you. Being certain so far only of the background, I doubt my capacity to lay a play in it, likewise the capacity of Broadway to accept such a play even if one were well made. It grows more obvious to me year by year that Broadway is not interested in fine distinctions, least of all in spiritual ones. Our theatrical capital would be likely to avow that it knew all about Indians, feeling that they were done once for all in wood by Mr. Cooper, and in trochaic tetrameter by Mr. Longfellow. If Parkman suggested something to me a great many bored auditors who had never read Parkman would inquire by what right I made the monosyllabic Indian eloquent, and what possible originality or novelty I thought I had achieved in picturing the Jesuit as devoted or the Indian as a noble savage.

Nevertheless the history of the Jesuits is fascinating on its own account and I feel richer mentally for knowing it. If I change my mind on better acquaintance with the material and do find a play in Pontiac or Father Joques, the play will probably be its own reward and cost the Theatre Guild a lot of money. This will sound pessimistic to you but I don't mean it that way. It's the business of the playwright to please both himself and his audience and I have looked long and hard at that Broadway audience and found only a narrow margin of over-lapping between me and it.

Thanks for your letter and for thinking about me on the St. Lawrence. We do very well for strangers.[2]

Sincerely

1. In 1937 Anderson bought a farm near Hudson, Maine. Brown had proposed two play subjects for Anderson, both drawn from Francis Parkman's histories, one focusing on the Indian Pontiac, the other on the Jesuit Father Joques (November 1, 1937; T). The story of Pontiac is found in *The Conspiracy of Pontiac and the Indian War after the Conquest of Canada* (1870), that of Father Joques in *The Jesuits in North America in the Seventeenth Century* (1867).

2. Anderson did not undertake a play on either subject.

58. TO RAY LYMAN WILBUR [1]

New City
December 9, 1937

Dear Dr. Wilbur:

Stated briefly as possible, my suggestions for the use of the open air theatre at Stanford are these:

That Stanford University establish a national theatre festival, possibly to be called the Festival of Dionysius, after the Greek fashion; that the University offer three prizes of $1,000 each for three poetic tragedies, with no restriction on style or subject or author save that the author be a resident of the United States; that these three tragedies be performed on successive days by Stanford students under the supervision of the Dramatic Department, and an additional reward of $500 be given to the author of that tragedy which wins most votes from members of the audience who have seen all three plays; that on the fourth day the program should consist of three one-act satyr plays written by students of Stanford University and burlesquing either one of the three tragedies previously given or any tragedy well-known to the audience, and that a small cash prize be voted by the audience to the winning play. In these last plays I should personally wish to encourage the use of the animal chorus and the traditional burlesque trappings with which the Greeks took off their own tragedies.

These suggestions make a radical departure from what is customary in the modern use of the outdoor theatre, especially in the emphasis on poetic tragedy, in leaving out revivals altogether, in providing for large cash prizes and in the national scope of the competition. I think these departures are all justified. Poetic tragedy has always been the highest aim of the theatre and the young men and women who are now attacking dramatic writing have begun to make attempts in that direction which, if encouraged, may lead to the production of a national drama worthy of a great nation. Mr. Titterton of the National Broadcasting Company and Miss Helburn with her Bureau of New Plays both assure me that a large proportion of the manuscripts they now receive are in verse and not bad verse at that. It seems to me much more important to emphasize this tendency than to draw on the ancients for the usual program of revivals. It is worth noting also that good prose plays are fairly certain of a hearing on Broadway whereas a play in verse is so far a bad commercial risk. I know of several worthwhile plays of this character which should be submitted and are worthy of a production.

The amounts I suggest for the prizes will no doubt meet with criticism but they are not too large if we wish to encourage the use of verse on the stage. The writing of a poetic tragedy is a long and arduous task and even those who are able and willing to attempt it are at present restrained from embarking on so hazardous an enterprise with so little prospect of financial return. This country has spent huge sums on theatres and theatre equipment for the use of students in production technique but has neglected almost completely to provide an incentive for the writing of plays which should fill such theatres. Without the plays the theatres become a dead weight, empty auditoriums provided with a profusion of mechanical equipment for the projection of an art form which we have forgotten to encourage. If the theatres are worthwhile, if the equipment is to be useful, we must somehow stimulate the talent that will give the theatre something to project. The play is the spirit of the theatre and without it the equipment is dead.

In regard to the national scope of the competition, it seems to me that the advantages are obvious. Such a scheme would make Stanford the center toward which all aspirants for distinction in poetic drama would turn. This would be especially true if the prizes were offered for one production only and all other rights to the manuscripts were left in the authors' hands. It would hold out to the writer an opportunity to see his work in performance, to display it to possible commercial producers and to finance himself through that doubtful period when he is trying something for which the market is at present most uncertain.

This is only my personal outline of what I should like to see in an outdoor theatre. No doubt it would have to be modified if adopted and some of the details are probably unrealizable, but in the main I think it would be good both for Stanford and the theatre in general.

It was a great pleasure to see you in New York and to discover that you share some of my own enthusiasm for the theatre as a center of national culture. I haven't included in this letter any discussion of the possible study cycles which we mentioned which would take up concurrently the theatre, the music and the painting of different civilizations in different historical periods, but that was as much your idea as my own and you can state it better than I can. Whatever comes

of this scheme, or if nothing comes of it, be sure I shall continue to
wish you well at Stanford.

Sincerely

1. Wilbur (1875–1949), secretary of the interior (1929–33) in the Hoover
administration, was for the balance of his career president of Stanford University
(1916–41). Margery Bailey inspired him with the idea of using Stanford as an
instrument in the creation of a national drama and arranged for him to meet with
Anderson during a trip to New York City shortly before the present letter.

59. TO JOHN F. WHARTON *

New City
February 18, 1938

Dear John:[1]

I have been so drowned in a difficult play that I haven't come up
to answer letters in more than a month. However, I must tell you that
I think you have done a beautiful job with the Articles of
Confederation, which appear to be both clear and complete.

There are two minor points I'd like to talk over with the Board
before signing my copy and burning my bridges. The first concerns the
individual author's right to bargain for outside talent and to sell his
play elsewhere in case he feels it necessary in order to get the best
production. I believe we'll all stay with the group whenever we can
and that the bargaining should be left with the individual, for stars are
hard to approach and hard to deal with at best and I should feel at a
grave disadvantage with the Lunts or Cornell if my hands were tied. A
star or a director might like a play yet dislike to change producers, and
be unwilling to offend us by saying so. Our mutual interest in our
investment should be sufficient to hold us together without an
ironclad clause. You say in your note that you think the Board would
always be lenient in such matters, but the Board is of course a variable
and I'd rather depend upon free co-operation than a loose construc-
tion of the law.

The other point I wanted to mention is that if no play is to be
produced until it is complete and the Board is to decide when a play is
complete, then it is in the Board's power to decide which plays shall be

produced and which shall not. Perhaps the Board should make this decision but the states-general didn't seem to feel that way when last we met, and if we do delegate that power to the Board, perhaps we should say so openly.

When I finish this play I am working at, I shall get very serious about that one-set inexpensive comedy which is to keep so far under our budget requirements that it will look like a garter-snake marching through Washington Square arch.[2]

Sincerely

1. The Basic Agreement for the Incorporation of the Playwrights' Company is given in Wharton, *Life Among the Playwrights*, pp. 270–77. The document, signed by Wharton and the member playwrights on April 12, 1938, was drawn by Wharton, and he had sent a draft of it to Anderson, who was at work on *The Duquesnes*, an unfinished play (*Catalogue*, p. 68).

2. Anderson's next play was not a "one-set inexpensive comedy" but *Knicker-bocker Holiday*, an elaborate and expensive (and moderately successful) musical, his first play produced by the Playwrights' Company.

60. TO MARGERY BAILEY

New City
March 5, 1938

Dear Margery:[1]

The months go by and become years and still I haven't written to you. I won't try to apologize even though my conscience will probably bother me forever because of my complete neglect of you when I had heard that you were ill and felt very certain you were depressed. I'll begin at the beginning and try not to cover all the ground.

The Souvenir seemed to me a producible play, with a little work, whereas the other two did not. Also it had some fairly good poetry.

As for Wilbur and the contest festival, I gave him what I thought might fill his theatres, though I wasn't at all sure.[2] Certainly I can't take responsibility for the quality of the plays that come in. I will continue to do my poor best in regard to the verse play contest, even to coughing up money if necessary, at any rate, I don't want you to have to borrow from the bank. As to your three choices, I don't want to try to write anything; I'm trying so hard to write a play that I don't want to be interrupted. I doubt that I shall have time for a vacation and certainly I won't lecture on any subject. You may, of course, use any part of the Carnegie text which appeals to you.[3]

In regard to the judges, I wish I could escape reading the plays but I have nothing to suggest and don't know how I can get out of it. Nobody else will read them or care whether they're read or not.

I haven't written Sandoe yet but found his paper excellent, myself hardly deserving of it.[4]

I guess that's all except my gratitude and my fervent wish that you are never ill again.

Sincerely
Maxwell

1. During the previous fall Prof. Bailey had sent Anderson the three best scripts from the verse play competition at Stanford, including *Souvenir de la Malmaison* by Dorothy Dow, winner of the 1937 Maxwell Anderson Award. More recently she had asked him to take part in the awards ceremony at Stanford in the fall of 1938.
2. See no. 58.
3. "The Arts as Motive Power," delivered as the Founder's Day Address at Carnegie Institute, Pittsburgh, on October 14, 1937, and on October 17 published in the *New York Times*, sec. 11, p. 1, cols. 6–8, p. 2, cols. 1–5 (included as "Whatever Hope We Have" in *The Essence of Tragedy and Other Footnotes and Papers*, 1939).
4. James L. Sandoe, "The Case of Maxwell Anderson," *Colorado College Publication* 30 (April 1, 1940): 73–82. Sandoe, at the time librarian at the University of Colorado, had participated in Prof. Bailey's drama workshops at Stanford during the summers of 1935 and 1936, and with the invitation to the 1938 awards ceremony Prof. Bailey had included Sandoe's paper.

61. TO GUTHRIE MC CLINTIC [1]

New City
March 5, 1938

Dear Guthrie:

Within a day or two you will probably see an announcement of a producing organization formed by a number of playwrights of whom I am one. The idea is similar to that of the project which came to nothing several years ago, though the playwrights involved are not all the same.[2] The formation of this organization will naturally have some bearing on our understanding, but I hasten to assure you that the participants leave themselves free to produce outside the organization, and that I hope we shall work together often in the future. In fact, of the playwrights involved I am the only one who is entirely satisfied with his producer and director, and I would not join such a group if I were thinking of my own productions and my chances of success. They are probably better with you than elsewhere.

If I thought I could go on writing plays with machine-like regularity, I wouldn't make any change at all, but either the theatre is falling to pieces around me or I am falling to pieces inside it. Maybe it's the critics that discourage me, maybe it's the general atmosphere around Broadway, but to write anything at all is like pulling teeth nowadays, because I cannot avoid anticipating the reception it will get. I find this same impediment in other playwrights of the association and a number of us have decided to combine to keep up our spirits, to make, if possible, the center of opinion not so continually adverse. The other playwrights in our association have either been on the point of withdrawing from the theatre altogether or wondering how soon they would be in that frame of mind. If we can talk each other into going on and perhaps help a little with the structure of each other's plays, the theatre as a whole should benefit and individually we'll be better off.

So far I have no play for next year except the one which I am currently writing for the Lunts, the one which started out in France and has moved so far away and changed so completely that you will never recognize it.[3]

What I really want to get at is that I hope we won't separate over this reorganization because I shall always want to have you direct all my plays.

Sincerely

1. McClintic (1893–1961) was the producer/director Anderson turned to following his difficulties with the Theatre Guild over *Valley Forge*. Beginning with the next play, *Winterset*, McClintic produced and directed most of Anderson's plays until the formation of the Playwrights' Company, and thereafter directed several of them, including *Key Largo*. Announcements of the formation of the Playwrights' Company were to appear in New York papers on March 8, 1938.

2. There had been several such attempts during the past decade. Elmer Rice, in *Minority Report* (1963), notes one involving himself, Anderson, Philip Barry, and George Kelly (P. 375).

3. Probably *The Duquesnes*, an unfinished play featuring a highly successful husband-and-wife acting team such as the Lunts (Alfred Lunt and Lynn Fontanne). For *The Duquesnes*, see *Catalogue*, p. 68.

62. TO ROBERT E. SHERWOOD *

[New City]
[March 8, 1938]

Dear Bob—[1]

I've tried writing those lines—and done it very badly. My only
excuse for sending them is that I can't explain what I meant about the
motivation any other way. —But I also realize now that if these
motives are placed at the climax they'll have to be stressed a little more
in the other scenes which involve Mary as a symbol, and that the
atmosphere of the play changes somewhat when the pattern is brought
out clearly. Perhaps the change isn't for the better. Perhaps bringing
out one pattern injures the more complex design—and even makes the
whole less convincing.

I'm writing a note to John in this mail,[2] telling him that the
collapse of that picture sale[3]—along with other calamities, including
an income tax decision—has made it improbable that I shall have ten
thousand to invest this summer. It's rather embarrassing to confess
this, after pressing so hard for our own investment, but a number of
things have happened to me—all of them unforeseen. We'll probably
have a chance to talk the matter over before you go. It may be that I
could work with the Playwrights' Theatre without taking an actual
share in its management or profits. This seems not to be my lucky
year—

As ever,
Max

1. Sherwood had sent a draft of *Abe Lincoln in Illinois* and had pointed to his
special difficulty with Mary Todd Lincoln as a symbol (a problem he discusses in the
published preface to the play).
2. John F. Wharton.
3. David O. Selznick had reneged on a commitment to buy the film rights to *The
Star-Wagon*, saying it might be held to plagiarize the just-released picture *Turn Back the
Clock*.

63. TO MRS. F. DURAND TAYLOR[1]

New City
April 5, 1938

Dear Mrs. Taylor:

The Marlowe legend has tempted me more than once but most definitely when Hotson's book came out. Lately I have thought of him as the symbol of modern loneliness and loss of faith, but always the fact that he was a writer and that I have a prejudice against writing about writers, turns me aside from any real consideration of the story. It may be that there is new material or a new light on the old material that would allow me to see a play in Marlowe's life, and since you so generously offer the fruits of your own thinking and the matter has somewhat haunted you, I should like very much to know in some detail what kind of story and meaning you have founded on Dr. Hotson's researches. No doubt, as you suggest, the concept would refuse to grow if transplanted, but something in what you say may turn out to be just the catalytic agent I have needed.

Your letter went a long way about in reaching me and came only yesterday. I thought of calling you at once for a letter like that is rare to any of us. I conquered that impulse, being a little shy myself about breaking down barriers, and contented myself with looking up the three articles which you mentioned.[2] I gather that you are interested in Marlowe's possible use of the theatre as a springboard into importance and higher politics and I am not at all sure that I like that approach to the subject, but I should like to know what meaning these ghosts have had for you. Lest another letter should go wandering, my address is New City, Rockland County, New York.

Sincerely

P.S. I am keeping your book for a couple of days to study your underscorings.

1. Marjorie F. Taylor of East Orange, New Jersey, had written to Anderson about her idea for a play based on the life of Christopher Marlowe (March 15, 1938; T). Her three-page letter, sent to him in care of the Author's League of America, outlined characters and situations, and with the letter she sent a copy of J. Leslie Hotson, *The Death of Christopher Marlowe* (1925), saying that it contained the core of her idea for the play and that she had been haunted by the idea since her student days at Hollins College in the twenties. Her hope was that Anderson would be attracted to the idea and

write the play, and her letter contained a statement absolving him of any indebtedness to her. She asked only for tickets to opening night.

2. J. Leslie Hotson, "Tracking Down a Murderer," *Atlantic Monthly* 135 (June, 1925): 733–41. "Kit Marlowe's Murder 'Out'," *Literary Digest* 85 (June 13, 1925): 27–28. Horace Gregory, review of *The Works and Life of Christopher Marlowe*, R. H. Case ed. (New York, 1932), *New Republic* 71 (June 22, 1932): 159–60.

64. TO JOHN F. WHARTON

New City
April 22, 1938

Dear John:[1]

When I saw you the other day I realized that you had been from the first more deeply concerned about your own good faith than I could possibly be, and my misgivings must have seemed both heartless and thoughtless. My excuse must be that I didn't know you very well, that legal ethics are often baffling and sometimes disillusioning to the layman and that one learns to be astonished at nothing in a business deal. In the last analysis there is nothing to rely on but personal probity and from now on I shall rely on you implicitly.

Sincerely
Max

1. Wharton represented John Hay Whitney, who financed David Selznick's motion picture producing company. Selznick had recently withdrawn his offer to buy the film rights to *The Star-Wagon*, a sale Anderson had hoped would finance his entry into the Playwrights' Company, and Anderson at first thought that Wharton was involved in Selznick's act of bad faith.

65. TO JOHN F. WHARTON

New City
May 18, 1938

Dear John:[1]

So far I haven't been able to hit on any title for our venture that sounds acceptable even to my ears. However, I'm glad the old one is unavailable if Sidney didn't like it. There should be a certain unanimity toward the label.

I seem to be getting along very well with the operetta[2] but it's a new form for me and I can't be sure. Kurt Weill returns from the coast in about ten days and I expect to be able to show him a completed script, subject to revision, after we have talked it over. He plans to go to work on the music as soon as he gets here. I shall not want to submit the script to the playwrights until the revisions are completed, probably about the middle of June. Burgess Meredith has read the first half and says he wants to play the lead. On the other hand, I should want him to take the best part he can get and my script doesn't absolutely require him.[3]

Let's hope inspiration falls from the clouds on somebody in regard to that name. If anything occurs to me I'll let you know at once. Thanks for talking to Alfred Sturt[4] and for you bulletins on general progress. I shall set down the 42nd Street address for use after the first of June.

Sincerely
Max

1. Members of the Playwrights' Company originally named the company the Playwrights' Theatre. In a letter of May 12, 1938 (JFW), however, Wharton informed Anderson that Playwrights' Theatre was not available because the New York secretary of state judged it in conflict with the names of several other theatrical organizations. Its unavailability would please Sidney Howard, Wharton added, because Howard had not liked Playwrights' Theatre.

2. *Knickerbocker Holiday.*

3. Meredith had played the lead in *Winterset*, *High Tor*, and *The Star-Wagon*. In the Wharton letter cited above, Wharton told Anderson that other producers were submitting scripts to Meredith for production next season. Eventually Meredith refused the lead (Brom Broeck) in *Knickerbocker Holiday*, and for production Anderson revised the script, shifting the focus to Peter Stuyvesant (played by Walter Huston).

4. Sturt, Anderson's business secretary, was also an insurance agent, and earlier in the month Anderson had sent Sturt to Wharton to arrange insurance for the company.

66. TO ELMER RICE *

New City
June 26, 1938

Dear Elmer:[1]

First of all let me thank you for your telegram which is the only word I have had from the playwrights about my script so far and most encouraging. I think you will like it better when you see it next for I am doing a good deal of rewriting, especially in the first act. Weill's music is the best I have ever heard for any musical show, better even than Sullivan's. If the words are only half as good and we have the right actors, we should come off very well. I've had a lot of casting and production problems to consider and am therefore very late with this letter but you needed a vacation anyway so perhaps I'll be forgiven.

This House—and I like the title by the way—held me from beginning to end and should play just as well as it reads. Everything you write is so alive and so commanding that there is never any faltering of interest. But when I looked over the script today I felt, as I had when I read it first, that an audience would be in doubt as to what you meant to convey. I am not even certain that I know what impression you meant to leave though I think I can make a pretty big guess at it.

I feel a bit hesitant about making definite suggestions but after all that is what our organization is for and I shall hope to get the same kind of thing from you whenever you have an idea you think might help. To be brief, I was dissatisfied with three things; first, I didn't know why the ghosts came back and they never told me; second, the old man's death appeared accidental which results in a fortuitous end to your second act; and third, your last act presents no answer to the indictment Frank brings at the end of the second.

I don't know how you would go about clearing these matters up, in case you thought it necessary to do so. Please forgive me if I suggest the way in which I'd go about it if it were my problem. I don't know any other way to make my meaning plain.

The big scene at the end of the second act begins as it must with a statement of the young people's side of the question. They don't want the house sold and they have their reasons for it. Then the old man has his say and the words you have given him are thrilling and beautiful. But now I think the ghosts should have their innings and prove their right to be in the play. One of them—I don't know which one—should say that they are all there for only one reason, because they had all known and loved this particular bit of earth, because what they are is bound up with its fresh, individualistic, pioneering freedom, and with a way of life which will be known no more in this neighborhood after this sale. Now this Frank knows and he doesn't answer him, but there should be another speaker, perhaps Harriet Stone, who says that the dead have one wisdom the living never appreciate, a knowledge that death is necessary because as we grow older we harden into fixed ways of thinking and lose elasticity of mind necessary to meet a new day. Frank is old; he wants to keep things as they were; perhaps his place is more with the ghosts themselves than with the young living who are pressing on ahead. It is the realization of this truth striking home to his brain that brings Frank down.

The last act ought to give an answer to Frank's indictment and this is how I saw it coming about: The other ghosts have disappeared, satisfied with the saving of the house, but the ghost of Frank, still posing the old question, comes to Connie to ask how this modern regimentation of farm and factory is any improvement over the Bund itself. Connie's answer is that there is a new kind of pioneering for every age, that as it was the problem of the early settlers to preserve life and liberty in a wilderness, it is the problem of her generation to preserve the freedom of the individual in the midst of social organization. No matter how the problem is solved, the important thing to keep is a man's independence in his world, whether he be a laborer or a capitalist, and this is what the play is saying.

This is all said very baldly and not very well. You will probably throw it all out but it may suggest something to you which will answer the difficulties I mentioned. You will note that nothing I have suggested would alter the structure, which is very effective as it stands, and whatever comes of any advice I give all I shall want to see is the best play you can write. This letter is of course between ourselves.

When you have any notes for me regarding *Knickerbocker Holiday* I hope you will set them down without fear or favor and send them on as quickly as you can for I want to incorporate all the advice I can get.

Good luck to you in the West.

Sincerely

1. From San Francisco Rice had sent Anderson a draft of his current play, then called *This House* but changed to *American Landscape* for its production by the Playwrights' Company and publication in the fall of 1938. He had also sent an enthusiastic telegram after reading *Knickerbocker Holiday*.

67. TO MRS. F. DURAND TAYLOR

New City
November 10, 1938

Dear Mrs. Taylor:

Your last inquiry about Marlowe is dated August 6th which means that it arrived just as I was going into the sausage machine with a new production.[1] We have now emerged, wrapped and neatly labelled, but with the usual conviction that I will never be the same. My friends and well-wishers tell me that I must go away somewhere and forget and whether I forget or not I shall probably go away. I expect to come back on or about Thanksgiving and shall drop you a note at that time in the hope of arranging a meeting in New York. I am sorry about these delays because I am still hopeful about what might be done with Kit.[2]

Sincerely

1. *Knickerbocker Holiday.*
2. According to a letter from Mrs. Taylor to the present editor (July 7, 1971), she met with Anderson in December, 1938, for a three-hour lunch at the Algonquin Hotel in New York where they discussed the possibilities of a Marlowe play. She further remembers that about a month after the meeting Anderson wrote her to say he had decided against doing a play on Marlowe because he lacked time for the necessary research.

68. TO GILMOR BROWN [1]

New City
November 10, 1938

Dear Mr. Brown:

You have my permission to use the plays you name at the $50 a week royalty and I hope the venture turns out well for you in case you embark on it. May I suggest that *The Buccaneer* is hardly up to the others in structure or quality? I should think *Outside Looking In* would be a better choice, but of course that's up to you.

I'm afraid it would be impossible to let you have a new play, partly because I don't know when I'll have one ready nor what it will be about, but also because a play has a better chance in New York if it tries out with the New York cast and comes into the city keyed up for the opening. There have been exceptions but it seems to be less of a gamble to go through the regular routine. It does occur to me that the three one-act plays on revolution would make an evening in the theatre and might serve you as the equivalent of a new play. Two of them, *The Feast of Ortolans* and *Second Overture*, were published in Stage Magazine; the third, *The Bastion of St. Gervais*, I would have to send you in manuscript. [2] You are welcome to use these if they appeal to you.

All good wishes for the festival.

Sincerely

1. Brown (1887–1960), founder of the Pasadena Playhouse in 1918 and director of it until his death, had written to Anderson in preparation for the fifth of his annual Midsummer Drama Festivals at the playhouse, to be held in 1939. The four previous festivals had been devoted largely to Shakespeare and Shaw, and the fifth was to be devoted to Anderson. It ran for eight weeks in 1939, June 26 to August 19, and included eight plays: *Elizabeth the Queen*, *Valley Forge*, *The Wingless Victory*, *The Masque of Kings*, *Both Your Houses*, *Gods of the Lightning*, *Winterset*, and *The Star-Wagon*. At the time of the present letter, however, Brown intended to play *The Buccaneer* during the week eventually taken by *Gods of the Lightning*.

2. For "The Bastion Saint-Gervais," unpublished, see *Catalogue*, p. 64.

69. TO MRS. FLORENCE B. HULT[1]

New City
November 12, 1938

Dear Mrs. Hult:

I have felt guilty for years because I haven't been able to get a hearing for Gottfried on the New York stage but there is always something in his work—a lack of experience in the Broadway theatre or too poetic an aim, I can't put my finger on it—that stands in the way of a possible production. He is too good a poet and too fine a person to be rejected but when a manager reads his script the question he always asks is whether it will make money, and I can't truthfully say yes myself.

You write most discerningly about my own plays—I don't think anybody else ever made the comment about *Elizabeth*—the inference, when you come right down to it, that nobody gives up his own world for love. I have a feeling that my own plays have suffered a great deal from being written to a demand but that's the only way plays can be written profitably and I have tried to make an intelligent compromise between my soul and my living.

I have written to Lois Austin,[2] very tardily, having just got my play on,[3] and will see her some time this month, though it's very doubtful that I can be of any help this season.

My best to you both.

Sincerely

1. Wife of Gottfried Hult (1869–1950), professor of Greek at the University of North Dakota during Anderson's student days there. Anderson became a close friend of the Hults and credited Prof. Hult with introducing him to Greek philosophy. Prof. Hult also wrote poetry, publishing two books of verse (*Reveries*, 1909, and *Outbound*, 1920) and a collection of poetic dramas, *Inverted Torches* (1940).

2. Niece of the Hults and an aspiring actress.

3. *Knickerbocker Holiday.*

70. TO HELEN DEUTSCH [1]

New City
November 25, 1938

Dear Helen:

I have just finished reading Robert Newman's play "Ghost Town." The verse has depth, intelligence and beauty. Individual lines often have a haunting quality but unfortunately they don't always forward the plot or develop the characters. They *reveal* the characters, which is different. The main weakness, however, is in the structure of the story. Even after thinking it over I cannot be sure on which side one's sympathies are meant to be enlisted. Mr. Newman has presented two brothers, equally attractive and equally interesting, and a man, Kerry, who seems to occupy the middle ground. Which one is the protagonist? Perhaps he was showing both sides and playing for the middle, but somehow I don't think this is so. He must have had a definite point of view and therefore every aspect of the play should have furthered this point of view. An audience, though more intelligent than we commonly believe, must nevertheless be led very slowly and carefully from one step to the next, following the author by the nose, as it were, so that even when the audience does not agree with the author, it is carried along by his inexorable logic. In conventional form this is achieved by the device of the hero. But in this play I cannot decide who is the hero. I couldn't possibly offer any structural suggestions without being sure on this one important point.

I feel, too, that the characters are not clearly defined. Though Mac and Don stand for different points of view which are clearly enough stated, I do not understand them as persons either singly or in relation to each other. The drama must be between people and not between ideas. What is it between these two brothers that separates them and brings about their antipathies? Somehow they have no flesh to cover their minds. The same is true of the girl who is only a symbol in the minds of the men and therefore a symbol in the author's mind also. Or perhaps I should have turned that about.

You know all this, of course, and I am not writing an essay on playwriting for your benefit. I am assuming that you intend to pass this on to Mr. Newman and am really writing it for him.

As ever

1. Helen Deutsch (c. 1900), play-reader for the Theatre Guild, had sent Anderson the verse play discussed in the letter, Robert Newman's *Ghost Town*. Newman (b. 1909), later a novelist, began as a playwright, and *Ghost Town*, written in 1937–38 and not produced or published, interprets a current TVA dam-building project in terms of the freeing-of-the-waters theme in the Grail legend. Two brothers, its implications explained to them by an observant bystander (Kerry), choose sides about the dam, one opposing it as a threat to the traditional life of the community, the other supporting it as a promise of new vitality. Don, opposing the dam and impotent, loses his girl friend to his brother Mac, who makes love with her on the night he sets the dam in operation (from two Newman letters to the present editor, September 24, and October 8, 1975).

71. TO LAURENCE MOORE[1]

New City
December 5, 1938

Dear Mr. Moore:

I am afraid there is very little that one playwright can do to help another toward finding a more accurate and illuminating means of expression. Your play shows thought and undoubted talent but as you say in your letter the verse is often unsatisfactory for the stage. Not that it isn't good verse, as modern verse goes, but it's certainly too cryptic to be understood at one hearing. It's almost as if when you cease writing prose, you cease to communicate, whereas the verse should communicate just as directly and more forcefully than the prose. Structurally your play seems to me to hold together very well and your characters are interesting and ably developed.

I am forwarding your script to Miss Louise Sillcox of The Dramatists' Guild with the recommendation that if there are any extra scholarships floating about you could get one. This probably won't mean a thing to you but I'm making the suggestion.

Sincerely

P.S. There is an annual verse play contest held by Stanford University and you might enter your play.[2] There are no strings attached and you retain all rights. The contest is in charge of Professor Margery Bailey.

1. An aspiring playwright, Moore had sent Anderson his verse play *April is the Cruellest Month* for comment. Written for the Federal Theatre Project (see *90 New Plays*, Play Bureau Publication No. 4, December, 1936, where the play is described as a

"poetic tragedy of two misfits in a crumbling civilization"), the play had not been produced, and Moore feared that its chorus was awkward and its verse unfunctional as dialogue (Moore to Anderson, November 3, 1938; T).

2. Moore did not receive a prize in the Stanford contests.

72. TO ALBERT H. GROSS [1]

New City
December 5, 1938

Dear Mr. Gross:

I shall of course be glad to sign any memorandum against Nazi leadership drawn up by Thomas Mann and would be willing to lend myself in any effective way to strengthen the protest. But I am not effective as a speaker—I'll have to leave that phase of it to those who are better qualified.

Sincerely

1. Gross, with the theatrical agency A. & S. Lyons in New York, was helping to organize support for Thomas Mann's campaign to arouse American public opinion against the Nazis. In the fall of 1938 Mann had come to the U. S., and he issued several public statements like the one referred to in the present letter. Gross, along with Dorothy Thompson and others, planned to have a statement by Mann signed by people prominent in the arts and supported by them with speeches at Carnegie Hall on December 18, 1938, but that particular meeting did not take place.

73. TO PAUL MUNI [1]

[New City]
[Early December, 1938]

Dear Mr. Muni—

Elmer Rice was kind enough to let me read the letter you wrote to him a few weeks ago, and also his answer to it. As he has warned you I now have a play in mind which I would write for next year if I felt some assurance that you would play it. It is, to be frank, a play about Napoleon, following him through from twenty years old to the return from Elba. The actors who could play it as it should be played are so few that I can think of only one in this country—yourself. And a play is an investment of time that one doesn't like to make unless there's a fair certainty of being able to cast it.

But I should like to write it this winter and I should like to have you play it next fall, and so I'm writing to ask in a preliminary way what the chances are. Naturally I wouldn't want you to commit yourself to a play which isn't yet on paper, nor would I want you [to] go into my play in preference to one you liked better—you might like Elmer's better, for example—but I would want to be sure that you could be free to play a season in New York if you liked my script, and that the project was likely to interest you. I have faith enough in the story I have in mind, and in the underlying idea, to gamble on your willingness to play the Napoleon role once the play's written and you've read it.

I'm aware that Napoleon hasn't been a popular figure on the stage, and that he presents difficulties, but I think I know why he hasn't been popular, and I think there's a way around the difficulties. He had a likeable side which has been neglected, and his passion for power grew out of a youthful passion for freedom so inevitably that the steps can be traced without loss of sympathy with him. There was a long period when his youthful dream was buried under success and cynicism, but he came back to his vision in the end. It's this development, his gradual corruption by power and his awakening when it's too late that I'd try to dramatize.

I shant conceal that I await your reply with some anxiety, for though the subject has begun to take hold on me I won't dare to begin on it unless we can come to some tentative understanding. If you feel encouraging about the notion I'd plan to have the script ready to show you in March.

Sincerely,

1. Muni (1896–1967), actor who first achieved stardom in Rice's *Counsellor-at-Law* (1931), spent most of the thirties in Hollywood starring in numerous motion pictures. He wished to return to the stage, and Anderson wished to secure him for a Playwrights' Company production, preferably of an Anderson play.

74. TO PAUL MUNI

New City
December 31, 1938

Dear Mr. Muni:[1]

I think I'd better take your word for it and drop the Napoleon venture, at least for the present. There truly isn't anybody else to play it that I know of. And lest you should be concerned about it, let me confess that I feel a certain relief in getting out from under the subject for it involves an enormous amount of research and I fear I was intending a certain amount of violence on Napoleon's character in order to make it possible for me to write about him.[2]

At the moment I am casting about for a subject that might possibly interest you, though what I've found so far isn't good enough. Meanwhile Elmer Rice has a story in mind which ought to make a good play for you and among us all The Playwrights' Company ought to be able to turn out something to bring you East next fall. At any rate I hope you'll keep your plans sufficiently fluid so that if a good script comes your way in the spring you'll be able to say yes to it.

I am very grateful to you for your honesty in this matter. I think we'd enjoy working together. Let's hope something comes out of these preliminaries—if not this coming year then soon.

Sincerely

1. Muni had rejected the Napoleon play proposed in no. 73.
2. Anderson did not write a play about Napoleon. After considering other possibilities, he wrote *Key Largo*, in which Muni played the lead (King McCloud) in the fall of 1939.

75. TO MARSTON BALCH [1]

New City
February 18, 1939

Dear Mr. Balch:

The acting version of "High Tor" supplied by Brandt and Brandt is probably the version that we arrived at during rehearsals. For the stage it's probably better than the printed text but I confess that I like the first draft best and therefore printed it.[2]

You speak of Van's closing line "in both versions" as ambiguous and you quote the line as "but I can hardly wait for that". The original closing line was "but I can hardly wait" and the "for that" was thrown in by the actor to make the meaning plain to himself, I suppose, and crept into the stage script.[3] The outcome for Van is simply that he moves out "Port Jervis way". His explanation to Lisa is certainly not to be taken literally, more or less as an excuse. The Indian is more symbolic than realistic but he should dress as a modern Indian would dress, in fairly cheap hunting clothes. Just how fluent his diction dares to be is a question for the actor and director.

Sincerely

1. Balch (b. 1901), active in the National Theatre Conference and coauthor of *Theater in America* (1968), was director of the university theater at Tufts and had written to Anderson in preparation for a production of *High Tor* that he was to direct in the spring of 1939, asking particularly about the textual differences between the two versions of the play, the acting version and the Anderson House version.

2. As was his custom after the formation of Anderson House Publishing Company in 1933, Anderson used the preproduction text of *High Tor* for the Anderson House edition of the play, and in plot and thematic emphasis it differs from the acting script, now available from Dramatists Play Service and in Joseph Mersand, ed., *Three Dramas of American Individualism* (1961).

3. The acting version ends with "for that"; the Anderson House edition does not.

76. TO PAUL ROBESON [1]

New City
March 3, 1939

Dear Mr. Robeson:

Harold Freedman has promised me that he will send you a copy of "Aeneas Africanus" and I want to put a note in the same mail for you, explaining as well as I can what our project is, why we need you and how far we intend to depart from the original. In looking over the field for a story for another musical, Kurt Weill and I came across "Aeneas" and decided that we would like to put that next on our list if we could get you to take the leading part. Without you, frankly, I shouldn't think much of the project. With you I think it would make an excellent and most unusual musical play.

The story as you'll find it in the original is a mere skeleton and wouldn't have body enough for a play. Also it has no theme and the central character is hardly complex enough or distinguished enough to hold a play together. In addition, the story has no climax and no central scene.

Although I haven't worked out a plot in detail, it's my intention to make it the story of a man who was born a slave and had never been obliged or encouraged to make an ethical decision for himself. Finding himself free but entrusted with valuable property which was placed in his hands for safe-keeping by a master to whom he owes no duty save that imposed by loyalty and friendship, he is tempted to consider the property his own. After a long, unrewarded search for the man who was his master, he finally decides to hunt no further and makes himself respected in his own world as a free man, even acquiring a competence by his management of a stable of horses built up from the progeny of the original racing mare with which he was entrusted. At this point he encounters again the man who was his master, but fails to reveal himself, justifying his conduct by reflecting on the years of labor for which he was never paid. Too late Aeneas discovers that the man and his family are now in want and that there is nothing left out of their fortune except what he, Aeneas, has saved for them. He sets out in his search again, having discovered that his freedom brings with it responsibilities as a person which he never had to worry about before.

The love story of Aeneas should run parallel with the main story. The girl from whom he parts when he sets out on his long trip has remained with the man who was his master. He has been searching for her as much as for his own integrity throughout his long journey and his temptations.

I hope this won't sound to you like a discouragingly serious story and I assure you that it won't include propaganda of one kind or another. Essentially it is the story of a man in a chaotic world in search of his own manhood and his own rules of conduct, but I mean to tell it, of course, somewhat lightheartedly with whatever humor and grace I can muster and with Kurt's music.

However, I should hesitate to go to work on it without some assurance that you will be free to do it because, although there may be other people who could act the part, I don't know of anybody who could both act and sing it and the script might be wasted completely if you were not available.[2]

Sincerely

1. Robeson (1898–1976), singer and champion of Negro rights, came to prominence as an actor in a revival of O'Neill's *The Emperor Jones* in 1925. Hoping to secure him as the lead, Anderson here outlines a play based on *Eneas Africanus* (1919) by Harry Stillwell Edwards (1855–1938), editor of the *Macon* (Georgia) *Telegraph* and friend of Joel Chandler Harris. In Edwards's story Eneas, a former slave, wanders through the southeastern states for eight years after the Civil War trying to locate his home plantation, which is just south of Atlanta, supporting himself the while by preaching and horse racing. His exploits are given in letters and newspaper accounts sent to his former owner by people who have encountered Eneas, and the last episode shows his happy arrival at the plantation with the owner's silver, including a wedding cup that has been in the family since colonial days, on the wedding day of the owner's daughter.

2. Robeson rejected the play, saying he did not wish to perpetuate the stereotyped image of the Negro as an Uncle Tom (letter to Anderson from Robeson's wife, March 29, 1939;T). Anderson and Weill worked on the play in 1939, then resumed and completed it in 1945, changing the title to *Ulysses Africanus*. For the play, unpublished, see *Catalogue*, pp. 78–79.

77. TO SIDNEY HOWARD [1]

[Spring, 1939]

DEAR SIDNEY IT'S AN ENCHANTING SCRIPT PACKED WITH MORE SHEER INTELLIGENCE THAN ANYTHING I'VE READ IN YEARS. IT SUFFERS A LITTLE BUT LESS THAN YOU MIGHT THINK FROM BEING AN IDEA PLAY. IT SEEMS TO NEED MINOR CLARIFICATIONS AND ON THE STAGE ITS PROBABLY DEPENDENT ON BRILLIANT ACTING BUT IT'S CERTAINLY WORTH THE INVESTMENT AND A PIECE OF WORK TO BE PROUD OF FOREVER

M. A.

1. Howard was the only one of the playwrights who had no play during the first season of the Playwrights' Company, and to the relief of all the members he had just finished a play for the second season, *Madam, Will You Walk?*

78. TO VICTOR SAMROCK [1]

Hollywood, California
May 31, 1939

Not having read the Daudet story I can only say of Elmers play
that it seems to me beautifully and charmingly written but with an
essentially undramatic story and one which has lost much of its
poignancy by reason of the vaster and bitterer tragedies that intervene
between us and the rather dim and minor tragedy of the Franco
Prussian War[.] It would probably never get justice from the public or
the critics[.] I am also very much afraid that this is not the moment to
mention the Franco Prussian War which was lost by the French to the
Germans[.] I am at the Hollywood Knickerbocker for a couple of
days[.] Will send a permanent address later[.][2]

Max

1. Samrock (b. 1907), business manager of the Playwrights' Company, had sent
Anderson the script of Rice's latest play *The Siege of Berlin*, based on Alphonse
Daudet's short story "Le Siege de Berlin." The story focuses on an old French veteran of
the Napoleonic wars whose family attempts to shield him from the reality of French
defeat in the Franco-Prussian War by creating a fictitious version of the war in which the
French are victorious. As he sees Prussian troops marching down the Champs-Elysees,
however, he realizes that the siege of Berlin, in the version he had gotten, was actually
the siege of Paris. And with the cry "Aux armes! aux armes! les Prussiens," he dies. In
March, 1938, Hitler had occupied Austria. That fall at the Munich conference he won
Czechoslovakia, which he invaded in the spring of 1939. Three months after the present
telegram he signed a nonaggression pact with Russia and invaded Poland, beginning
World War II.

2. The remaining members of the company felt as Anderson did about Rice's play,
and it was not produced or published.

79. TO SIDNEY HOWARD

22506 Roosevelt Highway
Malibu, California
June 7, 1939

Dear Sidney:[1]

Thanks for the letter, which pretty closely parallels my second
thoughts on *Key Largo* and clarifies what I have left to do, or a

beginning on it. Just to indicate what I've been thinking I list the changes I have in mind. (1) Rearrange the prologue so that King wins the argument more definitely. (2) Make Murillo's relation to Alegre more believable. (3) Let King get something out of his confession to d'Alcala and Alegre, an accession of courage that enables him to face Murillo at the end of the first act and postpone the decision. (4) Let Alegre send Gash where he will find the Indians—out of her feeling for King, and in order to hang the prospect of their return over the action during the ideological argument in the second act. (5) Establish Hunk as a jumpy character, a trigger man who is likely to make a mistake. (6) Slow down the end, letting King explain to Murillo exactly why he must do as he is doing—to insure the escape of the Indians, to reverse publicly what happens at the end of the first act, and to save Alegre finally from Murillo.

You are certainly right about Burgess—and I had the same fears.[2] Being out here has one advantage—I shall be able to see Muni and can attempt to cast the part elsewhere if he's not interested. As for Longmire, I wrote the part with Zita Johann in mind, and have practically promised it to her, so I don't like to switch now. I'm not sure I'd be gaining anyway, except in youth. I'm inclined to think Zita has more stops to her instrument than Longmire has—though none too many at that.[3]

John mentions Cagney and Garfield.[4] I had thought of Garfield, but I don't like his diction. Cagney is a possibility. As for Margaret Webster's direction, I don't know her work. And I have no way of finding out about it before we start.[5]

John also says that you are still not quite certain of your last act.[6] I haven't seen the play since the first revision, but I can reiterate a couple of points which I hope you haven't forgotten. One is that the audience should be conscious all the while that Brightly is a demon who is affecting those about him. It seemed to me you were letting them guess a little. Also, I hope you end with a lover's knot, maybe rather bizarre, but quite convincing. And maybe Brightly should discover compassion at the end. Since he ought to know everything. I'm very happy about that play—even at this distance in time and geography, and only hope it's well cast. It will depend on its actors as much as mine does, and the best are none too good.

The criticisms have helped a lot—especially since you and John have somewhat illuminated each other's remarks.

Love to you and Polly.[7]

Sincerely,
Max

1. Howard had sent Anderson a letter about *Key Largo* suggesting that (1) the play's central character, King McCloud, seemed realistic about saving his life in the Prologue but cowardly about it in Act I; (2) at the end McCloud's climactic realization (that one who is afraid to die is dead already) came too fast for its full impact to be felt; and (3) the character of Alegre was insufficiently developed (June 3, 1939; T).

2. Burgess Meredith had played the lead in *Winterset*, and Howard feared that if he also took the lead in *Key Largo* the similarity of situation in the two plays (two young people vs. the underworld) might be emphasized and Anderson unjustly charged with repeating himself.

3. Adele Longmire had played Ann Rutledge in Sherwood's *Abe Lincoln In Illinois*, and Howard had suggested her for Alegre in *Key Largo* as part of an effort to keep promising actors and actresses under contract to the Playwrights' Company. Zita Johann had appeared in a number of plays and motion pictures. In the production of *Key Largo* Uta Hagen had the part of Alegre.

4. In a letter of June 3, 1939 (T), Wharton had suggested James Cagney (who first gained attention as an actor with the role of Little Red in *Outside Looking In*) or John Garfield for the part of Murillo, the gangster in *Key Largo*. In the production Frederic Tozere had the part.

5. Wharton had also suggested Margaret Webster as director for *Key Largo*. Miss Webster had had considerable directorial experience, especially with Shakespeare, Shaw, and Ibsen. Guthrie McClintic directed *Key Largo*.

6. *Madam, Will You Walk?*, a contemporary version of the Faust story with Dr. Brightlee as the Mephistopheles figure.

7. Howard's wife.

80. TO PAUL MUNI

22506 Roosevelt Highway
Malibu, California
June 24, 1939

Dear Mr. Muni:

This letter will confirm our agreement, made yesterday, that you will play King McCloud in *Key Largo* for the Playwrights' Company during the 1939–40 season, reporting for rehearsals on or about October first (or somewhere between September twentieth and

October fifteenth), remaining with the play if it is successful until the first of June, and re-opening in the fall if we both consider that business warrants. It is agreed that you are to receive star billing and that your compensation during the run of the play will be fifteen hundred dollars a week against ten per cent of the weekly gross.

Sincerely

Maxwell Anderson

81. TO BROOKS ATKINSON[1]

New City

August 21, 1939

Dear Brooks Atkinson:

It's flattering to be regarded as a poet, though I don't think of myself that way, knowing very well that I'm only a practical playwright who has had the audacity to use verse in an effort to improve his plays. If I were a better poet maybe I'd be dreamier and less hard-headed in politics. But why a poet or artist should regard the extension of government as a benefit I can't see at all. A poet or artist is able to function only in a free society; his vision and the effort toward his vision are only possible where men are free to act and think without despotic repression. Arbitrary power in any form is his enemy, whether it be the power of a bank, a corporation, a labor official, a conquerer, or a government. It is fashionable nowadays to believe that economic justice is obtainable by means of an extension of governmental power into economic fields; but a poet or artist who knows history or even watches current events is aware that government control of industry leads inevitably to political despotism, under which no artist can function worth a damn.

But even as I write this I realize that this is exactly what I said before and you weren't convinced. Probably our political difference runs deep. To you the evils of capitalism appear more real than the evils of collectivism. Perhaps in the end it comes down to what we think the race ought to go toward. It's my opinion that the evils of capitalism are the evils of the jungle, the evils of collectivism those of the ant-hill. And since we must choose between them I prefer the jungle. After all, we evolved from the jungle. Nothing will ever evolve from the ant-hill.

But I think it was the tone of your criticism that disturbed me more than the content. You know that my opinions are not purchaseable, but it seemed to me there was a touch of New Deal acrimony in your voice, especially in the reference to the Manufacturers' Association—as if to imply that any opinion which opposed the obviously high functions of the Roosevelt administration could hardly be honest.[2] Perhaps you'll say I expect too much of a critic, and I do expect a lot of you, for you have always seemed to try to give an unbiased opinion in matters pertaining to the theatre. But politics is another jungle, and we'll just have to hope that the best man sometimes wins.

Sincerely

1. Atkinson (b. 1894), influential drama critic for the *New York Times* (1925–60) whose other work at the time included *Henry Thoreau: Cosmic Yankee* (1927), had written an antagonistic review of *The Essence of Tragedy and Other Footnotes and Papers* ("Ruminations of a Poet," *New York Times*, June 4, 1939, sec. 9, p. 1, cols. 1–3). The review focused on one essay in the book, "The Politics of *Knickerbocker Holiday*," and criticized Anderson for his Thoreauvian attack on Roosevelt's extension of governmental power over the lives of individual citizens. In an unlocated letter Anderson challenged the review, and in reply (June 14, 1939; T) Atkinson admitted that the review had been written from a point of view favorable to the New Deal but maintained that poets in particular should support the New Deal because of its humanitarian intentions.
2. In his review Atkinson had said: "Probably Mr. Anderson does not aspire to be the poet laureate of the National Manufacturers Association, but there is nothing in [his] political sentiments to disqualify him."

82. TO POLLY HOWARD [1]

Hotel Dorset
New York City
[September/October, 1939]

Dear Polly—

I didn't quite realize till I heard it read today how wise and witty *Madam, Will You Walk* is. Now that I've passed my mid-century mark and spend a good deal of time looking ahead into darkness I appreciate what few fixed stars of belief men have been able to hang up against the sky—and Sidney nailed them beautifully in the court scene.[2] Man's destiny is to give the universe a reason for existing—to be the unique custodian of the heroic. One can embroider on these things, but there's nothing more to say. It's all summed up here in a few brief apothegms. I kept thinking as I listened, this is one of the very few noteworthy plays of our time. Perhaps the most brilliant and significant any of us will ever do. I felt like thanking Sidney, and since I couldn't I'm writing you.

Sincerely

1. Polly, widow of Sidney Howard who had died in a farm accident on August 23, 1939. That fall the Playwrights' Company attempted a production of Howard's latest play, *Madam, Will You Walk?*

2. Act II, scene 3. Anderson's next sentence is a close paraphrase of the key thematic speeches in the scene.

83. TO ARCHER MILTON HUNTINGTON [1]

Hotel Dorset
New York City
October 3, [1939]

Dear Mr. Huntington—

The other day you said you thought poetry should be impersonal, and at the moment I couldn't think of an answer. But the matter bothered me, and I make a counter-proposition. Dramatic and even epic poetry is necessarily impersonal, but lyric verse is a brief short-circuit of emotion, and the individual emotion is felt directly behind it. The more universal his subject the wider the appeal may be—but universality shouldn't be mistaken for impersonality. Not that it's important, but you had me on the ropes for a moment and I like to keep things straight in my mind.

Rehearsals of *Key Largo* began yesterday, and we are now in New York— at the overleaf address.[2] I don't like it much though, and will spend a long week-end at New City.

Sincerely
Maxwell Anderson

1. Son of Collis P. H. Huntington, builder of the Central Pacific Railroad, Archer Huntington (1870–1955) was a multimillionaire poet, scholar, and philanthropist interested in projects related to conservation and Spanish culture. Among his activities he renovated the American Geographical Society, founded the Hispanic Society of America, and published the manuscript text of *Poema del Cid* (1897), a verse translation of it (1907), and notes to the poem (1908). He lived near Anderson on South Mountain Road out of New City.
    2. The hotel.

84. TO LELA CHAMBERS

> Hotel Dorset
> New York City
> [October 8, 1939]

Dear Lela—[1]

Lee came to see us a week ago. We all liked him very much—and especially since he didn't complain at all about his own situation but did put in a word for Keith whenever he got a chance. He says he thinks Keith ought to get a break in regard to schooling, and also that Keith is probably carrying a pretty heavy burden right now, considering his health. I don't know whether Keith's had an examination or not, but Lee has a notion he may be anemic, and it's quite possible, for both Quentin and Terry have had that trouble and even when boys look big and healthy they can be short of hemoglobin. —That isn't what I was going to say, however. I just want you to know that it wasn't because we were disappointed that Kenneth didn't try to keep Keith in Buffalo this year. It was because Anderson House didn't make any money, and I can't promise to do anything about it either, unless *Key Largo* goes well. If it does I'll help Keith to go back to Buffalo—or some college—next semester. Maybe you and Dan can help with it, though I know you have a thousand things to do with your money. —I just wanted Keith to know this so he wouldn't feel there was no way out.

> Love to you all
> Max

Maybe I'll see you in Buffalo. There will be seats if you come—[2]

1. Lee and Keith were sons of Mrs. Chambers. Until the current semester Anderson and his brother Kenneth had supported Keith, the younger of the two, at the University of Buffalo with proceeds from Anderson House, the publishing company they formed in 1933. Lee, financially unable to attend college, was working on Long Island and was shortly to join the army.

2. *Key Largo* was to begin its out-of-town run in Indianapolis on October 30, 1939, and reach Buffalo in mid-November.

85. TO WALLACE A. BACON [1]

New City
October 20, 1939

Dear Mr. Bacon:

It's hard to convey how unusual it is to receive a good play in the mail. As for a good poetic play, that had never happened before, and so I hope you will forgive me for delaying so long to read "Savonarola". It's an excellent play and the verse is excellent.

It has two faults from my point of view which may prevent a Broadway production or success. The first is a lack of introductory relieving humor of the sort even Shakespeare found necessary for most of his tragedies. For some reason an audience insists on an occasional light touch, a relief from thinking or emotion. The other deficiency is more fundamental. Aristotle would say that your hero has no tragic fault and I would add that the lack of a tragic fault eliminates the possibility of a recognition scene for your climax. I am sending you a little book of essays which includes "The Essence of Tragedy" because that paper will tell you more exactly what I mean. [2]

Even though I make these criticisms, however, "Savonarola" is a fine play and I am glad to have seen it. If you are ever in New York and would like to get in touch with me, I live at New City and my telephone number is 2202.

Sincerely

Ms. under
separate cover

1. Bacon (b. 1914), who gave the Margery Bailey Memorial Lectures at the Ashland (Oregon) Shakespeare Festival in 1973, spent his career in the Department of English and Speech at Northwestern University, where his chief interests lay in the

literature of the English Renaissance and oral interpretation. At the time of the present letter he was a graduate student in English at the University of Michigan and had sent Anderson his play, *Savonarola* (pub. 1949).

2. *The Essence of Tragedy and Other Footnotes and Papers* (1939).

86. TO POLLY HOWARD

Athletic Club
Indianapolis, Indiana
[Early November, 1939]

Dear Polly—[1]

This is a hard letter to write, because it might be construed as hard-hearted, and I don't think there's any of that behind what I want to say. But when I left Sam's apartment the other day I took with me a conviction that unless something was done quickly we might come to the production date of Sidney's play unready to meet our audience and too confused and worn-out to be able to retrieve our mistakes.

I had been worried about the script because I couldn't imagine how any man could take over Sidney's work and do the revamping which one always counts on from an author before rehearsals start. When I heard the first reading I felt that Bob had by some miracle of sympathy been able to effect the necessary changes with little dislocation and no falsifying of Sidney's intention. It seemed to me then that the unbelievable had happened and that the play would get the audience it deserved, even without Sidney's hand to make revisions. I don't think you have realized quite how fortunate the play has been. No other playwright could have done the work Bob did, and without that work the play wouldn't have been ready for production, because it wasn't in final shape, as Sidney knew.

I know you feel it your duty to Sidney to keep the play as nearly his as possible. I know that Bob feels the same obligation, and that you have differed only over the words that must be used in revision. I don't think you know how deeply Bob has been torn between his responsibility to the play in the theatre which naturally requires alterations, and the play as his friend left it in manuscript, not quite ready to be produced. The task of making alterations during rehearsal is never easy. It calls for spontaneity under pressure. And when the pressure comes not only from the necessities of the theatre but also from an emotional cross-wise pull the task is well-nigh impossible. Much as I sympathize with your desire to keep the play as it was I can only say that unless we look the other way for a while and let Bob function he'll be paralyzed entirely and the play will suffer.

You may answer that the play will suffer unless you are able to make certain restrictions, and that may be true. One never knows about plays, whether they'll go or why. But at this point I think you should either turn the responsibility over to Bob entirely or take it over yourself. The way things are going we are likely to emerge from rehearsals with more nervous wreckage than accomplishment.

I say this quite honestly liking Sidney's play more than I like my own,[2] and only hoping the production will honor his memory.[3]

Sincerely
Max

1. Following Sidney Howard's death, Robert Sherwood attempted to revise *Madam, Will You Walk?* for its Playwrights' Company production, but he met continuous opposition from Polly Howard, who wished no changes in her late husband's script.

2. *Key Largo.*

3. Problems remained in the script and developed in the cast, which featured George M. Cohan. When Cohan resigned during the Baltimore tryout in mid-November, the company cancelled the production. (T. Edward Hambleton and Norris Houghton produced *Madam, Will You Walk?* in 1953 and in 1955 the acting script was published by Dramatists Play Service.)

87. TO VICTOR SAMROCK

Hotel Statler
Cleveland, Ohio
[November 7, 1939]

Dear Victor—[1]

Do you think the enclosed might be effective as a hand-bill to be distributed with programs? I'd be willing to begin with the opening night of *Key Largo.*

McDermott gives us a rave review here.[2]

Best to the office
Max

1. With the present letter Anderson included the following statement, which became an insert in the programs for *Key Largo*:

PLEASE

Probably the worst enemy of the New York theatre is the cougher in the audience. New York has the most courteous and attentive audiences in the world and a majority at every performance give the play every possible chance, but there are nearly always a few who make no secret of their bronchial afflictions. This is both thoughtless and discourteous, and can be a great detriment even to a good play.

According to medical opinion a cough is controllable. It follows that if those who suffer from colds or throat irritation will only provide themselves with cough drops and a little will power, we can all be more sanguine about theatrical futures on Manhattan.

THE PLAYWRIGHTS' COMPANY

2. William F. McDermott, columnist and drama critic for the *Cleveland Plain Dealer*, developed the point that *Key Largo* "will almost certainly be a success and, more important, it will deserve success" because of its effective treatment of a noble theme, the "struggle for an ideal that will give life meaning" (*Plain Dealer*, November 7, 1939, p. 6, cols. 1–3).

88. TO QUENTIN ANDERSON [1]

[1939][2]

Dear Quentin—

The question is bound up with the perpetual insoluble problem of mankind—how to set up necessary governments without delegating more power than any man, or set of men, can be trusted to use without encroaching on our equally necessary individual liberties. It's because I believe the problem insoluble that I hold out for compromises and temporary arrangements, such as the system of checks and balances within the government and the balance of power between government and independent business enterprises. Any authority which obtains complete control over our economic life will have absolute power, and will use it as absolute power has always been used in the past. Such control might be attained by the great corporations if the government's power were allowed to dwindle too far. But if the government, to curb the corporations, swallows our economic system, then the government has a monopoly of political and economic powers—and the result is such a slave state as the present Russia or Germany.

That's all—

Max

1. Anderson's son, who joined the English faculty of Columbia University in the fall of 1939.

2. In an undated note to the present editor Quentin Anderson surmises that the letter was written in the late thirties or early forties. Its content suggests that the letter is associated with the controversy between Anderson and Brooks Atkinson over *Knickerbocker Holiday* and the New Deal (see no. 81), and the date has been assigned on the basis of that probability.

89. TO MARGERY BAILEY

[New City]
May 18, 1940

Dear Margery Bailey—

Your letter found me reading the sonnet variorum again—the one on which you collaborated with Frank Hill and Professor Alden.[1] It's one of the books I look through every once in a while—nearly always finding something new—or something I've forgotten. There is truly a kind of after life in books. Professor Alden has been gone many years, and yet I hear his voice and feel his personality behind his writing as strongly as if he were alive. Of course, I've seen and heard him—and without those memories the life I could give him—or feel from him—would be less definite, yet something of him would be there—and perhaps even more accurately conveyed without the slight falsifications which voice and appearance may inject. I didn't care much for Alden when I knew him, but I'm very fond of him now.

This is applicable (or appropriate) in no way I can think of—I was merely reading the variorum when your letter came. And your letter was most exhilarating. I've had rather little favorable comment on *Key Largo* except from my own company of playwrights and a few theatre people here and there. To the most articulate body of opinion —the critics'—it was mostly rather a bore. The comments, though I didn't read them, I gather to have been along the line of "Oh, don't start that again!" Now I have resigned myself to the fact that the critics never know about anything—but the truth has a corollary (I never could spell)[2]—that an author never knows either. I can't lay your opinion to my soul without knowing very well that it may be a flattering unction—and God knows a man is tempted to hope that the most intelligent are those who find virtue in his work.

Lately I've made a compromise with my conscience—just in order to go on. I assume that I am trying to do something which neither the critics nor the public is likely to understand—something therefore which neither can judge, and which will have to wait for a decision later on. When neither my face nor my voice is around to distract opinion. And when I get a letter like yours—which may be once in two or three years—I say to myself—this may possibly be a hint of what posterity will think of it—may possibly. But I naturally remember that posterity may not think of it at all.

Without such a word once in a while, though, I'd be entirely without hope—so I leave you to imagine how many times I've read your birthday letter—and will read it again. I'm fifty-one.

Maxwell Anderson

1. Raymond MacDonald Alden, ed., *The Sonnets of Shakespeare, from the Quarto of 1609 with Variorum Readings and Commentary* (1916). Alden (1873–1924) was professor of English at Stanford (1899–1911 and 1914–24).

2. In the original, "corollary" is attempted and crossed out several times.

90. TO PAUL MUNI

New City
July 10, 1940

Dear Muni:

Your last letter to me seems to indicate that you think maybe "Key Largo" should have had better fortune than it had. I am inclined to think that's true, but I'm certain it wasn't the casting that was at fault. There was something a little wrong with the play or with its timing which made it a little less than popular. But you held it up magnificently and gave it a far longer run than any of us expected. More than that, I'm glad we worked together because that's the only way people get acquainted in the theatre these days, and we think we have found two very good friends in you and Bella.[1] All the members of the Playwrights' Company agree that you will have first chance at any play we write which seems to have a part for you.

Good luck and good fortune to you both.

As ever,
Max

1. Muni's wife, the actress Bella Finkel. She sometimes appeared in plays with him but had no role in *Key Largo*.

91. TO DOROTHY THOMPSON [1]

New City
September 8, 1940

Dear Dorothy Thompson:

The Playwrights Company has tried several times to organize a repertory theatre but has always met with insuperable obstacles. It's our conviction that the theatre, to be healthy, should be able to pay for itself, also we have never felt financially able to support a repertory which could not stand on its own feet. But when we try to put such an organization together we always discover that the costs would outweigh the income—even at the most sanguine estimate. New York productions are geared to bring in an income over a considerable period of time. You can't possibly make back your production costs on a play in two weeks. It's seldom that you can do it in six weeks. A repertory company would have to begin with a rush of productions—all of them gambles, as everything is in our theatre—and no likelihood of getting the investment back within several years, if at all. I don't know of anybody who could afford to sink money in such a venture—and, frankly, I have my doubts of the soundness of any scheme that doesn't at least promise a return.

Perhaps your theory is that your actors will not cost as much, nor your productions, as is usual on Broadway. We've had some experience with that. We honestly try to hold down the cost of production to a minimum. But if you want an acceptable production, with actors the public will pay to see, you can't proceed inexpensively.

And I don't agree with you that a playwright can't do his best work on Broadway. The theatre is always part of a civilization, and that limits its scope. But within the limits of what our civilization calls for we are free to do the best we can. —I shall watch your venture with every hope for its success, and I shall be willing to help in any way I can, but I couldn't honestly be part of the venture, for I have had to say no to the same proposition from within our own ranks.

Sincerely

1. Thompson (1894–1961), newspaper columnist on foreign and domestic politics and wife of Sinclair Lewis, had asked Anderson to join her in an attempt (unsuccessful) to establish a repertory company in New York.

92. TO REGINALD GAIMSTER [1]

New City
October 12, 1940

Dear Mr. Gaimster:

I am afraid the paths of poetry in the theatre are rougher than anybody can imagine who hasn't been over them. I am walking a little lame myself these days having made the mistake, I fear, of examining the fundamental principles of Christianity at a time when men should be examining their weapons. This play was in rehearsal when your letter came or I should have answered it earlier, and perhaps more optimistically.

The quality of your verse seems excellent in these samples and the play may be excellent for all I know but a play on the subject of peace would not only be a bad risk but one that no producer would assume. On the other hand the capacity for verse which might be spoken from the stage is so rare and in your case so unmistakable that I should like to see your manuscript. If there is any substance in your ambition you will write more plays than one and perhaps the tide will next time not be against you.

Sincerely
Maxwell Anderson

1. Gaimster, an aspiring playwright who did not produce or publish any plays, had sent Anderson a portion of his play *The Timely Voice*. The play, in verse, focused on Woodrow Wilson's struggle to keep America out of World War I (Gaimster to Anderson, August 10, 1940; T). Anderson's reply came shortly after the decision to close his own play, *Journey to Jerusalem*, which had opened on October 5 to negative reviews.

93. TO HAROLD FREEDMAN [1]

New City
October 30, 1940

Dear Harold:

The play I have had in mind tells the story of an American actress and a French journalist. After years of separation, partly through misunderstanding, they have met in Paris in the spring of 1940, have married, have made a one-day visit to Versailles for a hurried honeymoon, and are found there at the opening of the first scene of the play. Raoul, the man, must return to Paris at once, because the paper for which he writes has hesitated to attack Hitler and his influence is needed if the editors are not to anticipate the conquest of Paris by the Germans. He has been begged by many to cease his attacks on the German leader, which have been spectacular, and has written an answer to these apostles of appeasement as his most recent contribution to the paper. Before they leave Versailles, however, the lovers agree to come every year to a corner of the gardens which they have adopted as especially their own.

In the second scene of the first act Louise is in her room in the Paris hotel. Paris has fallen. There is no service. Raoul has been missing for three days. He was last seen at the office of his newspaper. An old friend comes to see Louise, a friend who has been estranged for years, but who comes to renew the old allegiance because the days have grown desperate, and folk of good will should stick together. Besides, he has news for her. It has come by chance to his ears that Raoul has been taken by the Gestapo, and interned. There is nothing to do but try to obtain an interview with some German official who may know where the prisoner was taken.

The third scene is Louise's interview with the official who caused the arrest. He begins most hopefully, saying that of course in so minor a matter the imprisonment is only a form. They chat amiably. Then the dossier is brought. The officer frowns. This is a trifle more serious than he thought. It would be wiser, in fact, if Louise gave up hope of seeing Raoul again. When she in astonishment asks why he reveals that Raoul has been under surveillance for many years—that he has mortally offended some of the higher powers in the German state, and that his punishment will be severe. If she continues to love him her punishment will also be severe. Louise demands how she is to be punished. The answer is quite frank. She will try to see her husband, and she will many times think she is about to succeed, but always she will come to a closed gate, and the gate will not open. Her husband will know, each time, that she is at the gate, and will expect each time to see her, for hope springs eternal, but he will never see her. Louise has money outside Germany, outside France, and though the German state has no direct hold on her, it will, the officer assures her, gradually take from her all her fortune, for she will pay for a thousand schemes to rescue her husband, and every scheme will be betrayed. But each time her husband will expect to be rescued, will believe that she has succeeded. And it is his torture that each time she will fail. Louise says that there is no time for such malignity. He informs her that the conduct of their torment will be turned over to a man who has come to hate them both. "We have time for everything," says the officer, "and we think of everything. Now, will you take your American passport in your hand, take ship for the United States, save your wealth and your sanity, and evade this torture?" "No," answers Louise, "I will stay here." "Of course," says the officer, "we knew that. As I said, we think of everything."

The second act begins with a scene in Louise's room—now denuded of luxuries. Nearly a year has passed. She has spent all she has on schemes for Raoul's release. One by one they have failed, and she has been officially notified by the Gestapo of why and how they failed. But at last she has succeeded. Raoul has been freed; her last scheme has worked. She has heard from him. It was his own handwriting, and he will come to her apartment this evening. She makes what meagre preparations she can—and at the hour when he has promised to appear comes instead the German officer. But not to disappoint her. He comes to say that it is indeed true that Raoul is being released, only there has been a slight delay because of the usual

red tape. However, he is being released, not because her scheme has
succeeded, but because even the hearts of the Gestapo leaders have
been touched by her faithfulness and the endurance with which she
fought to save her lover. If she will come with him to the camp outside
Paris they will meet Raoul together. She doubts his word but goes.

The second scene of this act shows Raoul with a cell-mate who
lies on a cot in a stall of what was once a horse stable. His cell-mate
has been tortured and cannot move. Raoul is constantly torn between
an agonizing desire to see Louise again and an inability to conceal
resentment and contempt for his captors. He has been a student of
anthropology and his comments on the facial angles and racial descent
of the guards drive them to a frenzy. However they have not touched
him so far; his torture is evidently to be mental. A guard comes to
inform him that he is to be released—that Louise is waiting at the gate.
He tells the guard that this is a lie; that it has happened too often to
deceive him now. The guard says that he is to remain or go to the gate
as he pleased—there is no compulsion. Raoul, knowing that he is
being duped, still goes.

The next scene shows Louise before the gate, and several men are
actually led out and released. When the last has gone and there is no
Raoul, the officer appears perturbed. Finally he goes inside. When he
returns he tells Louise that he has seen her husband, and told him that
she is waiting for him, but that the meeting is as far away as ever. He
then points out to her that all he promised has come about. They have
taken her money, and they care no more about her. She can leave for
the United States at any time. She bursts out at him with what she
thinks of the world his kind has made—then returns to her room.
Here she looks at herself in the mirror, wondering if she has been
changed so much by misery that she has nothing left to offer Raoul
even if he were free. There is a knock at the door, and a man appears
who has another scheme in mind for freeing her husband. She says no
angrily; then she calls him back. She still has one ring which she has
saved to pay their way out of France. She knows she is a fool to trust
anyone or to try again. She struggles to regain control of her life—to
leave France and escape from nightmare, but she cannot let go. Her
love and hope compel her to try everything that offers. Because there is
always the chance. —She gives the man her last money.

The last act is in one scene. It is the day of the year when she and
her husband have appointed to meet in the corner of the park. She has

not heard of her last scheme. She goes to the park, not with hope now but to keep a spiritual tryst with one she will never see again. The old friend who has stood by her throughout the year goes with her. And while they sit watching the loiterers in the park she questions him and drives him to confess that he too worked for the Gestapo. His family is held as hostages in Germany, and he has been compelled to become a spy. Her last scheme, too, was hollow, for he knew of it. Then he goes, leaving her on the bench, an old and broken woman. A cleaner of the park, a fellow with a stick who picks up papers, sits beside her, and though she does not see him she sees a tear fall on his hand. She reaches into her purse blindly to find a coin for him, which he takes. Then she rises to go, but he starts to tell his story—of how once he promised to meet a woman here, and hoped she might be there today. It is Raoul, and their one bitter year apart has so changed them that they did not know each other. Each remembered the other as youthful and gay. But now they see through the disguise. The last scheme had worked. The last man she trusted had been a Gestapo man, as she feared, but for once a heart had been touched. He had done as he promised. Raoul, though free, dared not go near her rooms. And now it seems to them that they have won—that all that has been done to them was impotent and of no account, because somehow they did hang on and come through.

This is only a story outline, leaving out background and character —and minor figures which would fill in the picture. Even the motivation is sketchy as I tell it here. But I think it would make a moving story.

Sincerely
Maxwell Anderson

1. Freedman (1897–1966), in the Dramatic Department of Brandt & Brandt literary agency in New York, became Anderson's agent in 1933. Prior to that time Anderson had had no agent, but difficulties with producer Jed Harris over production rights to *Both Your Houses* led him to Freedman. Until his death Freedman remained Anderson's agent, and Anderson valued him highly as a person and as a business representative. The present letter outlines the play that became *Candle in the Wind*.

94. TO S. N. BEHRMAN

December 6, 1940

Dear Sam:[1]

It's probably an ancient cliche, but it came to me like a revelation when we were discussing your play after the first reading that there would be no excuse for literary effort if human nature could be reduced to a formula. Literature is a continual reexamination of humanity—its status, motives, failings and ideals—and if it were made according to any set of rules it would come out constantly with the same result. There should be no rules in literature except those concerned with effectiveness. *What* the writer is trying to say must be left always to the insight and intuition of the writer. Don't let yourself be argued logically into any revision which offends or fails to square with your inner conviction—or which violates your own mood. No writer can justify himself logically. He can only defend himself by force majeur. You write the best comedy our theatre has ever heard—and comedy has its own Delphic laws which cannot be analyzed and are above control. Instinct is above all theory in such matters. Producers are always thinking they have playwrights on the hip when they ask "What does it mean?" and the pw doesn't know. But he should never be asked that question. He shouldn't know, and if he does he is not a playwright who will be remembered, for he has said something easy. The only question which a playwright should be asked is, "Do you really want it that way? Does it seem right to you, or as near right as you can get it?" No change should be made that isn't made to satisfy the playwright's own soul and conscience.

"Which some professing have erred concerning the faith. Grace be with thee."

Also luck, love, health and your own way.

MAX

1. Members of the Playwrights' Company had recently discussed Behrman's *The Talley Method*, which the company would produce on February 24, 1941, and Anderson had argued that Behrman should make some thematic alteration in the play.

Part III

ACHIEVEMENT
AND
CONTROVERSY
1941–1953

I have long maintained that it is the function of the theatre, above and beyond entertainment, to help men think well of themselves and their activities—to point out and celebrate whatever is good and worth saving in our confused and often desperate generations.

—ANDERSON *to*
the NEW YORK THEATRE CRITICS
September 15, 1946

95. TO HELEN HAYES [1]

New City
March 3, 1941

Dear Helen:

Well, dreams seldom come true. At least it's seldom the person a play's written for is free to play it when it's put on. "Mary of Scotland" was one of the fortunate exceptions. Alas, though I'm no prophet, I had seen you in "Twelfth Night", and it seemed likely to me that you'd be required in that role next season whether you had signed for it or not. Demand has its imperious way. —In this and similar fashions I try to rationalize my disappointment out the window, but I must confess that I wrote in that book no more on the day when I got your letter. Probably I'll start again, but so far I can't make progress.

Nevertheless I want to thank you again for your Viola. If I were an actor I'd play nobody but Shakespeare. He was Merlin. He could really work miracles. The rest of them—well, they tried hard—they still try—but there was only one wizard. [2]

As ever

1. Miss Hayes (b. 1900), actress and wife of playwright Charles MacArthur, was a friend and neighbor of Anderson. As an actress she had come into prominence in the twenties, then starred in *Mary of Scotland*, and Anderson was presently writing *Candle in the Wind* with her in mind for the lead. She was playing Viola in a revival of *Twelfth Night* with Maurice Evans, however, and had recently told Anderson that the popularity of the production made it likely that *Twelfth Night* would be continued next season, when *Candle in the Wind* was to be produced.

2. *Twelfth Night* did not carry over to the next season, and Miss Hayes had the lead in *Candle in the Wind*.

96. TO DONALD OGDEN STEWART [1]

New City
March 11, 1941

Dear Mr. Stewart:

As you are aware, labor leaders are not persecuted in this country. Indeed, they enjoy a large share of immunity under our laws and from the present administration. Communism is dangerous, however, in men who occupy key positions in industry, for American communism is a conspiracy to overthrow our democratic government and is at present working in cooperation with the Nazi war on civilization. If Mr. Bridges is not and has not been a communist, he has nothing to lose by an investigation. If he is or has been one he should not be allowed to occupy his present position. My impression is that many communists are taking cover under tolerant democratic laws which they would destroy if they were in power.

I would like to ask you a question. Can you assure me personally that Mr. Bridges is not and has not been a communist?

Sincerely
Maxwell Anderson

1. Stewart (b. 1894), humorist and screen writer, and also president of the League of American Writers, had written to Anderson asking his support for Harry Bridges, president of the Maritime Union on the West Coast and at the time under investigation as a communist by the House Un-American Activities Committee.

97. TO GEORGE MIDDLETON

New City
April 21, 1941

Dear George:[1]

Please forgive the delay in answering your very simple question. I looked up the lines from *Valley Forge* in the original manuscript and found that they had been written merely as part of a speech and without preparation. They did not end the play—several other speeches followed. When the play was presented, however, the following speeches were cut out, leaving the lines on liberty for the curtain. I am afraid I can't tell you any more about it.

I certainly wish you well with your autobiography and intend to read it.[2]

Sincerely
Maxwell A.

1. In connection with *These Things Are Mine: The Autobiography of a Journeyman Playwright* (1947), Middleton had asked Anderson about the closing lines in the production of *Valley Forge*: "This liberty will look easy by and by / when nobody dies to get it." As was his custom after the formation of Anderson House, Anderson published the preproduction text of *Valley Forge*, and that text does not end with the lines on liberty.

2. In *These Things Are Mine* Middleton used the present letter to make the point that with plays "production is fusion" of diverse considerations and opinions (p. 69).

98. TO GORDON K. CHALMERS[1]

New City
April 21, 1941

Dear Prof. Chalmers:

The truth is I can't think of any way to accept your invitation without reservations that would destroy my usefulness on a commencement program. I should like very much to come and talk to the young people at Kenyon and to you but on June 9th I may not be within reach of Ohio and you naturally have to make your plans some time in advance.

If I had any turn for speaking and could deliver a lecture without any preparation my own attitude toward such an affair might be different but I am easily flustered on my feet and cannot speak well without a manuscript. A manuscript requires an original impulse and considerable work. Just now I don't have the impulse, wouldn't know what to say and would have to go to work without an idea. The paper which you and Mrs. Chalmers heard at the Modern Language Association contained the one thing I have had to say in essay form in many years. Most of the time I am content to write plays and embody whatever ideas I have in them.

I hope this won't seem an ungracious rejoinder after so sincere an invitation. At any rate I am telling the exact truth and my regrets are also sincere.

Yours,

1. Chalmers (1904–56), president of Kenyon College from 1937 until his death, had heard Anderson read "The Essence of Tragedy" at the 1938 meeting of the Modern Language Association and had invited him to speak at Kenyon's upcoming commencement.

99. TO VAN WYCK BROOKS

New City
April 21, 1941

Dear Brother Van Wyck:[1]
    (At least is science, philosophy and religion,
    and sometimes literature and the arts)
    I shall come to the luncheon. I won't understand what's said. I have a philosopher son who teaches at Columbia[2] and I can't follow him when he begins on Aquinas but I should like to see you and the others again.

Sincerely
Maxwell Anderson

1. In September, 1941, the second annual Conference on Science, Philosophy and Religion was to be held at Columbia University. Louis Finkelstein, president of the Jewish Theological Seminary of America, organized the conference (see no. 101), and he along with Brooks, Anderson, and Lewis Mumford were planning the part of the program devoted to literature and the arts.
2. Quentin, a member of the English department at Columbia.

100. TO THE PLAYWRIGHTS' COMPANY

New City
May 26, 1941

Dear Company:

I have little confidence in my wisdom in business matters, remembering the times I have pulled and hauled in the direction of one deep end or another, but I must say how I feel about moving picture backing while there's still time. Financially it seems we couldn't lose if we were backed by R.K.O. or Warners. I'm not so sure of that, because we might lose financially if we lost faith in ourselves and something of that sort might happen if Jake Wilk[1] were reading our scripts in advance and arguing about the investment. But, supposing we couldn't lose financially, wouldn't we be selling out the theatre to the pictures? When the Dramatists Guild was founded the idea back of it was to prevent Hollywood domination of Broadway. This idea may have narrowed down to an argument over picture options and sales, but the basic notion remains the same. If we accept picture backing we shall have surrendered the central citadel of the theatre to Hollywood. It's all very well to talk about retaining control, but in the end the control will go with the money. It always does, as John[2] knows. I should feel pretty sick about our company if it got itself into that position.

On the other hand it's true, as John suggested long ago, that we'd be wiser to gamble less—to take in outside backing that would guarantee us against loss even though it also cut down somewhat our possible profits. I couldn't object to money of that sort if it were put up by people who had no other interest in our affairs beyond wanting to make money out of the company. Our present stockholders are not in the entertainment business, have some respect for the theatre, and don't try to influence us. Harold[3] says more money is available from people of this sort. We could lose little in reputation or in self-esteem if we took more capital from such sources. But if any representative of R.K.O. or Warners had the right to inquire what the hell happened to that last hundred thousand our morale would suffer dangerously.

If it came to a choice between financial failure and surrender to the pictures I think I'd choose financial failure. Of course that may be just an old family prejudice, but it runs deep.

Sincerely
Maxwell Anderson

1. Jacob Wilk, at the time eastern story editor for Warner Brothers Pictures.
2. John F. Wharton.
3. Harold Freedman.

101. TO LOUIS FINKELSTEIN [1]

[New City]
[July 17, 1941]

Dear Mr. Finkelstein—

Several times I have sat down to write that brief clarifying paper of which we spoke, and always I have given it up in despair. Whenever I look straight at what I believe it disappears, and I can only get a glimpse again by turning to something else. I thought that by carefully stalking my altars I might perhaps get close enough to explain myself to myself before they could dissolve, but I've come to the conclusion that there's a defect in my philosophic center of vision. The thing I try to look at is there but I can see it only with the tail of my eye. Add to this difficulty my complete ignorance of modern philosophy and its language and you will see that I'm inadequate to the task you set me.

And when I read a paper such as Krutch's my lack of equipment for the job becomes paralyzingly evident. Krutch climbs among unsubstantial things sure-footed as a goat, never dislodging a concept. He lays down names and steps on them and they hold him up. I haven't the shoes for walking in clouds. I go through and fall. I certainly can't lead a discussion in such company. It will be all I can do to follow. After the planks are laid.

Sincerely
Maxwell Anderson

1. Finkelstein (b. 1895) joined the faculty of the Jewish Theological Seminary of America in 1919 and in 1940 became the seminary's president (until 1951, afterward chancellor). Also in 1940 he organized the Conference on Science, Philosophy and

Religion, in the early forties an annual conference held at Columbia University. The second conference was held in September, 1941, and in preparation for it Finkelstein had met through the spring with Anderson, Van Wyck Brooks, and Lewis Mumford to discuss the part of the program devoted to literature. Joseph Wood Krutch of the Columbia faculty was to present a paper at the conference on the role of the arts in modern society, and Anderson had said that he would prepare a paper on his own basic beliefs and how they operated in his plays.

102. TO BROOKS ATKINSON

Hotel Hay-Adams House
Washington, D.C.
[October 12, 1941]

Dear Brooks—[1]

My wife read me your letter over the 'phone, and I want to thank you for your quick and open-hearted response to that Rutgers paper. It was written hastily last Sunday, and I had no chance to revise it, hence a number of chinks and loop-holes which I'll try to patch up. Among them the case of *Pal Joey*, concerning which I have a theory.[2] As for the main thesis I do believe it with all my heart, though I feel a bit embarrassed at having spoken so publicly of what might have been better kept to myself. I've sometimes thought that a religion, like a vice, was more effective when practised in secret—in the opposite direction, that is.

But the theatre has more to be proud of than it seems to realize—and civilization owes it more than it will ever know.

Sincerely

Max

1. On October 10, 1941, his son Quentin read a paper by Anderson at a Rutgers University symposium on the arts. The paper, which became the title essay in *Off Broadway* (1947), developed the thesis that "the theater is a religious institution devoted entirely to the exaltation of the spirit of man," and that it "is as much a worship as the theater of the Greeks, and has exactly the same meaning in our lives" (*Off Broadway*, p. 28). Anderson was in Washington with *Candle in the Wind*, and Atkinson, who attended the Rutgers symposium, immediately wrote to him praising the paper and requesting it for the *New York Times*, which published the paper as "By Way of Preface: The Theatre as Religion," October 26, 1941, sec. 9, p. 1, cols. 5–8, p. 3, cols. 1–5.

2. In the paper as read at Rutgers, printed in the *Times*, and included as the preface to *Candle in the Wind* (December, 1941), Anderson cites *Pal Joey* (musical, 1940, based on a collection of John O'Hara stories) as one of several modern plays that "subject our fundamental beliefs to the acid test of ribald laughter" in the manner of Greek satyr plays (*Candle in the Wind*, p. xiv). But for its two later appearances, in *The Bases of Artistic Creation* (Rutgers University Press, 1942) and in *Off Broadway*, he deleted *Pal Joey* and reduced the discussion of satyr-like modern plays (*Off Broadway*, p. 32), without however changing the thesis of the essay.

103. TO LELA AND DAN CHAMBERS

[New City]
[November 2, 1941]

Dear Lela and Dan—[1]

I sat here for a long time trying to call you, but I couldn't make myself do it—I was afraid to try to say anything. Then when I did call you'd gone to Olean. There's nothing anybody can say though when somebody you've loved as much as Lee is gone. —I keep thinking of things he said and did. There was nobody sweeter or gentler or humbler. He wanted Keith to have a chance, so he sent him money out of his little pay. When Ralph was ill he came all the way to New York from out on Long Island just to let me know. And he'll continue to be Lee as long as we can remember.

I've got myself tied up in rehearsals of a new scene this week and can't go to Hinsdale. I know you'll forgive me. I'll come later.

My love to you both—and to all the boys, and to Lee—

Max

1. The day before the present letter Lee Chambers, oldest son of Lela and Dan, had been killed in the crash of his Army Air Force training plane in Ohio. *Candle in the Wind* was Anderson's current production.

104. TO BROOKS ATKINSON

[New City]
November 2, [1941]

Dear Brooks—[1]

I want to thank you for printing those final paragraphs—and for doing it so graciously and cleverly. Also I want to make it clear that I wasn't referring to you when I spoke of the joyous assassination. You're an honest man, I know. What you naturally want from me, after all my thunder in the index, is a great play, and you're disappointed when you don't get it. I'm disappointed in myself in the same way—disappointed every year, and more this year than most because I didn't even try for it. I tried for propaganda against Hitler. Maybe not very effectively, but that's what was in my mind. And I still haven't given up hope that I'll write that great play—in spite of my own limitations and some adverse conditions—before my pen and brain are worn clear down to the gristle. Again thanks.

Sincerely
Maxwell Anderson

1. Anderson's anti-Nazi play *Candle in the Wind* opened on October 22, 1941, to reviews unanimously hostile. Atkinson's review, though milder than most, represented the prevalent view that "in spite of the unity of conviction on both sides of the footlights, 'Candle in the Wind' somehow lacks dramatic fire" (*New York Times*, October 23, 1941, p. 26, cols. 2–3). Anderson objected (unlocated) to the "joyous assassination" of his play by the critics, and Atkinson devoted a second column to the play and its attendant essay, "By Way of Preface: The Theatre As Religion," which he had run in the *Times* (see no. 102, n. 2). The second column appeared on the day of the present letter, and Atkinson organized it as a contrast between the play, which was dull, and the essay, which was "the most vital thing that has been written about the theatre for a long time" (*New York Times*, November 2, 1941, sec. 9, p. 1, cols. 1–3).

105. TO LELA CHAMBERS

[New City]
December 15, 1941

Dear Lela—[1]

I've wanted to write to you and Dan several times, but it always seems I can't say anything because of thinking about Lee. There's just nothing to say in the face of such a loss. And to speak of it brings back that dull pain that one feels on waking.

I had a letter from Avery the same day I got yours, and I sent him a wire for the company. Keith's reaction to the war is pretty general, I guess—and what one would hope for. If those fools on the other side insist on fighting us our boys have to take up the challenge. We don't pretend to like the business, though. It's an evil game, which we play because it's forced on us, but we have to play well enough to win or we all lose together. I think if I were young enough I'd go into the service now. My pacifist days are over. —Alan and Nancy are living in New York City now. He's been transferred to Governor's Island, Fort Jay, and can come home every night. So they've been very fortunate. We haven't heard from Terry since the war started. No doubt a rash of enlistments will break out at Amherst.

I hope you won't think I forgot you because I didn't write. I can't see a uniform without remembering Lee. When my own boys come home I hold on to them as long as I can, and you can imagine why. We all go sooner or later, but these wars take the boys first. I'd go quite happily myself instead. I'm 53 today. At that age I can be pretty sure I'll never do better than I've done, and so I could leave any time.

Love to you and Dan—
Max

1. Lee (recently killed in an army training accident), Keith, and Avery are sons of Lela and Dan Chambers. Alan and Terry are Anderson's sons.

106. TO AVERY CHAMBERS [1]

New City
February 5, 1942

Dear Avery—

Thank you for your letter. I've thought several times of writing you, but somehow most of my letter-writing is done when I'm lying awake at night, and the letters never get on the page or in the mail. But mainly what I wanted to say was that I admire you for your courage and your valiant attempt to wring some kind of education out of these thorny times into which you were born. And you've done it, too. Your recent letters show a spiritual awakening which is the essence of all education. You're grappling with the problems of the earth, and nobody does more than that. —Maybe Fiderlick has helped you with that. Such a man is essential to an education. He'll inspire you all your life, and that's probably all the return he wants for what he does. That notion of his that all of us are gods in embryo—at least when young—that's a good basis for thinking—and I agree with it.

I wish I could send you a copy of my poems,[2] but I haven't an extra one. It's been out of print a long while and I haven't been able to locate any except the one I have. But I send my hopes and good wishes for you in the army or elsewhere. If you see or write to Keith please send him the same from me. And don't be sad about the army service. This is the only world we have and we must live in the world as it is. If you want to be a writer there's no better preparation than experience of life.

No better boys ever came along than you four—and I know I'll be proud of you, Avery, no matter where I hear of you. Let me know what happens—

Love
Max

1. Avery (b. 1920), third son of Lela and Dan Chambers, was attending Drake University and had told Anderson about a stimulating teacher, James J. Fiderlick (1893–1968), professor of drama and founding director of the Drake Theatre.
2. *You Who Have Dreams*.

107. TO EDWIN P. PARKER, JR. [1]

March 11, 1942

Dear General Parker:

Since returning from the Fort I have been reflecting that you might be able to use a half hour comedy skit on some of those camp programs, and that I might be able to repay your hospitality to a certain extent by writing one and turning it over to you.

At the moment I'm thinking of a dramatic picture of barracks at reveille time. Humorously treated, of course, but accurate enough to be recognized. If it were funny enough I think the boys would like it and it could be used in more camps than one. It has occurred to me that I could make the sketch more authentic and probably more effective if I could have the help of one of your public relations boys in preparing the script. Would it be possible for somebody like Hargrove to come to New York for two or three days to work this thing out with me? I shall try to write it whether I can get help or not, but one of the men who slept in the same barracks and knows all the procedure, could certainly add to the local color.

Best regards to you and Mrs. Parker.[2]

Sincerely,

1. Gen. Parker commanded Fort Bragg, North Carolina, which Anderson had visited the previous month gathering background material for *The Eve of St. Mark*. Francis Marion Hargrove, at the time an enlisted man at Fort Bragg, wrote the soon to be published *See Here, Private Hargrove* (1942), to which Anderson contributed a foreword.

2. Parker sent Hargrove to New City during the next few weeks, and with his help Anderson wrote "From Reveille to Breakfast" (see *Catalogue*, p. 39).

108. TO RUSSEL CROUSE AND CLIFTON FADIMAN [1]

New City
March 29, 1942

Dear Crouse, Fadiman, et al.:

If I know what your letter to the President means I'm afraid I can't go along with you. The people of a democracy should never ask their government to do all their thinking for them, even in time of war, and a fair share of the thinking of a nation is done by its writers. If we want our country to win we must not abdicate and turn over our functions to a sort of coordinator of literature. The strength of a democracy is in its flexibility, and government thinking is not exactly resilient. Much as I admire Elmer Davis I would not trust him nor any man or board to decide what should be said aloud in the United States during the next few years.

When you speak of word-warfare, of "the words that will influence our fellow citizens, our allies, and, in the end, our enemies", there is an unfortunate implication that our fellow citizens and allies are to be told what is good for them, and that somebody should be delegated to decide what is good for them. I think the people should be told the truth at all times, subject to the necessity of withholding military information from the enemy. A free people will defend itself best when it knows what's going on. Hitler cannot tell his people the truth, but that's his weakness. It may bring him temporary advantages, but it will destroy him when the truth catches up with him. A free people is capable of free discussion of uncensored news, and that's its strength. Let us continue to be a free people.

If you mean only that there should be a clearing house of writer talent which could help in the war effort, I'm inclined to agree, but I doubt that the letter says that.

Sincerely

Maxwell Anderson

1. Crouse (1893–1966), journalist and playwright, and Fadiman (b. 1904), essayist and editor, had written to President Roosevelt on behalf of the Authors League of America supporting the creation of the Office of War Information and the naming of Elmer Davis, journalist and fellow member of the league, as its head. Before sending it to Roosevelt, they sent the letter to other members of the league for their signature. Roosevelt created the Office of War Information, with Davis as its head, in June, 1942. The OWI was an object of controversy from the start, being seen as an agency for objective information by some and by others as an instrument for propaganda and censorship.

109. TO LELA AND DAN CHAMBERS

New City
June 1, 1942

Dear Lela and Dan—[1]

I've been thinking a lot about Lee lately, and I know you have. And it occurs to me that I'd like to dedicate this play I'm writing to him. It's not about him, though there's a lot of the hill in it, and there's a character that's like him, but there are a lot of soldiers and the problem of the play is the soldier's problem which Lee, with so many other young men, have had to face. They faced it for us, too—and Lee specifically faced it for our family before a lot of people quite understood.

The Eve of St. Mark—that's the name of it—isn't finished yet, but should be within a week or two. As soon as there are copies I'll see that you have one.[2]

Love
Max

1. Anderson would shortly complete *The Eve of St. Mark*. Much of the play is set at the Chambers's home and farm ("the hill") near Hinsdale, New York, and their son Lee is the model for the character Quizz West.
2. *The Eve of St. Mark* was published in August, 1942, with the inscription:
Dedicated to Sergeant Lee Chambers—
one of the first to go, one of the first to die
that we may keep this earth for free men.

110. TO LEE NORVELLE [1]

New City
June 2, 1942

Dear Dr. Norvelle—

Since I am coming within sight of the end of my play I shall soon be able to send it to you and to make business arrangements with the Theatre Conference. My notion is that I should convey the amateur rights to the Conference, covering the whole country except the area around New York which might be reached by our metropolitan critics.

My reason for making this exception you will readily understand. The value of the Conference to me is that it can present my play to the country before it has been seen and blasted by the New York firing squad. If amateur productions were made within accessible distance the squad would make the journey and pounce on the production and my whole object in giving you the play would be nullified.

Also it's possible that after *The Eve* has been presented throughout the country I'd want to try a professional production in New York. If that came about I'd be obligated by my contract with the Playwrights' to turn my play over to them for its metropolitan representation.[2] If it were successful in New York it might then be sent on the road. But even that would not, it seems to me, conflict with the amateur ownership of the play, which would continue in your hands. So far as I know there is no real competition between touring company and amateur performances.

I hope this plan meets with your approval. At present I see no other which could be reasonably followed. The Conference is not equipped to make professional productions, and I can't pledge myself that a professional production of *The Eve* won't be called for. So far it seems to me to be the best play I've written in years. And one reason it's good, I believe, is that I've been thinking of the country as a whole, not of the New York first nighters.

Now, as to the try-out in Indiana which you mention as a possibility: If I thought a try-out would be good for the play I'd certainly be glad to have you make the first presentation there. But that's another thing I'm trying to leave behind. I've been going through try-outs for nearly twenty years, and my conclusion is that they're usually bad for the play, and always a hell which no play or author or set of players should have to go through. A try-out sometimes improves a production, sometimes even improves a script for production in a certain city where the requirements are fairly well known, but it always destroys literary value, always degrades quality and adds theatrical clichés. It would please me better if, instead of trying for a smooth script, machined and trimmed, you could try for simultaneous productions, as much as possible, in the cities that intend to present the play this fall. I shall not ask that any theatre stick absolutely to the words as they are sent out. I have no objection to cuts and minor alterations. I should only like to stipulate that each program state on whose authority the changes are made.

I hope you won't think me captious or arbitrary in any of these matters. I have high hopes for both of us in this venture. If things go as well as they may we could begin to see our way toward a much more national theatre. And if this production succeeds other playwrights will want to try similar ventures. Some have already said as much to me. They'll all be watching results.

Sincerely

1. Norvelle (b. 1892), in the Speech and Theatre Department at Indiana University and director of the university theater, was to become president of the National Theatre Conference later in the year. The conference, an organization of college and community theaters formed in 1932 to encourage the development of the noncommercial theater in America, was seeking production rights to new plays by established playwrights in an effort to break the hold of Broadway on new play production. Paul Green, current president of the NTC, and Norvelle had begun the effort by negotiating with Anderson for the rights to his next play, *The Eve of St. Mark*.

2. The play was produced in New York by the Playwrights' Company on October 7, 1942, by which time it had had over seventy-five amateur productions arranged by the National Theatre Conference.

III. TO LEE NORVELLE

June 16, 1942

Dear Norvelle:

Looking over my play[1] yesterday I decided I didn't want to show the last scene to you the way it is. On the other hand I wanted you to have some notion of what the play would be like, and so I'm sending you the first ten scenes. The eleventh and last will follow as soon as I complete the revisions, which should be within a week. If you can go ahead with your plans on the basis of what's enclosed, please do so. The last scene is not difficult. I merely want to do it another way.

I'm inclined to think you're right about revisions, and it will be a great relief to me if you will take care of requests to be allowed to make them. Also the ten per cent charge for handling the play is reasonable. There are two or three matters I want to ask you about—or propose. One is cooperation between you and Barrett Clark[2] to the extent that he can offer the play to groups that do not compete with yours. I know this may require some working out, but if there's good will on both sides it shouldn't be too difficult. Frankly, I want the play shown as widely and as early as possible—and if Barrett's list could be added to yours it would be good both for the play and for me. However, I want it understood that the amateur rights to the play belong to the Conference, and that Barrett's releases will have to come through you. Another thing is the right to cancel our contract after one year if I wish to do so. I don't expect to exercise the right, but I think it would be only fair that I retain it. I'm leaving it to Harold Freedman to work these matters out with you, but if you are dissatisfied, please appeal to me at once. As for that circle which we shall have to draw around New York to avoid the critics, I fear it will have to be larger than you anticipated. They have been known to rush to Boston and Washington to see a try-out. I think all cities of the Atlantic seaboard within that range should be asked to delay production until after some decision is made about production in New York City.

I'll send the manuscript to Kenneth as soon as it's complete and he'll rush the printing. I know every day counts with you. You are of course at liberty to proceed with your necessary publicity. I am asking Bill Fields to announce for the Playwrights Company that *The Eve of St. Mark* was written for the Conference and for production throughout the country.

Sincerely
Maxwell Anderson

1. *The Eve of St. Mark*.
2. Director of Dramatists Play Service.

112. TO ARCHER MILTON HUNTINGTON

[August 10, 1942]

Dear Archer—[1]

A friend and neighbor of ours, Mrs. Ruth Reeves, wants to talk with you about a project she has for popularizing Central and South American textile designs in North America—and she has asked me to try to arrange an interview with you. Now I don't know, of course, whether or not your interest in things Spanish extends to South America, but if it does, and if you think that a better understanding between the western continents might result from our adoption of some of our southern neighbors' decorative styles, then Ruth Reeves may have something to say that would interest you. You have probably heard of her. She has travelled a good deal in South America and is a recognized authority on the graphic and pictorial arts as practised below the canal. The Metropolitan has promised her an exhibition if she can get together a collection of basic designs, and it's the making of such a collection which she wants to discuss with you. She's an intelligent and able woman, and sensitive. She could meet you in New York, and won't waste your time.[2]

I think I have a good play coming on this fall—one that I'd not be ashamed to show you.[3] If it turns out well I'll let you know. Mab sends best greetings to you both—and so do I.[4]

Sincerely

P.S. High Tor[5] is on the market, for [blank]. It could be a state park—or the quarry could buy it. Probably it's no use trying to hold back the march of industrial machinery, but if you want to give a chunk of that sum I think I could raise the rest over here.[6] —M. A.

1. Huntington had an extensive interest in Spanish culture, and Anderson's neighbor Ruth Reeves (1892–1966), artist and student of handicrafts as cultural expressions, had studied Inca arts in Ecuador, Peru, and Bolivia on a Guggenheim Fellowship in 1941.

2. Huntington's reply (August 15, 1942; T) said that, though interested in Mrs. Reeves's work, he would be out of New York for some time and could not see her. Mrs. Reeves had no exhibition at the Metropolitan Museum of Art, though she had exhibitions at several other museums.

3. *The Eve of St. Mark*.

4. Huntington's wife was the sculptress, Anna Hyatt Huntington.

5. Mountain overlooking the Hudson River near Anderson's home.

6. High Tor was put up for sale in the summer of 1942 following the death of its owner Elmer van Orden on February 19, 1942. The Hudson River Conservation Society, in competition with several traprock companies, attempted to raise money to buy the mountain, and in February, 1943, they made the purchase. The price of the property is not given in the surviving draft of the letter, but the Society paid $12,000 for it. Anderson was chairman of the Rockland County Committee To Save High Tor, which worked with the Hudson River Conservation Society and raised $5,000 of the $12,000 purchase price. In May, 1943, the society turned over the property to the Palisades Interstate Park Commission, and High Tor was made a state park.

113. TO LELA AND DAN CHAMBERS

[New City]
August 17, 1942

Dear Lela & Dan—[1]

Terry went away in the bus from Haverstraw today with about 150 draftees. He's to report to Governor's Island for medical and induction if they want him. Probably his eyes will keep him out of anything he'd like—he wants to get into the air force or near it, but has little chance of that. He'll take his two weeks furlough in any case.

I'm writing to tell you that *The Eve of St. Mark* goes into rehearsal a week from today and will open toward the end of Sept or the beginning of October. Now, I don't know how you'll like it on the stage, but I want to invite you to the N.Y. opening, and for a week or so in these parts at that time. If that's a time when you can get away we'd like to have you. Maybe Ethel and Ralph[2] should come too, and we'll all see something of N.Y. town. It's a long time since we'd done anything together.

The pigs are thriving. We've had more rain [than] this region ever saw in its life. Oceans! I'm enclosing a check for Keith and one for Avery[3]—just for spending money. Love—and please come.

Max

1. *The Eve of St. Mark* contained characters modeled on the Chambers family, was set in part on their farm in western New York, and was dedicated to their son Lee, recently killed in an air force training accident.
2. Another of Anderson's sisters and her husband.
3. Sons of Lela and Dan.

114. TO EDWIN P. PARKER JR.

December 19, 1942

Dear General Parker:[1]

Thank you for that very reassuring letter about "THE EVE OF ST. MARK". I had hoped it wouldn't disappoint you when it appeared. I only wish you might see it in New York, where it has the advantage of an especially excellent production.

And now that I find you were not annoyed by the results of your kindness to me last spring, I gather courage to ask if you would help me out again. I plan to visit the colored troops in a Southern camp this winter if nobody objects, and perhaps you won't mind if I turn up again at your headquarters looking for advice and directions.

In fact, this letter is in the nature of warning that unless you discourage me, I'm likely to turn up at Camp Butner early in January.[2]

Sincerely,

Maxwell Anderson

1. Parker, who had commanded Fort Bragg when Anderson visited the base in February, 1942, gathering material for *The Eve of St. Mark*, was now commander at Camp Butner, North Carolina. During the first week of December he had seen a production of the play by the Carolina Playmakers at the University of North Carolina, and on December 8, 1942, had written to Anderson in praise of it (T).

2. Anderson visited several camps in Virginia and North Carolina during January and February, 1943. From North Carolina he went to England and North Africa, however, and the play that resulted from the trip was *Storm Operation*, a play that grew out of the stay in North Africa.

115. TO GERTRUDE ANDERSON

[At Sea][1]
March 23, 1943

Mab darling—

It's 9:40 in the evening—we slept and were waked for dinner—and ate it—despite our vows—and are now given a half-hour to write a note and send it before the censorship clamps down. It was certainly hard to say goodbye in that cold shed of a pier—both of us half-sick and depressed by the bitter day. Somehow the whole venture takes on a futile air when subjected to the scrutiny of actuality. How can it be a good thing to embark on this particular voyage—when there are so many interesting things to do nearer home? It's a kind of a test of a fellow—whether he can interest himself in something near at hand or must be looking restlessly at a distant pasture. But then I come back to the present state of the world—and the fact that I must get a breath of its desperation before I can write again.

You'll be lonely for a while—till I come back, I hope—but not half as lonely and lost as I feel away from you. It's really hard for me to go and not see you for months. If I didn't feel a real need to do it I'd never have got this far. Dolce far niente[2] never means much to me. But you and our home and the days we've built up together mean a great deal. I feel a constant pull in my solar plexus back toward that place and you. It will bring me back as soon as I can come.

Tell Hesper I shall be hoping to get V-mail from her—and from you, too. She was very sweet over the phone.

All my love, darling
Max

1. Anderson was on board the *Pinto*, a Portuguese ship sailing under the flag of the Colonial Navigating Company. Leaving New York, he sailed to Lisbon via the Azores. From Lisbon he flew to London, later flying to North Africa, then sailing back to Boston. Robert Sherwood, director of the Overseas Branch of the Office of War Information, had obtained permission for Anderson to make the trip, and the next several letters (through no. 125) provide a detailed account of the trip.

2. Loafing.

116. TO GERTRUDE ANDERSON

[At Sea]
April 1, [1943]

Darling—

About an hour ago we sighted the Azores, and now we are beginning to go round the headland into the harbor. I have been told that we can mail letters and perhaps even send a cable from here. So far I've kept up my diary daily, but written no letters because the day of mailing seemed so far away. But there may be a chance only today to get a word off. The Azores, when we first saw them, were highish—mountainous—but as we got closer we saw that they were farmed right up to the top, with an intricate pattern of patch-work brown and green fields.

It's been a long, mostly calm, sometimes boring voyage. My cold has hung on so that part of the time I've stayed in my bed reading practically all day—but I've met a lot of young men from the Board of Economic Warfare and the O.W.I. and the State Dept., and they all seem surprisingly bright and well-equipped. Somebody is doing some good picking in Washington. My hands are still cold from standing in the wind to watch the Azores, but it's not really cold here. In fact, we've been pretty far south during the whole voyage. I'm pretty well sun burned. Also I've quit taking quinidine! There must have been some allergen in what I was eating. For the last four days I haven't needed it. Maybe I'll find out what was the trouble.

Now, looking from the other side of the ship, I find there's a high, peaked, snow-capped mountain, rising seven thousand feet or so from the sea. Most beautiful—with cloud draperies. We've stopped now—waiting for a pilot, perhaps—just pausing here between the islands.

We've had lunch. It's now a quarter of two and we're all waiting for a chance to go to Horta.[1] During lunch a boy came round bearing a placard. It read

> PEASANT NOTICE (meaning pleasant)
> Passagers will be allowed to go ashore on the following conditions:
> They must return until seven.
> They must not leave Horta.

Gabby[2] and I were among the first in line to get in the launch, but the waves were so high that the little boat went away without passengers. Now we're all hoping that it will come back—or that the ship will edge up to the pier.

I'm not at all sure whether to mail this here or not. If there were a clipper coming through soon it might go right away. But it might hang around in the Azores a long while. At least I'll be able to send a cable from here.

I miss you darling. I wish you could have come along. If I can possibly arrange passage for you from London I will.

I love you, darling
Max

---

1. Main port for the island of Fayal in the Azores.
2. Gabriel Pascal (1894–1954), Hungarian producer-director who came to England in the thirties, won the esteem of Bernard Shaw, and was entrusted with the

filming of several of his plays (*Pygmalion*, 1938; *Major Barbara*, 1940; *Caesar and Cleopatra*, 1945). At present he was returning to England to make war documentaries.

117. TO GERTRUDE ANDERSON

Ponta del Gado[1]
April 6, 1943

Darling—what a relief to get a cable from you—and such a good one! One doesn't realize how much of a shell he's accumulated and how tense he's got till something like that comes along—and the whole world takes on meaning again. I can't imagine how you caught me here—for I knew nothing about stopping at the Azores when we sailed. You must have got in touch with the agents and obtained the address from them. Anyway it came like rain to sailors in a life-boat. I've just been talking to a lot of sailors and I know something about how that felt to them. A lot of English and Norwegian boys who were torpedoed and managed to get to Flores[2] were picked up by the *Pinto* and I talk with them as much [as] I can. Today I was part of the afternoon in the bar with the two captains—English and Norwegian— and since then I've been playing chess with one of the Norwegian crew down in their quarters.

We're in Ponta del Gado—to which you sent the cable. It's a largish little city. We're not allowed ashore here because it's a military zone. But we have been able to buy fresh fruit from huckster boats alongside—and yesterday we were allowed to go ashore at another port—Angra de Heroismo—which means heroic anchorage.[3] There we walked about in town and had lunch and I bought a cheap cap and some honey and a little wicker basket—square, with a cover—for laundry. The lunch was wonderful. I went with Barnes and Shey, O.W.I. fellows, and Mrs. Maund, whose husband was the commander of the Ark Royal.[4] She has offered to put me in touch with naval authorities in London.

While in Angra de Heroismo yesterday I sent you a cable from the Post Office—and one to Quentin. It took a couple of hours and the censorship was so complete that I felt that the whole affair was a futile gesture. Like sending up a Roman candle and expecting it to attract your attention in New City. In Horta they were very hurried about censoring, so I was able to get a real message through.

April 8[5]

Yesterday I was sick—I don't know what from unless it was a dinner Gabby cooked for his table and invited me to attend. It was chicken paprika and good—perhaps I was ill from the native food or fruit purchased in Angra de Heroismo. Anyway I slept most of yesterday and today I'm all right. Also we hear now that we're to be in Lisbon Saturday morning. Even so the voyage will have taken much longer than was advertised, and I'm not exactly sure why. It may be that the stops in the Azores were anticipated by the agents, though they certainly said nothing about them. And we did lose time going back to Flores to pick up the survivors there. Our course through the Azores has been something like this:

There was a rumor to the effect that we were not supposed to go to Horta at all, and that may be true, for we did no trading there—and though there was a lot of American seamen, survivors of torpedoing, we didn't take any of them aboard. I talked to some of the seamen in the Cafe International and they were very homesick for America. Some were from Brooklyn, some from West Virginia—most of the men in their ships had been lost.

We weren't allowed ashore at Flores, but we did pick up a good many English and Scotch sailors there, and I've been spending a good deal of time with them. They were well taken care of by the natives, who are all Catholics and all Portuguese. The islands are extraordinarily beautiful to look at.

When we got to Angra de H. we were allowed ashore again, and there we picked up a lot more survivors and unloaded a good deal of wheat. In Ponta del Gada, where your cable reached me, we stayed longer than anywhere else, but were not allowed to go ashore. More survivors were taken on, and more wheat taken off. Altogether we seem to have turned into a sort of tramp steamer for a time, operating among the islands. But I'm very glad of it, for I've got to know something about the torpedoings and could write a play about the merchant marine if I ever wanted to.

You will wonder what I do with myself with all this time on my hands—and I begin to wonder myself. My cold has been a real problem to me. I was sick in bed for a while, and ate little. Then when I began to stir around I ran into the most interesting assortment of young men I've met for a long while. All going abroad for the American gov't. With them I talk and play chess and walk the deck. There are three American girls with the group, going over as secretaries, etc. Then there's Mrs. Maund, who sits at my table and whose husband, as I told you, commanded the Ark Royal before she was sunk. She's all right but veddy bloody English. She's been away from her husband for three years, and was hoping for a cable from him on their anniversary, which was day before yesterday. When I got a cable and she got none she was really blue for a while.

I think I might actually have worked on the ship if I hadn't had such a really tough cold. I'm not quite over it yet. And the usual aftermath of cold sores has descended on me—so I'm not a pretty sight. It doesn't matter, though. Everybody seems to know who I am and is quite nice to me. Even the Portuguese captain, who speaks some English, has gone out of his way to be affable and helpful about letting me go ashore. Of course I went only when all could go, but it was partly because of my petition that we got off at Angra.

I managed to get some laundry done on the boat, so I'm not in such a bad way as might be. Anyway it's become a joke with all of us that we have to put our dirty clothes back on. —My diary I've kept up every day, and it will tell you more than I can get into letters, I guess. But there's nothing to tell except that I've missed you and Hesper and felt myself in a sort of helpless vacuum from the beginning. It's not wasted, because the Azores and the survivors are wonderful experience. But it's personally quite empty. Here's one detail. I have three kinds of money in pocket now. Different pockets, of course. About fifty American dollars, about 1500 Portuguese escudos, and 3 British pounds. The pounds I got by accident, because an American (no, English) woman wanted to change some pounds for dollars. The escudos are worth less than 5 cents each, so they don't represent great wealth. I'll need them in Portugal, and for tipping the *creados* on the ship. Cabin boys, bath steward, waiter, perhaps others. I've had to learn a little Portuguese. For example, *fash favór* is please. *Monte obligado* is thank you. And what little French I knew has come in handy. And little is right. But it usually doesn't take much. Wanting hot water to shave, for example, I asked for aqua chaud—and got it!

Those books we bought the night before I left have proved life-savers. Not only do I read them but I lend them out—have conducted a [illegible] library. First I plowed through *The Idiot*, which occupied nearly a week—then the life of Lincoln. I'm now reading *The Turn of the Screw*. And several of the books are in circulation. A very nice old English woman, Mrs. Hackett, is reading *The Idiot* and I've told her to keep it. Several people have read the little pocket readers, and Steinbeck's *Pastures of Heaven* have circulated completely out of my ken. *They Call it Pacific* has gone the rounds. And Irwin Edman is now in use. The only one I've held on to tightly is the Lincoln collection.[6]

Apr. 9—Our last day at sea, if all these predictions are correct. Somehow as we get nearer to land and to a possible post office it seems more fun to write a letter. When we were so far at sea there just wasn't much point. I keep reflecting, though, that from now on there's a third party to all our correspondence—and that's the censor. I don't mind, but unless my letters happen to get into a diplomatic pouch they'll probably be covered with black deletions—for I'm not quite sure what's censorable and what's not. Bramsen tells me that his mail will go with the uncensored from Lisbon and that mine probably will, too. If these pages arrived unscathed you'll know that I made contacts there.

This ship is alive with children, English children going home, and though they're basically well-bred the confinement of the voyage is finally getting to be too much for them. They're all on edge and excited—and their mothers and aunts are not much better. Especially the wives who are going back to their husbands after two or three years' absence. That long a time is really too much of a strain on any relationship. They feel nervous, and unhappy about having gone away—a bit defensive. Especially now that England has come through without an invasion, and they could have stayed put without risking the children too much. But they didn't know it would be that way. They were pretty well convinced that an invasion was possible. And maybe it was. It just didn't happen.

Lisbon—Apr 10. So this is Portugal! It's a quarter of eleven and it's been a long day. Last night I sat watching the dancing till after eleven—and just then a cabin boy came around with a placard which said, in effect, 1. Please set clocks ahead two hours. 2. All passengers will come to the 1st class bar at 7 A.M. I set my watch ahead, and it was then 1:15. Got to bed at 2:00, woke at five to hear the boat stopping in calm water. We must have taken on a pilot and then gone on up the river Tagus. At seven I was at the bar and was informed that we would be received at 8:30. The customs and other clearances didn't hold me long, but they kept Gabby because of certain stockings and cigars until we were too late to get to the bank (this is Saturday) and I couldn't get escudos enough to buy my plane ticket to London. Our priorities are here and we could have left tonight or Monday at seven if we'd been able to raise the Portuguese cash. It never occurred to me that a British company wouldn't take either travellers' checks, or pounds or dollars. No, they must have escudos. Nearly five thousand of them to buy a ticket to London.

Well, we dashed around from one embassy to another, finding out all these things, and there was no word from you at the American embassy. We went to the Hotel Avez—I sent you a cable—and had a nap, and then a walk through the side streets, and then a long dinner —what a change after the execrable food on the boat—and now I've come up to my room ready to sleep. Had to take a double room with Gabby—but we were lucky to get it. It was his influence—and it was he, I believe, who got me the priority for London—that got the room for us. There is a terrific pressure for places to stay. But he's a trial to live with. —I'm so weary and sleepy I keep miswriting words. —I wish you were here to make this place exciting. It keeps reminding me of Havana. Barefoot women with baskets on their heads and children selling lottery tickets and sacred emblems and funny high white-cream architecture. Look I'm all going to pieces.[7] I'll write more about it tomorrow. I can't be sure yet whether I'll mail this in Lisbon or England. It depends on the service one anticipates. I don't know when planes go or how.

London, Apr. 14—Well, I didn't write the next day. Things happened too fast, I guess. I did manage to make notes in the little journal to cover the time. What occurred in essence was this: The O.W.I. forgot me in Lisbon entirely—didn't even send my name to the consul, and I'd be stuck there for months if Gabriel hadn't worked the matter from the British end—and got a priority for me. But he had no money at all—and so I paid everything. Now that we're in London he may have money again—and be able to repay me—but so far I'm not sure. We're at the Claridge—which is tres expensif. Got on a plane yesterday morning and flew six hours over the ocean, landing at Bristol. Crossing England was a delight—it was so green, so well cultivated, so somehow gentle. —Today I must get my food card and identification card and a hair-cut and see Beaumont and go to the American Embassy, hoping for news of you there. For nothing arrived in Lisbon—just nothing. I suspect the Portuguese.

The Claridge, Apr 15—Darling, I begin to get terribly lonely! Just no news at all since that one cable in the Azores. But I got the O.W.I. to send you a notice that I had arrived. Maybe I'll get some word from you tomorrow. They say any cable that the censor finds suspicious or that sounds as if it were sent by a new arrival is held about ten days. —At last—your cable came!

Apr 16—That passage was interrupted by a call from Willy Wyler,[8] who invited me to go out to the coast—in the middle of the night—to see the beginning and end of a sweep over the continent. Said yes—we started at 1:30 A.M.—drove till four, got a few hours sleep, got up early, saw the planes start, waited about nervously all day till they began to come back. The colonel in command was going crazy because more than half were overdue—when they began to come in. Some landed at other airports but they all got home safely. A friend of Wyler's was killed in another sweep today, however. —There go the air-raid sirens—the Germans are coming! I will not go to a shelter. I'd rather stay here.

Well, it was a real air raid, but it's over. Gabby and I sat talking through it—and then put the lights out to look out the window. It was bright moonlight—but with clouds. Plenty of bombs and ack-ack.

Today Gabby organized his new film company—with the greatest financier in England[9]—really—and is again sound financially. They are making me a director of the company. —Would you like to live in

England for a while? Everybody seems to want me to stay here. They seem to think I could earn a living, too. But I guess I'd want to get back. Gabby's idea is to get you over here as a scenario writer.

Saturday April 17—I've been sort of holding on to this letter hoping there was some way to get it into a quicker mail service than is likely if one simply drops it in a box. But so far I haven't found any such thing—and maybe I'll end by just mailing it and trusting that it gets through fairly quick. Today—or rather this afternoon—I'm quiet here and alone for the first time. Gabby has gone for the week-end. So perhaps I can get something said that would explain my quandary to you. It's quite unlikely that my play will go on.[10] It must have an American cast, and there's no chance of getting one here—or bringing one over. Or small chance. Now I'm planning to go to North Africa because I don't think I'll find material for a play in England. However, I do have material for a picture—about the survivors—and Gabby wants me to do that right now and have it ready to be the first picture he makes here. Also he promises to get you over here to help me with the scenario, as I said. I don't believe I'd be happy here for long, but at the moment we'd be nearer the center of things than we are in New York. At least nearer the center of where one gets materials. This is really a war front, here in London. One finds that out on a first inspection. But it doesn't seem too unsafe for Hesper—and the spirit of the people is so wonderful that one feels honored to be a member of the English speaking fraternity. There is one rather serious drawback, however, to your coming over. Gabby says he thinks he can get you here, but is doubtful about getting you back till the war is over. That would certainly be more than a year.[11]

Sunday—Apr 18—Darling, I guess I'll have to mail this soon, or it will grow out of all bounds. Somehow or other I'll put it in the mail tomorrow, first making an effort to discover which pouch goes most rapidly. Today I went out to Keats' house in Hampstead, with Garretson, Wyler and the Editor of The Stars & Stripes—who is called Llewellyn—a major, as is Wyler.[12] It was very nice to see the house and garden again, uninjured in the midst of a pretty badly bombed London—though the caretaker told us there had been three fire-bombs on the roof and the house was nearly lost at one time. We drove down to the bombed area below St. Pauls—and that's really something devastated. But somehow London goes right on, and quite confidently now.

Midnight—I had dinner with Wyler—and food here, by the way, is a bit scanty and without much variety. It's good for me, though. After dinner Wyler took me to see some people with whom he was to play gin rummy. Among them was Ellen Drew, who was supposed to play the girl in my play.[13] She is married to Major Bartlett, whom I had met in Hollywood and also in Washington. —Let me confirm now a few things about scarcities here. If you come over you should bring plenty of stockings, for you will get none here. Bring or send some candy. There is no fruit here except once in a while rhubarb—if that's fruit. Bring a supply of vitamins.

I have just today worked out in my mind a story about merchant marine survivors which I think will make a good picture. It would even make a play, but if Gabby wants a picture immediately I may write it for him and earn some pounds to live on. You would be coming, if you come, to work on scenarios for Gabby. Arthur Rank, who is financing him, begins to grow in importance as I hear more rumors about him. Till now he is really a dominating financier. Owns not only the whole film industry in this country but other industries as well. Rank's influence is so great that he would be able to bring you over if he felt you were needed—or so Gabby says.

I've talked now with a lot of men who have been here nearly a year—leaving wives and children in America. They are all pretty unhappy about it. Not so much because of the distance as because the difficulty of communication magnifies the distance. It's so hard to get a word through quickly. One feels really cut off. I feel it already myself —and even though I'm seeing and experiencing the most exciting things I could hope for here there's always an ache in me that keeps wishing for home and you and Hesper. And it will get worse—and not better. In all this dislocation of the world, and in the storm of violent death we feel round us here, it's the women and children at home the men cling to. Wyler showed me the pictures of his children with such pride. Victor[14] was so happy to hear even bare reports of Anne and the children. I know now that the pain at one's heart can become overwhelming.

I love you, darling,
Max[15]

1. Chief port on the island of Sao Miguel in the Azores.

2. The westerly island among the Azores.

3. Chief port on the island of Terceira in the Azores.

4. The British aircraft carrier *Ark Royal* went down off Gibraltar in November, 1941. In the spring of 1941 planes from the *Ark Royal* had participated in the bombing and sinking of the German battleship *Bismarck*, and in November the *Ark Royal* was torpedoed by the German submarine U-81. The *Ark Royal*, commanded by Captain L. E. H. Maund, sank while in tow to Gibraltar. In referring to Mrs. Maund in the letters, Anderson spells her name several ways, none of them the spelling adopted for this edition, which gives the name as spelled in newspaper accounts of the sinking of the *Ark Royal*.

5. Because of the impossibility of mailing letters on board ship and the uncertainty of mailing them at his various stops, Anderson wrote the present letter and several of the following ones in journal fashion, dating each entry and adding it to earlier portions of the letter. The present composite letter, beginning on April 6, has succeeding entries on April 8 (*Pinto*), April 9 (*Pinto*), April 10 (Lisbon), April 14 (London), April 15 (London), April 16 (London), April 17 (London), April 18 (London), and April 18 midnight (London).

6. *They Call It Pacific* (1943) by Clark Lee (1907–1953), Associated Press reporter, describes the war in the Pacific. Irwin Edman (1896–1954), professor of philosophy at Columbia University, published several books during the preceding decade, most recently *Fountainheads of Freedom* (1941). "The Lincoln collection" is probably Carl Sandburg, *Abraham Lincoln: The War Years* 4 vols. (1939).

7. "Architecture" in the previous sentence had been written incorrectly, written over, then scratched out and written again. Several words in the last few sentences show similar revision.

8. William Wyler (b. 1902), American motion picture director, was at the time a major in the U.S. Army engaged in the production of documentary films about the war.

9. The financier J. Arthur Rank (b. 1888), director of about a hundred companies in Great Britain and America, including financial institutions and motion-picture producing companies.

10. *The Eve of St. Mark*.

11. Note added at top of page: "Gin rummy is the great game here, just as at home."

12. Albert Henry Garretson (b. 1910), formerly professor of law at Colgate University, was at the time (1943–44) in the Economic Warfare Division of the American Embassy in London. Since 1946 he has been professor in the School of Law, New York University, Washington Square, and has had several State Department and United Nations assignments. Ensley Llewellyn was editor of the military newspaper *Stars and Stripes*.

13. Ellen Drew (b. 1915), American actress who played mainly in motion pictures.

14. Victor A. Rapport (b. 1903), formerly professor of sociology at the University of Connecticut, was at the time a major in the U.S. Army stationed in London. After his military service (1940–46), Rapport went to Wayne State University in Detroit as a dean.

15. Note added at top of page: "Llewellyn, the editor of the Stars and Stripes here, asked me to send thanks and greetings to Milton C. [Caniff, author of the comic strip, "Steve Canyon," and neighbor of Anderson on South Mountain Road]—and tell him his strip is extremely popular—though sometimes too hot to handle."
Note added at side of page: "1:30 A.M.—There's just been another air raid by

moonlight—guns going off all around. A small raid—nobody pays attention."

Note added at top of first page of composite letter: "If you do come by Lisbon—stay at Hotel Avez—AVEZ—and ask to see the asst. manager, Mr. Armada—who speaks excellent English—a friend of Pascal's. Take his advice. —Carry plenty of money—preferably in a money belt. You can carry excess baggage on the plane if you pay for it. If the Avez is full ask Armada where to go. Don't stay in the Avenito [illegible].

118. TO GERTRUDE ANDERSON

> Hotel Claridge
> London
> April 26, [1943][1]

Darling—

It's so hard to write when one doesn't know how soon the letter will go or when it will be delivered. Such a barrier has been raised that one feels really cut off. That broadcast to America which I made last night I did largely because I hoped you might be able to tune in on the short-wave, and we could have at least a one-way conversation. But things go so slowly I'm not even sure you got my cable about the broadcast and not at all sure your short-wave set could pick the thing up even if you knew about it. If you did hear it you caught up on a lot of my activities which would take a long time to describe, like the visit to the bomber station, the waiting around for messages, the attitude of London civilians and all that. —The letter I sent over to Victor last Monday may have got off to you promptly—and you may get it soon—maybe it will take weeks or months, for the censor may find things in it to blot out. Anyway I'll start as near as I can where I left off. My diary, which I've kept so far, is a great help—if I didn't have it everything would be blurred. And, darling, please be patient with me if I tell dull things—I begin to feel the way all the men over here seem to—that I just must get into some kind of personal touch with home —that I can't say anything very real because it's so far—and yet I must let you know how I get along. Well—that's not very clear. I'm just so baffled with this wall of silence between us it gets to be a pain.

Well, anyway—in my last letter I must have said something about seeing the Keats house, for the letter went the day after I'd been there. The day the letter went—Monday the 19th—I made a short broadcast to the U.S. Didn't have time to warn you of that one. Tuesday I was reading Wyler's script for his air picture,[2] and saw Brewster Morgan —had dinner with him, in fact. Wednesday I got a cable from you saying you would like to live in England if I could arrange it. I did my best to do so by finishing the synopsis of a picture about torpedoing survivors and turning it over to Gabby.[3] If that is done Gabby says Arthur Rank can get you over here as my assistant. But I told you that. On that day too I had lunch with Russell Lane, who has put on all my plays out in Madison, Wisc., and is now with the Red Cross here. He wanted the army to put on *St. Mark* here—and since a commercial production seems impossible I gave him permission to go ahead.[4] He went to Gen. Rogers at once, and Rogers wants to do it in London, in one of the regular theatres, with soldier actors and for soldiers. It would be a non-profit making venture, as I said in my cable to you today. And I like that much better than the first plan. I don't want to be offering a war play to the English for money. I'd rather give it to them. They've earned all we can give. Russell Lane, by the way, turned out to be the greatest Anderson fan I've ever encountered—really considers me the great American playwright—which, as I told him, came to me as a new idea.

On Thursday I wrote the 15 minute broadcast which you may have heard me deliver last night—and appeared on another broadcast —a sort of Information Please. On Friday I tried to cable you some flowers because it was Shakespeare's birthday—but it was also Good Friday, so the shops were all closed. Had dinner with Terence Rattigan, who wrote *Flare Path*, still running here,[5] and the script of Wyler's picture. On Saturday Garretson and Chaffee, two fellows from the Bureau of Economic Warfare, got on a train with me to go to Oxford and Stratford. We walked all over Oxford that day and that night slept in students' rooms that hadn't been altered since the founding of the University. Pretty bleak and monastic. Went on to Stratford next day. It was closed up tight as a cartridge—on Easter Sunday—but we managed to get into nearly all the places I wanted to see. Trinity Church, where the bard is buried, is really a beauty. Built in 1220, or there abouts. And there's the tomb of the great man in the chancel, like you've always heard tell, and his bust, and

"Good friend, for Jesus' sake forbear"

cut into the flag where his bones lie—and his daughter and his son-in-law buried beside him. He was really a laird in his own country. Only the Shakespeares and their kin lie in that chancel! All the others lie in lesser ground, or outside the church. And this was not because he was a great poet but because he owned the tithes of Stratford, having acquired them by purchase.[6] The bust is most disappointing. As much so as folk say. But the church is a thing of beauty. The birthplace looks quite authentic—and the Nash house, where his son-in-law lived. The Avon is a tiny little river.

Came back to London to make that broadcast—which was at 2 A.M. Monday morning here—and at 8 P.M. Sunday evening in New City. In consequence I missed a lot of sleep and slept late this morning. This evening I went to dine with a Rev. Mr. Spencer and his family. I met him when Herbert Agar asked me to make a speech[7]—and it turned out I was to speak at a Federation of Churches—or something like that—and Spencer and I agreed that some other bloke might be a better choice.

Tomorrow night I'm having dinner with Victor again—and the night after with Capt. Dan Selko, a friend of Kenneth's—who also works in the B.E.W. Thursday Brewster Morgan wants me to go to the theatre with him. The theatre, here, begins at 6 P.M. and ends about nine. People have dinner after the theatre. This is because of raids, blackouts, etc. But the theatres are all jammed. Everything goes.

April 27

Dear—I'm going to send this off today, hoping it goes through fast. And it occurs to me you'll be wondering why I'm still in England. It's this way. If Rank wants me to write that sea picture I'll stay here and do it—for that's war work, too—and try to send for you. If that picture doesn't hold me I'll try at once to get transportation to a point nearer the fighting. I haven't seen Gabby in three days—there's been a long Easter holiday, four days of it—and he hadn't even been able to get my synopsis typed to show to Rank the last time I saw him. But the decision should come soon. —And if I stay in London I'm going to move out of the Claridge to 34 South Molton St., which is near the Claridge and the Embassy. A flat that costs little. I love you, darling. And I'm terribly lonesome for you. Give Hesper my love, and tell her

to write to me. I hope for a letter from you soon. I've had none yet—
not even the Lisbon one.

Max

Darling—

I didn't mail this today after all, because I think maybe it will go
quicker the way I'm sending it. And though I met Victor for dinner
tonight—also his superior, Col. Lord—I thought I'd add another
word and wait for the better chance. Victor and Lord were in good
spirits about the war. They have to deal with questions of supply, and
they say it's just a matter of mathematics—sooner or later, now—the
allies will win. We then had dinner at a sort of club where the food is
nicely cooked and we sat around talking till nearly 10:30. Tell Anne
that her Victor is certainly well and hearty, but that he hangs on every
word of news from home like a small boy—even though the news I
have is still the same as ever. Col. Lord's family is in Washington, and
he's been here since early last summer. So I really shouldn't complain
much yet. But he's an old army man, and seems resigned to the
situation. A very interesting fellow, though—the man who talked old
man Kaiser into building cargo planes.[8]

I'm hoping for a cable or a letter tomorrow. And hoping you
heard my broadcast, I guess. I'll leave a bit of space here to fill
tomorrow.

—April 28—

Dearest—your cable came as I hoped—and you heard the broadcast—
as I hoped— and I'll just have to wait for letters. It's not your fault if
they don't come through. This one I'll take over to Herbert Agar, who
is supposed to be going home soon. He'll show it to the censor and
take it with him—if his packet isn't too full. And that reminds me—
maybe I'll be going home myself one of these days—or you'll be
coming over. I'll have dinner with Arthur Rank Thursday—and on
Friday will cable you. All my love—

Max

1. The letter is another of the composite letters, and the dates of its entries are April
26, April 27, April 28, 1943.

2. During the next few years Wyler directed several "air picture[s]," and the one
referred to here cannot be positively identified. Perhaps it was *The Memphis Belle*, the
next one produced after the date of the letter, released in 1944 by Paramount Pictures.

3. No record of this script has come to light, either in Anderson's manuscripts or in Pascal's pictures.

4. For details of the production, which Lane directed, see Appendix I, no. 3. Lane (b.1899), professor of drama at the University of Wisconsin before the war, remained in London after the war as an actor.

5. *Flare Path*, Rattigan's war play, had closed in New York the previous January after only fourteen performances, but in London was having an extended run.

6. The tithes, fixed rents originally paid to the priests of Holy Trinity Church in Stratford, were in Shakespeare's day in the hands of the Corporation of Stratford. He purchased the lease on a large portion of the tithes on July 24, 1605, for £ 440, and thereafter it brought him an income of £ 60 to £ 100 annually.

7. Herbert S. Agar (b. 1897), American journalist and author (books include *The People's Choice*, 1933, Pulitzer Prize for American history), was at the time Special Assistant to the U.S. Ambassador in London.

8. The cargo plane developed by Henry J. Kaiser was the HK-1, a "flying wing" capable of transporting 120,000 pounds of cargo up to 17,000 miles. It passed flight tests and became operational in June, 1943.

119. TO GERTRUDE ANDERSON

Hotel Claridge
London
May 2, 1943

Dear— I don't know whether or not I can send V-mail, because I have no APO number—but at least I can write on the paper. I've sent long accumulated letters to you so far—two of them—and the first one, mailed from London, you received. The second I sent off by Herbert Agar, and you should get it soon. A previous letter was mailed from the Azores. —At present I'm trying to do several things at once. 1st—trying to arrange to have my play[1] produced in London for all soldiers—anybody in uniform and their dates—and simultaneously all over the United Kingdom by groups of soldiers in the camps and separate units. 2nd—there's a producer here who has the mad idea of putting on *The Wingless Victory*—and I've been discussing that. In fact I've given permission.[2] 3rd I'm writing a script for a descriptive short picture by Wyler which consists of shots of actual bombings of Germany and the French bases. 4th—I'm trying to arrange my passage (and get permission to go) to North Africa. Cabled Bob about that today.[3] 5th (this *is* piling up) I'm seeing Arthur Rank on Thursday eve about the survivor picture. He has told Gabby that he would need you to work on the script with me, and that if I will stay and do the story for them he will arrange about your passage. I haven't been able to talk it over with him myself, so I can't get it clear about whether or not Hesper could come. Rank says that he wouldn't insist that I write that picture immediately, and that if I want to go to North Africa first he'll be happy to get the script later—but he wants to sign a contract with me now.

All this has led to infinite complications in seeing people and trying to learn things and straighten out unexpected difficulties. One runs into jealousies and army procedure and prejudices that drive him mad—but I guess things are getting into some kind of order. Brewster Morgan is in charge of army liaison here—with O.W.I.—and he's doing what he can to smooth my way to Africa. I still feel that that trip is imperative if I'm to get the background for another play—the play I want—though there are plays and play materials everywhere.

Had lunch yesterday with Shaw's secretary, Miss Patch—and there's a character. She's been with him only 22 years.[4]

Oh, darling—it may actually come about—that you get here— and we learn about England together. I'm doing my best to bring it about. I only hope you're not sorry. I love you, darling,

Max

I have written a new scene for *St. Mark*, to put in place of present dream scenes.[5] And a new speech for *The Wingless Victory*. I have taken a little studio place to write in and which is a more or less permanent address—it's 34 South Molton St., London, W 1

1. *The Eve of St. Mark*.

2. *The Wingless Victory* was produced in London by a group including Wanda Rotha, Manning Whiley, and Mary Merrall. It opened on September 8, 1943.

3. Robert Sherwood, at the time director of the Overseas Branch of the Office of War Information.

4. Blanche Patch, Shaw's secretary from 1920 until his death in 1950, whose *Thirty Years with G.B.S.* (1951) recounts the association.

5. For the new scene and the two it replaces, see Appendix I, no. 3.

120. TO GERTRUDE ANDERSON

[London]

May 6, 1943[1]

Darling—Your first letter—the first to arrive, not the first sent—came day before yesterday, and I've read it several times. I'll wear it out reading it if the mails continue to be so slow. Then yesterday came a letter from Hesper in a bold flowing style, quite new from her, and a letter from Alan in Hollywood. We really should number our letters, for they arrive out of order. Garretson, for example, received two from his wife day before yesterday, and they were numbered 4 and 10. So she had written at least ten and he knew there were others coming to fill in gaps.

This is the day, as you know, when I'm to have dinner with Rank and get something started about your priority. It's not going to be possible to tell you the decision before this letter goes, but perhaps I can get an indication from him of what the chances are for you. I shall have a good opportunity to send this the early part of next week—and won't be able to write during the week-end—so I must try to set down what news there is today and tomorrow. Saturday and Sunday Wyler and I are visiting a bomber field, and we'll be pretty busy. I think probably I'd better turn my letter over to the censor Friday night to be sure it gets through in time to catch the boat I'm aiming at.

This morning I ate an egg—a wonderful egg and toast and tea for breakfast. By the way you'll have to give up your first thing in the morning drink if you live in England. There's all the coffee you want, though. And I think the present food situation in this country is actually a healthy one. At any rate I feel very fit, and I could eat less to some advantage.

Gabriel called me in excitement yesterday. His company had been financed, and he was able to pay back what he owed me. So I'm well fixed—will even have enough to pay my way to No. Africa if my priority—and permission come through. So far no word of that. The O.W.I. have cabled Bob and so have I, so perhaps something will happen suddenly. If I go I'll manage to get a cable to you somehow, no matter how rushed my departure. Maybe I'll have to set out without my African kit. The trunk hasn't arrived yet. Garretson's came yesterday, and so did Miss Ives'. But they had started before the Pinto sailed.

Darling, I've never in my life talked to so many interesting people and seen so many interesting things in such a short space of time. Since I came to London there's been a constant flow of things to do and see, till I've been almost bewildered—and occasionally unable to choose among different experiences that offer themselves. It's truly an exciting and inspiring country. But one can't be in more than one place at a time. This week-end I'd like very much to look at a fighter field and talk to some of the pilots. They're the boys who drive the raiders away every time they try to reach London. But Wyler wants me to go with him to live with the bomber pilots and since I've promised to write that continuity for him—I'm doing that.

Last night I had dinner with Michael Redgrave, who is playing in *A Month in the Country*, and Manning Whiley, who has just closed a long run in *Rain*. Whiley wants to put on *The Wingless Victory* here in September, and Redgrave is to direct it. Miss Rotha, who played the lead in *Rain* for 13 months, wants to play Oparre. In fact she's so mad about the part she's turned down other things just on the chance of my allowing her to do it. I think they'll do a good job. I'm going to do some re-writing for them. The sets are brilliantly designed—really romantic and beautiful, judging by the drawings.[2]

I'm having lunch today with Harvey Gibson, who is the head of the Red Cross (Amer) here.[3] What I want of him is that the Red Cross arrange to pay for the theatre where Rusty Lane puts on *St. Mark*. It seems that if the army puts the play on it's impossible to charge admission. But if Gibson wants to he can probably arrange the theatre rent under lend-lease rules. This afternoon I'm going to see The Ambassadors, a theatre which Gabby says would be good for *The Eve*, though rather too small for ordinary commercial productions. It's practically the only one available. Theatre business here is terrific —for everything.

By the way, I've written a new scene for the London production of *St. Mark*. Maybe I'll include a copy in this letter and you can get Victor to put it in the New York production if it's still worth while. It's a dream scene that takes the place of the two dream scenes already there. Or it could be put in place of the scene with the girl.[4]

If you haven't my permanent address in London—if it wasn't in my last letter—I'd better include it here. It's 34 South Molton Street. In case I go to Africa I'll move out of Claridges and put my things in the So. Molton flat. I've kept the Claridge room only because they take telephone messages and you know that address. It's not very expensive. The little flat costs almost nothing. And Garretson is a very nice boy, a brilliant sensible mind and we're good company for each other.

If you should be coming—and want to cable money over here to have when you get here I've opened an account—in my name, of course—at The National City Bank of New York, 11, Waterloo Place, S.W.1., London. I'm not sure you'll need to send any. If I work for Rank or Pascal I'll be able to earn a living here—and if you work for one of them you'll have your own income. I'll know more about that tonight.

Mab, dear, I haven't told you what a thrill it was to get your letter. After so many days in that vacuum you were talking about. It makes the world look so different to be reassured—to know that you're there and just as lonely as I am. —I can't quite make up my mind whether I want to live here or not— but I know it would be fun to be here with you. You'd really love it—and we'd have wonderful times together. So if we do manage to meet here—and our stay lasts a long time—I don't think we'll ever be sorry.

—Well, I had lunch with Harvey Gibson, who is the head of the American Red Cross here—and he says he will guarantee that we get a playhouse for *The Eve*. That's a great relief, for we're not allowed to charge admission. —Before I forget to tell you—let me put in a word about luggage. I think the air-lines have put an end to the excess baggage out of Lisbon. You will be able to carry only 44 lbs. And Hesper the same if she were along. However, Mr. Gibson rather disheartened me about your passport. He said that his wife was the last wife to sail from the U.S. for England to join her husband. There is a strict army and embassy rule that husbands and wives must not be sent to the same theatre of war. If you were just a scenario writer, without any connection with me, you'd get the permit right away on Rank's request.[5]

Gabby told me this afternoon that I could have any amount I wanted as an advance on the life-boat story. It seems I *could* make a living here. And I'd like to write a play to go on in England first. But if you can't come I'll feel like going home as soon as I've seen North Africa. Another aside—there are no copies of my plays over here. Could you send a copy of the 11 verse plays?[6] Whiley says I'm practically out of print and unobtainable in London.

Friday morning. [May 7, 1943]

Well, darling, it begins to look as if it might happen. It's 6:30 A.M., and I'm not able to sleep any more, so I sit up in bed to write the news. I had dinner with Rank, who is a plain North-countryman, in spite of his wealth, and he seems to have taken to me greatly. We talked at length about the theatre and pictures, and he developed a great desire to have me stay in this country, at least long enough to do a picture—the survivor story—for Gabby. He had his lawyer in, and we went over the possibility of your coming, for I told him I was unwilling to remain here long without you and that your help was essential if I were to settle down to write a play and a picture here. The lawyer said he thought your coming was quite possible if you were needed to work with me. I'm going to talk to him today about Hesper. But if he can get you over he can get Hesper too, I believe, for the main difficulty seems to be the husband and wife prejudice in the State Department and the high command. However, I have experienced something of the power of the English picture-companies in the transportation field. Gabby and I stayed only three days in Lisbon. And lots of folks wait there for months for a plane. Gabby has discovered it was Rank's gang that got us here so fast. I'll send you a cable today, indicating what may happen. And Smith, Rank's lawyer, will cable his message to the states about you—and things will start moving. You would probably have to come by the Pinto—a long journey—and you may have to wait, as I did, for things to happen —but the matter is now in train.

It might be a long absence, for the going back is a real difficulty. And so you would have to leave the house and our affairs in charge of someone else. Maybe Nancy would move over. If she would you could put her name on our bank account and let her have a list of the monthly checks, etc. With some responsiblity too for making decisions, such as helping Lawrence and Lillian if he's drafted. Or Quentin could take over these matters if Nancy didn't want to move. Either would be satisfactory to me—and so would Meg. All three seem to be fairly permanent residents of the road.[7]

If I do go to No. Africa you may arrive here in my absence, in which case I'll have parked my things at 34 South Molton St., and you could always stay there if Claridges had no room for you. There's only one bed in my room, and beds are at a premium here, but you could get along there at least till you found something else. The landlady's name is Mrs. Daftis, and she's very nice. Garretson you'll like I know. He has the other room of the flat. The cooking arrangements, by the way, are in my room, and consist of an electric plate and some pots and pans and dishes. Garry and I have only made tea there. —You'll have to make up your mind not to be too particular about food, anyway, and Hesper will want to carry her B-complex, etc, in quantity, and you'll get used to the rooms being heated in the English fashion—they like them much cooler than Americans—and this too with nothing sheer on your legs. Some of the women here have a real nostalgia for American nylon but the Scotch soldiers go about with nothing on their shanks below the kilts and a girl can get used to the same.

One other reason occurs to me for having another name on the Spring Valley account. If we should need to cable for money somebody would have to get cash to send. You could bring a good-sized sum with you, just to be sure you weren't stuck on route—and could cable Spring Valley or New City in case of emergency. I doubt that I'd be allowed to help you from here. You might possibly be stuck in Lisbon, God forfend, and people have been known to run out of money there. If you and Hesper and I live here I'd plan to earn enough to live on. It wouldn't be much—nobody has much after taxes—not even Rank— but we could easily live on little here because we'd have no establishment beyond a furnished flat or something of the sort.

It's 7:30 AM and I've been writing for an hour, trying to remember what advice to give about the journey, for it's possible I'll not have a later chance to write about it. If I hear you're on the Pinto I'll cable the Hotel Avez in Lisbon to reserve a room for you. The manager is a friend of Gabby's. Or the assistant manager. The food on the Pinto is pretty bad, but the Avez makes up for it.

—It occurs to me maybe Miss Grieser would accept extra baggage to send to me—even if she couldn't for you—and you could send extra baggage that way. You'll certainly need a trunkful of things if you're here for the winter—and Hesper too. There are a lot of things you'd never buy here and would have to bring—nearly all winter garments. If you do send a trunk would you include in it a couple of dozen jars of that Squibb product I have been using? They don't have them here. —Be sure to eat lots of oranges on the ship. They're good for you.

4:30 PM Friday—Darling, I must take this over to get it started, and will only add a word. May you keep safe! I'll never forgive myself if I advise you badly and you come to harm. Before you get this you'll hear from me by cable. All my love, dearest, to you and Hesper—thank her for those sweet letters. I've had two from her. It would be wonderful to see you here—both of you—

Max

Saturday, May 8—7:30 A.M.

Darling—

I kept this last night, after all, because I found I could mail it this morning. Last night I made a speech—on the American theatre, not very good, but I got to know some people out of it and it was passable. Got home so late I didn't write any more. This morning the paper announces the capture of Bizerta and Tunis[8]—so now I don't know whether I'll go to Africa at all. It may be too late to get a notion of what it was like—and so far I've heard nothing from the powers that be concerning permission.

Wyler is not going to the bomber field today as he planned, but Major Jack Whitney is, and it seems I'm going with him. But first I must mail this and talk something over with Gabby. He's pushing me to decide to do a picture for him in England, and I keep saying that I won't stay long enough for that unless it's definite that you're coming over. And I wasn't able to get hold of Rank's lawyer yesterday to hear what he thought—or had concluded—about Hesper. I'll try to do that this morning, but probably won't be able to reach him before this is mailed. It seems to depend on just how much influence Rank has, and though he has a great deal such a request might go too far. At any rate you'll have found out from me by cable before this can cross the Atlantic. —My trip to the same bomber station, which I visited last time, will probably hold me till Monday morning. I saw Whitney in the elevator here the other night. He's in the air intelligence service —more or less the same sort of thing Burgess will be with.[9]

These last days I've been so really dated up that I've had to hurry from one thing to another—but it's all so fascinating I can't bear to turn down any chance. This morning I was wakened by the air raid sirens, so there must have been German planes about. I heard no bombs, however, only some distant ack-ack guns.

Sweet, I know you must be in a puzzled mood, unable to move on this matter of your coming, and wondering why no definite word comes through. But I'm baffled, too—and just have to wait on the movements and decisions of people who don't move fast and may not all mean what they say. I won't stay here for a long period, though, unless you can come. And I've made that clear. Also—it's tempting here—they offer me so much—but I don't want to end up an expatriate. I'll have to be an American writer to the last.

But I'm doing all I can—and you'll hear. All my love, dear—

Max[10]

1. Another of the composite letters, written from the South Molton Street address in London, its entries dated May 6, May 7 (6:30 A.M. and 4:30 P.M.), and May 8 (7:30 A.M.)

2. *The Wingless Victory* was produced by Bernard Delfort at the Phoenix Theatre in London, opening on September 8, 1943. Redgrave (b. 1908), British actor and director, directed the production. Wanda Rotha, international actress born in Vienna, had the lead (Oparre), supported by her husband, the British actor Manning Whiley (b. 1915). *A Month in the Country*, in which Redgrave was starring, was an adaption by Emlyn Williams of the Turgenev novel that had opened on February 11, 1943. And *Rain*, in which Rotha and Whiley had played, was the 1922 dramatization by John Colton and Clemence Randolph of Somerset Maugham's story "Miss Thompson."

3. Harvey D. Gibson (1882–1950), president of Manufacturers Trust Company of New York, had taken a leave of absence in 1942 to become American Red Cross Commissioner to Great Britain.

4. For the new scene, see Appendix I, no. 3. Mrs. Anderson sent the scene to Victor Samrock, Business Manager of the Playwrights' Company (her cover letter, June 1, 1943, W), but apparently it was not inserted into the New York production of the play.

5. Note added at top of page: "Perhaps Miss Grieser will send luggage for you, by boat."

6. *Eleven Verse Plays*.

7. Nancy, wife of Anderson's son Alan, who was in the army in California at the time. Lawrence (Lillian was Lawrence's wife), Anderson's youngest brother. Quentin, Anderson's son; and Meg (Margaret), Quentin's wife.

8. On May 7 the U.S. II Corps and Eighth Army compelled the surrender of the Germans at the North African city of Bizerta and the British First Army captured Tunis. The Allied army under the British Gen. Alexander moving from the west and the British army under Gen. Montgomery moving from the east had crushed the German army under Field Marshall Rommel, and the capture of Bizerta and Tunis signaled the end of German resistance to the Allies in North Africa.

9. Burgess Meredith (b. 1907), Anderson's neighbor in Rockland County and actor (lead in *Winterset*, *High Tor*, *The Star-Wagon*), had entered the army earlier in 1943 (until 1945) and by July was stationed in London.

10. Note added at top of page: "Later: Gabriel says he thinks it better to ask for you first and then mention Hesper—we may do that. He still thinks Rank is able to arrange the whole matter. So what I hope is a good voyage for such precious freight. Max"

121. TO GERTRUDE ANDERSON

[London]
May 11, [1943]

Mab darling—

Another letter from you today—and one from Hesper. I've had three from her now—two from you, one from Alan. I'm trying to get the mail that went to Lisbon, but so far it's not here. —It was wonderful to hear that my long London screed had reached you and you at least knew what had happened. I sent another letter which was pre-censored here and carried by Agar—then another by the head of the O.W.I. here. So far I don't know how fast they went, of course. I'm going to write several pages tonight, have them censored as fast as possible and try to get them off by a Red Cross official who is going home on a mission. So much happens that I can't even try to set it all down. It seems as if I hear and see new and startling things every day. And my poor little one-page diary just can't contain even the exterior facts.

The last letter I wrote you stopped, I think, with my evening with Arthur Rank. Since then I've tried to make out whether or not his lawyer was really going to work to get you here—and I can't be quite sure. Talking with the lawyer over the phone yesterday I got the impression that he had made all the necessary preliminary steps, but I wasn't sure how much pressure he was prepared to bring. Then today and yesterday Gabby and I talked about the picture he wants me to write at this moment—and I told him that I was very doubtful about starting anything of that sort till I was sure you were coming. He began to assure me at once that if he urged Rank very hard Rank could certainly put it through leaving the impression that he would have to keep after Rank and his lawyer.—As things look now I shan't get to Africa. If I stay I'll be staying in England, with the possibility of jumping off if something happens near here and I can get permission to go. I can write a picture and make a good deal of money—but I wouldn't be gathering material if I did that. And I do want to have a play for the fall. So far I have two possibilities for the theatre. One, the survivor story and the other about the Flying Fortress. This week-end I spent at a Fortress field—met Sir Stafford Cripps there, by the way[1] —and talked with many and many a pilot. Even had dinner with the enlisted men of a pilot's crew—and heard them babble enthusiastically about their ship and their captain—and their methods of fighting the Germans and getting safely home. It's beautiful stuff. I just don't know yet what I want to do. —Perhaps I shouldn't write another play about the war. Perhaps I should do a picture for Rank instead. It would be easier to decide these things if I knew what was going to come of your priority.

I must tell you how your letter got here. I was out having lunch with Russell Lane, who is going to direct *St. Mark* for the army here, and Gabby. When I got back there was an envelope under my door from Victor. A letter had arrived for him from Anne. He opened it and there was only a letter for me from you. He said he hated me heartily for a while in spite of your very graceful apology. Hesper's letter was in with yours, of course.

And Nancy has gone to visit Alan! That's news—and quite a trip for so young a child.[2] But it's the easiest age for travelling in some ways.

I had lunch with Jonathan Cape one day,[3] and he's been very nice to me. Put me on the track of my publishers here—the Bodley Head. I found their office today—but they had not one book of mine. Several people who have wanted to put on my plays here have been unable to get copies. I find I have considerable reputation in London, but it's all hear-say. Nobody—or very few—have seen a play of mine—or read one. Yet in one of those bomber crews I talked to the other day there was a gunner who had read *The Eve* before he came over. He'd got hold of it in a university library. And he was already a veteran! Had made twenty-three flights over enemy territory!

By the way—you will see Quentin. I'm reading a book which I'd like to recommend to him—*Modern Man in Search of a Soul*.[4] I've only begun it, really, but it seems to be a very intelligent and greatly modernized discussion of analysis and its relation to everyday living. —I shall mail you, before I forget it, a couple of photos of myself giving a copy of my play to Col. Orter for the use of the armed forces in the United Kingdom. Victor tells me that he sent Anne a copy of *The Stars and Stripes* with a picture of me on the front page.

This business of bringing Hesper over—versus leaving her there —has me a bit confused. No doubt you feel the same way. If she were able to come there'd always be the risk involved. It's always possible for even a Portuguese ship to go down—"by accident," of course—

and we'd feel responsible. But if you came you'd probably stay for the duration—and it's not quite possible to imagine you here for a year with me—and Hesper at home. So I'm more at sea about that than about anything else. But if it turned out well I'd like it very much. And of course the chances are it would turn out well. The English schools are an unknown quantity to me but I rather think they're good.[5]

One cable came from Terry—saying he was still waiting in Goldsboro for something to happen.[6] That was dated Apr 26th. He said he was writing, and he may have, but no letter has come. For that matter I've had only 2 of yours, and you've sent more, I know. That's the only communication that has come to me via the American Embassy. The letters you sent to that address just haven't arrived. But I have told you that other people's letters appear to arrive helter-skelter and in reverse order most of the time.

Since I wrote you I've seen some plays. Three or rather two and a quarter. Saw Coward's *Present Laughter* first night, and *Heartbreak House*, which features Deborah Kerr, the girl for whom Gabby wants me to write the picture, and the first two scenes of *A Month in the Country*.[7] The Coward play is funny but cheap. Picture of a great playwright, obviously Coward, and played by himself, who is so over-run by visitors and letters and girls who have lost their latch-keys and want to stay the night with him that he finally cuts the gordian knot by going back to his first wife. *Heartbreak House* is clever and funny and somewhat dated. But Shaw will allow no cutting or changing. I saw a letter of Shaw's to Gabby today in which he said he wanted very much to meet "Anderson," but would have to put it off till his wife is better. *A Month in the Country* was so boring I left. The theatre here is exceedingly prosperous, and in a terrible slump artistically. Quite a lot of American plays running—old ones—no really good English ones. But everything goes. It's almost impossible to get a theatre. Old things —*What Every Woman Knows*, and Drinkwater's *Abraham Lincoln* and *Watch on the Rhine* run on and on. Even the picture version of *Gone with the Wind* has been running here for years. *Flare Path*, which failed quickly in N.Y., is nearing the end of its first year here.[8] It's mainly comedy they want. The tone has sunk a lot since the beginning of the war.

Sweet—I'm terribly lonely, and feel like starting off for home the moment I can get a chance—and yet I feel too that this is where I must be if I want to learn a lot of essential things. So I grit my teeth and cling to my determination to stick with it till I've really soaked in enough of the war and this atmosphere so that I'll be able to report on both. I know that if I took a plane this week and landed at New City —I'd be so happy I wouldn't care about anything else. But later I'd be sorry. I keep remembering that I was like a fish out of water at Fort Bragg—yet that was an invaluable week I spent there.[9] And this has already been immensely valuable. Those poor lads at the flying stations, how lonesome they get for their girls and homes! But they love flying. And the things they do are simply magnificent. I've heard enough tales of heroism, told quite casually and unemotionally, to last the theatre for years.

I'll be seeing Gabby tomorrow about that picture and you'll probably get a cable one way or another soon.

All my love, darling,
Max

1. Cripps (1889–1952), prominent in British governments before and after the war and early in the war ambassador to the U.S.S.R. (1940–42), was at the time Minister of Aircraft Production (1942–45).

2. Nancy, wife of Anderson's son Alan, who was in the army on assignment in Hollywood to make war documentaries. Their son, Alan, Jr. (b. February 22, 1943), was not quite three months old at the time. Nancy and the child lived on South Mountain Road, not far from Anderson's home.

3. Jonathan Cape (1879–1960), founder and head of the English publishing firm Jonathan Cape Ltd.

4. Carl Gustav Jung, *Modern Man in Search of a Soul* (New York, 1934).

5. Hesper (b. August 10, 1934) was nearly nine.

6. Anderson's son Terence was in the army stationed at Goldsboro, N.C.

7. Noel Coward's *Present Laughter* had opened at the Haymarket Theatre in London on April 29, 1943. Shaw's *Heartbreak House* (written 1913–16, first produced 1920) in its present production had Deborah Kerr (b. 1921) in the role of Ellie Dunn. For *A Month in the Country*, see no. 120, n. 2.

8. *What Every Woman Knows*, James M. Barrie's play, was first produced in 1908. John Drinkwater's *Abraham Lincoln* had been produced first in 1918. And *Watch on the Rhine*, Lillian Hellman's play, was still running in its original production, which began in 1941. Margaret Mitchell's *Gone with the Wind* (1936) had its first motion-picture adaptation in 1939. For *Flare Path*, see no. 118, n. 5.

9. In February, 1942, Anderson had spent a week at Fort Bragg, N.C., and then visited other military bases in preparation for writing *The Eve of St. Mark*.

122. TO HESPER ANDERSON

[London]
May 11, [1943]

Dear Hesper—

I've had three letters from you and it's beginning to be high time you got at least one from me. It's hard work to write letters but it's lots of fun to get them. Imagine me sitting in a small hotel room with nothing in it but a couple of tables and a couple of beds—one I sleep in and the other is covered with books—and I'm just sitting here trying to remember what you look like while I write you a letter.

Let me tell you a story I heard about two gunners in a B17—a Flying Fortress. There are ten men in the crew. Pilot, co-pilot, navigator, bombardier, radio man, two waist gunners, one tail gunner, one under-turret gunner and one engineer. They fly so high and it gets so cold up there that they have to wear electrically heated clothes. Otherwise they would freeze solid. And there's no air to speak of up there so they have to wear oxygen masks constantly. If the oxygen mask comes off and the man doesn't get it back on quickly he loses consciousness—and pretty soon he smothers. Well, once a Fortress was in a battle up there and one of the waist gunners was wounded and fell down and his mask came off. The other gunner grabbed the walkie-oxygen tank and went over to the wounded man and gave him a few whiffs, and he came to. But then the second gunner had passed out for lack of oxygen, and the first one, the wounded one, gave the other a few whiffs. He came to and by that time the wounded one was out again. They went on like that, giving each other drinks of oxygen, till they were out of the battle and somebody noticed them and dragged them over to their own masks where they could breathe again. That isn't a very funny story but it's one of the best I've heard about the war.

I certainly hope it works out so that you and mother can come to England, because I know you'd both be so excited about coming and about being here. But if you can't come then I'll want to come home as soon as I've had time to see a few more American soldiers and learn a few more things about England. I went down to the British Museum today because I wanted to see the Elgin Marbles again. They are the Greek statues that Keats wrote about. But the Museum is closed now.[1]

Mother tells me you've been learning some poems, and that reminds me of the time when you were learning "The Eve of St. Mark."[2] We've had the kind of spring here that is described in that poem. Cold, drizzly, foggy, torpid, soggy, aguish, windy—everything that mother doesn't like. And not much heat in the houses, so she'd have been freezing. However the weather began to look a little better today. You asked whether my cold was still following me around like a shadow. It was about the worst cold I ever had, but it's about gone now. I'm glad you're over "peek-eye" as you called it. And I'm glad you're learning to skip rope. If you ever want to be a prize-fighter that will be invaluable.

It's getting later and later here. Twenty minutes past eleven. That means it's twenty minutes past five where you are. Why, you haven't even had dinner yet. And where Alan is it's only twenty minutes past two.[3] That's ridiculous. Demi-morale has just had lunch. Alan is still working at Warner Brothers. And here I'm thinking of going to bed. Maybe I'd better write to Alan first. I haven't written to him yet.

Goodnight, Hesper darling.
Daddy

1. For one of its periodic cleanings.
2. Keats's unfinished poem that stands importantly behind Anderson's play of the same title.
3. Alan was in Hollywood at work on war films. His wife and infant son ("Demi-morale") were visiting him there at the time.

123. TO GERTRUDE ANDERSON

[London]
May 18, [1943][1]

Mab darling—

I've been in such confusion lately that I haven't tried to write. Anything I can say about my plans would change within hours—and by the time I sat down to tell you something it was no longer the case. Saturday your two cables came, saying you'd given up coming over for the present. I tried to answer and then maddeningly my cable was held up (in N.Y.) for insufficient address. Not merely held up, cancelled. Then I got off another, and in the same moment met Peter Cusic— Edla's husband—and he sicked me on the Ministry of Information, saying he knew people there who could get me to Africa. I went to see them, thinking I might make my trip and then go straight home. They were very encouraging, said they would arrange it in about a week— and I thought I was set. (There goes an alert—the 2nd since I sat down here.) So I began to get ready to go. That was Saturday. —Sunday I was happy and took a walk in Hyde Park, listening to the orators, since I'd get to Algiers. Monday I went to Lloyd's bank and found the Bank of England won't let me take money out of England without a special permission which may take time to get. Then I went to see Col. Tuppen of Public Relations, and he told me he had asked Eisenhower's permission to send me to Africa but hadn't received it yet. Went then to Brewster Morgan[2] who didn't like it at all that I had gone to the British for help and told me there was no use trying to leave unless I got the word from Eisenhower. I'd be stranded forever in Lisbon. Coming home I got a call from the Ministry of Information—and they have a seat for me on the Friday plane but they say I'd better not go without the permission—so now I have transportation and can't use it. The petty jealousies of gov't officials are really quite extraordinary. Every one defending his own little bailiwick of power—and trying to gather allegiance to himself by being nice to everybody—or seeming to be. The rivalry between the Red Cross and Special Services over the doing of my play[3] was disheartening to observe. On the whole I like the head of the Red Cross here—Mr. Harvey Gibson—about as little as anybody I've met. Why they have to pick big business men with no ambition except for themselves to run such an organization I can't fathom. There are plenty of intelligent and generous people in the Red Cross here, but the big boss has to be one of the Wall St. wrecker gang.

I do know how you feel about the passport difficulty, darling— and I think there was no use quarreling with them about it. The best I can do now is to make plans for coming over again, and bringing you and Hesper for part of each year. It's a delightful country to be in—at least it would be if you were here too—and I've never before felt I could take part so easily in so many ventures. That is, I feel as if I'd be welcome here. And you'd fit in just the same way. Of course I don't mean to change countries. But England doesn't really seem foreign when you've been here a while. If I only had time to see a little of the country before I leave. I haven't had time to go to Scotland! And each day I'm rushing about on some futile errand connected with trying to get somewhere. Or to do something for somebody. Sunday I was re-writing the *Wingless Victory* for the production here. Today I was trying to think about that continuity for Wyler, but never got started. One spends so many hours going from one dreary office to another. Just trying to get arm-bands—for example. The correspondents here wear another, less conspicuous one—but they're all gone—can't get any more. And every day I go past the American Embassy—hoping for letters or my extra baggage. So far nothing. Not one piece of mail (or freight) have I received out of all those visits. If I do go to Africa soon I'll have to go without that tropical equipment—and I can't buy even cotton socks at the moment. But believe me I'll go—with anything I happen to have on—if the word comes through.

Wed. [May 19, 1943] 3:20 A.M. —Dear—I was wakened by terrific gunfire all about—and in the darkness I couldn't remember where I was. It was so strange to try to figure out my relation to that crackling, smashing confusion. It's faded away now. I can barely hear it in the distance. I heard planes overhead—and bombs were dropped—where I have no idea, but uncomfortably close. It's light moonlight. I'm about to put my light out and look out.

Midnight—Wed., May 19, [1943]
Darling—an alert has just sounded again—it's another brilliant moonlit night. So far I hear no ack-ack or bombs—not even in the distance.

First let me thank you for a sweet and beautiful letter that came this morning—it's the one you wrote after you heard the broadcast, and it contained a clipping about Terry. I've had a later letter, but I was most happy to get this one, because it said so many things I wanted to hear, and it at least gave me an intimation of what those early letters that haven't come must be like. I hope I get them sometime. It's a temptation—you know me—to turn round now and go home to you, for I'm as much in love with home as you are with travelling. And I miss you terribly. Everywhere I go I look for your face, and—because you aren't there the place is empty.

And now I'm on the point of making a major decision. I have the visas and the seat on the plane. At nine in the morning I shall go to the British Overseas⁴ and ask them if they're prepared to sell me through tickets to the destination I've had in mind all along. If they are I'll be tempted to buy the passage and start on Friday, leaving it to Brewster Morgan and Col. Tupper to get permission for me to enter Continental Africa. You will hear from me about money anyway, if I go, for I still haven't got the Bank of England to release any of my funds—even the traveller's checks which I brought in with me. And since I'm getting up early I'd better go to bed. Goodnight—dear lover. I hope you have the cable I sent today. I want a word from you before I start.

May 20, [1943]—11:45 A.M.

Darling—I went over to the British Overseas and bought a ticket to Gibraltar good for tomorrow. Then I came back and asked Col. Tupper if he'd heard from Gen. Eisenhower, and he had not. I went then to Brewster Morgan—and he said well, perhaps I'd better go and he'd try to get my permission quickly so that I wouldn't be stuck too long on the Rock. So he called some people about my itinerary among them the American transport officer here, who, as soon as he heard I was going with the British said "What's the matter with us? Why doesn't he go with the American Army Service? We've got lots of space?" Well, when I heard that I began to reconsider my Gibraltar plan—for the American planes don't stop at all, and I'd get much more directly where I want to go. So I finally decided to wait here a while longer for the Eisenhower word. I can turn in the ticket, so nothing lost. Not even time, I guess, for this route is less round-about, and once I get my army clearance I shouldn't be hung up any where. It's better to have a little more time here anyway. I heard the London cast read *The Eve* last night—with the new scene—and it was really exciting. It sounded like a good play—and they're good actors. Happy and eager. The new scene is a great improvement. And today we go to see some people about the Haymarket Theatre—we're likely to get it for the month of July. After that we don't know. *The Wingless Victory* people haven't got a theatre yet but are determined to start in Sept. anyway. I'm having lunch with Victor Rapport today. He called—had heard from Anne, says that on May 10th you'd had only the one letter. Something must have gone wrong.

May 21, [1943]

Darling—the permission has just come through. I don't know yet when I start, but the transport folks said yesterday there were plenty of seats on the planes—so it shouldn't take long. I begin to feel breathless—on the verge of a hop so breathtaking. My trunk hasn't come yet—so I have no African equipment, but I'll try to buy a helmet and some light socks and let it go at that. I'm keeping the room at 34 South Molton St., and giving up my place at Claridges. Garretson will pick up any messages that come here for me, and will act as my agent and friend in general. His address is A. H. Garretson, 34 So. Molton, office 40 Berkley Sq.—he's connected with the Amer. Embassy—a Bureau of Econ. Warfare man. My bank account here is now at Lloyds Bank, 62 Brook St., London. £643. You'll hear from me, of course, from Africa. I may possibly come home directly from there—or may come this way if it seems to be quicker or preferable.

Yesterday afternoon I attended a sort of board meeting at Rank's office. He was very busy and hurried, but he seemed greatly disappointed that I was not staying longer in England, and fell in at once with my suggestion that I spend 3 winter months of each year here to help with scripts. He said, "put it down in black and white—anything you want." I said, "I don't know whether I'll want much of anything—perhaps expenses." We left it that way.

Midnight—Friday—[May 21, 1943]

Your telegram came—and darling I shall keep safe if I can and come home to you. Maybe this will be the last letter I get off before I go toward N. Africa, for I shall probably get about the first plane that has a vacancy. And Ed Murrow[5] is leaving for the States soon by a fast route—so I may decide to get this over to him early in the morning, let him show it to the censor and take it with him. But maybe I'll just air mail it. Or give it to Victor. The one I gave him seems to have gone most rapidly.

I'm feeling very happy about this trip today. Already it's given me an immense store of background and material—and two possible plays. But the play I want to write is the story of Anglo-American relations in Africa and elsewhere—and so I must go south to get that straight in my mind. If I do it Gabby wants to produce it here next fall—with Rusty Lane directing. Maybe we can work out a trans-Atlantic system. At any rate this one play I have in mind should be as good in London as in New York. And since I want it to be largely comic it should be good at least in one of the two cities.[6] —It may be an illusion—and I may never get around to the projects I have in mind—but I do feel a stirring of many impulses—and perhaps I shall really get around at last to writing that really great play. I dream of that still. But if I never get to that, well, I shall still have come as close as I could. If I wanted to flatter myself and think I had done something already I've had plenty of temptation toward that here. I've met a number of really fine people who take me much more seriously than I'll ever be able to take myself. I can only hope there's something in it—or will be before I'm through.

Darling—I love you always—wherever I am—and will get back to you as fast as I can. May the winds and tides be auspicious and let me see you soon.

Max

May 22, [1943], 2:30 AM

Darling—I went to sleep about 12:30, and at 2:30 I woke and couldn't sleep, so I was reading. Then the alert sounded and I've been sitting at the window watching for searchlights and listening to the guns. Sitting there I tried to think out an epitaph for a modern. It would run something like this:

> *The psychologists, analyzing thought,*
> *come upon flesh and matter; the*
> *physicists, analyzing matter,*
> *reduce it to something no more*
> *ponderable than thought. Something*
> *of this there was here.*

Shucks, it's no good. I'll go back to bed. —On second thought I think I would like to have that on my tomb-stone.

Dear—It's now 12:30—and I'm to have lunch with Willie Wyler—so I'll just write a word about this morning. It's been quite eventful. First I got a bottle of whiskey to take over to Miss Ives at O.W.I., and she made some phone calls for me. (The whiskey was a present. She couldn't get any.) As a result of the calls I found I could go whenever I wished. Put my name down for Monday. Went then to see a heart specialist (Army—formerly Johns Hopkins) because my quinidine is running low, and I wanted if possible to take some extra to N.A. He examined me thoroughly—seems to know more about hearts and fibrillation than Friedberg,[7] —says it's caused by scarring. Results probably from early rheumatic fever. And does shorten life. So I'll have to stay on quinidine or digitalis the rest of my days. It doesn't really matter. If only I can write that great play. —That letter from the boy at Chapel Hill, translator of Ibsen, was at the Embassy this morning.[8] The first mail I've ever received there and it was sent on April 3rd. Was marked "Insufficient postage for transatlantic air mail" so it probably came by boat. I think I'll get Victor to send this letter off. —Oh, yes, to get back to the quinidine. I can get a little more but not till Tuesday eve., so I may postpone my start till I have that supply.

One heartening thing I do learn. My tour of N.A. may not take too long, for I'll be sent about by air. Since my bag hasn't arrived I must go today and buy some tropical clothes.

—That letter from the boy in Chapel Hill was really touching. He feels the way Rusty Lane does—the one who's doing *St. Mark* here. Wish it were true.

10 P.M.

The Embassy called to say there was a letter for me, and I walked over to get it. It was written Apr 11 on V mail paper and is marked "insufficient postage for transatlantic air mail." You hadn't yet heard of my arrival in Lisbon. But it's rather nice to get these letters gradually. One has fun piecing everything together. And Hesper's remark was sweet. She wrote me later to say that she did miss me.

I went alone to the officers' mess for dinner, and, as always happens, a fellow sat down beside me and we began to talk. It turned out he's writing a book, a soldier's impressions of England, and he came over to the hotel with me to show me some of it. He was rather diffident about the whole thing, but some of the chapters were very good and so I encouraged him to finish it and send it to Bill Sloane. As a matter of fact I gave him your address and said if he sent it to you you'd give it to Bill. His name is Lt. Frank M. Kearns. You'll probably receive a MS.[9]

I couldn't get any clothes today, and will have to wait till Monday. Saw Pare Lorentz[10] at the transportation office and he said I'd better get the light uniform here. It'll be hot as hell in Algiers. I sent you a cable this afternoon saying my trip was delayed and would you send a hundred to Algiers. Thought that would at least give you a notion of where I might be. It was sent about 5:30 P.M. At that time it's 11:30 A.M. in New City. You should get it today, may have it by dinner time, any way. Tomorrow I'm to have breakfast with Wyler—he's to spill to me all he thinks about the air force—he's made two sweeps over Germany or France lately—and I'm to write a continuity for his picture. I'll work all afternoon—and get it done, for I'll have no more time.

Sunday

Dear—I've decided to put stamps on this and send it off air mail—and get off a shorter one before I leave Tuesday. Today I'm working all day with Wyler on his film, writing the continuity, taking notes and seeing pictures of flights. Have been with him all morning and will see a film with him in a few minutes.

I'm waiting here now for Willie to call and we'll go over to the studio together—we're looking at a lot of film of operational flights—wonderful things; I've seen some.

I love you, sweet. Thank you for dear letters I've got—and the others that haven't come yet. We'll compare notes when we get together. Kiss Hesper for me. —There's Willie's ring—Goodbye, darling—

Max

1. A composite letter, the dates of its several entries being: May 18 (Tuesday); May 19, 3:20 A.M. (Wednesday); May 19, midnight; May 20, 11:45 A.M. (Thursday); May 21 (Friday); May 21, midnight; May 22, 2:30 A.M. (Saturday); May 22, 12:30 P.M.; May 22, 10:00 P.M.; May 23 (Sunday).

2. Morgan (1907–60), before and after the war a radio and television producer with CBS, was at the time Chief of Broadcasting and Communications for the Psychological Warfare Group of the American 12th Army.

3. *The Eve of St. Mark*.

4. British Overseas Airways Corporation (BOAC).

5. Edward R. Murrow (1908–65) had become European director for CBS news in 1937 and during the war became famous for his daily "This is London" broadcasts, which began with the chiming of Big Ben.

6. *Storm Operation*, the play that resulted from Anderson's trip to North Africa, was not produced in London.

7. Anderson's physician in New York.

8. Kai Jurgensen (1916–71), at the time a graduate student in the Department of Dramatic Arts at the University of North Carolina. With Robert F. Schenkkan (b. 1917), a fellow graduate student, he had translated *Peer Gynt* and *The Wild Duck*

during 1941 and 1942, though the translations were not published until 1966, when Jurgensen was a member of the faculty at the University of North Carolina and Schenkkan was president of the educational television network in Texas.

9. Kearns's manuscript was not published. William Sloane, an editor with Henry Holt Publishing Company (1939–46), in 1946 founded the publishing company William Sloane Associates, which (in association with Anderson House) published Anderson's second collection of essays, *Off Broadway* (1947), and two of his plays, *Anne of the Thousand Days* (1948) and *Lost in the Stars* (1949).

10. Lorentz, film critic (*Censored: The Private Life of the Movies* [1930]) and documentary film maker (*The Plow That Broke the Plains* [1936], *The River* [1937], *The Flight for Life* [1939]), was at the time with the Overseas Technical Unit of the Air Transport Command in London.

124. TO GERTRUDE ANDERSON

76 Rue Gallioni, Algiers
Aboulker residence
May 30, 1943[1]

Darling—

Things have happened so fast this last week that I haven't written down a word—and hardly thought a thought. For one thing I haven't been alone. I can't really remember when I sent off the last letter to you, but if I begin a narrative with last Tuesday I'll be covering a lot of ground. When the permission to go to Africa finally came through from the army things didn't pause. I could have left Sunday night, but had a few things to do—among them the continuity for Wyler's film—so I picked Tuesday. Monday I spent writing the continuity, Tuesday I moved everything to South Molton St and in the evening took a train to the airport. It was a sleeper and when I got to the station Wednesday morning I found that I could have the day to myself—wouldn't go out till evening. Well, it just happened that I was then near the bridge that Tam o' Shanter rode across, so I went to see that and to visit the birthplace and "Alloway's auld haunted kirk"—which was a ruin when the poem was written and still is.[2] That evening at ten o'clock we climbed on board, thirteen of us, and set out for the south. There were no sleeping accomodations, of course, and the toilet facilities were public and meager. There was considerable quiet fun over the fact that you had to move a certain French officer's feet every time you wanted to (as the British officers say) "splash your boots." A general was with us. He held out till the middle of the night—then his aide borrowed my flashlight and escorted him to the facilities. The French officer who slept so near the drains never woke up throughout all this. He had the only good bed—a packed up rubber boat—and he slept soundly. I stretched out on three aluminum "bucket-seats" and slept a little between one and four with somebody quietly kicking me in the face from time to time. It was an eleven hour trip, and we descended at nine in the morning at Marrakech, somewhere in No. Africa. No food en route except a cheese sandwich and a cup of water. There were many memorable things about that trip. I have never seen such cloud formations or such sunset effects as we got that first evening—as we flew over Ireland. Then the next morning we flew over clouds for a long time after sunrise—just white fleece rolling below us forever—and when it parted we caught a glimpse of blue sea far below. But— happening to look down one time I saw—not blue sea, but African fields—purple, yellow, red, burned brown mostly, like southern California; and obviously merging into desert. The further south we went the more desert-like things became. No towns through this region, only occasional 'dobe houses, red or brown clay, with walls about them of the same material—blistering hot in the midst of a great blistered area. At nine we came down at the Marrakech air-port and finally got onto a bus and drove a blistering hot way into a town on the edge of the Sahara. Really an oasis place. Seven of us were put in one room in the Casino (evidently the French had intended to make this place into a sort of Agua Caliente) where I got a few minutes sleep, then woke up to see as much of the place as we'd have time for before leaving. Drove about in a native rig—horses and an ancient contraption—with some fellow passengers, saw the bazaar, the native market, the Sultan's palace, now deserted, and then managed to wangle a room in a hotel along with Jim Cook, a War Shipping Board man. The filth, the poverty, the disease, the below stairs humanity of the place were quite sickening, and of course there was no water for baths, or toilet paper, nothing really ready for civilized occupation. How these people live: I've seen them picking over garbage pails in the alleys in Algiers, but Marrakech was a step beneath anything one quite believes. A sort of bad dream. It's hard to imagine applying democracy to such a population. Yet the workman-ship on the sultan's palace—who had 365 wives—was really incredibly beautiful—and in Marrakech I bought a couple of hand-bags, one for you and one for Hesper. Very fine leather work.

Just to get the time straight it was Tues. evening when I left London and Wed. evening when I got through looking at Burns relics and took the plane for Africa. Thursday morning we were in Marrakech. Thursday night I slept at the *La Mamounia*, an elegant hotel on the edge of the decline and fall of civilization, and Friday morning we began a series of hops in the general direction of Algiers. Fez, Casablanca, Oran, then here. It took all day, and at seven in the evening Jim Cook and I had just managed to get a billet from the army and a lieutenant had lent us two cots and two blankets to set up in a room which was empty for the night. We had decided to go without dinner because it was too late to get into the officers' mess, but then a sergeant came upstairs and told us we were invited to eat with the family who owned the house. It's a well-to-do family of many brothers and brothers-in-law, French and Jewish and very happy. They took us in at once, gave us an excellent meal and plied us with wine and brandy. The family name seems to be Aboulker, and they've given up the top floor of their city home to American and British soldiers. The billeting office had sent us here, and we've now slept two nights on those borrowed army cots with no pillows and no mosquito-netting. We're near the top of a hill here, and a long way from the center of the city, which makes transportation a difficulty. The view of the Mediterranean which we get on the way up and down is worth a lot of trouble, though, and the city is so crowded that we're lucky to have cots at all. Army officers are often reduced to sleeping on the floor. They say Algiers was built as a city of 250,000—and it now contains 500,000 civilians, to say nothing of the soldiers. And there must be 200,000 of them.

This is a terrible pen—I'll change it. —This is better—and I hope more legible. I've gone back to my old gold pen, but for some reason my hand doesn't retain its cunning. I write as if I'd never tried before. Very clumsy. Maybe it's the heat, maybe it's just lack of practice. To get on with the narrative—yesterday Cook and I went down to the junior officers' mess with Captains Potter and Hill and Lieutenant Schlanger, who are billeted on this floor also. —Along with many others, British and American. There was no water in the morning, but I had been warned by Schlanger that there might not be, so I had saved a quart in an empty Johnny Walker bottle. We came up the hill, shaved with that quart of water, and set out in the heat to locate our offices. I found O. H. P. Garrett, head of O.W.I. in Algiers,[3] and had lunch with a few of the OWI men in their own mess. When I tried to send you a message saying I was here I met with blank refusal, both from the Red Cross—which I finally located—and from my own office. I finally persuaded them to try to tack on a message concerning where I was to Miss Grieser. I hope she'll telephone you. At any rate this zone is entirely military and no private messages go out. I can write a letter and that's all.

After a talk with Garrett, and with C. D. Jackson, O.W.I. head in Africa,[4] I began to realize that the O.W.I. had nothing or little to do with my coming to Algiers, and was a bit astonished that I had got here. It came out then that the Public Relations office had probably arranged the whole matter, and Jackson suggested that I meet Commander Butcher, Eisenhower's aide,[5] and ask him for anything I wanted in the way of contacts, etc. It's been suggested that I might visit some of the rest camps where the soldiers who were in the thick of the fighting go to recuperate, but I may not need to ask for anything. Captain Hill and Capt. Potter, who live here, were in some of the scrimmages and Potter had his whole battery killed around him, escaping alone; also last night Cook and I had dinner with some enlisted men in a signal and communications group. I made friends with the top sergeant, who is a Keats enthusiast, and intend to see him again. He and his buddies drove us through a corner of the native quarter of Algiers—it seems there was a picture that used it for a background—and then we came home. A long talk with Potter about his experiences in the war, and then bed—or cot—after midnight. Up early this morning, which is Sunday—to officers' mess with Hill and Potter. Then a long talk with Cook, who is a Christian Sciencer—and then to write this letter. I've been writing a long time—and very badly—it's nearly twelve. I'm writing at Capt Potter's desk now. He has a nice room, has been here a long time. He says he writes to his wife every day. Just to keep in touch. Just to try to remember. Everything begins to seem so far away. I'll go to lunch now. Then this afternoon I'll try to catch up on sleep. —

Thursday P.M.
June 3, [1943]

Darling—

Again I have been snatched so rapidly from one activity to another that I haven't been able even to write my notes of what goes on—and no letter to you. But the letter begins to be a doubtful matter, as there's no way to send anything faster than I'll go myself. I feel terrible about not letting you know where I am, but I wasn't prepared for the censorship situation here. When we reached Marrakech I tried to send a word from there, but there seemed to be no facilities for it, so I had to let it go. Arriving here, that was my first thought, but again I couldn't reach anybody who seemed to know about telegrams, and as I told you I met only blank refusal at the Red Cross. Talking with Jackson, of the O.W.I., and Col. Phillips, of Public Relations, I find that there's a new ruling in the matter. No personal notifications or messages are supposed to go out at all—though up to last week the rule was not so strict. I arrived just in time to be blacked out completely—and I'm not even sure Miss Grieser got the notice of my arrival. I shall try again, now that I know people better, to slip a word in somewhere for you.

Now I must try to remember, for myself as well as for you, what's been happening so far. My first impressions were just a North African blur—made up of dust, heat, sunshine, crowded streets, military cars dashing up and down, ships in harbor, veiled women, more dust, more heat, delay, crowded offices, lifts that won't work, ten men in one billet, mosquitoes, no water in the taps, no baths, cold water shaves in water saved in a Johnny Walker bottle, French officers, British officers, American officers, salutes, Moorish castles taken over for supply depots, California sunshine, Scotch and English accents, crowded buses, paper francs, misdirections, desperate attempts at French, getting lost, walking miles in the heat to get money changed, trying to locate the American consulate, dinner with American soldiers at their stand-up mess, officers' mess, stories of fighting, stories of narrow escapes, a supply sergeant and a top sergeant who have adopted me as their special care,[6] frustration in outer offices, dirty clothes, no water, no laundry, Moslems on street cars, dirty Arab boys with and without shoe-shine boxes, officers yelling "Alley!" at same, the Kasbah, the native market, dirty Arabs in black, dirty Arabs in white, dirty white veils, never, by any chance, anything clean, except the officers'

uniforms on that day when they first put on their summer tans. I saw
General Eisenhower on that day,[7] and he was really clean and cool. I
could go on with these impressions and add soldiers in knickers, 8th
Army boys, so tanned they look like natives, horrible drinks in native
cafes while one talks to soldiers of the 8th and 1st Armies, drivers
honking down narrow twisting streets while the natives move casually
out of the way, atabrine pills supplied by the 1st sergeant, mosquito
netting supplied by the supply sgt., who stole it from the navy,[8] French
chatter everywhere, Arab chatter, a plethora of money in the army,
nothing to buy in the stores, a corporal named Alfred, in charge of this
billet, who polishes my shoes, which are white with dust, and talks
longingly about dairy-farming in up-state New York—a great longing
on the part of all the boys to go home, to get out of this obnoxious
Arabian place, a general hatred of John L. Lewis, a general feeling that
the miners should get in the army once and find out what it's like.[9]

But while I have time I must try to remember my days
successively. Monday I went again to see C. D. Jackson, who took me
down to Col. Phillips and turned me over formally to Public Relations,
Col. Phillips and I had a little talk about what I want to find out and
he agreed to set me on my way—asked me to come back that
afternoon and go up with him to see Eisenhower's aide. Went back,
Phillips wasn't in, so I didn't see him. Had dinner with Sergt. Simeon
Snider and 1st. Sgt. Peter Hromchak, at their mess. They drove me
home in the weapons carrier. Next morning I went to see Phillips
again. We had a chat and then he said, "Gen. Eisenhower will see you
this morning if you want to go up." I went and talked half an hour
with the C. in C., who is most enthusiastic about what I'm trying to
write about. He suggested some material for the story. I had lunch
with Snider in his mess at the Palais [illegible]. Tuesday evening I had
dinner in a native restaurant with my sergeants. Yesterday—
Wednesday—I was all day with Commander Butcher—Col. Gault,
Col. Torrance—who dictated a partial history of the N.A. campaign to
me—and in the eve. I had dinner with the sgts again. Oh, yes, lunch
was with Mr. (Captain) Kalloch, of the War Shipping Board. Today I
had breakfast with Lt. Jones, who is here to arrange entertainment for
the British troops. He came down with me on the plane. Lunch at the
officers' mess with Capt. Head and Captain Hill. Tried to get an apt.
to live in, with Hill's help. Then came home to take a much needed
nap and write this letter. I'm sure I've left out half—but it wasn't

wasted. It will all be there when I need it for material. At 4:30 I'm to be at the St George to get some more history from Col Torrance. Then I'm going to dinner with Major Bruskin (P.R.O.) who is going to get some correspondents to talk about the part of the campaign they saw. And so I must hurry. But before I lay down my pen let me say that I have been able to arrange how I'll get back. Around the middle of the month I'll start for home and you. It's been too long already. I'm grateful that I can learn—and that it's that soon.

Sunday, June 6 [1943] or thereabout

Darling—

Thursday evening I drove out with Bruskin, and those two correspondents to a hostel on the beach, where we ate plenty and they talked about the front line. Friday I saw Marshall Tedder and he gave me a history of the strategy in the Mediterranean—especially from the point of view of an airman.[10] Saturday I talked a long while with Capt. Ruwct, who led a company at the time of the landing. Today I drove out to the beach with Sgts Hromchak and Snider—and Capt Head. Had dinner with the sergeants. Found that I'm to get my tickets tomorrow and leave Tues. for Casablanca. Lt. Col. Phil. Cockrane is in Casablanca—and I hope to see him there. I'm beginning to know my way around this place a bit, but I'm very happy to get out of it. It will be wonderful just to be on my way home. You can't imagine how enviously the boys look at me—how they all long for the United States. I'm luckier than I deserve.

Friday night—I forgot to say—we had a considerable raid here—and I've never seen such fire-works as the anti-air fire put up. The whole sky was illuminated with patterns made by the tracer bullets.

Oh, darling—I'm so weary of travelling about. I want to see you and home.

Casablanca, June 9

Darling—I'm now in Casablanca—and without my luggage—all because of my own foolishness, I suppose. I got on the plane this morning at Algiers, and we flew to Oran—then stopped and the crew said we'd stay there an hour and a half. Said we'd leave at 12:15. Well, I took them literally, I suppose. I should have sat and watched that plane like a hawk, but I found a seat in the shade and got acquainted with a colonel and got a sandwich and strolled into the waiting-room at 12:05. "How about my plane?" I asked. "They're just taking off," somebody shouted. I started to run across the field, somebody got a jeep and caught up with me and we dashed for the plane— appropriately named "Snafu." Well, as we drove up to the wing the door slammed in my face, the propellers turned and it was too late. I wangled my way onto the next plane, and got to Casablanca at 4:30, but my luggage has gone on to Marrakech. I considered going on down there to get it, but the pilot promised to bring it up with him tomorrow morning, so I stayed here. I'm in the officers' quarters of the American Merchant Seaman's Club—and I've been lent pajamas and have bought myself a razor and a clean shirt. Also I've just been bitten by a mosquito, so I'd better close up and get ready for bed. Soon I'll be getting on a ship, darling. Home will look mighty good to me. Oh—and I got your wire—the Tribune one—so you did know I was in Algiers.[11] I was sick yesterday—but that's another story—I'd better go to bed now.

June 11 [1943], Friday.
    Darling—As usual there's been plenty going on since I wrote that last line. I'll try to catch up. The sleeping that first night was rather hectic here—because the seamen have a way of getting a bit tight and noisy and I was in a room with a lot of them. Last night was better. —Yesterday I got up at six and got all shaved and scoured. It was my first real bath in Africa. Then I went out with Woodhouse (one of the men in charge here)[12] to the airport and was lucky enough to get there just as Lt. Tector was arriving back from Marrakech. And the lad was as good as his word. He had taken the trouble to hunt up my luggage, get [it] on his plane and bring it back here. The pilots on these courier planes are really wonderful fellows. Only my officer's coat was missing, and I was so glad to see the rest of the stuff that I didn't worry about that. —Then I started out to get my passage on the ship—and found that I had to go to several places—among them army headquarters. Going there I ran into the C.O. of this post and area—and he took me to lunch along with several officers. One of them was going out to the prison camp here—full [of] Germans and Italians, and offered to take me along. I went with him—it was Maj. Maguire—and met Major Morgan who went with us. The camp was huge. I'll have to tell you about that later. Anyway Maguire offered to

help me with the passage, and this morning I went to his office and found that he had collected all the official signatures necessary except the consul's. I went and got that myself. It remains for me to see a certain Lt. Smith who allocates space on ships. That I'll do later this afternoon. Meanwhile I have just had lunch with Maguire and Woodhouse and Kaplin and a French officer who also helped with my ticket and who told us his story of his escape from France. It was unbelievable and hair-raising. His name is Jean de Bretauil.

Let me come back now to that cable of yours. On the day before I was to leave Algiers I was sick. The reason was merely that I hadn't eaten any candy for a long time and was [un?] used to sugar. I went to the PX and got some things I needed—and one thing I didn't need at all—a bar of Babe Ruth. It was awful stuff, but was rather starved for sweets, I guess, for I ate it, and almost instantly got one of those attacks of indigestion. That was Monday afternoon. I ate nothing that night and nothing all the next day—just lay in bed. About 5 in the evening a little native boy came to my quarters and told me I must come with him. I was so sick I didn't want to go, but I finally followed him out into the sun and away over across the enclosure was a Frenchman in uniform. I crossed the compound in my pajamas and he handed me a telegram—the only one I got in Algiers. It was from you and said "Tribune says you arrived. Blessings and love." I began to get better then. 1st Sgt. Peter Hromchak came over in the evening bringing a can of pears and about 8 that night I felt good enough to eat some of them. Next morning Hromchak and his supply sergeant, Simeon Snider, came over with the weapons carrier and drove me to the air port in style, carrying my luggage and saying goodbye with as much affection as if I had been their own papa. I got along really well with the enlisted men. Anyway I found or made a lot of good friends among them in Algiers. Here I've had to concentrate on officers because that passage is my first concern. It seems to be well in train now. Tomorrow I intend to start visiting men in hospital, among them, I hope, some German and Italian prisoners. I hear such conflicting reports about them I'd like to find out a bit for myself. By the way I ran into Edward Trever (he uses his old name Tolleland in the army) at the airport. He's very enthusiastic about army life, says he'd never go back to acting now. I've collected the names of so many soldiers who want me to send or take verbal messages home that I'm going to have to spend a day or two telephoning to relatives. But I'll be happy to do it. It's about all one can do for these boys over here—and they're happy just thinking their folks will hear about them. It's 4 o'clock and I must get ready to go to the dock for that last permission.

Saturday, June 12 [1943]—

Darling—Now I'm all set to go and just waiting for word to come aboard. Will probably get it tomorrow evening—or Monday. Just when we sail I don't know, of course. But it's at least arranged that I go. Today I went to the 6th Hospital to talk to wounded soldiers. They were very friendly. A lot of them will be on the same ship with me, very likely. This is getting to be a very long letter—and no way to send it—so I'll stop and go to sleep.

Sunday, June 13 [1943]

Darling—This is a quiet Sunday in Casablanca—quiet, hot and humid. Last night the heat was the worst so far and the mosquitoes really got me. Tonight I've been promised a netting over my cot. If I don't come home with malaria it'll be just good luck. Thirty per cent of the population is said by the medics to be infected and if a mosquito bites a carrier and then you you get it almost certainly. However, I won't count on it.

Today is the day I might get a call to come on board—today or tomorrow morning. Somehow I seem to be in a period of suspended animation waiting here for that word. I know the voyage will seem long and not too safe, but it's the last lap of the journey home and I can't keep my mind off it. I understand how these boys look back at their homes now. They want only one thing— to get this war over so they can go home. And of course the end is coming nearer. Pantelleria capitulated day before yesterday—and Lampedusa has now surrendered.[13] The way is being cleared for an assault on the mainland somewhere. —I'm going to write a short letter to mail from here—just in case this one gets lost. And give in it the names of the people I've known best in N. Africa. Then in case anything went wrong on that voyage home you'd know somebody who could relate my African trek.[14]

Monday, June 14 [1943], early

Darling—Last night came a call asking me to report to a certain pier at a certain time, ready to travel. So I'm really to start home!

Somehow it seems so far away now that even the beginning of the voyage seems unreal, as if it couldn't happen. But maybe it will.

Wednesday, June 16 [1943]

Went on board at 6 on Monday, watched them loading. Watched them again all day Tuesday as we lay in port. Ate on the ship and slept here. Cabin with Weston Haynes, naval photographer. Took on a lot of wounded, some wounded prisoners. Many able-bodied prisoners. Italians wait on our tables very happily.

Thursday, June 17 [1943]

Darling—I'm sitting here at the moment in a life-jacket, awaiting instructions. They're holding "Abandon Ship" drill, and we were told to wait in our cabin for instructions. But it's been half an hour now and nobody comes. Weston Haynes, the Assoc. Press photographer, is asleep in his chair. This morning I went around with him while he took pictures of wounded Americans and we also went in among the German prisoners, but they were eating and very crowded, so no pictures were taken there. I went in merely as assistant camera-man, carrying bulbs and film.

Saturday, June 19 [1943]—

Darling—Yesterday I did a lot of exploring about the boat with my photographer room-mate. Saw the galleys and the hospital quarters and the prison quarters. Saw the German officers heiling and shaking hands on the after-deck. When we sailed there was a great shortage of help in the galley and the dining-room. Now that has all been solved by the Italian prisoners. They are all happy and smiling about going to America and they bring you coffee with an eager willingness that would earn fabulous tips ashore. —The Germans, however, are moody and surly, are not trusted out of rifle range, and are not even asked if they wish to help. —Yesterday at 4:30 we were being followed by a submarine, according to one of the officers, but we ran away from it. Our course is far south. Flying fish skitter away from our bow like flights of little birds or grasshoppers.

Sunday, June 20 [1943]

Darling—It's the evening of Sunday—and now I think it's the 20th of June. We're steaming through sub-tropical ocean, with flying fish spraying out from the bows on both sides. Little ones, like locusts, larger ones, the size of robins. Our voyage is longer than we expected because we've come a long way south—and now it seems we won't get in till toward the end of the week. My guess is that we're in the Carribean, somewhere south of Cuba, at the moment. —I've been sitting all evening in the center of a group of C.B.'s at the bow of the ship, hearing their version of Freetown, Africa.[15]

Tues, June 22 [1943]

Darling—Yesterday was midsummers day—and to the best of my observation this wonderful old ship turned north. It's a beautiful job of shipbuilding, this vessel, and gives me great respect for American ship designers. Yesterday I talked much to sailors, wounded men and flyers. We bought a gallon of ice-cream and consumed it. First since leaving home. Last night's sunset and evening star were perfect. The sunrise in the sea was perfect this morning. And of course—we're all happy—we're headed for home.

Have been talking most of the morning with Fletcher Martin, one of the painters who went out on the project that Henry is with. Only he painted in Tunisia. Saw Gen. Biddle there.[16]

June 25 [1943]

Darling—Now it is announced that we shall dock in Boston. That's not so good for most of the folk aboard—and of course it makes my journey home more complicated. I'll send a wire or call you from the Hub. All this while there's been no way of saying a word of my whereabouts.

8 P.M. —And now it seems we're to get into Boston around noon. So I may perhaps reach home tomorrow night. It seems far far away. But closer, closer than it was.

1. The present letter, written in fourteen entries, covers extensive travel (from London to Algiers to Boston). The first entry, written in Algiers, Algeria, on Sunday, May 30, covers his trip from London. On Tuesday evening, May 25, he had departed London via train, to arrive at Alloway, Scotland, the next morning, Wednesday, May 26. That evening he took a flight from Alloway and arrived the next morning (Thursday, May 27) at Marrakech, Morocco, where he spent the day and night. On Friday, May 28, he flew to Algiers, stopping at Fez and Casablanca in Morocco, and at Oran, Algeria, on the way. The second and third entries were written in Algiers, on Thursday, June 3, and Sunday, June 6, and they narrate his activities in that city. The fourth entry was written in Casablanca on Wednesday, June 9, and it recounts his last

day in Algiers (June 8) and his flight on the ninth to Casablanca. Entries five through eight were written in Casablanca on June 11 (Friday), 12 (Saturday), 13 (Sunday), and 14 (Monday), and they give his experiences in that city. On the evening of June 14 he boarded a ship in Casablanca harbor for America. The ship sailed on Wednesday, June 16, and docked at Boston around noon on Saturday, June 26. The last six entries give his experiences on board ship and were written on June 16 (Wednesday), June 17 (Thursday), June 19 (Saturday), June 22 (Tuesday), and June 25 (Friday).

2. He was, that is, at Alloway, Scotland, birthplace and home of Robert Burns (1759–96), whose poem "Tam o'Shanter" (1791), he refers to and quotes (l. 32 in the poem).

3. Oliver H. P. Garrett (1898–1952) before the war had been a newspaper man (with the *New York Sun*, *Evening Globe*, *Evening Post*, and *World*) and writer. His film scripts include *A Farewell to Arms*, *Moby Dick*, *A Duel in the Sun*, and the winner of a 1934 Oscar, *Manhattan Melodrama*. His *Waltz in Goose Step* (1938) was an early anti-Nazi play.

4. Charles Douglas Jackson (1902–64), before the war an executive in Time, Inc., had been assistant to the U.S. Ambassador to Turkey, 1942–43. From early 1943 to 1945 he held several governmental posts, including the O.W.I. position. In 1952–53 he was special assistant to President Eisenhower, and in 1954 U.S. delegate to the Ninth U.N. General Assembly.

5. Harry Cecil Butcher (b. 1901), agricultural expert and CBS radio executive prior to the war, entered the navy in 1942 and became Eisenhower's aide early in 1943. His book, *My Three Years with Eisenhower* (New York, 1946), recounts the association.

6. Sgt. Simeon Snider and 1st Sgt. Peter Hromchak.

7. The visit with Eisenhower, on Tuesday morning, June 1, is described later in the letter. For a fuller account of the interview, see *Catalogue*, pp. 40–43.

8. The pills, a drug used to combat malaria, were supplied by Peter Hromchak; the netting, by Simeon Snider.

9. In 1941 President Roosevelt had reached an agreement with organized labor that for the duration of the war labor disputes would be settled by arbitration, without strikes, in order not to interfere with the war effort. John L. Lewis (1880–1969), president of United Mine Workers, offered the first major challenge to the agreement in the spring of 1943, when he insisted on pay increases that went beyond the government's wage/price controls and threatened a strike unless his demands were met. The conflict between Lewis and Roosevelt reached a head in May and June, 1943, when some locals in the UMW did strike and returned to work only on direct orders from Roosevelt.

10. Arthur W., Air Marshall Lord Tedder (1891–1967), at the time deputy supreme commander of Allied Forces under Eisenhower, had been commander of the English Royal Air Force in the Middle East since the outbreak of the war.

11. The wire, quoted later in the letter, mentions a *New York Herald-Tribune* story telling of Anderson's arrival in North Africa. But the Late Edition of the paper between May 28 (the day he arrived in Algiers) and June 8 (the day he received the wire) does not include the story.

12. James Woodhouse, with the War Shipping Administration in Casablanca.

13. Preparing to invade Italy, the Allies took Pantelleria, an Italian held island off the west coast of Sicily on June 11, 1943. Lampedusa, off the southern coast of Sicily, surrendered to the Allies the next day.

14. See no. 125.

15. Capital of Sierra Leone.

16. Fletcher Martin (b. 1904), painter and book illustrator, had been in North Africa as war art correspondent for *Life* magazine, and an exhibition of his work opened at the Midtown Galleries in December, 1943. "Henry" was presumably Anderson's friend and neighbor, the artist Henry Varnum Poor (1888–1970), who had designed Anderson's home on South Mountain Road and also illustrated *High Tor* when it was published. No record has come to light of his association with *Life*. Anthony J. Drexel Biddle (1896–1961) had been U.S. Ambassador to Poland in 1939, then ambassador to the French government in exile from 1940 to 1944.

125. TO GERTRUDE ANDERSON

[Casablanca]
June 13, [1943]

Darling—

I'm writing this short note to mail from N. Africa just in case my long letter should happen to be lost. Of course I expect to get home, but if I shouldn't and no record was saved you'd like to know who my friends were in this theatre and what I did here.

For ten days I lived in the same room with James Cook—a wonderful fellow—I'm very glad I met him. Then in another city I've met two of his colleagues, James Woodhouse and Abraham Kaplin. They've been very kind to me. 1st Sgt. Peter Hromchak, Sgt. Simeon Snider, and Lt. Chester Schlanger were all good friends to me in this region.[1] Their addresses are

Mr. James Cook
War Shipping Administration
A.P.O. 512, c/o Postmaster, N.Y., N.Y.
James Woodhouse, Navy 216—N.Y., N.Y.
Abe Kaplin, Navy 216, N.Y., N.Y.
1st Sgt. Peter Hromchak
296th Signal Installation Co., A.P.O. 512, N.Y., N.Y.
Sgt. Simeon Snider, same address.
Lt. Chester Schlanger
A.P.O. 512, N.Y., N.Y.

I could give other names, but that should be enough. I've been most fortunate in friends wherever I've gone here.

I'm purposely not including any details in this note, because they might be censorable.

I love you, darling—and I think I'll get home.

Max

1. Cook had come down with Anderson on the plane from England, and they had shared a room in Algiers, where he also met Hromchak, Snider, and Schlanger. He met Woodhouse and Kaplin in Casablanca.

126. TO DWIGHT D. EISENHOWER [1]

July 1, 1943

Dear General Eisenhower:

After talking with you in Algiers I went about a good deal among enlisted men in North Africa trying to find out what I could about their interests and their morale and their diversions. Of course news from home comes first, and news of the world probably second, in keeping up morale, but their diversions are also important—and in this field it seemed to me that what was offered to them could be vastly improved. There is an occasional show given, but it's usually pretty brainless and incompetent. Now I know from experience that soldiers as well as other people like a little meaning mixed in with their entertainment, and I know too that the morale of an army is improved when the fighting man gets an occasional unobtrusive reminder of what he's fighting for. The theatre is the perfect medium for making such suggestions, and it's not being used that way. I've noticed that what the soldiers like best of all is a humorous play about their own lives and problems. When they get even a taste of that sort of thing they really respond. And so I want to make a brash suggestion. There are good playwrights around, some in the army, who could write short plays for the men, plays they could put on for themselves (and that's something they like to do, too) when they happen to have a little time on their hands. One such playwright is Sgt. Sidney Kingsley, playwright and director, author of *Dead End*, *Men in White*, and this year's prize winning *The Patriots*.[2] He'd be intensely interested in a job of that sort. He's now in the Provost Marshall's office, 1st Army

Headquarters, Governors Island, New York. Serial number 32061838.
You'd find him an able man, likeable and sensible, capable of taking
charge of a whole program of entertainment for an area. His C.O.
feels the same way about him and has recommended him for a
commission in Special Services—but at the moment that department
unfortunately has no commission to hand out.[3]

I'm extremely grateful to you for your kindness and for
stimulating suggestions concerning the play I'm planning to write.[4]
You helped me more than you will ever know, just by being the leader
you are, and with the vision you have.

Sincerely
Maxwell Anderson

1. Eisenhower (1890–1969), supreme allied commander in Europe, was at Malta
planning the invasion of Italy.

2. *The Patriots*, produced by the Playwrights' Company on January 29, 1943, won
the Drama Critics' Circle Award for the 1942–43 season. Kingsley's *Dead End* had
been produced in 1936, *Men in White* in 1934.

3. Kingsley, (b. 1906), drafted in 1941, was commissioned a lieutenant in
September, 1943, and assigned to Special Services.

4. *Storm Operation*.

127. TO HAROLD ANDERSON [1]

New City
July 27, 1943

Dear Harold—

After a silence of so many years, during which everything has
happened, practically, that could, I take my pen in hand to report that
I have turned farmer in a small way and like all other farmers I'm in
trouble. That is, I haven't enough feed to tide me over the winter, and
no prospect of getting it. It occurred to me that feed might be
purchaseable in your vicinity and there might be no law against your
buying some for me and shipping it this way. Maybe I'm wrong, but
maybe not. Anyway you'll owe me a letter now. I have two cows, a
horse and about five voracious pigs, to say nothing of the chickens—
less than a hundred.

My trip to England and No. Africa was full of sights and sounds—too numerous to mention. I learned a lot—so much that I may not be able to write a play. A playwright shouldn't know what's really going on. He's palsied by reality.

We're all well. I'm twice a grandfather.[2] Terry's in New Mexico in an air corps ground crew. Al's a top sergeant in *This Is the Army* Co. and going shortly to England or Africa.[3] Quentin is teaching in Columbia. Hesper's almost nine—started a diary today.

As ever

Max

1. Anderson's brother, who lived in Des Moines, Iowa.
2. Quentin's daughter, Martha Haskett, was born February 22, 1942; and Alan's son, Alan, Jr., was born February 22, 1943.
3. *This Is The Army*, a musical review assembled by Irving Berlin and produced by the government for the Emergency War Relief Fund, had opened in New York on July 4, 1942.

128. TO THE PLAYWRIGHTS' COMPANY

[New City]
October 21, 1943

An Open Letter to THE PLAYWRIGHTS' COMPANY:[1]

The greatest need of The Playwrights' Company at present is a vigorous and vehement opposition to President S. N. (synonym mad) Behrman, recently re-elected for a third term and obviously campaigning for a fourth. In his mad reach for power, we can be certain that he will let nothing stand in his way. This may be our last opportunity to speak freely. At the last Playwrights' session, President B. remarked to me that if I dared lift a voice against his candidacy, my words would be torn from their context and twisted in such a way as to destroy me. "I rely," said the power-swollen President, "on your inexperience in political chicane, your noble nature and your innate decency. I shall destroy you." Gentlemen, this is our President. I tremble for our democratic principles. *Every argument used by Behrman in favor of a third term is equally applicable to a fourth, a fifth, a sixth!* Is there to be a Behrman dynasty?

Mr. Behrman scoffs at the idealistic records of possible opponents and chooses to stand on the McKinley platform. He boasts of his life-long adherence to the principles of sound money, acquired, evidently, during the campaign of 1896. Any deviation from devotion to sound money he regards as Byranism. He has made it plain that while he runs the company, it will have only one goal—the acquisition of hard cash. Yet, by his own standards, he has signally failed. It was he who prevented the company from buying a theatre, and he boasts of this at a time when theatres are at a premium and every theatre in the city has doubled in value. The Playwrights' Company was organized with a capital of $100,000. That sum is now reduced, according to the auditors' latest figures, to $59,782.03. And this sum, dwindled and inadequate, is available only in depreciated currency.

We have been brought to this by Mr. Behrman's fanatical adherence to a nineteenth century financial doctrine first promulgated by the notorious Mark Hanna—the Pennsylvania boss responsible for the imitation marble columns in the capital at Harrisburg, paid for by the voters, of course, at the cost of real marble.

I hesitate to dwell upon the inroads made into Behrman's higher nature by his crude monetary interpretation of the world. But I must, in justice, point out that he spoke only mildly against Mr. Sherwood's removal to Washington in a close election year.[2] Shortly thereafter, Mr. B. quietly manoeuvered himself into a dictatorial position among the voting stockholders and took advantage of Sherwood's absence to write a play for the Lunts.[3] It is to be noted that, though other members of the company have their ups and downs, Mr. Behrman is always unobtrusively solvent. Where he gets his money is beginning to puzzle some of his colleagues not so blessed as he with an eye to the main chance. Perhaps it will be remembered that Mr. B., alone among us, has been known to show irritation at the presence of auditors in the outer office. "What are these people doing here?" he has been heard to mutter. It is a short step from Mark Hanna to Teapot Dome. Who was it who inaugurated the custom (now followed by others in self defense) of dipping into the petty cash for taxi fares and charging lunches to the company? Gentlemen, without vision, the people perish. And Mr. Behrman visualizes nothing beyond the dollar—the pre-Spanish War issue of the dollar.

MAXWELL ANDERSON

P.S.: I no longer trust Pinto, Winokur & Pagano.[4] Mr. B. has touched these men, and they are no longer to be trusted. If they have not been corrupted, it is not because they have not been approached. I fear that if our financial status were honestly investigated, it would be found as hollow as Mark Hanna's marble.

M.A.

N.B. I find that Mr. S. N. B. is at Saratoga. Is it necessary to say more.

M. A.

1. A tongue-in-cheek attack on S. N. Behrman during his campaign for the presidency of the Playwrights' Company. The office was ceremonial, and Behrman and Anderson staged the campaign to raise morale at a time when all of the playwrights were despondent about their work. At a meeting of the company on October 14 Behrman made his campaign speech, "viciously" attacking each member in turn (given in Wharton, *Life Among the Playwrights*, pp. 102–5), and Anderson sent the speech to an absent member, saying "it's too good to miss" and adding that "it need hardly be said that Sam was re-elected by voice vote" (Anderson to Madeline Sherwood, for Robert Sherwood, October 14, 1943; W). In the present letter he responds to the speech, attacking Behrman with arguments drawn from the opposition to Roosevelt's precedent-breaking third term.

2. Sherwood, now an assistant to President Roosevelt, had begun the association as a speech writer for Roosevelt during *his* campaign for a third term.

3. The Lunts, who had starred in three Sherwood plays (*Reunion in Vienna*, 1931; *Idiot's Delight*, 1936; and *There Shall Be No Night*, 1940), then starred in Behrman's *The Pirate* during the 1942–43 season.

4. CPA firm, auditors for the Playwrights' Company.

129. TO DWIGHT D. EISENHOWER

[November, 1943]

Dear General Eisenhower —[1]

This is my attempt to write that play we talked about in Algiers. It's not what I hoped it would be, of course. Nothing ever comes up to one's hopes. Also a play, as everybody knows, can't show much of a campaign, being limited to glimpses into the lives of a few characters at moments of decision, glimpses which we can only hope will indicate and perhaps illuminate the vast background behind their lives.

And a play about Americans under fire carries a tremendous burden of responsibility. It attempts to speak for men who speak so well for themselves in their deeds and in their blunt and vivid language that nothing said behind the lines can approach that curt eloquence. Even if the writing and the production turn out luckily the scope of the war's effect on those involved must be conveyed largely by inference and by virtue of the imagination of the audience. Yet the great problem of the civilian nowadays is to understand the men and women who have borne the heat and burden and death and wounds of this war, and so I offer "Storm Operation" to you and to the public, hoping it will go some little way toward interpreting between the battle-front and our homes.

Sincerely
M. A.

1. In Algiers the previous June Eisenhower had encouraged Anderson to write a play celebrating Anglo-American military cooperation (for details of the interview, see *Catalogue*, pp. 40–43), but *Storm Operation*, the play that resulted from the trip to Algiers, focused on the demoralizing effect of the war on those engaged in it. The present letter accompanied a script of the play.

130. TO ALEXANDER D. SURLES [1]

[New York City]
November 22, 1943

Dear General Surles —

I have finally finished a play about the North African Campaign, dealing largely with Anglo-American relations. I talked to General Eisenhower about it in Algiers and have no doubt that it is on the line of what you would like to have said. I am mailing you a copy of it today and would have sent one before, but I have been revising and wanted you to have a rehearsal copy. The name is "Storm Operation".

As you will have guessed, I want to ask you a favor in connection with the production. We have already come on many questions which cannot be answered except by a military expert—mostly questions of usage and the correct equipment. The Prologue and Epilogue, for instance, take place in an invasion barge and we want to make sure that our routine is not obviously incorrect. You probably have pictures that would cover all the situations that bother us. You may even have at your disposal a young officer full of encyclopedic information who could take one glance at what we are doing and tell us whether or not we are wrong.

I haven't seen you since my trip to England and Africa, and let me thank you again for making the journey possible and for all favors past. I have tried to report truthfully on what I saw and I hope you will find the play a good job.

Sincerely,

1. To obtain permission to enter North Africa Anderson had agreed to secure War Department approval of any play that resulted from the trip. Gen. Surles was Director of the Bureau of Public Relations in the War Department, and with the present letter Anderson sent him a script of *Storm Operation* for War Department approval.

131. TO ALEXANDER D. SURLES

[Baltimore, Maryland]
December 7, 1943

Dear General Surles —[1]

I am of course changing or deleting the passages in Storm Operation to which you refer. In regard to the Australian nurse I am consulting with Sherwood. Whatever his opinion, it seems wise to eliminate all reference to her origin and to change her uniform sufficiently to make identification impossible. My whole intention is, as you know, to further the friendship and cooperation of the Allies and I shall welcome any further suggestion along those lines. None of these changes will injure the play in the slightest, and I am honestly grateful to your bureau for your friendly assistance.

Sincerely
Maxwell Anderson

1. Surles had replied to no. 130 with a tactfully phrased demand that several changes be made in *Storm Operation*. Anderson must delete the pregnancy of an unmarried American nurse (Kathryn Byrne), a scene in which an American soldier kicked a Moslem who was praying, and a scene in which American and English soldiers mistreated German prisoners of war. He should also change a prominent character, the

Australian nurse Thomasina Grey, making her less disillusioned and less promiscuous in her relationship with the British Captain Sutton. But Surles had referred the question of nurse Grey to Robert Sherwood of the Office of War Information, who would check with British and Australian authorities to see whether they would be offended by the play (Surles to Anderson, December 6, 1943; W). Anderson was in Baltimore, where *Storm Operation* was beginning its try-out run at the Maryland Theater. His agreement with the War Department (see no. 130, n. 1) compelled him to revise the play as Surles indicated.

132. TO KATHARINE S. WHITE [1]

[New City]
March 17, 1944

Dear Mrs. White:

Your letter waited for me at the office and I didn't get it till yesterday. I feel very apologetic for having put you through all this. My information about Fish was small but vague, and I certainly should have looked up my facts before bursting into dithyrambs. It's a lot more difficult to revise than to write a first draft. Whether I can rearrange the poem to fit the facts without taking all the edge off it, I don't know. It might be very funny to have a footnote to every line and I'm inclined to think that many would be necessary to clear matters up. I hope I won't have to give the whole thing up but a political document should be black and white and there's nothing clear about Mr. Fish's position in space or politics.

I want to thank you personally for the way you have gone about this matter. I think you must be the conscience of the New Yorker. [2]

Sincerely
Maxwell Anderson

1. Mrs. White, wife of E. B. White and collaborator with him on several books, was an editor of the *New Yorker*. During the 1944 elections Anderson headed a committee in his congressional district to defeat Hamilton Fish for reelection to the U.S. House of Representatives, and about March 1 he had sent a verse satire on Fish to Mrs. White. Her reply (March 7, 1944; T) said she wanted to use the poem if Anderson could revise it to reflect the complications that had resulted from the redrawing of New York congressional districts, complications (mostly geographical) that she explained at length.
2. The poem as revised was published as "Mr. Fish Crosses the River," *New Yorker* 20 (May 13, 1944): 28.

133. TO LELA AND DAN CHAMBERS

[New City]
June 9, 1944

Dear Lela & Dan—[1]

Terry took Meg and Nancy to New York this evening to see *Othello*, and Mab is in town too, so I am alone here with Hesper, who has finally gone to bed. Your letter, with the enclosed copy of Lt. Corpenning's, came this morning, and all day I've been carrying it around with me—not wanting to show it to the children or even talk about it. I'm no good at such a time as this. All I can feel or say is just a dumb misery. And that was one reason why it wouldn't have helped for me to go out and see you. The terrible necessity of the invasion and what our boys have to go through has got me down. Leland Stowe[2] said something on the radio tonight that came near what seems like the truth to me. He said, why is it that the living never seem to be worthy of their dead? I feel so unworthy. And the nation around me seems so far from knowing or perceiving what is being given and done for us. We shall remain a free nation because of this bloody business they go through, and a good life isn't possible except in a free nation, but we're not cleansed, we're not dedicated, we're not better, any of us, for what the boys have gone through to save our freedom. They're cleansed and dedicated. That was in Keith's letter.[3] But then look at the political jockeying, and the race prejudice and the small damnable envies that run all through our free society. Are we saved so that we can go on being like that? Even the army—perhaps the army, most of all—has learned, and will learn nothing from its dead. Perhaps some learn. A few come out of it knowing what was given and how much it meant. —But there was that wonderful statement of the Gettysburg address—and after it the horrible mess of carpet-bagging and the Grant administration. Men go on bartering over the fresh graves.

I tried writing a poem for Keith, but it wasn't within a million miles of what I wanted to say. So I gave it up.[4] —I shall send that address to Alan at once. He's somewhere south of Rome still, and might by chance know or be able to find out something.

This is a silly kind of letter to write.***[5] [Terry] spoke about wanting to write to you—but sat looking at the paper a while and couldn't say anything. He said one thing—you either give everything or you have it pretty easy. There's nothing in between.

Forgive me for this if you can.
My love to you both—

Max

1. In March, 1944, the Chambers's son Keith, a bomber pilot flying combat
missions from one of several fields at Foggia, Italy, had been killed when a plane from
another field collided with his shortly after take-off. But the Chambers did not learn the
details of his death until much later. On March 30, 1944, they were notified that Keith
was missing in action. In early June a death notice arrived without details, sent by a Lt.
Corpenning. Desperate for information, the Chambers sent Corpenning's letter to
Anderson with the hope that he could forward the name and address to his son Alan,
then a soldier in the vicinity of Foggia. Three days before the present letter the
Normandy invasion had begun.

2. Stowe was in Europe as war correspondent for the American Broadcasting
Corporation.

3. With the original notice that Keith was missing in action, the Chambers had
received his "in case" letter, a letter written to be sent in case one were killed or missing
in action. In his letter Keith emphasized that he fought out of conviction and became a
pilot by choice, and he charged his parents to maintain themselves "in health and spirit
until the end of this chaos, never giving a thought to any end except our triumph" (held
by Lela Chambers).

4. Later finished as "Last Letter" and sent to Mrs. Chambers on July 7, 1944. In
four stanzas the poem depicts the bomber pilot "Guiding the great wings / Facing our
death" and gives to the pilot's death the meaning it had in Keith's letter ("Last Letter,"
held by Lela Chambers).

5. Four sentences concerning a family member deleted at the request of the holder.

134. TO DWIGHT D. EISENHOWER

[August, 1944]

Dear General Eisenhower:[1]

Storm Operation is my attempt at that play we talked about in
Algiers. It covers only a tiny fraction of the campaign in North Africa
and reveals no more than a glimpse at the problem of Anglo-American
and other racial relations. It conveys no more than a hint at the
upheaval in our thinking and the destruction of preconceptions
concerning other peoples which is certain to follow any close contact
with their soil and their homes. But I have tried to be honest and
accurate, and I can only hope that the story of these few lives at

moments of decision will indicate the larger background and the enormous consequence of decisions made behind the scenes.

Sincerely

Maxwell Anderson

1. The present letter, written after *Storm Operation* was censored by the War Department and produced unsuccessfully, accompanied a published copy of the play.

135. TO THE EDITOR [1]

[Early November, 1944]

To the Editor:

If there is such a thing as a life or death election this one coming up deserves to be called just that. The United States will emerge from the war with many times the power and responsibility we had in 1940. Power without wisdom is calamitous, and when a nation has great power without great wisdom its sons pay for its mistakes with their lives. If ever there was necessity for wisdom in Washington it is now and in the immediate future. That is the issue in this election: how to send to Washington or retain there enough brains and character in House, Senate and White House, to keep the peace of the earth for us at least during the next few decades. For the peace of the earth is going to be very largely in our keeping, whether we like it or not. We must play a part, and a great part, among the nations, and we must deal both honestly and wisely with our neighbor sovereignties, or war will come down on us all again—ten times magnified, ten times as bloody.

Now I am not an expert in international affairs, but we must all go to the polls next week and pass judgment on the men who seek to represent us in Washington. Probably no one of us is expert enough to choose well every time he pushes down a lever, but we must do our best. And one special responsibility rests on us of the 29th District, because it just happens that the whole country, and a large part of the English-speaking world, will watch what we do about Ham Fish. The Congressional election in this 29th District is second only to the Presidential contest in news value and significance. And our choice is a simple one. If we elect Gus Bennet to Congress a sigh of relief will go up all over the United States. For if we do that it will mean that the man who has fought tooth and nail against every advance toward international understanding, who has been counted on for twenty years to advocate the wrong thing, the mistaken thing, the trouble-making thing in foreign affairs, will at last be out of our national councils. I am not exaggerating when I say that the election of Hamilton Fish from this district would make us a laughing-stock throughout the United States. His name stands, and he has stood in Congress for twenty-four years, for all that is futile, silly, blundering, and inefficient. He has become a comic-strip character, a caricature of every bumbling, meaningless Congressman who was ever laughed out of Washington.

Of the great issue now before us, the life or death of our children, Fish knows nothing and has learned nothing in all his time in public service. His international thinking is still the nineteenth century variety. If you listen to his speeches you hear no discussion of policy—only personal defense, evasion and attack. He has never contributed anything. He has nothing to contribute now. He cannot possibly change and begin to produce the wisdom we need in high places. He can only go on as he has in the past, a figure of fun to the casual observer, but in truth a grim portent of tragedy over the horizon—a tragedy which we shall help to bring on ourselves if we choose to be represented by such a man and such thinking.

And how has Mr. Fish kept his seat in Congress with all these disadvantages? The answer is plain. He is a shrewd and ruthless machine politician. He does favors, offers patronage, gives clam-bakes, joins clubs, controls purse-strings, runs an office which keeps track of who wants this and who can get that. He is a broker in benefits for his political friends. This is usual though not admirable among politicians, but with him it's a business. He makes it a full-time job. He represents, not the citizens of his district, but the machine of that district. If he goes to Congress from the 29th it will be the Newburgh County machine, with twenty-four years of local log-rolling and back-scratching behind it, that sends him. The voters of Rockland, Sullivan and Orange will repudiate him. He doesn't have his machine working well in those counties yet. But the Newburgh machine will plump for him as always, in return for past rewards, and he is hoping to drag us all along with it. If he got in we might be saddled with him as long as he lived, for some of the machine-politicians, even in Rockland, are already working for him. They'd like to see him elected because he's the kind of representative who passes the gravy. He said as much in his first Nyack speech.

If we elect Gus Bennet to represent us we shall not be sending an errand boy to Washington to do the odd jobs of his political friends. We shall be sending an honest man to apply his high intelligence and human sympathy to the great problems of our time. Bennet's outstanding characteristic is his honesty. He has refused over and over again to evade responsibility or equivocate. Whatever he does in Washington will be honestly, intelligently and fearlessly done. We shall not have to apologize for him.

But Mr. Fish? Well, he has been saying the Rockland opposition to him comes from Communists and pinks. This he knows is a lie. I myself am not a member of any political party, I vote Democratic or Republican as I please, but I have lived in Rockland County since 1922, my children have grown up here, and my grandchildren are beginning to grow up here. I don't want to suffer the shame, and I don't want Rockland County to suffer the shame, of being represented in Congress by Hamilton Fish.[2]

Sincerely

MAXWELL ANDERSON

1. Hamilton Fish, long a U.S. Congressman from New York, had taken the German side during the years leading up to World War II. He had opposed Lend Lease, Selective Service, and other preparations for war, and had made a much-publicized visit to Germany as guest of Hermann Goering and other high Nazi officials. In 1944 New York's congressional districts were redrawn, and Fish's new district, the 29th, retained Newburgh County and added Orange, Sullivan, and Anderson's home county, Rockland. In the August primary Fish defeated Augustus W. Bennet for nomination as the Republican candidate. Then Bennet, a lawyer without previous congressional experience, opposed Fish as an Independent in the November general elections. Anderson sent the present letter to several newspapers in the 29th district shortly before election day, November 7.

2. In the general election Bennet defeated Fish for the congressional seat.

136. TO THE PLAYWRIGHTS' COMPANY

December 26, 1944

Dear John, Sam, Elmer, Bob, Victor and Bill:

There seemed to be some doubt in the minds of the majority at the last meeting as to where or why the Playwrights might lack anything as a producing organization. I have some dubious opinions on both sides of the question that I'd like to put on paper because I'll never get them said otherwise.

Our organization was a declaration of independence from producers. Nobody is happier than I am to be independent. We can write as and what we please, without fear of finding no outlet on Broadway; we have an organization that does its utmost to put our scripts on without compromise or falsification; our relations with actors and theatre employees are honest and fair; and we are in a position to talk to any manager or producer on a basis of equality. These are benefits no one of us would give up. When Sam talks to the Guild he does so from our secure emplacement. They know he doesn't have to have them unless he wants them.

But I can understand why he might want them. We have nobody in our organization who does the work of a producer. Victor is our business manager, the best there is. Bill handles our publicity, and he's the best there is at that. Either one might be capable of acting as producer for us, but they never have because that is not their status. John has been invaluable in holding us together, but he is a busy man, with interests largely outside our company. As playwrights, we do not act as producers for each other. A producer, good or bad, if he's a producer at all, puts his full time on the work. He's constantly on hand, and on call, working on scripts, casting, theatres, and the thousand and more things that go into making a success of a play. We read each others plays, and our advice on scripts is probably the best there is as far as it goes. But it's brief and sporadic. We hold brief, sporadic and hurried meetings. Somebody's always looking at his watch before we've covered all the major production problems that must be settled—and as for the minor problems, they are hardly dealt with at all.

What we need, and need urgently, is a production head, preferably a genius, constantly on the job of getting our plays ready for the market. It's a full time occupation even for a genius, but failing a genius, it's a full time occupation for the best man there is in the field. If we found such a man, one we'd all trust, he'd want a large share in our profits for what he did. But I think he would more than pay for himself by enabling us to turn out a much larger proportion of successes. If we do not find such a man, and perhaps most of us don't want him around, it's inevitable that the place will be filled from time to time from the outside. For the Guild and Max Gordon,[1] with all their drawbacks, do work constantly at producing plays, and we do not. We write them.

This situation, of course, makes many more difficulties for some of us than for others. Those who have executive competence and can deal successfully with the succession of disasters that usually lead up to an opening see little need for a trouble-shooter in the shop. This is probably a fundamental difference of opinion, and one that will continue. I would no doubt bitterly resent some of the activities of any producing executive we found. But I would still think I needed him. And since he would be working for me and not I for him, I should not have lost any of the autonomy I so highly prize. No outside producer of recognized importance would come into our organization on such a basis, but a young man with his name still to make might well do it, and we'd very likely be as good for him as he for us. I have no names to offer, but the man exists. I think we should set out to find him.

Sincerely,

Max

1. Prominent Broadway producer, who had also produced the motion-picture version of Sherwood's *Abe Lincoln in Illinois*.

137. TO JOSEPH WOOD KRUTCH [1]

December 27, 1944

Dear Mr. Krutch:

I am reading your Johnson with great pleasure—and approaching the end of it with much more than the usual reluctance with which one faces "all last things". Perhaps some of my enjoyment is due to a recognition of a couple of fellow pessimists, but that's certainly not all. You have done a superb job. I have never been able to read Boswell through. I find him insufferable. But this story has for me the fascination that novels long ago lost.

Sincerely,

1. Krutch (1893–1970), a wide-ranging writer on the faculty of Columbia University since the early twenties, was currently Brander Matthews Professor of Dramatic Literature. He had written extensively on the drama, including *The American Drama Since 1918* (1939), and on other subjects as well. His *Samuel Johnson* had just been published.

138. TO JOHN F. WHARTON

[Hollywood, California]
March 18, 1945

Dear John—[1]

I'm sending the contracts with Bergman to Victor today. Her husband insisted on an escape clause in case the strike made it impossible to finish her picture in time, but she does intend to come—and is much excited by the whole project.

Forgive me if I differ with you completely in the matter of outside producers.[2] You assume that an outside producer can be of no value. That's a matter of opinion, just as the value of a star is a matter of opinion. If a playwright thinks an outside producer is valuable, the thinking makes it so. We have cooperated with other producers to get a hoped-for value. Any hoped-for value is justification for such cooperation. In my opinion it would be both unnecessary and destructive to reorganize the company to enable us to use a bargaining power *which we have used in the past with complete freedom.* At this moment I don't like or want to work with any producer except our own company, but at the moment I made up my mind that some such producer was valuable to me or my play it would be the natural, legal and profitable thing for the company to help me work out an arrangement with that producer, just as it would help me if I wanted a certain star. It may be the opinion of the company that the star is of no value, or that the outside producer is of no value, and we may advise

to that effect, but I see any failure to go along with the playwright's
wishes as an absolute denial of the company's basic agreement.

As ever

Max

P.S. Just one more word. You say that one of the objects of the
Plawrights' Company is "to produce their own plays without the
conflict that has so often ensued between the manager and the
playwright." This present argument, as I see it, is a conflict between a
playwright and his producer, made all the more galling because he is
committed to one producer, and committed in order to avoid just such
conflicts.

1. Anderson was negotiating with Ingrid Bergman to take the lead in *Joan of
Lorraine*, and her husband, Peter Lindstrom, acted as her business representative. Miss
Bergman was engaged in several pictures about this time, and a strike (settled on the day
of the present letter) by actors and stagehands in New York and Los Angeles threatened
to prolong her picture work beyond the starting date for a fall production of *Joan*.

2. The argument referred to here, an argument within the Playwrights' Company
concerning the use of outside producers by member playwrights, grew out of S. N.
Behrman's desire to have the Theatre Guild produce his next play, *Dunnigan's
Daughter*. For details of the situation, see no. 141, n. 1.

139. TO INGRID BERGMAN [1]

[Los Angeles, California]

April 23, 1945

Dear Ingrid—

Since I find myself unable, because of a rule of the Dramatists'
Guild, to promise you any part of the picture rights in *A Girl from
Lorraine*, or even to promise legally that you will play the part of Joan
in the picture, I want to assure you personally that I shall do
everything I can to make certain that you do play that part and that
you play it under the conditions you prefer. It needs no contract to
bind me to this. I'd be a fool not to insist on having you if you're
available. Nobody else could do the play or the picture to my
satisfaction.

I know, too, that you are making considerable financial sacrifice in taking time from pictures to do the play in New York, and that you would not act in the play at all if you were not confident that you would play the same role in the picture. It's my understanding, therefore, that you are signing with the Playwrights' Company for a period of seven months only, including rehearsals, but that you will extend the period to eight months in case you are entirely satisfied with the conditions of the picture sale.

As you know, I am so happy to have you for the part of Joan, and I appreciate so well your enthusiasm and cooperative spirit, that if there is ever any way in which the contract irks you or becomes difficult for you I shall be glad—and the Playwrights' Company will be glad—to make any feasible readjustment. It's my belief that we shall never quarrel over terms in this venture. We are only too happy and grateful to have you with us. And so—good fortune!

Sincerely
Maxwell Anderson

1. Miss Bergman (b. 1915), Swedish actress, had come to the United States in 1939 and had acted mainly in motion pictures (among them *Casablanca*, 1942, and *For Whom the Bell Tolls*, 1943), though she had initially appeared on Broadway in revivals of Molnar's *Liliom* (with Burgess Meredith) in 1940 and O'Neill's *Anna Christi* in 1941. Anderson went to Los Angeles in February, 1945, and remained until June negotiating with Miss Bergman to do his Joan of Arc play on stage and as a motion picture. Entitled *Joan of Lorraine* when produced and published, the play was known as *A Girl from Lorraine* at the time of the present letter (for the several titles, and versions, of the play, see *Catalogue*, pp. 43–46). The negotiations with Miss Bergman were filled with difficulties, and the present letter introduces an early one, a problem in the contract sent to Wharton in March.

140. TO INGRID BERGMAN

Hotel Bel-Air
Los Angeles, California
[April 25, 1945]

Dear Ingrid—[1]

This letter is written to confirm our verbal understanding concerning the possible moving picture to be made from my play "A Girl from Lorraine." Since you are to play the part of Joan on the stage I naturally want you to play Joan in the picture also, and you assure me that you wish to do so, and will do so if it can possibly be arranged. In return for this assurance I give you my word that I will not put the play on the market without your consent, but will hold the rights in the hope that you and I together may be able to work out a project for producing the picture ourselves. If, during the course of the New York run of the play, or later, we agree that it is better to sell the play, then I shall be free to sell it, but not otherwise. It is also understood between us that if you are satisfied with my handling of the picture rights you will add a month of playing time to the contract you are signing with the Playwrights' Company, making the contract for eight months, including rehearsals.

Sincerely
Maxwell Anderson

Agreed to[2]

---

1. On the day of the present letter Anderson's diary (T) notes: "Lunch with Ingrid at studio. Talk of doing the [Joan] picture ourselves."
2. Appended for Miss Bergman's signature. She agreed to these terms and, according to the 1945 diary, signed a contract embodying them on May 7: "Ingrid and I drove to the beach. Sitting in the sand she signed the contracts—changing the dates to May 7." This was the second in a long line of contracts that extended well into the next year. *Joan of Lorraine* went into rehearsal on October 3, 1946, and as late as June 21 the 1946 diary (T) shows Anderson still negotiating the length of playing time in Miss Bergman's contract, with him then insisting on not less than four months.

---

141. TO MEMBERS OF THE PLAYWRIGHTS' COMPANY

[Los Angeles, California]
May 24, 1945

Dear Bob, Sam, Elmer & John—[1]

Since I'm still working on revisions that I want to talk over with Ingrid I'm not returning quite as soon as I hoped, and I want to make one point in this encyclical argument of ours. I can't for the life of me see why Bob should regard the Playwrights' Company "as a sort of agreeable club" in case one member of the company wanted the cooperation of another producer on one play. It seems to me that the company was formed to serve the interests of the members, that those interests are certain to differ in some ways, and that the company should be flexible enough to meet situations such as this present [one] with considerable calm. Is it a matter of principle with us that there shall never be an outside producer in on our plays unless he brings a star in his hand? If so, I think it's a silly principle and I don't hold with it.

In fact, I refuse to lose interest in the Playwrights' Company no matter what happens. I want it to grow, prosper and take in more territory. I want to produce my plays with it and share my hopes and fortunes with it so long as I'm capable of writing plays. Certainly we shouldn't quarrel over anything small. Certainly we shouldn't be thinking of losing members at a time when what we need is to take more in.[2]

Nostalgically
Max

1. Within the Playwrights' Company an argument had arisen concerning S. N. Behrman's desire to have the Theatre Guild produce his plays. His previous play, *Jacobowsky and the Colonel*, had been rejected by the Playwrights' Company, then produced by the Guild on March 14, 1944. At the time of the present letter he wished to have the Guild produce his next play, *Dunnigan's Daughter*. Sherwood led the opposition to Behrman, and in a letter to Anderson of May 9, 1945 (T), Sherwood had written: "I for one would not be interested in the continuance of this Company if its partners regard it solely as a sort of agreeable club, the members of which prefer to conduct their professional affairs elsewhere."

2. Behrman allowed the Theatre Guild to produce *Dunnigan's Daughter*, in December, 1945, and in June of the next year he resigned from the Playwrights' Company.

142. TO GEORGE [CUKOR?][1]

[New City]
[Fall, 1945]

Dear George—

Kurt is now enthusiastic about the possibilities of a musical based on this new Jefferson story, but I am loathe to complicate my life and my season with a musical—especially since the play with Ingrid is a major job—so we're giving up that idea. I mention it only because it does have the kind of background in which you might find place for music and for musical interludes. You will note that I have omitted the Lincoln episode, also the Indians and the negro, sticking to a story line that involves the theatre and the Jefferson-Tessie-Claire triangle, with the young Polly and old Jefferson as supporting characters.[2] Rip Van Winkle was not a great success till later than I indicate, but Jefferson did try it out and put it aside for a while for the re-writing that put it in its present form.[3] I have done a little preliminary tinkering with dialogue, but won't get serious along that line till I hear from you as to whether or not this outline comes near what you'd like to use. If you don't like it—or if you think it's not in shape to show to the studio—please let me know exactly what you think is wrong.

Please give my best to Kate if you see her.[4] I'm still brooding over the fact that I have no play to offer her—now that she wants a play. If you have an idea for one let me know. I'd drop the picture instantly and go to work on it.

Sincerely

Max

1. Cukor (b. 1899), who directed the original production of *Saturday's Children*, went to Hollywood during the thirties and became a director for MGM. The picture outlined in the present letter was not made, but Anderson's script focused on Joseph Jefferson (1829–1905), American actor raised in a family of actors and most often associated with *Rip Van Winkle*. Jefferson published his autobiography in 1890, and Anderson's 1945 diary, at July 6, notes: "I read Jefferson's autobiography. Wrote some trial pages. Dinner at Kurt's—Talk with Kurt about . . . Jo Jefferson."

2. The Lincoln episode is prominent in the autobiography. In 1841 Jefferson with his father's troupe arrived at Springfield, Ill., where they were met by a prohibitive tax on theatrical performances. Lincoln, thinking the tax unjust, took the matter to court and succeeded in having the tax removed. He accepted no pay for his work, and the penniless troupe looked on him as their savior. Except for "old Jefferson," Joseph's father, the other people and episodes mentioned in the letter are not clearly present in the autobiography or other accounts of Jefferson's life.

3. Following its publication in *The Sketch-Book* (1819), Washington Irving's "Rip Van Winkle" was frequently dramatized. Jefferson adapted the tale first in 1859 and again in 1860, but was dissatisfied with both versions as they were staged with himself in the title role. In London in 1865 playwright Dion Boucicault (1820–90) made a new version for him, and it was an instantaneous success with the English at its opening on September 4. The next year Jefferson repeated the success in New York and then devoted himself almost exclusively to the play until his retirement in 1904, when he had become so celebrated in the role that he was known as America's Rip Van Winkle. In

1895 he published the play with a preface that traces the development of his version of *Rip Van Winkle*.

4. Katharine Hepburn (b. 1907), who had wanted to do *Joan of Lorraine*.

143. TO INGRID BERGMAN

Playwrights' Company
New York City
October 20, 1945

Dear Ingrid—[1]

This is a business letter which I don't like to write, but it has to be done sometime, so here goes. Victor Samrock tells me that the contract which you signed to do Joan is not acceptable to Actors Equity—the actors' union in New York—and that therefore I really have no contract with you to do the play. Equity objects to some of the clauses inserted by Mr. Dan. I'm asking Victor to redraw the contract in a way that Equity will accept, and send it to you for your signature.

Also, now that the play is definitely off until next year I would like to make a pre-production sale to pictures. It's not, as you know, my fault that the production is delayed, and I would frankly like to make an income out of it this year. All your conditions could be met. According to the rules of the Dramatists' Guild the bidding would have to be open among all the major companies, but it would be possible to retain for you the choice of the director, the producer and any other control you desired. You could have any salary you wanted to name. I am quite certain, and so is Harold Freedman, that we could get a very large price for the picture rights now. After the opening the price would depend somewhat on how the play was received.

You know how much I want you to do both the play and the picture. You are the Joan I hope for. And I know you want to do it. But it's not good business or even good friendship to have no contract, as at present, so we must get that matter settled. —To show my good faith in the matter let me say this. Kate Hepburn is in town and anxious to do a play. She has always wanted to do Joan. She will play a play a whole season and then on the road. She does not demand a quarter of the author's share in the picture rights. She could do the play this year. You and I have no contract legally because of the interference of Mr. Dan. Yet I am not showing the play to Kate. I am going to wait for you. You are the one for Joan. —Considering these things don't you owe it to me to allow an immediate picture sale? Please let me know at once how you feel about this?[2]

Sincerely

Max

1. Originally scheduling *Joan of Lorraine* for production in the fall of 1945, Anderson had to postpone the production until the following fall in order to accommodate Miss Bergman's motion picture schedule (during 1945–46 she made *The Bells of St. Mary's*, *Spellbound*, *Saratoga Trunk*, and *Notorious*).

2. Miss Bergman did not consent to an immediate picture sale, and *Joan of Arc* (the motion picture adapted from *Joan of Lorraine*) was not made until 1947–48, with Miss Bergman in the title role.

144. TO S. N. BEHRMAN

October 26, 1945

Dear Sam—[1]

Forgive me for being so late in thanking you for that note about my play. The note came in time to save me from an overwhelmingly adverse vote—and I know that you wrote it at a time when you were desperately trying to do something with your own play. At the moment I'm wondering whether I shouldn't give up on that one—and not go any further toward a production. A playwright is always caught between the need to protect his own concept and the need for criticism. He must have both—and when to fight for his concept and when to give up—who can decide except the madman in between?[2]

I was sorry I couldn't come down to see your play. I want to see you soon, anyway. My best (I slip this in slyly) to Elia.

Love

Max

1. Behrman's *Dunnigan's Daughter*, then having a try-out run in Washington, was produced by the Theatre Guild and directed by Elia Kazan. Anderson supported Behrman in his wish to have the Guild produce the play, but other members of the Playwrights' Company objected, and the controversy led to Behrman's resignation from

the company. Anderson was revising *Truckline Cafe* after its rejection by the Playwrights' Company.

2. The following February Anderson produced *Truckline Cafe* with Elia Kazan and Harold Clurman, and Kazan directed the production.

145. TO LOUIS KRONENBERGER[1]

[New City]
November 21, 1945

Dear Mr. Kronenberger—

Reading your article in *Commentary* this afternoon I find myself asking why you omit from your list of causes the one basic reason for the present impotence of the theatre. You say "In a time of crisis we may partly excuse a lack of art." You diagnose "a lack of discipline, of aspiration, of maturity, not to speak of talent." Surely you know that the trouble goes deeper. For the first time in our history the majority of thinking people have come up against a crippling lack of faith. There is no faith, political, religious, social or personal, that remains unshaken nowadays—and it seems to me this is just as apparent in the young people as in old fellows like myself. Now a good play cannot be written except out of conviction—for or against—and when convictions wobble the theatre wobbles. No matter what his other equipment may be, if a dramatist has no faith he cannot fashion a play. The era of good playwriting is an era of confidence—usually, in retrospect, mistaken—confidence that runs through playwrights, audiences, actors and the whole structure of society. Every play, even a farce or a mystery or a comedy of manners, must uphold or attack some standard of loyalty or behaviour. But we are beginning to wonder whether there are standards based on anything firmer than a desire to survive. We are edging toward that frame of mind which has meant the end of a good many epochs of the theatre—to say nothing of civilizations. And it's likely that there has never been such a general disintegration of beliefs and morals as now. Men and women, one and all, are in the unfortunate position of having to live by unproveable, improbable and generally nonsensical propositions which their busy, logical brains are constantly attacking and bringing to the ground.

And when logic has won, and the man—or the civilization—is entirely cynical—then the man or civilization is ready for the eternal junk-pile. Novels and poems don't necessarily die at such a time. Novels can be made out of pure gossip; poems can be made out of pure despair. But a play cannot exist without some kind of affirmation.

The fission of the atom adds to our confusion, of course. With unlimited power in a few hands it grows doubtful that democracy can operate much longer, and democracy—a faith that the people will somehow feel and find their way, even though blindfold—was about all we had left to cling to. Only the insensitive and the fanatics remain unconfused at present—and they don't write good plays.

Sincerely
M. A.

This requires no answer. I don't answer letters and I don't expect it of other people.

1. Kronenberger (b. 1904), who was to become a professor of theater arts at Brandeis in 1953, was for much of his career the drama critic for *Time* (1938–61). He published extensively, on historical subjects and contemporary culture as well as on the drama, and at the time of the present letter he had contributed an article to the first number of *Commentary* on "The Decline of the Theater" (*Commentary* 1 [November, 1945]: 47–51).

146. TO FRANK D. FACKENTHAL[1]

March 8, 1946

Dear Mr. Fackenthal:

It will give me great pleasure to be present at Columbia to receive the degree of Doctor of Letters on June 4th.

I have always had an aversion to the medieval symbolism of the cap and gown but now that I have very little hair on the top of my head, I see that there is a point in the costume. I[t] makes elderly men more presentable. And the same, I suppose, goes for honorary degrees.

But, seriously, I have an increasing respect for Columbia. Having two sons there,[2] I receive very constant and accurate reports. You

appear to have a real university, and at a time when it has become
almost impossible to maintain any standards.

Sincerely,
Maxwell Anderson

1. Fackenthal (1886–1968), associated with Columbia University in various
capacities since entering as a freshman in 1902 and during the early forties a member of
the committee that directed the Manhattan Project for atomic research, was at the time
acting president of Columbia (1945–48) and had invited Anderson to receive an
honorary degree from the school. Anderson had been unable to accept a similar
invitation in 1943, when his trip to London and North Africa took him out of the
country at commencement time, but he did accept the present invitation.
2. Quentin, who had taught there since 1939, and Terence, who was enrolled in
Columbia College that year.

147. TO ARTHUR S. LYONS [1]

[New City]
July 9, 1946

Dear Mr. Lyons:

Kurt Weill has told me about a conversation he had with you
about a possible picture production tie-up for The Playwrights'
Company in California. I have been thinking for some time that it
would be wise for us to produce and supervise our own pictures, and
that if we could make a business arrangement with some firm in the
west which gave us access to production facilities, we should be in a
far better position to control what is done with our plays when they
are transferred to the screen. I wonder if you would be willing to write
me in some detail concerning what your firm would have to offer and
how we could cooperate to make those of our plays which look like
good picture properties into pictures of which we could be proud—
and at the same time retain some financial interest in them.

The most important item in any such arrangement would be the
control we kept over the making of the pictures. We would want to
have a free hand in choosing writers, directors and actors. And we
would want to retain control of the copyrights. But I feel that some
business approach is possible, and since you are on the ground and

have thought the matter over, I'd be very glad to hear from you as to what plan you think is feasible.

Sincerely
Maxwell Anderson

1. Lyons, president of A&S Lyons, a talent agency in Hollywood, was also associated with David Loew in Producing Artists, Inc., a company for producing motion pictures.

148. TO S. N. BEHRMAN

August 1, 1946

Dear Sam—[1]

I miss you. Nothing reconciles me to losing you from the company except the news from Lawrence that you have finished one play and started another. If resigning has that effect on you you should do it often.

And I keep in touch with you by way of the New Yorker. You might try reading *Hamlet* with the S.p. in mind. Or *King Lear*. Or *Othello*. Or *Paradise Lost*—to say nothing of *Genesis*. A whole literature has been lost here somewhere.

Anyway—though in this theatre a man sees the folks he's working with, and no others usually—I hope to see you

Love
Max

1. Behrman had a letter in the current *New Yorker* ridiculing Edmund Wilson, who asserted in a review of Oscar Wilde (*New Yorker*, June 29, 1946, pp. 69–77) that Wilde's fiction must be read with the author's syphilis in mind. For syphilis Wilson used the term *Spirochaeta pallida*; and in his letter Behrman took up the term, using initials, and mocked Wilson's contention for its arbitrariness by interpreting a Wilde fairy tale in terms of S. p. (*New Yorker*, August 3, 1946, pp. 63–65). Earlier in the year Behrman had resigned from the Playwrights' Company and resumed his association with Lawrence Langner and the Theatre Guild, a loss that Anderson felt deeply.

149. TO ARTHUR S. LYONS

August 2, 1946

Dear Mr. Lyons:[1]

It's a bit difficult to get the playwrights to consider your suggestions at the moment, because Sherwood is in London and Rice is involved in three productions—two of "DREAM GIRL" and the musical of "STREET SCENE". A copy of your letter has been sent to both of them, however, and we're to have a full meeting this month sometime after Sherwood returns and can go into the matter then.

John Wharton and Kurt Weill and I have read the letter and talked it over unofficially. John said he thought it was the first proposal of the sort that we could consider seriously, and although he didn't have time to go into details, he left me with the impression that he would be satisfied with the conditions as he understood them. He felt that certain objections would be raised but that they could be overcome.

Kurt and I, discussing the project together afterward, agreed that the difficulty most likely to be encountered was indicated in your statement that the playwright should have a "strong voice" in the selection of directors, writers and players. We felt that we would have to have much more than a strong voice; we would have to have a controlling voice—and as you know whoever controls the money controls also the artistic direction of the production in hand. You would have to be safe-guarded against waste or extravagance, but we would have missed our aim altogether if we were not actually making the decisions. And since we would be working on a profit-sharing basis, we'd have as much incentive as you to be careful of expenditures.

All this is preliminary and off the record, however. As soon as my group makes up its collective mind, we must try to arrange a meeting and draw up terms. And I want to thank you for thinking the matter out and putting it in writing. That was an obvious, but a difficult and essential contribution, and you did a good job on it.[2]

Sincerely,

1. The New York production of Rice's *Dream Girl* had opened on December 14, 1945, and another production was to open soon in Chicago. *Street Scene*, originally produced in 1929, was being adapted as a musical, Rice providing the libretto,

Langston Hughes the lyrics, and Kurt Weill the music. The adaptation opened in New York on January 9, 1947.

2. The Playwrights' Company did not reach an agreement with Lyons for the production of their plays as motion pictures.

150. TO S. N. BEHRMAN

New City
August 29, 1946

Dear Sam—[1]

What a tender skin Mr. Wilson has! He can't bear it that one of his remarks should be taken in a light-hearted fashion. You were supposed to brood reverently.

At the risk of being over-fatuous I shall repeat to you what my old mother used to say to me about my recurrent "lung-fever." She pointed out to me that the fat boys had most of the bronchial troubles. And lately I've discovered that if I eat no bread nor anything made with flour the pounds peel off me. I repeat this old wives tale as one fat boy to another.

I wouldn't sell that Bangor place to a friend.[2] It's mostly musk-rat swamp surrounded by a deer-fence. The rats go under and the deer go over, leaving nothing inside but a slow-deep stream full of fish that bite and pull in so easy that no sportsman gets any fun out of them.

Well, I wish you were back in the company. I shall try to get you back in—or organize another one and get you into that.

I write this in the middle of the night—not being able to sleep. The curse of over-fifty is indecision. I could have used a little of it usefully when under fifty.

Love to you and Else—
Max

1. Edmund Wilson had replied in a huffy fashion (*New Yorker*, August 24, 1946, pp. 69–70) to Behrman's ridicule of his idea that a writer's physical make-up affected his work (see no. 148, n. 1).

2. Several acres outside Bangor, Maine, that Anderson had bought in 1937 for vacations and was now trying to sell.

151. TO THE NEW YORK NEWSPAPER AND
MAGAZINE THEATER CRITICS [1]

[New City]
[September 15, 1946]

Dear Mr. _____

The tickets enclosed are not for the opening night of *Joan of Lorraine* but for some weeks later in the run, and I write this letter to explain that the Playwrights' Company has made this change from the usual schedule at my request. It is my conviction that a small group of the theatre critics of New York have become, without intention perhaps, but no less absolutely, a board of censors which a play must pass to achieve a run. And since New York is the only play producing center for the country these same critics constitute a censorship board for the theatre of the United States. There was a time, not so long ago, when a play might, and sometimes did, live down a set of adverse notices and find an audience, but the costs of production and operation are currently so high that this has become impossible. Plays now live or die by your verdict and that of your fellow reviewers. And since it seems to be the opinion of a majority of the critics' circle that it is a critic's duty to destroy whatever play he does not like, and destroy, if possible, the reputation of the playwright along with his play, since the circle has the whole power of the metropolitan press behind it and can operate in security, with no chance of adequate discussion or reply, any play, whatever its merit or demerit, can be blasted off the stage, never to be revived, if a few of the men who occupy positions similar to your own happen to find it unamusing.

This is not a democratic process. Under these conditions the public never gets a chance to discover whether or not a play is worth seeing. Plays are struck down on the opening night, or blown up on the opening night, with very slight consideration but complete finality. The public, reading tens of thousands of words of praise or dispraise, naturally attends or stays away as advised by the newspapers, and hits and failures are so arrived at. How and how much the uncensored judgment of the public would differ from that of the critics is a matter of opinion. My own observation makes me certain that the public would accept many more plays, many more playwrights, and a far wider range of subjects, if it were allowed to choose for itself. It would be more tolerant both of what is cheap and of what is serious, for the theatre public contains audiences of many kinds—over-lapping but almost infinite in variety. Left to themselves these audiences would find out and support the plays that suited them, with the result that the theatre would take in vastly more territory, and reach both higher and lower than it can under the present system.

For the critics, in the main, speak for one audience only. They represent a little group of theatre-wise, newspaper-wise, cafe society-wise people, who go to first nights as former generations went to church, to show themselves and their clothes, and to be in on whatever is new. Most critics have the additional disadvantage of being graduate journalists, sharing the disillusions, the aversions and the general cynicism of their profession. It would be hard for them to show enthusiasm for any mortal achievement even if they did not one and all acquire, after a certain number of premieres, the critics' occupational disease—an acute allergy to all theatrical representation.

Very little has been said or written about the agony which critics suffer in the theatre, but any experienced reviewer knows how real that agony is, and how far it disables his judgment. His seat on the aisle is like a dentist's chair to him, and he sits in it with the apprehension of a patient who has been drilled repeatedly to the quick. He suffers through acts and scenes only because he is paid to do it and because he takes a professional pride in the reports he writes of these sessions in hell. Nothing but novelty or music or fast-moving comedy can take his mind off the routine of torture. He can give good reviews only to plays that distract him from his pain. Moreover, he has never chosen the play he is witnessing. He is the perpetual deadhead audience. He is there out of duty. If, with all this, he is ever capable of having a good time in the theatre, it's in the nature of a small miracle. The stage itself should be, must be, occupied by professionals. The professional audience is death.

The critics are of course not responsible for this combination of circumstances that peculiarly unfits them to judge plays and then sets them up as judges with absolute power. But the condition exists. I have long maintained that it is the function of the theatre, above and beyond entertainment, to help men think well of themselves and their activities—to point out and celebrate whatever is good and worth saving in our confused and often desperate generations. The human race, coming this year to a crossroads as deadly as that of Oedipus, is compelled to search its thoughts and emotions, and to ransack all possible sources of wisdom, for a way forward among doubtful paths. It must choose quickly, with inadequate evidence, and it must not be altogether wrong. Whoever has a word to say about where we are or where we are going should be allowed to say it now while it may still have some value. If it were possible to write for audiences—for men and women who go to the theatre because they want to see and hear the play, and not for any other reason—the stage would certainly attempt these major questions, and the audiences would listen carefully, knowing what straits we are in, and what the penalty is if we take a wrong turning. But most of the critics seem unaware of this crisis, and unaware of the bitter necessity which men now feel for some faith, some at least half-hope, some confidence, to take them through the immediate days and (if we are to have them) years. And since the critics are unaware, and it has become impossible to write for audiences without first pleasing the critics, the first and almost the only concern of the actor and playwright in our theatre is to alleviate the aisle-seat anguish of the professionals. To do this it is necessary to avoid whatever is serious, treat all affirmation as bad taste, and entertain briskly without faltering.

I know that you will say you favor the fullest and freest operation of the theatre, without restrictions on subject, treatment or talent. Unfortunately, the censorship of which you are part does not operate that way. Under the guise of a protection against artistic incompetence it has set up and maintains a general control over what may be seen on the stage. Like all other censorships it degrades and diminishes the art it sets out to serve. It has kept many of our best playwrights out of the theatre for many years. It turns on the younger playwrights with special fury, making no attempt to find or nurture talent, but only to annihilate any writer who does not talk loud enough or funny enough to compete with the eternally whirling dentists's drill on the critical molars. It has ousted so many playwrights, actors, producers and directors from Broadway that our theatre sinks yearly to a less and less impressive fraction of what it used to be, and the role of the critic himself dwindles along with the institution he gradually destroys. Lesser men have taken over most of the critical assignments because there is hardly enough theatre left to be worth a city editor's attention. Though this reduction in size is not the work of the critics alone—for there have been other parasites gnawing at the timbers—they have had a major and determining part in the destruction. And as their power has increased they have used it less wisely and with less mercy.

You will have gathered by this time why the tickets enclosed are not for the first night. I want the public to see my play and form its opinion before you have given yours. I know that this is a good deal to ask, because it takes the power of life and death out of your hands and puts it into the hands of the audience. But nearly every one of you has admitted, either in print or in private, that the critics have too much power, more than they want or should have, and has indicated that he would be happier without so much responsibility on his hands and so much weight attached to his words. I believe the majority of your number will agree with me that in a democracy the men and women who pay for their seats and go to the theatre to get something for themselves out of the play or the acting should decide which plays are worth their while.

If I did not take the theatre very seriously, if I did not believe the freedom of the theatre just as important as freedom of the press or freedom of speech, I should not go to this trouble myself nor put you to the trouble of altering your first-night arrangements. But I do believe the theatre important and its freedom important. I believe it should be judged by the public and not by a subsidized group. As I see the matter, I am trying to arrange for a plebescite to replace the ruling of an arbitrary and prejudiced court martial which doubles as its own firing squad.

Sincerely

P.S. Since the critics that write for immediate publication constitute the real censorship it would have been possible to make a distinction between these (mainly newspaper) reviewers and those whose opinions are printed later on. Also there are some able and conscientious men among the critics who would rather make a fair appraisal than a wise-crack, and exceptions could have been made in their favor. But any such attempt at discrimination would have been open to question. To give this method an honest trial it must be all or none, and I have asked the office to be quite impartial.[2]

1. The present letter, written in connection with *Joan of Lorraine*, represents Anderson's response to the critical reaction to his most recent play, *Truckline Cafe* (unpublished, see *Catalogue*, pp. 77–78). *Truckline Cafe* had opened in New York on February 27, 1946, to reviews unanimously condemnatory and in the main vitriolic. A

few days later, in a newspaper article, Anderson appealed over the heads of the critics for public support of the play ("To the Theatre Public," *New York Herald Tribune*, March 4, 1946, p. 10, cols. 1–2), but because of sparse attendance *Truckline Cafe* closed on March 9. On March 18 Anderson's 1946 diary noted that "all day [he was] trying to write a preface for *Truckline Cafe*—on the present critical situation. Not much good—what I've written." On April 24 he returned to the writing of *Joan of Lorraine* and immediately began to develop the argument against the critics and the plan for withholding their opening night tickets that are embodied in the present letter. According to the 1946 diary he wrote a first draft of the letter on April 27–28, another on June 13–15, then revised the second draft on September 15. An autograph note heading the final draft indicates that the letter was sent: "A Letter to the Theatre Critics of New York—Sent with the Tickets to *Joan of Lorraine*."

2. The critics ignored the letter, attending *Joan of Lorraine* on opening night and making no reference to the letter in their enthusiastic reviews, but Anderson did not forget the matter. Recasting it, he published the letter as "The Mighty Critics" in the *New York Times* (February 16, 1947, sec. 2, p. 1, cols. 1–2, p. 2, cols. 1–2), thereby stimulating a separate controversy (see letters no. 152 and 153), then used it as the leading essay in *Off Broadway* when that book was published in the summer of 1947. In 1948 he envisioned a similar plan for circumventing the critics in connection with *Anne of the Thousand Days* (see letter no. 160).

152. TO E. B. WHITE [1]

March 1, 1947

Dear Andy—

If you, of all people, could miss completely the point of what I had to say about the critics, the theatre must be inexplicable to laymen or I must have done a poor job of explaining. You say you choose the plays you see. No doubt you do, but you choose them from among those the critics let live. Any play the critics say no to dies, and if you look for it the next week you don't find it. Your comment implies that you believe the critics are always right, and that you and the public should be protected from any play the critics don't like.

You say you "will settle for this play-reviewing force in preference to the force that tries to stand between me and Brooks Atkinson." But what force tries to stand between you and Brooks Atkinson? Do you mean that I am trying to exert such a force? I said, and meant, nothing like that. I said that Mr. Atkinson's opinions should not have the force of law, which they have at present. They have that force, as I tried to make very clear, only because theatre costs are now so high that overwhelmingly good opinions in the press are essential to a play that is to run.

What I did not say in my article, but what I should think would occur to you as a journalist, is that it is sadly injurious not only to the public but to the critic himself when a critic's opinions have the effect of a statute.

You say that I complain that critics are chosen for their readability. I made no such complaint. I enjoy readable critics as much as you do. But I maintained, and still do, that it is most unfortunate that critics chosen for their readability should become, whether they like it or not—and many of the more intelligent among them do not like it—judges and censors whose lightest words operate as legislation on Broadway. A critic has no obligation to be fair. A judge has.

You say that what degrades and diminishes the art of the theatre is a bad play. Have the critics never acclaimed bad plays? Have they never decried good ones? Public opinion is the only trustworthy court for such questions, and the way things are now set up there is no possibility of appeal from the critics to the public.

I agree most heartily that "if democracy means anything at all, it means that secrecy is mischievous." It also means that monopolies, whether in opinion or anything else, are mischievous.

As ever

Max

1. White (b. 1899), a prolific writer whose books include children's stories, a manual of style, and collections of his poems and essays, was long associated with the *New Yorker* and responsible for its "Talk of the Town" column. For a short time he also conducted another column, "Turtle Bay Diary," and in that column on the day of the present letter (*New Yorker*, March 1, 1947, pp. 78–79) he had taken vigorous exception to Anderson's recent attack on New York theater critics ("The Mighty Critics," *New York Times*, February 16, 1947, sec. 2, p. 1, cols. 1–2, p. 2, cols. 1–2). White defended the critics as safeguards against mediocrity in the theater and attacked Anderson for preferring secrecy to a free and open discussion of plays.

153. TO E. B. WHITE

March 10, 1947

Dear Andy,[1]

Personally I'd have read the Turtle Bay Diary for at least six years if I'd lived so long. As it is I find myself on the look-out, as I dodge through the New Yorker, for that peculiar unabashed lucidity which seems to be your own. Maybe I'll distrust it a little more in the future, because it seemed to me that you pulled a rabbit-punch after the bell rang, but I don't know either. A man's whole life is lived on a basis of insufficient evidence.

I guess what I wanted to say was that I never like my own work very much by the time it gets on the stage. But if people want to go to it the critics shouldn't stop them.

Yours, with the usual incomplete understanding

1. In a playful attempt to mollify Anderson, White had replied to no. 152 by saying that "Turtle Bay Diary," which he had hoped would run for six years, had closed after only two performances.

154. TO ARCHER MILTON HUNTINGTON

Hotel Bel-Air
Los Angeles, California
April 27, 1947

Dear Archer—[1]

It meant a lot to me to get that letter from you. I try not to have illusions about myself and what I've done—though without a bit of ego nobody would do anything—and I want to give at least as much credit to others as I'd take for myself if we shifted places. However, I did think I had said something significant—not new, of course—in the play, and that all the commentators had missed it. It's gratifying when a fellow with a good brain says there is something there and I wasn't just fooling myself.

We're ensconced in this palatial and unpalatable hotel, probably for some time—since this picture means a lot to me financially and I'd be wise to see it through the works.[2] But I haven't forgotten our appointment for September, and hope to have a new play written to show you. That's not a threat, however. I hate reading MS. and understand that in others. Mab sends her love to Anna and to you— and so do I, though you'll probably throw it right back in my teeth, enriched with profanity.

Sincerely
Max

1. Huntington, in a letter of April 15, 1947 (T), had congratulated Anderson on *Joan of Lorraine*, which he had just read. He thought that Anderson was especially well suited for philosophizing by means of history and that he had made a powerful contemporary play out of the Joan story.
2. *Joan of Arc*.

155. TO UPTON SINCLAIR

[Los Angeles, California]
June 4, 1947

Dear Upton—[1]

I have learned after many battering years in the theatre that one has to be completely honest about the plays he reads—otherwise he'll find himself involved in productions which he doesn't believe in and to which he can give nothing. I found *A Giant's Strength* well-built and well-written, and in parts moving and fascinating—but I was disappointed. Inevitably, no doubt. When you write about the atomic bomb you're certain to say what should be done about it—which will always sound like propaganda—and you are certain to indicate a solution—which, since the future is unknown, will always sound hypothetical and unconvincing. This would happen to anybody who chose this subject. It's not a criticism of your playwriting but only of your choice of material.

One other weakness is inherent in the subject itself. Nobody has yet worked out a solution. You carry your people through an imaginative experience—and carry the reader along with you most of the time—but in the end all the lad can say is: Stop killing each other. Well, that's been said. Jesus said it, and so have many others, including the Quakers, and the wars get bigger and more final. They make playwriting sound like a morning lark in the Mammoth Cave.

Nevertheless I enjoyed reading the play. I hope you'll write more.[2]

Sincerely
Maxwell Anderson

1. Sinclair had recently sent Anderson his play, *A Giant's Strength* (published by the author, 1948).
2. His *Autobiography* (1962) says that in all Sinclair wrote thirty plays (p. 306), but none were produced professionally.

156. TO ROBERT E. SHERWOOD

Sierra Pictures, Inc.
Hal Roach Studio
Culver City, California
July 26, 1947

Dear Bob:[1]

After our talk on the phone I am inclined to think you're getting the same advice from every direction, and this letter may be quite superfluous. Nevertheless, I'll set down the two or three notes which seem to me most essential.

First, let me repeat that it was a great pleasure and like a breath of fresh air to read the play. It has, like everything you do, good firm writing and thinking and imaginative wit.

Second, (I repeat this though everybody has said it) if men don't want to live like the gods and will choose, instead of immortality, our usual misery, death, disease, even war, rather than monotonous perfection, then the reason is that the best doesn't come out in men or nations until they are challenged and meet the challenge and somehow manage to fight their way through.

Third, when this comes to an open issue between the gods and the man, he should know why he's leaving, and should say it. They should know why he goes and the half-mortal girl should know why she goes. Perhaps the heaviest penalty should fall on her. She should have to give up her immortality and Ares should warn her of this.

Fourth, perhaps there should be two girls involved, on[e] wholly a goddess, the other half-mortal. In this case, he would, of course, fall in love first with the goddess, then find himself drawn to the other.

I am a little confused, not by the play, but just philosophically, about the meaning of the theme. If what we are struggling toward is what the gods have—control, security, poise and immortality—and if we don't want these things when we arrive at them, what is it that we want? But, no doubt, that's too much to ask at this moment.

And you will have thought much more about this than I have. If anything further occurs to me I'll write to you before we come east. The sooner I can talk it over with you the better I'll like it. I think it will be a beautiful play. It needs that missing scene.[2]

Affectionately,

Max

1. Sherwood had sent Anderson *The Twilight*, one of several plays he wrote in an attempt to return to the theater following the war and the writing of *Roosevelt and Hopkins* (1948).
2. *The Twilight* was not produced or published.

157. TO THE EDITOR, *New York Herald Tribune*

New City
January 9, 1948

To THE NEW YORK HERALD TRIBUNE:[1]

Kindly allow me to answer the letter from Mr. George Polk, which you published January 7th, about my reports from Greece. I wrote five articles on the situation in Greece for the Herald Tribune. Only two were printed in New York, and those two badly garbled in transmission. If all five had been published as I wrote them my position would have been made much clearer. However, Mr. Polk does gather correctly that I believe the present government in Greece, though far from perfect, should be supported, and that a victory for the Communist guerillas in Macedonia would be a disaster for all free men. The Greek people have earned and deserve a better government than they have, but if Mr. Polk believes that reforms in Greek

government would end the crisis there he is more naive than a
newspaperman has a right to be. Russia will not be satisfied with, but
will make war, declared or undeclared, against any government in
Greece except a Communist government.

The earth is now divided, at Russian insistence, and despite
American and British attempts at reconciliation, into two antagonistic
areas. One consists of Russia and her captive satellites, the other of the
nations which operate mainly as capitalistic economies. Within the
zone of Russian dominance, the individual has no rights the state is
bound to respect. In all countries of the capitalist group there is an
attempt to guarantee the liberties which are set down in our own Bill
of Rights. Russia and the other Communist-controlled nations are run
like armies, from the top, without freedom of speech, press, thought
or action. There is probably an occasional failure in the discipline, but
that does not affect the overall intent. In the capitalist group of
nations the freedoms which are guaranteed by law can only be
approximated, could never be attained, even by the best and wisest
administration imaginable. They are not attained in the United States,
they are not attained in Switzerland, they are not attained in Norway
—and they are not attained in Greece. Greece, on the frontier between
communism and capitalism, and fighting a communist rebellion which
is supported by all the nations along her northern border, has done
very well to keep any of the freedoms which men hope for in a
peaceful society. But she has kept a great many of them. She has a free
press, free speech, a free theatre, freedom of political opinion, a free
economy. That rebels have been executed and imprisoned there can be
no doubt. That injustice has been done many times there can be no
doubt. With the best will in the world authorities are not always just,
and after the training for violence necessitated by the last war,
combined with the ancient vendettas which Greece has inherited from
her past and the ruthless pressure of Russian power in the north, one
can hardly expect to find the best will in the world in the Athenian
government. Yet the difference between Greece and Yugoslavia can be
said to be infinite. It is a difference not in degree but in kind. In
Yugoslavia, or in any communist state, there is no attempt to establish
individual freedom. In Greece the attempt is made, and though not as
successful as in the United States, where we have everything in our
favor, it gives to the citizens of Athens, Crete and Salonika at least a

thousand times the liberty currently available to the slave populations of Moscow and Belgrade.

To the communists here and elsewhere there's nothing wrong with the Russian methods, for the communists have made a religion of slavery and appear content to see Russia enslave the earth. But if Mr. Polk is on the side of liberty against oppression, let him look again at those 400,000 refugees in Macedonia, driven from their farms and herds by military bands that profess to be Greeks but make their raids from across the border and retire to the refuge of Yugoslavia or Albania when they have finished their work of burning villages, running off cattle and impressing young men into service. Let him ask himself why there is no rebellion in Greece except in territory that can be reached overland from a communist country. Let him ask himself why there is no communism, but fierce opposition to it, in Crete—the part of Greece most badly battered by the war, least able to rebuild its cities, its agriculture or its tiny industry. Russia is a long way from Crete, and the thinking in Heracleion is a long way from Russian thinking.

The thinking in Athens is a long way from Russian thinking, too. Athens is a city of intellectuals, of political discussion, of passionate disagreements, of fortune and poverty, good luck and bad. But on one political subject I found a substantial agreement. Nearly everybody in Athens believes that if there were an election tomorrow the Greek government would be swung further to the right, further away from Communism than in the last election. Whatever the majority may think of their present government they would rather have it than the despotism that has conquered the Balkans and washes in over the Macedonian boundary.[2]

Maxwell Anderson

1. For a production of *Joan of Lorraine* in Athens, Anderson had visited Greece, November 1 to December 15, 1947, and had toured the country and sent back reports to the *New York Herald Tribune*. He cabled five reports, only two of which were published in the New York edition of the paper: "An American Observer in Greece," November 28, 1947, p. 26, cols. 5–7; and "The Plight of the Greek People," December 1, 1947, p. 22, cols. 5–7. (Two others were carried only in the Paris or International edition: "Freedom in Greece," November 25, 1947; and "The Conflict in Greece," November 27, 1947. The fifth, on the abiding interest in the drama among the Greek people, was not published at all.) In the published reports Anderson maintained that the Greek government, since it was democratic, deserved American support in its war against communist guerrillas operating in the north of the country. Anderson's position

was then attacked by George Polk, foreign correspondent for CBS in Athens. In
" 'Outright Injustice' in Greece" (*New York Herald Tribune*, January 7, 1948, p. 24,
cols. 6–7), Polk said that the Greek government was corrupt, unjust, and unpopular
and that Anderson's picture of it was pure "fiction."

2. The present letter was published as "An American Playwright Looks at Greece,"
New York Herald Tribune, January 18, 1948, sec. 2, p. 7, cols. 3–6.

158. TO ALAN PATON [1]

New City
March 15, 1948

Dear Mr. Paton:

I hope I can convey to you, at so great a distance, something of
the emotion with which I read "Cry, the Beloved Country" and which
many Americans must feel now as they read it. For years I've wanted
to write something which would state the position and perhaps
illuminate the tragedy of our own negroes. Now that I've read your
story I think you have said as much as can be said both for your
country and ours.

When I read the book I had just finished the second act of a play,[2]
a play that I hope to finish later. But the Kumalo story took such hold
on me that I decided I'd like to try to arrange it for the stage—and
would like to do it now, while the mood was still fresh. The other play
can wait. I'm sure that we can get together on the business
arrangements, for these things have been done before and your
representatives and mine seem to agree that the contracts which are
being sent you are usual and fair—but the purpose of this letter is to
explain how I would go about making the story ready for the theatre.

My first concern would be to keep as much as possible of the
dialogue and the story structure, just as they stand. Your effects are
both powerful and delicate—and both the power and the delicacy
could be lost in an ordinary dramatization. And to keep the plot and
the dialogue in the form you gave them would only be possible if a
chorus—a sort of Greek chorus—were used to tie together the great
number of scenes, and to comment on the action as you comment in
the philosophic and descriptive passages. Of course, I should have to
put some of that comment into verse, but some of the lyric prose could

be lifted out intact and set to music. Kurt Weill, who would make the musical setting, is as enthusiastic about the book and about this dramatic method for it as I am. We have worked together before, and you no doubt know of him.

It would be our task—as we see it—to translate into stage form, without dulling its edge or losing its poetry, this extraordinarily moving tale of lost men clinging to odds and ends of faith in the darkness of our modern earth. For the breaking of the tribe is only a symbol of the breaking of all tribes and all the old ways and beliefs.

Perhaps I should explain also that Kurt Weill and I are both members of the Playwrights' Company, that we are our own producers and would be in complete charge of the production, and that we are planning, if we receive your permission, to stage the play in New York next fall. But the permission must come first, naturally, before we go to work.

In any case, and no matter what you decide, I want to thank you for writing the book. I don't read novels any more. This is the first I've read in a good many years. But it's more than a novel, and I think it can be as touching and tragic in the theatre as on the printed page.

Sincerely
Maxwell Anderson

1. Paton (b. 1903), South African writer, teacher, and political leader whose career has been devoted to racial equality in South Africa, first attracted attention outside his own country with the publication of *Cry, the Beloved Country* by Charles Scribner's in February, 1948. He wrote the novel during the latter half of 1947, while inspecting Scandinavian and American prisons, and Anderson heard about the novel in December, 1947, from Dorothy Hammerstein, who along with Anderson was sailing from England to America. On March 1, 1948, Mrs. Hammerstein brought Anderson a copy of the novel, and during the next few days he and Kurt Weill decided to dramatize it, the dramatization becoming *Lost In the Stars*. (For a detailed account of how Anderson became acquainted with *Cry, the Beloved Country*, see Laurence G. Avery, "Maxwell Anderson and *Both Your Houses*," *North Dakota Quarterly* 38 [Winter, 1970]: n. 8, pp. 18–19).

2. *Anne of the Thousand Days*.

159. TO THE EDITOR, *Atlantic Monthly*[1]

New City
August 30, 1948

Dear Sir:

It's an excellent thing that the radio should, through such men as Don Hollenbeck, check on the accuracy of the press, but perhaps someone should also check the accuracy of Don Hollenbeck. When he writes that to me "the problem" (of Greece) "was all Red" he is indulging in the kind of simplification that makes tabloids unreliable. My articles in the Herald-Tribune were written in an effort to come a little closer to the truth than the American press—and radio—seemed to me to be getting. My impression was and still is that the Russians won their greatest propaganda battle in Greece. They succeeded in convincing a large number of American newsmen that the present Greek government is fascist, tyrannical, unjust, and without support from the people, that the Communists in the north are high-minded crusaders for reform, and that a Communist regime in Greece would be an improvement over what goes on there now. The only point I tried to make was that even the most ramshackle representative government is better than any Communist government, and that too many critics of Sophoulis[2] and the men around him were innocently following the party line up, down and across the isthmus.

The people of Greece, when I talked with them, were well aware that their government was not perfect. They looked with longing, as some Americans look now, back toward the democracy of Thomas Jefferson. They are well aware that Greece has always been a Mediterranean nation—that is, it has been governed, from the earliest pages of Herodotus on down, by a mixture of corruption, envy, heroism, malice, the sudden illuminations of genius, and the lust for power. They are now pulling together as best they can under a coalition cabinet which got in as the result of an election, and which (though it is not a government to be proud of, any more than the government of Jersey City is) has been slowly setting the nation on its feet after a series of war efforts and disasters such as no other people has been called upon to endure in this century.

A great deal has been said to discredit the Greek elections. I don't know, of course, how honest they were. I do know that they were far more honest than any election ever held in a Communist country. An agricultural director in Heracleion, Crete, who had lived in the United States and taken his degree at Cornell, was one of the official observers of the polling in Heracleion. He told me that in his opinion the Greek elections were not as honest as you would expect an election to be in Ithaca, New York, but about as honest as you would expect in Chicago.

I don't know, of course, how much injustice there has been in Greece, but I note that Secretary Marshall[3] has recently stated that Greece and the present Greek government are not being fairly treated by the American press. I note, too, that Dwight Griswold, the director of AMAG in Greece, does not believe that there have been many, if any, undeserved executions in Greece under the existing regime.[4] I remember that even the Athenian liberals who were most critical of the Sophoulis government maintained that their courts were upright and incorruptible. And I wonder if our own government would stick so closely to the rules that protect the individual from state tyranny if we were fighting a Communist rebellion urged on and supported by a massive group of foreign powers. The procedures of the Un-American Activities Committee lead me to believe that if the Communist danger were as real here as in Greece our House of Representatives would be inclined to shoot first and investigate afterward. There is no "Un-Greek Activities Committee" in Athens.[5]

Sincerely
Maxwell Anderson

1. In its current issue the magazine carried an article critical of Anderson's position on Greece, "CBS Views the Press," *Atlantic Monthly* 182 (September, 1948): 49–51. The article, by Don Hollenbeck, commentator on a weekly radio program, "CBS Views the Press," maintained that Anderson had oversimplified the Greek situation and added that for Anderson "the problem was all Red" (p. 49).

2. Themistocles Sophoulis, premier of Greece from 1945 until his death in 1949.

3. George C. Marshall, secretary of state (1947–49) and author of the European Recovery Program, or Marshall Plan.

4. Griswold, in Athens as chief of the American Mission for Aid to Greece (1947–48), had supported Anderson's sympathetic view of the Greek government and attacked the American press for inaccurate coverage of Greece in "Reporting and Interpreting the News in Greece," *New York Herald Tribune*, May 2, 1948, sec. 2, p. 7, cols. 3–6.

5. The present letter was published in *Atlantic Monthly* 182 (November, 1948): 18, with a response by Hollenbeck, pp. 18–19.

160. TO THE NEWSPAPER DRAMA CRITICS
      OF NEW YORK [1]

[New City]
[September, 1948]

Dear Mr. _____

This is practically an open letter, since I'm sending it to all the first-night critics on the newspapers of New York City. For some years I've been trying, like many theatre workers, to find a way around the critics' first night—the opening night at which the critics appear in a body and can act as a firing squad to shoot down the play on view.

It's been my contention, and I think a majority of playwrights, actors, producers and theatre-goers agree with me, that the newspaper critics have a power which they should not have. At present they decide whether or not a play shall live. Because they're invited to first nights in a body, because of the enormous prestige and influence of the papers which publish their opinions, a play must die if they turn against it. And this is no democratic procedure. If delegates chosen by theatrical producers decided which newspapers could live we'd have the same situation in reverse. In a democracy the public should choose the plays it may see, as well as the newspapers it may read. And at present the newspaper critics choose the plays.

We have got ourselves into this fix—critics, audiences, producers and theatre workers alike—because a large group of the critics in our city are also reporters. As reporters it's their duty to rush to every opening and spread the news of what happened last night in the theatre. As reviewers or critics it's their duty to give well-considered and expert opinions of the play and the production. The first-string critics who are also newspaper men have done their best to fit themselves into this dual role, but the confusion of functions has had two unhappy results: it robs the public of its right to judge for itself— for any play the critics don't like is shot down before the public has a chance to form an opinion, and it robs the public of the matured consideration of the newspaper reviewers. Once these men have said their hasty journalistic say they're committed, and must stick by their guns. A thoughtful and careful literary judgment is in the circumstances impossible. What we get usually is something cock-sure, amusing, and off-hand. Now the critics are almost all men of good will, who wish only well to the theatre. It's their right to say what they think about the plays that open in our city. They would have a perfect right to be wrong occasionally—even as wrong as they are—if their lightest words were not lethal. What is needed is that their judgments should be rendered a bit later, after the play has attracted, or failed to attract, its public. Coming the morning after an opening, they often have the effect of a butcher's maul in the abattoir. And the power of the critics is so great that very few of those who might be hurt by it dare speak about it.

To begin to remedy the existing situation, to "break the cake of custom" at least in one instance, I'm writing this letter to make a suggestion. If the critics on the dailies were willing to attend the first night of ANNE OF THE THOUSAND DAYS as reporters only, withholding their critical opinions till two or three weeks later, the public would have a chance to decide the fate of the play before the papers had destroyed it or built it up. The public might throng to it, might stay away from it. In the latter case, the morning-after critics would never have to conduct the gruesome execution which is customary when a play is found guilty. The play would be dead and quietly buried before they got there. In case the public was pleased the reviewers' comments would come, somewhat as the magazine comments come now, as literary estimates. And that is what they should be. Will you, therefore, do me this favor on the night ANNE OF THE THOUSAND DAYS opens in New York? Will you send a reporter in your place, and give the audiences of the first few weeks an opportunity to think for themselves? Or, if you attend the first night, will you act as a reporter only, describing the event, and neither praising nor condemning the play?

In asking this I am deliberately discarding the great advantage which the play would have if the critics went all out for it. When they like a production they are, of course, the most powerful press agents in the world. But their power is not good for the theatre, which should be a democratic institution. They are not chosen by the public, cannot speak for it, do not represent it. I am also asking you, I know, to limit your own power, and that's a lot to ask—but in the arts no man or group of men should have the power to strike dead.

Please write to Mr. William Fields of the Playwrights' Company, 630 5th Ave., to say whether you will attend the first night or will designate a reporter in your place; and also, if you elect to come, whether you will attend as a reporter only or will insist on acting as critic, censor, and judge. A good many of your number have already said that your verdicts should be less absolute. Here is a method of making them less absolute. I think such action would begin to save the life of the theatre, and since the critics need a theatre if they are to remain in business, would be better in the long run for the critics too.

Sincerely

Maxwell Anderson

P.S. Mr. Atkinson protests that the critics do not have the power to strike dead, and cites instances of plays that have survived critical damnation. Well, there are instances of men who lived after being shot through the head—but not many.[2]

M. A.

1. The letter, which asks them not to go to *Anne of the Thousand Days* on opening night, was not sent to the critics. Anderson's 1948 diary (ND), at October 4 notes that he had a talk with other members of the Playwrights' Company "about opening night without critics. They thought it could be worked in a non-Shubert house—not with *Anne*. We *have* a Shubert house." *Anne* opened (to generally favorable reviews) on December 8, 1948, at the Shubert Theatre, one of the many theaters owned by the theatrical organization created during the first half of the century by Samuel, Jacob, and Lee Shubert. But shortly after deciding not to send it to the critics, Anderson recast the letter and published it as "More Thoughts About Dramatic Critics," *New York Herald Tribune*, October 10, 1948, sec. 5, p. 1, cols. 3–5.

2. Brooks Atkinson, drama critic of the *New York Times*, had outlined his position in a letter to Anderson, April 18, 1947 (T).

161. TO BROOKS ATKINSON

[New City]

December 29, 1948

Dear Brooks,[1]

Communication is so slow on these remote and slippery hills that I have only today learned that the advertisement you proposed was actually printed. I didn't see it, but I want to thank you both for a good jest and good will.

My position on these quote ads is fairly obvious, and no doubt you've guessed it, but I'll say it just to keep things clear between us.

Since I do honestly believe that the critics on the daily papers have too much power over the theatre, and since advertisements that quote the critics add to their power, I can't honestly favor the usual quotes even when to do so would mean a greater gain at our own box office. No doubt you noticed that no quotes were used for "Joan of Lorraine".

I shall drink an old-fashioned to your good health this evening. May we both live long enough to continue our feud through the next decade.[2]

Sincerely,
Max

1. Since he thought newspaper critics had too much influence on the stage life of plays, Anderson had not used remarks by the critics in advertisements of *Joan of Lorraine* or *Anne of the Thousand Days*, though critical response to both plays was favorable. But in the *New York Times* of December 24, 1948, the ad for *Anne* included the lines " 'Stirring drama . . . Passionate chronicle of Heroic people.'—Atkinson, *Times*" (p. 13, col. 1).

2. Responding to the present letter, Atkinson said that he had inserted the quotations from his review in the Christmas spirit and was glad the prank had not annoyed Anderson (Atkinson to Anderson, January 4, 1949, NYP).

162. TO JOHN F. WHARTON

New City
January 21, 1949

Dear John:[1]

I went back and re-read a good deal of "The Sky is Falling" because I found it incredible that so much sharp and beautiful writing had been wasted on a subject impossible for the Broadway stage—by a man who certainly knows his Broadway. This is Gar's best work, and most illuminating observation, yet even with perfect casting (in the mind's eye) it leaves the reader with a feeling of emptiness, no hope, nobody to like, nowhere to go, and a sense of unreality. It is also, though this would not matter if the reader were involved deeply, more of a character study than a play. It reminds me of the turn of the century Germans—Wedekind—or maybe Kaiser—and of Strindberg. It's despair, but somehow not the current despair.

And the woman studied is somehow out-of-date, somebody who went into the ash-can long ago. The issues are not clear, either. Does Gar mean to indicate that the Communist winning of China is a good thing? Does he mean that there is never too much Government control in a democracy?

It may be that Gar is evading his talent. He sets out to do something daring, bold, ruthless, and revolutionary. His talent is for form, a leaping but controlled imagination, the right thing at the right time. Kurt suggests that Tallulah could play the part.[2] But even so, would she be liked enough to be interesting?[3]

Sincerely,

Max

Maxwell Anderson

1. Garson Kanin (b. 1912) later became well known as a director with such plays as *The Diary of Anne Frank* (1955) and *Funny Girl* (1964), but he first came to prominence in the theater as a playwright with the long-running *Born Yesterday* in 1946. Wharton, wishing to bring Kanin into the Playwrights' Company, had secured a production of his *The Smile of the World*, which had a brief run during the month of the present letter, and now was circulating another Kanin play, *The Sky Is Falling*, among members of the company.

2. Kurt Weill and the actress Tallulah Bankhead.

3. *The Sky Is Falling* was not produced, though Kanin's next play, *The Rat Race*, produced by Leland Hayward in December, 1949, also focused on a woman at the brink of despair. Kanin was later to direct Sherwood's *Small War on Murray Hill* for the Playwrights' Company (1957) but did not join the company.

163. TO ALAN PATON [1]

[New York City]

March 17, 1949

Script and music finished. Great encouragement from Playwrights Company. Expect start rehearsals early September. Hope you can be in New York then. It happens we have used the ending you suggested. Best regards[2]

Max and Kurt

1. Anderson and Weill finished *Lost in the Stars* in February, and throughout the writing had corresponded with Paton about their dramatized version of his *Cry, the Beloved Country*. Their most significant departure from the novel comes at the end of the play, where the white man Jarvis, made to realize the humanity of the black man Kumalo, joins Kumalo at his home when Kumalo's son is executed. Paton, taking a suggestion from Anderson, had elaborated that conclusion in a letter of June 22, 1948 (T), saying that the coming together of the two men of different races was the most dramatic part of the story but emphasizing that, in order to be true to South Africa, their friendship must be stumbling and awkward.

2. Paton came to New York for final rehearsals of *Lost in the Stars* in October, 1949, and stayed through the opening of the play on October 30.

164. TO JOHN CAMPBELL CROSBY [1]

New City
April 13, 1949

Dear Mr. Crosby:

If the critic-shooting season is truly open allow me a brief response to your article on the subject. There is no closed season on playwrights. Any critic is free to open fire on any one of them at any time and from any position, as your remarks demonstrated. It's a bit unsportsmanlike, since the critic sits in a bomb-proof shelter and the playwright travels unarmed and unprotected across the open, but that's the way the game is played, and naturally that's the way the critics like it.

I agree with you that it's a shameful thing for a playwright to purchase space in a newspaper to argue that the critics have too much power. It's not courteous for a playwright to point out that there were no critics at all in the great days of the theatre and that in a democracy the audience, not the critics, should judge the plays. Moreover, I have a vegetarian attitude toward critics. I shall never shoot one. I feel toward them as I feel about the sacred bulls and cows that wander unscathed through the kitchen gardens of vegetarian India, making free with the truck and leaving an occasional deposit of useful compost. They should not be shot. They should not be put to work. They should continue on their witty, inaccurate, unscrupulous way, free to browse, gore and trample. It's good for the peasantry. It keeps them on their toes. It runs the fat off them and keeps them healthy.

By the way, Mr. Crosby, how do you take criticism? Your recent columns have not been up to your earlier standard. Your style is less sharp and your ideas less pungent. Were you a flash in the pan? Have you run out of amusing things to say?[2]

Sincerely,

MAXWELL ANDERSON

1. Crosby (b. 1912), since 1965 in London with the *Observer*, had before that a long career as columnist on the *New York Herald Tribune* (1935–65). His column on the day of the present letter criticized a radio program in which it was maintained that drama critics were unqualified to judge plays because they were not involved in writing or producing them. Crosby added: "It's an idea that has been kicked around for some time. It was most conspicuously and irritably advanced in a paid advertisement written some years ago by Maxwell Anderson in what might best be described as blank prose." The reference is to Anderson's "To the Theatre Public," *Herald Tribune*, March 4, 1946, p. 10, cols. 1–2, which attacked drama critics for their insensitivity to the public's concerns, not for their inexperience in play production. Crosby's column, a defense of drama critics, was entitled "Radio in Review: Critics Are In Season," *Herald Tribune*, April 13, 1949, p. 23, cols. 3–4.

2. Autograph note in upper left corner: "That's right. Put it in the basket. Continue the great tradition of American journalism. Never give a playwright an even break."

165. TO JOHN MASON BROWN

May 18, 1949

Dear John:[1]

A lot of this is quotation, but I can't think of any better way to say it. Forget the fifty dollars. This isn't work.

Sincerely

Maxwell Anderson

P.S. —By the way, I didn't write that dialogue you objected to in "Joan of Arc".[2] It was probably stuck in at the last moment during the shooting. You evidently don't know what goes on in the film business. The writer has no control whatever. If Ingrid hadn't insisted on taking out all human touches and making Joan a plaster saint the thing might have had some quality. She wrecked that one. She had the power to wreck it and she did. Moreover, she's completely unscrupulous. She doesn't keep her word and she has no respect for a writer's work.

1. Brown had asked Anderson for an article to run in the *Saturday Review of Literature*, and with the present letter Anderson sent him a passage from *Off Broadway* (pp. 33–35) with a new introduction, making an article that focused on the democratic nature of the theater. Brown published the article as "Democracy's Temple," *Saturday Review of Literature* 32 (August 6, 1949): 135.

2. *Joan of Arc*, the motion picture made from *Joan of Lorraine* and starring Ingrid Bergman, dropped the contemporary episodes from the play, and, though Anderson wrote the original film script, the script as filmed was written by Andrew Solt. In his review of the picture Brown had developed the point that "Although a talking picture is meant to be heard as well as seen, the words spoken in 'Joan of Arc' are so flat, jarring, colloquial, or undistinguished that the movie might have been better had it been a silent one" ("Joan and the 'Voices'," *Saturday Review of Literature* 31 December 18, 1948: 22–24).

166. TO JOHN F. WHARTON

[New City]
[May, 1949]

Dear John:[1]

As I read his accusation, Mr. Hackett appears to charge me with having plagiarized, or stolen, parts of three works of his: (1) a biography of Henry the VIIIth, (2) a novel about Anne Boleyn, and (3) a play about Henry the VIIIth. He does not make it quite clear which of these works he is quoting when he writes the list of phrases or ideas which he thinks I appropriated from him—but I wish to make one thing quite clear at the beginning. I read Mr. Hackett's biography of Henry the VIIIth, along with other histories and biographies, as part of my preparation for writing *"Anne of the Thousand Days."* I did not read his novel or his play on this subject nor did I know till after my play was finished that he had written the novel or the play. I affirm this quite deliberately, and I am willing to take oath to it. If Mr. Hackett accuses me of so much as looking into his play or novel—or even of hearing about them from others before my play was finished—he is accusing me of perjury. I did not know of either one, even by hearsay, before my play was complete and ready for production.

I first heard of Mr. Hackett's novel when Bretaigne Windust, who had been engaged to stage my play, brought the book to my house.[2] I did not read it then, and have never read it. As for the play, I heard about it later from Harold Freedman, at some time during the summer of 1948, when we were going over the names of actresses who might play Anne Boleyn. Mr. Freedman recalled then that Gertrude Lawrence had been considering a play on the subject of Henry and Anne by Francis Hackett. I have not read or seen a copy of Mr. Hackett's play. I have never discussed its content with anybody. Since this question came up I have been told by Elmer Rice and Robert Sherwood that they have read Mr. Hackett's play, but they did not show it to me or mention it to me earlier.

If I had known that Mr. Hackett had written a play about Henry the VIIIth before I wrote my play on that subject I would certainly have avoided reading his script. I have always tried to play fair in this matter of authorship, and I would consider it both unfair and unforgiveable for one playwright to read another playwright's work with an eye to finding something he might use. Moreover, after a quarter century spent in the theatre, I have learned that it is unwise for a practising playwright to read any unproduced play unless it is written by a friend or business associate. There are many plagiarism suits in the theatre, and if the plaintiff can point to the fact that the defendant has read his manuscript he can usually find some parallel to prove that lines or situations have been stolen. It's safer to read no scripts, and I come as close to reading none as I can and still remain a member of the Playwrights' Company.

Perhaps it will make my position in this matter somewhat clearer if I go over a few unflattering statistics relating my work in the theatre. Beginning in 1923 I have written and produced twenty-seven plays for the New York stage. Six of these were historical plays. Three of them, *Elizabeth the Queen*, *Mary of Scotland*, and *Anne of the Thousand Days*, dealt with the Tudor period of English history, the period I know best. I have not been invariably successful by any means, but it happens that all three of the Tudor plays have been successful. From my point of view it would seem not only unnecessary but foolhardy for me to take lessons in historical playwriting from Francis Hackett, who, according to his own testimony, has written only one play, and has not been able so far to get that one produced. My experience in the theatre has made me believe that good plays seldom go begging for a production. There is a great demand for any play that has a chance with the public. Somehow or other such plays do reach the stage.

Of the plays I have written four were collaborations and two have been dramatized from books. The royalties on the four collaborations were divided equally between the authors.[3] In the case of "Outside Looking In", which was dramatized from a book by Jim Tully,[4] an arrangement was made under which Tully shared the royalties with me. In the case of "Cry, the Beloved Country", which is planned for next fall, I have a contract with Alan Paton, the author, which guarantees his share in the royalties. It has been my intention in every case to deal openly and fairly with any author whose material I used, and if I had felt that my play about Anne was a dramatization of Hackett's material I would certainly have offered him a share of royalties. I did not feel any such obligation. I used his biography as a source-book only, and I studied so many other sources that it would have been quite impossible to discover the origin of speeches or scenes, even if historical material, derived from extant and available data, were copyrightable, and the property of individual owners. Mr. Hackett attempts to prove that certain speeches in my play about Anne were derived directly from his work—but on examination of his parallels I find not more than one or two that cannot be traced back just as easily to other source-books which I used. I find also that I took far more material from other histories than from Mr. Hackett's. When I planned the play and began writing it I was reading, not Mr. Hackett's book but a book by Martin Hume, "The Wives of Henry the VIIIth."[5]

Mr. Hackett maintains now that his biography of Henry is not a source-book, but that was not his opinion at the time it was published. In the *Foreword* to the 1929 edition he expressly states: "I have invented no dialogue. Thanks to the full diplomatic correspondence, I could stick to the record and yet quote direct speech." The *Foreword* says also: "No vividness excuses infidelity to the facts, and I have sought to base this history entirely on the material provided by the unselfish labor of a host of scholars, who, in matters of fact, must have the last word." My impression, after studying a number of authorities on the period to find background for my play, was—and is—that Mr. Hackett's book is a history, with no more originality than any other history, and containing very little material which could not be found among the many other histories and biographies which cover the same period.

Perhaps it would be useful if I were to give a brief account, as accurately as I can remember it, of how I came to write a play about Anne Boleyn. I keep a little day-book diary, and though it's rather sketchy it does quite often remind me of when and where I read a certain book or on what date I began or finished a certain play. Consulting this record I find that during 1946 I came back over and over again to the idea of a play about Christopher Marlowe. I read three biographies of Marlowe that year and re-read Hotson's book on Marlowe's death.[6] I also began to read about his period in the enormous eight-volume Pictorial History of England by George L. Craik and Charles MacFarlane, published in London by Charles Knight in 1838 and during the next decade.[7] On Dec. 21st I was reading in this history for Tudor background. On Jan. 9, 1947 I was still reading about Marlowe, the book being *"The Muses Darling."* Other interests intervened during the summer,[8] but Sept. 23 I find that I was talking to Burgess Meredith about the Marlowe play. The next day I find that I "woke at 5—thinking about Marlowe." On Oct. 2 I was again reading a life of Marlowe by Professor Boas. On Oct. 4 I was reading *Fanfare for Elizabeth* by Edith Sitwell. This is a brilliant study of the events that preceded Queen Elizabeth's arrival on the scene, and something of her early life. I read it for background for the Marlowe story. But the next day the diary reports that I had begun "to think of a play about the child Elizabeth." This shift took place partly because of Miss Sitwell's book, partly because I had begun to find Marlowe intractable as a character. I wasn't sure that I liked him, or that audiences would like him; in addition I couldn't think of any young actor who would be good in the part. On the next day, however, I had come upon another idea. The diary records that I was "studying the Tudor children—Children of Henry." "Children of Henry," as I thought of it, would have been a play about the three children of Henry the VIIIth by three different queens, after Henry and the three mothers were dead and the children—each one to govern England later—were living in the household of Catherine Parr, Henry's last wife, the one who survived him and was now married to Admiral Seymour. It was a bizarre, explosive household—three royal children, a step-mother who has been queen and a step-father who was both First Lord of the Admiralty and a pirate on the high seas. He was put to death in the end by his own brother, the protector, not for piracy but for attempting to make love to the adolescent Elizabeth. On Oct. 8 I record that I was still thinking of *"Children of Henry"* and

again reading "Fanfare for Elizabeth." On Oct. 16th I made a note
that I was reading about Anne Bullen, probably in the Charles Knight
history,[9] and by this time I had abandoned the "Children of Henry"
for the simple reason that I had happened to speak of it at the dinner
table and my daughter had casually informed me that the subject had
been covered, just as I planned it, in a book she had read as part of her
school-work—a book called "Young Bess."[10] Since it had been so
recently used I abandoned the notion of a play about Henry's
children, but on Oct. 20 I again record that I was studying "Fanfare
for Elizabeth" probably with the hope that there was a play
somewhere in the neighborhood. On Oct. 24th I went to Brentano's
and ordered some books, among them, as I remember it, Francis
Hackett's Henry the VIIIth, which was out of print and which I had
never read. Miss Lawlor, who waited on me, said she would try to find
a 2nd-hand copy. On Oct. 28th I was in New York City again and
Miss Lawlor had found a copy of "Henry the VIIIth" which I took
with me to the country. The next day I was reading it. On Nov. 1 I left
the United States to attend the opening of "Joan of Lorraine" in
Athens and did not return till Dec. 15th. On Dec. 17 the diary records
that I was reading a book called "Elizabeth and Leicester."[11] On Dec.
21st I was still—or again—reading "Elizabeth and Leicester." On
Dec. 22nd I read "Elizabeth and Leicester" in the morning and "The
Wives of Henry VIIIth" by Martin Hume in the evening. On Dec.
29th I was "just finishing Anne Boleyn's life in the Martin Hume
volume." On Jan. 3rd, 1948, the diary says: "Got an idea for Anne
B.—that the whole play takes place in her reverie, looking back." On
Jan. 4th and 5th I was reading about Henry the VIIIth, this time, as I
well remember, in the Martin Hume volume. For Jan. 9th there is this
entry; "To my cabin and worked out a tentative plan for 1st and 2nd
Acts of Anne of the Thousand Days." For Jan. 15th this entry: "To my
cabin in the woods to pick up a book to start a play in. The place
looked so inviting that I made a fire and began to write Anne of the
Thousand Days. Back for lunch at 1:30. Then to the cabin again and a
bit more writing. . . . Kurt came over. We talked about his play[12] and
mine. I read him my first three pages." Following the entries through I
find that I finished writing and revising Anne on May 26th, and took
the play to New York on that day to be typed.

I plod through these details because they make three things
evident. First, that I did not set out to write a play about Anne Boleyn,

but arrived at that subject after studying and considering several others; second, that I read a good many histories besides Mr. Hackett's on this same period; and, third, when I did find a plan for a play about Anne Boleyn its central idea, the idea that made it possible as a modern play, the idea that the entire action should take place in the minds of the leading characters, was not in Mr. Hackett's book at all, nor in any of the sources which I studied. I cannot emphasize too strongly that without this concept the whole play would have been impossible on the current stage, for without it *"Anne of the Thousand Days"* would have been a plain historical play, and of a vintage no longer acceptable to the theatre public. Without this idea I would never have thought the play worth writing at all.

Coming to Mr. Hackett's list of parallels I find he charges first that I stole the climax of *"Anne of the Thousand Days"* from his play on Anne. No doubt I have made it sufficiently clear that I have not read Mr. Hackett's play, but I should like to point out that there is another possibility here. Hackett says "the essence of the conflict between Anne and Henry, . . . centers on one issue—Elizabeth. That was the climax of my play. It is also the climax of Maxwell Anderson's. And Harold Freedman has always maintained that it made a superb last act. I have no doubt that he told Maxwell Anderson so. Certainly Behrman, who has money invested in Anderson's play, and Robert Sherwood both know it was superb theatre. I do not believe, however, that any source exists for this climax outside my play. And Anderson in my opinion derived his climax from the play I entrusted to Freedman."

Let me say again that nobody discussed Mr. Hackett's play with me, not Behrman, not Sherwood, not Freedman, nobody at all. As for my climax duplicating his, I doubt that very much. The climax of *"Anne of the Thousand Days"* is more complex than a mere struggle over the succession. But it happens that the climax of another play of mine, *"Mary of Scotland,"* produced in 1933, parallels very closely the episode Mr. Hackett indicates as the essence of his last act. In *"Mary of Scotland"* Queen Elizabeth comes to Mary demanding that Mary renounce her claim to the English throne as the price of her life. Mary refuses because her son is heir to the crown. In Hackett's play does Henry come to Anne demanding that she renounce Elizabeth's claim to the throne or die for refusing? If so Mr. Hackett could have taken his climax from my play about Mary, for it was successful, was

published, and could easily have come to Hackett's attention. It seems
very likely that he took this essential act from *"Mary of Scotland,"*
though the plagiarism must have been unconscious, for the similarity
would be too obvious to pass the most casual inspection. It appears to
me that, in his own confession, Mr. Hackett has lifted a pivotal,
original and effective scene from my early work. He points to his last
act as his best. And this theft may be the reason for its excellence.[13]

1. Wharton was defending Anderson in a plagiarism suit brought by Francis
Hackett on May 17, 1949. Hackett, associated with Anderson on the *World* in the early
twenties, claimed that Anderson's current play *Anne of the Thousand Days* plagiarized
three of his own works: a biography, *Henry the Eighth* (1929); a novel, *Queen Anne
Boleyn* (1939); and a play, *Anne Boleyn*, completed in 1942 but not produced or
published.

2. Broadway actor and director. H. C. Potter replaced Windust as director of *Anne
of the Thousand Days* before the play came to New York.

3. Three of the collaborations were with Laurence Stallings: *What Price Glory*
(1924), *First Flight* (1925), and *The Buccaneer* (1925). The fourth was with Harold
Hickerson on *Gods of the Lightning* (1928).

4. *Beggars of Life* (1924).

5. Martin Andrew Sharp Hume (1847–1910), *The Wives of Henry the Eighth, and
the Parts they Played in History* (n.d.)

6. The three biographies noted in the 1946 diary are: Frederick S. Boas,
Christopher Marlowe: A Biographical and Critical Study (1940); Leslie Hotson, *The
Death of Christopher Marlowe* (1925) (the book reread); and Charles Norman, *The
Muses' Darling* (1946).

7. The *Pictorial History of England* was also published in America (4 vols., 1846).
In the American edition vol. 2, book 6, covers the period of Marlowe's life.

8. From April 23 until August 9, 1947, Anderson was in California at work on the
script of *Joan of Arc*.

9. Bullen is given as an alternate spelling for Boleyn in the Knight (that is, the Craik
and MacFarlane) *Pictorial History of England*.

10. Margaret E. Irwin, *Young Bess* (1945).

11. Milton Waldman, *Elizabeth and Leicester* (1945).

12. *Love Life*, book and lyrics by Alan Jay Lerner, music by Weill, produced
October 8, 1948.

13. The countersuit suggested here was brought by Anderson against Hackett on
May 20, 1949, though for libel rather than plagiarism.

167. TO SAMUEL J. SILVERMAN [1]

New City
June 9, 1949

Dear Mr. Silverman:

Freedman's version of what happened in the case of BOTH YOUR HOUSES is correct, I think. He might have added that Harris held the play so long that though it was written as a satire on the Hoover administration it didn't come out till Roosevelt was in the White House. By that time the play seemed quite pointless.[2]

The SATURDAY'S CHILDREN business (which I had forgotten) was the result of a misunderstanding. While I was working on the WORLD several plays of mine were typed by Walter Lippmann's secretary. (He was also writing editorials for the WORLD at that time.) Among the plays the girl typed (her name was Orrie Lashin) were my first play, WHITE DESERT, and the collaborations with Laurence Stallings, among them WHAT PRICE GLORY. Miss Lashin told me she wanted to write plays, but couldn't think of a plot.[3] Rather carelessly, as I now see it, I gave her the plot of a play which I thought I would never write, and which she proceeded to put into some kind of play form. However, she obviously had little talent for playwriting and the project came to nothing. I did read her play and thought it pretty bad. This was sometime in 1924. In 1926 I remembered the plot and had lunch with Miss Lashin to ask her if she minded if I took a crack at the play. She said no, since the plot was mine anyway and she hadn't made a go of it. I then wrote SATURDAY'S CHILDREN, which went on early in 1927. At least two years later, when I was in California, some of Miss Lashin's friends persuaded her to sue me for stealing from her play. When I returned from California I saw her and her lawyer, explained these circumstances—which she accepted as the facts—and told her that I felt I had merely tried to help her, and was under no obligation. She said that though the story was mine and I had used nothing from her play she felt that her script had suggested atmosphere and background to me. I then offered a small settlement, I think a thousand dollars, largely because I had no evidence except her word and mine that I had suggested the story in the first place or that she had released it later.

At this time I had no agent, Mr. Freedman having become my representative afterward, when I was unable to come to any agreement with Jed Harris. It wasn't till the experience with Orrie

Lashin that I began to learn to be wary of trying to be helpful. I don't know where Miss Lashin is now.

I have located several plays on Anne Boleyn in the public library, and shall examine them for precedents. Meanwhile I try to put Fanny Holtzmann[4] out of my mind, so that I can get my work done. She is the kind of hornet that can make the horses run away with the mowing machine.

Sincerely,

P.S. By the way, I don't believe Hackett can retract what he said about me to the newspapers. The reporters who wrote the stories could, I would think, be called as witnesses in the libel suit against Hackett.[5] If they refused to swear what Hackett said about me was substantially what their papers published I would then have a case against the TIMES and the TRIBUNE. They cannot be free to print libellous allegations unless they can quote a source.[6]

1. Silverman, in John Wharton's law firm (Paul, Weiss, Wharton and Garrison), assisted in Anderson's defense against the plagiarism suit brought by Francis Hackett in connection with *Anne of the Thousand Days* (see no. 166).

2. Jed Harris, Broadway producer, held production rights to *Both Your Houses* during much of 1932 and did not release them to the play's eventual producer, the Theatre Guild, until January, 1933. The Guild produced the play on March 6, 1933, and it received that year's Pulitzer Prize in the drama.

3. With Milo Hastings she later wrote *Class of '29*, produced by the Federal Theater in 1936.

4. Hackett's lawyer in the *Anne of the Thousand Days* suit.

5. Anderson's suit against Hackett, filed on May 20, 1949, cited Hackett's remarks reported in two articles, "Hackett Contends Hit Play's Plot His," *New York Times*, May 18, 1949, p. 32, col. 1, and "Francis Hackett Sees His Books in Anne Play," *New York Herald Tribune*, May 18, 1949, p. 19, cols. 5–6.

6. After extensive negotiations between their lawyers, Anderson and Hackett dropped their charges against one another in April, 1950.

168. TO JOHN ARTHUR CHAPMAN [1]

[September, 1949]

Dear John,

Forgive me for not answering sooner your suggestion about the musical version of *Lightnin'*. I've been finishing revisions of *Cry the Beloved Country* and haven't looked up lately.[2]

But as for *Lightnin'*—which I saw with Frank Bacon—I'm afraid it's more Cole Porter's dish than mine. It's perfect material for a Broadway musical, and would lend itself to modern variations, but it couldn't possibly carry any meaning, and I find myself unable to take an interest in a play that doesn't say something. That is very possibly a weakness, but I have it and can't get rid of it. *Lightnin'*, however, will make a successful musical for somebody, and I hope you don't let the matter drop. Meanwhile, thank you for thinking of me.

Sincerely

M A

1. Chapman (b. 1900) had a long career with the *New York Daily News*, starting in 1920, and in 1943 became the paper's drama critic. He had written to suggest that Anderson make a musical out of *Lightnin'* (1918), through the twenties a long-running comedy by Winchell Smith and Frank Bacon, in which Bacon played the leading role of Lightnin' Bill Jones.
2. The final preproduction script of *Lost in the Stars* is dated September 9, 1949.

169. TO ARCHER MILTON HUNTINGTON

New City
March 14, 1950

Dear Archer—

Thanks for that letter about our songs from *Lost in the Stars*. And for wanting more so emphatically. At the moment I'm writing lyrics and other words for Mark Twain's *Huckleberry Finn*,[1] and so there may be more. I hope they're not a desecration of the original. It's happy stuff to work with. —It gave me an evening's delight to look through that book of photographs of Anna's work.[2] Now that it's summed up it looks as if she'd produced a torrent of beautiful things.

Anna tells Mab that you will achieve eighty years on Saturday. If I could figure out how you do it I'd try it myself, for I have a number of things I want to write. Not that I think it's very important any more—I'd just like to keep on earning a living and making marks on paper.

Come spring we'd like to come over to see you. Right now I'm pinned to my desk over Huck and Jim and the gaudy Dauphin.

Yours
Max

1. For a musical completed as *Raft on the River*, not produced or published. See *Catalogue*, p. 75.
2. American Sculptors Series, 3, *Anna Hyatt Huntington* (1947).

170. TO ARCHER MILTON HUNTINGTON

New City
July 1, 1950

Dear Archer:

It was heroic of you to plow all the way through that book,[1] giving me credit for holding myself in when I didn't quite come up to scratch. Those papers were written at odd times over a long period of years, each one for a separate occasion, and so they don't hold together very well and there is some over-lapping and repetition.

We both enjoyed the visit with you tremendously and I got something very definite out of it. That Socrates subject,[2] which I had been mulling for some time, got just enough encouragement from you so that I have been buried in Plato ever since. The old boy may prove an impossible hero; he's too perfect to be tragic but it's pleasant to read about him again.

If you ever break loose and start gallivanting about the country please come to see us. If you don't do that, it's likely to be another year before we get to Bethel again. My very best to Anna. Maybe she's not so good as Mab in argument but she does beautifully in bronze.

Let me hear from you when you are throwing off new works or ideas.

As ever,
Max

1. *Off Broadway*.
2. *Barefoot in Athens*.

171. TO BROOKS ATKINSON

[New York City]
August 8, 1950

Dear Mr. Atkinson:[1]

There seems to be so much confusion about the meaning of the Korean campaign and so much reluctance to meet the challenge of a third world war that I have decided to write down my version of our situation and state it in public, hoping to make clear that, little as we want any war, we can't refuse this one if Russia is fanatic enough to insist on it. If you agree with the statement well enough to sign it with me, please convey your acceptance as quickly as possible by wire or letter to me at this office. We hope to take a page ad in the Times for it on Thursday of this week.[2]

Sincerely,
Maxwell Anderson

1. On June 25, 1950, North Korea invaded South Korea and was largely victorious over the South Koreans and a small American force during the summer and fall, while Russian delegate Jacob Malik delayed U.N. action in Korea. Red Chinese troops joined the North Koreans in November, and on December 16 President Truman proclaimed a state of national emergency. Anderson, remembering Robert Sherwood's similar move just before World War II, took a full-page ad in the *New York Times* to rally support for American action in Korea (August 10, 1950, p. 19). In the ad he presented the Korean conflict as part of Russia's program for world conquest, and before printing it he circulated the ad from the Playwrights' Company office to a number of acquaintances for their signature.

2. Twenty-six others signed the ad with Anderson, but Atkinson declined, saying that the American people understood and supported the war, and that to say they did not could only encourage the Russians (Atkinson to Anderson, August 9, 1950; NYP).

172. TO BROOKS ATKINSON

New City
August 18, 1950

Dear Brooks—[1]

The more I think about it the more clearly I realize that that ad was only a sort of private declaration of war, and probably a little clumsy. I don't suppose anybody has the situation sized-up accurately, though maybe Walter L. came close to it in his definition of the present phase as a series of civil wars in which Russia will take the side of the rebels and we'll be trying to put the rebellion down. That's what's most infuriating in our position—we're going to have to smash most of Korea to save it from slavery, and it's going to make us most unpopular there.

No doubt you saw the Alsop article about the "business-as-usual" war.[2] That's perhaps a bit exaggerated but I think it's true that the country doesn't think it's at war. The crisis doesn't look immediate to us here—we're not shocked into action nor into making sharp discriminations between the loyal and the disloyal.

These are only opinions, of course. A fellow would really have to be a prophet to know what ought to be done next, and I'm no prophet.

Give my best to your wife. My wife doesn't agree with me either—and she says some of the things which you have written to me.

Yours
Max

1. Russian delegate Malik had argued against U.N. intervention in Korea on the grounds that the conflict there was a civil war. In his columns in the *New York Herald Tribune* Walter Lippmann took up the idea and projected a future in which Russia promoted civil disturbances throughout the world and used them as means of enslaving the countries involved. Lippmann thought it would be difficult for America to deal with those situations without wrecking a country in the process of defending it (1950: August 10, p. 21, cols. 1–2; August 14, p. 15, cols. 1–2; August 17, p. 19, cols. 1–2).

2. Writing from Korea, Stewart Alsop condemned American complacency about the Korean war in "Business-as-Usual War," *New York Herald Tribune*, August 18, 1950, p. 13, cols. 7–8.

173. TO JOHN F. WHARTON

New City
August 30, 1950

Dear John—

Thanks for your two letters.[1] Victor called me today and we agreed on Thurs. eve next week for a dinner meeting. I've been having a rough time trying to write a play[2] and at the moment am not sure that there'll be anything of mine to put on an arena or any other kind of stage with or without financing. Still we ought to discuss the financing problem in general, and I ought to find out a few things to tell our stock-holders. My present thought is that maybe we should all leave the theatre together and try to make a living at something else. But we can discuss that too.

Yours
Max

1. About the bleak financial condition of the Playwrights' Company.
2. *Barefoot in Athens*.

174. TO THE PLAYWRIGHTS' COMPANY

New City
September 5, 1950

Dear Playwrights—[1]

I wish to plead guilty with an explanation. I have written a play, but it was not written for production Manhattan and therefore we may not have to put it on. And since the difficulties of getting the money, the director, the theatre and the actors for a play are today almost insurmountable, no play should go into production unless the script is so convincing that it practically walks on the stage by itself. I'm not sure my play is that good. No playwright is ever sure his play is that good. He has to turn his script in and wait to see if it fights its way toward the spotlights.

Perhaps I should explain why the play was not aimed at New York. Three years ago, when I was in Greece attending the opening of

"Joan of Lorraine" there, I promised Theodore Kritas, who produced that play in Athens, that I would sometime try to write a play about Athens, for the Athenians. I have finally got around to writing it and am today mailing the script of "Barefoot in Athens" to him. I am also showing it to my own company, not at all sure it will be found suitable for local presentation. Maybe you won't like it enough to go through the hell of financing and worrying and grim trouble, which putting on a play entails. Maybe Mr. Kritas won't like it either, in which case I shall have had the fun of writing a play without ever having to go through the prolonged torture of casting, rehearsals, re-writing, try-outs, and first nights. Don't read it all if it doesn't hold your interest. Just shake your head and draw your hand across your throat. I'll understand.[2]

Sincerely,
Max

1. In August Anderson had written to the Greek producer Theodore Kritas, who staged *Joan of Lorraine* in Athens in 1947, saying that *Barefoot in Athens* "is being written primarily for Athens, and dedicated to the people of Greece" and asking if Kritas would like to consider it (Anderson to Kritas, August 4, 1950; T). Kritas replied affirmatively, and on the day of the present letter Anderson sent him a copy of the play. With the present letter he also sent *Barefoot in Athens* to the Playwrights' Company.

2. Kritas was enthusiastic about *Barefoot in Athens* and tried to arrange its production through the National Theatre in Athens (Kritas to Anderson, October 4, 1950;T), but the National Theatre, having scheduled *Anne of the Thousand Days* for the following season, did not produce *Barefoot in Athens*. The Playwrights' Company had reservations about the play, and Anderson revised it during the following spring.

175. TO ROBERT E. SHERWOOD

New City
April 24, 1951

Dear Bob:[1]

I'm having rather a hard time setting down my thoughts about your second version because I realize that you intend it for the Lunts and that pulls the story-line somewhat askew. Your characters are sound, your dialogue is wise and witty, your philosophy (or sociology or psychology) seems apt and impudent in a true comedy vein, yet I'm dissatisfied with the effort as something coming from you. And I'm not sure the Lunts will be able to do enough for you to make up for the influence they have on your playwriting. Yet they may, and you're so good at revisions that with the Lunts the chances are in favor of the project.

However, I can't help thinking about another approach to the story. As the play stands you shy away from your theme—which is a delicate one—and talk about it rather than treat it. Your theme is a defense of the bordello as an institution. I think this can be undertaken only lightly—as farce-comedy—but in those terms it would be quite possible. Your title—*Girls With Dogs*—suggests that attitude. Bronny's adventure is probably not a good central episode, but Helen and the doctor are both lonely, and their romance could be your main action.

Three or four points occurred to me while I was reading, and I'd better tell you what they are, just as impressions.

1. Maybe there are still too many scenes. The play gives the effect of being about a building, not the people in it.

2. None of the characters is central. We don't get inside any of them. And none of them changes enough during the play to make a turning point in the plot.

3. The big scene which we wait for is not a discussion of the issue which the play raises. We watch a castigation of a spoiled rich woman by an educated Mrs. Warren.[2] And since the expected argument is evaded the play is left without a meaning.

4. The worst trouble is that I can't find your main character. If it's Mrs. Montchauvet shouldn't the story begin with her and revolve around her? If it's the doctor shouldn't he be more than a spectator? If it's Bronny shouldn't he be a virgin when the curtain goes up?

5. Shouldn't the whole discussion be in a lighter vein? More like a Restoration comedy?

Forgive me if I'm making wild suggestions. I think the problem is soluble but not quite solved. The characters somehow don't get a chance to affect each other. They ricochet off each other, and sometimes strike sparks, but go on just as they were.

Ruefully,[3]

1. Sherwood had sent his play *Girls With Dogs* to Anderson.
2. Central character in Shaw's *Mrs. Warren's Profession* (1893).

3. *Girls With Dogs* was one of several plays Sherwood wrote in an unsuccessful attempt to regain his playwriting form following work in Roosevelt's administration during World War II. The play, scheduled for production by the Playwrights' Company in the 1951–52 season, was withdrawn, and it has not been produced or published.

176. TO JOHN F. WHARTON

New City
July 5, 1951

Dear John—[1]

I hope I'm not being difficult over this casting of Socrates, for I really want that play to go on, and every time a man's available there seems to me to be something wrong about him for the part, whereas when they're not available I begin to find them possible. Morley I considered, and decided against because he seems cool or cold—Cobb I find a hot or at least very warm actor who is all emotion but not enough brain. Alan has just discovered that Gwenn has set out on a tramp steamer trip and can't be reached till the end of July. Alan is now prospecting among other English actors—among them Felix Aylmer and Cecil Parker, as well as Barry Jones. It may be necessary for Alan to go to England.

I've looked over that stock transfer proposal,[2] and think your scheme is better. If there's a vote, I cast mine that way.

Please forgive me for not coming in for the reading of *The Idea*. My notions for re-writing or casting wouldn't be very relevant, since I wasn't enough in favor of the play to want to produce it.[3] Also I'm trying very hard to get the revisions done on that comedy of mine, and every time I have to read and consider a MS my concentration is gone.[4] Add to that I'm getting to be a chronic invalid and have to conserve my strength. I don't go to N.Y. City or anywhere else if I can avoid it. This puts a considerable crimp in my social life, which was never very prodigal. Never—well, not since I turned forty.

Sincerely
Max

1. Anderson's son Alan, who was to direct *Barefoot in Athens*, was looking for a Socrates, a role eventually played by the English actor Barry Jones. Others considered

for the part were Robert Morley, English playwright and actor; Lee J. Cobb, American who recently had played Willy Loman in *Death of a Salesman*; Edmund Gwenn, American who had an extensive career on Broadway and in Hollywood; and the English actors Felix Aylmer and Cecil Parker.

2. A business arrangement within the Playwrights' Company.

3. Edward Caulfield's *The Idea*, tried out by the Playwrights' Company in Boston on February 12, 1952, was not brought to New York. Caulfield produced no further plays, but three earlier plays had received short New York productions: *There's Always A Breeze* (1938), *And Be My Love* (1945), and *Bruno and Sidney* (1949).

4. *Adam, Lilith and Eve*, written with Rex Harrison and his wife Lilli Palmer in mind for the leads, was not produced because the Harrisons eventually wished more changes in it than Anderson was willing to make. For the play, unpublished, see *Catalogue*, pp. 62–63.

177. TO BROOKS ATKINSON

New City
November 3, 1951

Dear Brooks—[1]

I think you ought to come back and see *Barefoot in Athens* again before you write your second opinion. As you know, many things can go wrong on a first night, and some can never be corrected but some can. For one example, Socrates is not supposed to break down in the trial scene. The line written for him is "You lie!", and it's supposed to be cried out in anger, not in grief. On the opening night Mr. Jones surprised us, and himself, by weeping on that line. He had not done it before, has not done it again. But it sounded like an admission of guilt and altered the whole meaning of the play for that one evening. I wouldn't want you to change a line out of kindness, but I'm inclined to think we didn't get quite a fair trial at the opening. In fact, not fair at all, for there were many casual but damaging errors. If you want to come again, let Bill Fields know and he will leave tickets for you.[2]

Sincerely
Max

1. Atkinson's opening-night review of *Barefoot in Athens* had condemned the play as "highminded and pedestrian, sincere and perfunctory," and had even indulged in sarcasm, unusual for Atkinson, by concluding that the play was "not only barefoot but heavyfooted and slow" (*New York Times*, November 1, 1951, p. 35, cols.

2–3). Atkinson had however liked the trial scene (Act II, scene 2), thinking it the only scene in the play where Barry Jones made Socrates a sympathetic and moving character. Socrates's angry "You lie!" is a response to the charge that he hates Athens (II, 2; pp. 82–83).

2. Atkinson did not attend *Barefoot in Athens* again but, before receiving the present letter (Atkinson to Anderson, November 7, 1951, NYP), did write a second column on the play, based on a reading of the published text (*New York Times*, November 11, 1951, sec. 2, p. 1, cols. 1–2). In the second column he condemned the play again, concentrating on the conception of Socrates, a character who should be heroic but seemed petty, a weakness emphasized by Barry Jones, whose experience in Shaw plays made him portray the character as "light, pleasant, witty, and ingratiating."

178. TO VICTOR SAMROCK

[New City]
November 20, 1951

Dear Victor—[1]

Please pass this note along to the other members of the company. We've known for quite a while that Brooks Atkinson had a lot of power, but I think this last experience of mine was a pretty complete proof that without him a serious play has no chance. *Barefoot* had faults, and some bad ones, but it would have been successful, or at least had a run, if Brooks had voted for it. He didn't and it had to go. A serious play is a poor gamble anyway, but from now on I'd say nobody but one of Atkinson's favorites should try a straight play on Broadway. It isn't fair to the playwright or the actors or the investors. I'm certainly no favorite of Atkinson's and I shall therefore put on no plays while he remains where he is. This means that I won't be much good to the Playwrights' Company, for I shall have to find some other way to make a living. The company has been a home to me for so long that I shall miss it and miss you all more than I can say, but there's no use evading the facts. A lot of money was lost on *Barefoot* and I don't want to go through another such ordeal convinced from the beginning that a lot of money will be lost again. Also I don't want to take the company through it. I want to thank you all again, more than I can say, for standing by me during the difficult days—sometimes when I was pretty difficult myself.

How this decision should affect my business relations with the company I don't know. If it's better to leave my name on the books, I shall of course have no objection. If complete inactivity makes me an embarrassment to the organization I'll withdraw. I'd rather not take any part in producing plays from now on.

Max

1. *Barefoot in Athens* had opened on October 31, 1951, and was to close on November 24 after a run of thirty performances, losing $70,000.

179. TO ROBERT E. SHERWOOD

[New City]
November 29, 1951

Dear Bob—[1]

Your letter is so generous, as you always are, that I'm tempted to say all right, I'll go right to work on another, just for the pleasure of working with people I like so much. Anyway this is no time for me to make irrevocable decisions, and I guess I haven't made any. Inactivity, as you point out, is not always cause for dropping out of the Playwrights' Company—though you omit to say that you single-handed kept us on the credit side of the ledger for a good many years.

But I fear my problem will last longer than my present depression. It isn't only that I think the gamble isn't good enough for the investors when they put up the money for one by me. It's that the kind of theatre I have always written my plays for is gone or going. I have no hope that it will be resuscitated. Maybe, as you suggest, we'll discover other outlets for our work—outside New York, that is—but it begins to seem to me that what's wanted in New York is quick flash stuff, with plenty of shock or sex, and vapid musicals. That sort of thing was always wanted, of course, but it wasn't honored the way it is now. And there was occasionally room for something else.

It's true that I shall have to find a way to make a living outside the legitimate theatre, and some ways have begun to open up, so I shall sometimes be absent from Playwrights' meetings. I hope it's true that I'll always be welcome when I can attend.[2]

Yours,

1. Sherwood had urged Anderson to reconsider his decision to resign from the Playwrights' Company (no. 178), counseling that Anderson's depression over the failure of *Barefoot in Athens* was only temporary and citing his own record during the war years as evidence that one could be temporarily inactive as a playwright and still remain a member of the company.

2. Rice too had urged Anderson not to resign, and an autograph note at the top of the present letter reads: "Dear Elmer—I've written a note to Bob which really answers your note, too, so I send you this copy—Max"

180. TO JACKSON TOBY [1]

[New City]
November 30, 1951

Dear Dr. Toby:

Of course I shared that indignant reaction to a certain extent—at least for a while. However, one can't remain indignant for long at a time without losing perspective, and so I'm thinking of starting something else.

When you ask that the city be given another chance to see the play I can only answer in economic terms. The play cost $70,000—all of which was lost. I don't think we could find another set of investors to put up a second $70,000 to try again with a play which has once been damned and killed. So it will have to remain where it is, between covers.

Sincerely,
Maxwell Anderson

1. Toby, in the Department of Sociology at Rutgers University, had written to Anderson saying that he thought *Barefoot in Athens* a fine play and that he was indignant at the critics for their attacks on it. He thought the critics were not widely representative and urged Anderson to have the play produced again.

181. TO STEPHEN SONDHEIM [1]

[New City]
November 30, 1951

Dear Mr. Sondheim:

I'm sending your script back without reading it for a reason which will perhaps come to you as a shock—so brace yourself. If *High Tor* is done as a musical I may want to do the book and lyrics myself, and it would be unfair of me to read another man's work on the same venture. I'm sorry that this may make your work seem wasted, but I guess nothing's ever really wasted. That's the best I can do in the way of comfort. [2]

Sincerely,
Maxwell Anderson

1. Sondheim (b. 1930) was to become a well-known composer and lyricist, doing the lyrics for *West Side Story* (1957) and *Gypsy* (1959), and writing the music as well as the lyrics for *A Funny Thing Happened on the Way to the Forum* (1962) and *Anyone Can Whistle* (1964). At the time of the present letter he had made a musical adaption of *High Tor* and sent it to Anderson, hoping that Anderson would approve it for production.

2. A musical version of *High Tor* was done on CBS television, March 10, 1956, with book and lyrics by Anderson and music by Arthur Schwartz.

182. TO JOHN F. WHARTON

New City
December 5, 1951

Dear John—[1]

I won't try to go into that t.v. proposition fully till I see you, but I can offer one bit of information. If we had packaged that Celanese Theatre series we'd have taken in a commission of $80,000 in the first year which now goes to William Morris. Of course there'd be some expenses, rent, salaries, fees, etc., but if we packaged three programs and took in three times that commission the running expenses would increase only slightly.

Of course we could go into television without hiring Jerry Stagg, and I mention him only because he's the spectacularly successful man in the field right now, and all the other agencies and networks are trying to hire him away from Wm Morris. He'd be expensive, and he'd come to us only because we could give him a good deal of freedom and a firm name that he'd be proud of. But I think he'd be worth the investment.

It may be that Roger doesn't want to dip into television. It certainly would be a commercial venture pure and simple—but it looks to me to be something that we could do which would assure us a steady and certain return. And that's something the theatre no longer offers anybody. My best to you and Betty.

Sincerely

Max

1. Hoping to maintain financial stability, the Playwrights' Company made several unsuccessful attempts to enter the field of television play production. The Celanese Theatre, an opportunity the company missed, was a biweekly series of one-hour television productions of past Broadway plays. Developed by Anderson's wife Gertrude and Jerry Stagg of the William Morris agency, the Celanese Theatre attracted attention during the 1951–52 season for raising the standard of television offerings. It began on October 3 with *Ah, Wilderness!*, and *Winterset* was the third production, on October 31.

183. TO ELMER RICE

710 North Palm Drive

Beverly Hills,

California

February 13, 1952

Dear Elmer:[1]

This is certainly a thorny subject. Let me begin with a small point. You say that several of the Authors' League Council expressed "shocked surprise" that I should defend "blacklisting." You were present at that meeting and you know that what I said was that of all the television sponsors I knew the Celanese Theatre made the least use of *Red Channels* and was most inclined to be tolerant of actors who had been smeared as reds without deserving it. I can see that this might be deliberately twisted by somebody who wanted to smear me, but how you, with your legal training, could gather that I defended blacklisting I do not see. As for the article the *Times* man phoned you about, that was a similar defense of the Celanese people which I withdrew because I felt it was better for the Playwrights' Company if we didn't argue in public.[2] I have not defended blacklisting or *Red Channels*. I did say in my letter to you that there were people mentioned in *Red Channels* whose record of Communist affiliation was so long and so lurid that I would not want to be associated with them in any way and couldn't blame others who didn't like their atmosphere. This I wrote in a private letter to you. It was not a charge, not testimony. I have never accused anybody of being a Communist, but I reserve the right, as any free man must, of choosing my associates and steering clear of what looks to me like traitorous company. The same people looked traitorous to me before and after I read *Red Channels*. Choosing friends, associates, and even representatives is something we all have to do constantly without trial and with insufficient evidence. The difference between a private letter and a public accusation is something a lawyer should understand.

As to the legal status of the Communist Party, I believe you to be mistaken about that.[3] If you and I were caught conspiring to overthrow the government by force we'd be treated as traitors to our country and we'd deserve it. Every Communist party member is pledged to just such a conspiracy and deserves to be treated as a traitor. His activities are not political, but criminal. He does not deal with ideas. He studies a fixed code, a plan for violent revolution. You say that an accused man should have his day in court. I agree, and point out that the Communist leaders had more than half a year in court, and were found guilty. I remember too that Judge Medina specifically reminded the jurors that the evidence must show the defendants guilty beyond a reasonable doubt. You say that the law under which they were convicted is not a good law. It is your right to hold that opinion of any law.[4]

You note that we have both been cited by the Tenny Committee.[5] Two of the citations of my name I never authorized, but if I were cited many times I should all the more deplore the Authors' League resolution which lumps the innocent with the guilty.*****[6] Your mention of Socrates is apropos here. Socrates maintained the right of anybody to speculate and converse on any subject. He did not defend those who betrayed their country. You are actively defending Alcibiades and his sell-out to Persia.[7] The Communists are not questioning, philosophizing or speculating. They are agents of a foreign power who wish to defeat us and set that power over us.

As I see it the Communist Party is an international Ku Klux Klan devoted to the extirpation of all human rights and liberties among non-members and the destruction of all governments which it does not control. It has enslaved the peoples of Russia and her neighbors, it has murdered millions, it is conducting a war against the United Nations, it has undercover agents in every country trained to destroy and taught that any method that wins for their despotism is a good method. Some of these agents sit on the Council of the Authors' League and protest vehemently when their continued advocacy of Russian policy brings them into disrepute. I think it should bring them into disrepute. I think they should be ousted from any position of influence or honor which they hold. I think this should be done legally and deliberately, and why an honest man like yourself thinks it should not be done is what I cannot understand.

The heart of our argument, of course, is that you believe our local Communists to be acceptable citizens, while I believe them to be enemy agents, engaged in wrecking us from within. The evidence on this side is over-whelming. I think you are ignorant of it or prefer to ignore it.

Sincerely,

Max

1. At a meeting of the Authors' League of America on January 7, 1952, a resolution was adopted committing the league to defend any writer barred from work because of a listing in *Red Channels: The Report of Communist Influence in Radio and Television* (1950). Rice had supported the resolution and Anderson had opposed it, saying that like *Red Channels* it failed to discriminate between the innocent and the guilty. Anderson had also defended the Celanese Theatre, a television series for which his wife was script editor, against charges of blacklisting. The disagreement between Anderson and Rice continued in their letters, and Wharton in *Life Among the Playwrights*, pp. 209–13, gives the Rice letter to which the present letter responds. At the close of his letter Rice called the matter "a thorny subject" (p. 212).

2. The previous November Rice had denounced the Celanese Theatre, maintaining that for its production of his *Counsellor-at-Law* it refused to employ actors listed in *Red Channels* (*New York Times*, November 14, 1951, p. 33, col. 6). Rice and the Celanese Theatre debated the charge in the newspapers until February 24, when Celanese denied and denounced blacklisting and Rice rejoined the project (*New York Times*, February 25, 1952, p. 28, col. 6).

3. Rice had said that it was not illegal under U.S. law to belong to the Communist party (Wharton, pp. 209–10).

4. In a nine-month trial during 1949 eleven Communist party leaders were convicted under the Smith Act of criminal conspiracy to teach and advocate overthrow of the government by force and violence. Judge Harold R. Medina presided at the trial in the U.S. Circuit Court in New York, and among those convicted were Henry Winston and Gus Hall, national secretaries of the Communist party, and Robert Thompson, New York State chairman of the Communist party.

5. State Senator Jack B. Tenney, chairman of the California Senate Fact-Finding Committee on Un-American Activities, issued voluminous committee reports during the forties listing organizations designated as communist fronts and their members. Anderson is cited as member, Hollywood Writers' Mobilization, 1945; sponsor, National Council for Soviet-American Friendship, 1948; and signer, letter to Speaker of the House Martin from the National Institute of Arts and Letters protesting investigations by House Committee on Un-American Activities, 1948. Anderson was not associated with the first two projects.

6. Omitted are four sentences in which Anderson names several people, still alive at the time of this edition, and says they are members of the Communist party.

7. Rice had alluded to *Barefoot in Athens* and argued that Anderson was inconsistent in supporting freedom of speech in the play and opposing it in the current situation (Wharton, p. 211). Alcibiades, as a young man a disciple of Socrates, became an Athenian political and military leader during the Peloponnesian War and in 411 B.C. persuaded the Athenians to replace their democracy with an oligarchy in the hope (unrealized) of gaining Persian support against Sparta. Plutarch thus treated Alcibiades together with the Roman traitor Coriolanus in the parallel *Lives*.

184. TO JOHN F. WHARTON

710 North Palm Drive
Beverly Hills, Calif.
February 20, 1952

Dear John:[1]

Many thanks for your letter and for exposing yourself to this seemingly interminable correspondence. I don't like to go on with it myself, but I'm driven to do it by a growing belief that the Communists, while waging a real though undeclared war against us, have gophered themselves inside the U.S. into our key labor unions, into our government, into the publishing field, into journalism and into what many people call the entertainment field, which is where I work. And that they have so flooded our country with red propaganda that the liberals talk and write red propaganda without knowing they are doing it. I thought when in the east that Hollywood had more or less cleaned itself since the Congressional hearings began, but I was mistaken.[2] The majority of the studios are run by reds and party-liners. And they make a quiet point of hiring men who believe as they do.

You may be right in saying that if Congress defined Communism and its status under the law that would go a long way toward settling the dispute. It would probably separate the Communists from the liberals, which would be a major victory, for without the help of emotional liberals the Communists would be a minority everywhere and helpless. Meanwhile I am puzzled by your assumption that Elmer and I were arguing over our judicial system and that I advocated finding men guilty without trial.

Is there anybody who doesn't agree that a man should be assumed innocent until proven guilty? If there is he hasn't spoken up or appeared in the argument. But this maxim applies, as you know, only in courts of law. In other institutions, and in all private human relations, there are no rules of evidence and men and women usually decide as whim and prejudice and a superficial examination of facts convince them. Do you and Elmer mean that we should now begin to apply court procedure throughout our lives? I think we have to understand that there is an absolute difference between the decision of a court that a man is guilty and the decision of a purchaser that he would rather have another kind of automobile or another representative in Congress. There are no rules of evidence to guide the decision of an employer who has to satisfy customers or to govern the dissatisfaction of a customer who has heard that somebody is a Communist. These things are done off the cuff, like most of human life, and nobody can possibly invent a legal umbrella to protect us from casual injury by our neighbors.

Whether a Communist is a criminal or not, and whether or not there were actual Communists among the actors and writers who have lost jobs because they were accused of being Communists, still the employers have a perfect right to employ only the actors and writers who they believe are likely to bring a return in sales or prestige. As for the methods of choosing actors, nobody could supervise that. If there is a fellow traveller among the employers he also has a right to employ reds and fellow travellers—and refuse to employ others—as it suits his fancy. I see nothing difficult or abstruse about this.

I don't know what you mean by saying that injustice has been done because of private individuals taking over what should be a government function. Public opinion is not a government function. It's made up of a lot of private interests and factions, and it should control the government—and in the long run does. It was public opinion, steered by all kinds of special pleadings, including the *Times* and *Tribune*, which injured the actors and writers who lost jobs. Some of them may have deserved it. Some did not. Some of the people who get elected to Congress deserve it. Some do not. As soon as a man lifts his head and takes a stand of any sort people are free to discuss him and his views, fairly and unfairly, wisely or unwisely. There's nothing illegal or antisocial about *Red Channels*. It's a listing of people who joined red front organizations, with lists of the organizations they joined. If *Consumers' Digest* is legal this is legal. If employers or buyers want to use either, they are exercising only their right of choice in a free country and a free market. This is not black-listing. It is public information, which they use or not, as they like. I got inveigled into one or two Communist fronts myself, and I'm ashamed of it, and wish it hadn't happened, but it did happen. It's part of my record and so long as we retain free speech and a free press my record lays me open to attack. As does any man's. If you think the government could or should control any of these things I wish you'd let me know how.

Sincerely,
Maxwell Anderson

1. Wharton had joined Rice (see no. 183) in the argument with Anderson about communists and blacklisting.

2. The present hearings of the House Committee on Un-American Activities, chaired by John S. Wood, opened on March 8, 1951, and ran until November 13, 1952.

185. TO ELMER RICE

710 North Palm Drive
Beverly Hills, California
February 27, 1952

Dear Elmer—[1]

You certainly don't convince me. It seems to me that instead of answering me you set up straw men of your own and knock them down one after another. Probably my arguments look like that to you. And so we may as well agree not to agree.

Yours
Max

1. Rice's reply to no. 183 had attempted to refute Anderson's arguments.

186. TO ARCHER MILTON HUNTINGTON

[Agoura, California]
March 29, 1953

Dear Archer—[1]

When I found, last July, that Mab had been having what they call an affair with a young television executive I left home for a time and returned only to keep her going after she had tried suicide unsuccessfully. We weren't happy in the same house, however, and I left for California at the end of November, having decided to get a divorce and marry elsewhere.[2] Mab's television job fell through and she was unhappy—wanted me to return. Under the circumstances I couldn't, especially since I had managed to fall in love elsewhere. Mab's moods went from bad to worse, but I thought she was going to pull through and build a life of her own—and of course I did everything I could to encourage her to do that. Her suicide was a shock and not expected by anybody. It hits Hesper and me and the woman I expect to marry very hard. But I'm sorrier than I can say for Mab—and for what happened. It was all so unnecessary. I had been deeply in love with her.

I'll return soon to California. I intend to sell the New City place—have bought a house in California—may buy another in

Connecticut. In any case I shall hope to see you both when I return. Hesper is bearing up admirably, and time will do something for all of us. My address in California is a short and plain one. I put it at the end of the letter. My best to you and love to Anna.

Sincerely,
Max

Maxwell Anderson
Agoura
California

1. Anderson's wife Gertrude (Mab) had committed suicide on March 21, 1953.
2. Anderson and Gilda Oakleaf were married in Los Angeles on May 6, 1954.

187. TO ROBERT E. SHERWOOD

Apartment 1–D,
400 South Hauser Blvd.
Los Angeles, California
October 19, 1953

Dear Bob—[1]

After I got your last letter about *Devil's Hornpipe* I went over it again and realized that you were entirely right about the script as it looked then. But I knew, too, that there was nothing wrong with the original story—which was essentially the *Faust* story placed in our time. I had got off on the wrong foot, for a number of reasons, and produced something quite sour and disagreeable. With Rouben's help I started from the beginning, saving nothing but the background and the names of the characters—and we're getting near the end of a new version in which the story is changed, the motivations are different and the good people have enough brains to outsmart the devils at the end. The change is so complete that I think the whole is going to be both amusing and engaging. I expect to have book, lyrics and music pulled together within a few weeks and be able to bring them east in a script which—given a good presentation—will be successful.

But I am, as you will immediately see, in something of a dilemma. *Devil's Hornpipe* was announced by the Playwrights' Co., and then, as

Zolotow put it, "scratched".[2] No matter how good the script and the music, this, if I want to show what I have to another producer, is lethal publicity. Much as I dislike to put any of you to the trouble of reading the thing again I don't see any other way out of it. I should never have sent you that abortive first draft—but then if I hadn't I wouldn't have known how far I was wrong. I'll just have to ask you to forgive me and try to look at the new version as if there had been no former one. It may even happen, as I think in hopeful moments, that this one can set a new pattern for musicals.

The basic change I have made is this, that Danny, the lawyer hero, is not a fool. He has been poor, he is tempted by easy money, he takes it, he finds himself involved in a crime syndicate, and he fights his way out of it, bagging most of the mob in doing so. This doesn't sound very different, but it is. In the former version he was so easily deceived that he was laughable and not likeable. The compromise philosophy has been discarded. This is the old story of good, evil, temptation and error retrieved. Or corrected. And we have invented a new set of circumstances, both more convincing and funnier.

I have been offered a couple of pictures to do—you remember pictures?—so I could live if I stayed out here, but I'm hoping the musical is good enough to take me east. People are piling into this region like lemmings. I don't know what attracts them unless it's hope of a hydrogen bomb.

Give my regards to the men and boys at the office, and tell them I wish I were having the same.[3]

Yours,

MAX

1. Since Mab's suicide Anderson had been in Los Angeles writing a musical, *Devil's Hornpipe*, with Rouben Mamoulian, who had directed *Lost in the Stars*, and Allie Wrubel, composer and lyricist who worked mainly in motion pictures, including *Song of the South* (1947). The Playwrights' Company had rejected the first version of the play in August, and Sherwood had explained the decision by saying that *Devil's Hornpipie* was poorly structured and that the central character needed to be morally stronger and more interesting as a person (criticism recapitulated in letter cited in n. 3 below).

2. Sam Zolotow, theatrical reporter for the *New York Times*.

3. Sherwood replied that the company would be happy to consider the revised script (Sherwood to Anderson, October 21, 1953; W), and Anderson continued to work on it into December.

188. TO LELA CHAMBERS

[Apt. 1 D, 400 South Hauser Blvd.,
Los Angeles, California]
December 14, 1953

Dear Lela—

Day after tomorrow—and tomorrow I dimly remember is my birthday—I'm leaving for the east, and in going over the letters I've received out here I came across yours of August 23, still unanswered. Not because I don't think of you and remember you and yours as ever. No—just because life has got so complicated and difficult I can't quite keep up even with correspondence. Even when our years are broken clean in two there is work to be done, there are days to be lived through and mouths to be fed, as you know.[1] My work hasn't been going too well, and I've been working desperately hard at that. However, I am loved, and it's something not to be lonely. I won't try to explain it, but there is a woman of great beauty and sweetness who finds me worth while still and that has pulled me through.[2]

I'm going east to try to put on the musical I've been struggling over the last six months.[3] It's not quite in shape, and maybe it won't go on, but at least I'll get a decision on it and be able to start something else if this one is not to be. I'll be staying with Quentin when in New York City and with Alan when in New City. Alan's address you know. Quentin's is 400 West 118th St., N.Y. 27, N.Y.

Thank you for the news. The children sound wonderful—and they do make tomorrow seem worth going toward.

My best to Dan and love to you—and all those you love—

Max

Gilda is not going east with me—not at least till I know what my plans are—and it's quite possible I'll come back out here to work on a picture.[4]

1. Two of Lela's sons had been killed in World War II.
2. Gilda Oakleaf.
3. *Devil's Hornpipe*.
4. Anderson stayed in New York into January, when the Playwrights' Company rejected *Devil's Hornpipe* a second time. Anderson put the play aside and it was not produced or published, nor has a script of it come to light. But in 1958 it was made into a motion picture, *Never Steal Anything Small*.

Part IV

ACHIEVEMENT AND PEACE
1954–1958

*|Your play| puts the Book of Job into modern terms, and
. . . seems to say that a man who has everything that
constitutes success, and then suddenly loses it all, may find
that life still tastes sweet and is worth living when he is
reduced to base unflattered existence.*

*—ANDERSON to ELMER RICE,
March 8, 1955*

[Los Angeles, California]
February 7, 1954

Dear Bob—[1]

Since Miss Geffen's note hasn't yet come I shall be grateful if you let her know I'll appear and speak on May 26th and that I'm very sensible of the honor. Something in me likes the fact that there was no electioneering but let's not blind ourselves to the fact that nomination by R.E.S. carries weight. Still, I'd hate to be a man without friends, and I'm glad I have a friend at court. There was a time when I despised formal awards, but I know now that they have a place.[2]

By the way, I'm beginning to get a glow out of something else that has come about casually. When I saw Alfred at work and remembered what magic he and Lynn have I began automatically to think of plots they might play. And, thanks be, a story has occurred to me I think they'd like. I haven't begun work on it, or even planned it, and I know that others will probably play it if it's written, but it's a good idea with some nobility and some fun in it. Maybe I'll have it when I come east.[3]

I've been happier about *Ondine* than about anything else in the theatre for years.

Bob, I don't know what to say except again, many, many thanks—

MAX

1. Sherwood had written to say that the American Academy and National Institute of Arts and Letters had voted to award Anderson its Gold Medal for Drama in 1954 and that Felicia Geffen of the Academy and Institute would notify him shortly.

2. Though he planned to attend the awards ceremony in New York on May 26, Anderson was hospitalized in Los Angeles on May 23 and received the Gold Medal in absentia.

3. Alfred Lunt directed the current Playwrights' Company production of Jean Giraudoux's *Ondine* (in Maurice Valency's translation), which was to open on February 18, 1954, and Anderson had watched rehearsals on his trip east during the previous December and January. Lunt and his wife Lynn Fontanne had had the leads in *Elizabeth the Queen*, and the new play contemplated here is a sequel, *The Masque of Queens*, which treats Elizabeth's life from Essex's death to her own.

190. TO JOHN F. WHARTON

[Los Angeles, California]
February 27, 1954

Dear John—[1]

Here are the papers with, I hope, the signatures in the proper places.

I am hopeful that there'll be a play. If there isn't it will be because it takes more courage to write each succeeding play than the one preceding needed, and maybe there isn't sufficient heart for it.

But I'll try. Best to you—and those you see about.

Yours
Max

1. For his signature Wharton had sent Anderson the papers formalizing Robert Anderson's membership in the Playwrights' Company (Wharton to Anderson, February 25, 1954, JFW).

191. TO LELA CHAMBERS

[Apt. 1 D, 400 So. Hauser Blvd.
Los Angeles, Cal.]
April 14, 1954

Dear Lela—[1]

It's always good to hear from you—though I usually have the feeling of not deserving it. I'm not a good correspondent, largely because I have to write for a living—and so writing gets to be a chore.

I don't have a recent picture. Fact is, there isn't any recent one. But I can write to Bill Fields at the Playwrights' Co., and ask him to send you one. As for the work I'm doing at the moment, I hesitate to tell anybody what it is because it may come to nothing—and any information given out about it then becomes destructive. It is spoken of, or written of—as a project abandoned. And that has happened too often lately.

However, it's not likely that what you say to the Richburg girls will get to the N.Y. papers, so I'll venture to tell you what I'm at work on. I'm writing a play that has the title of *The Masque of Queens* and it's about the death of Queen Elizabeth—of England. The first Elizabeth —that is. The story runs that after she was stricken—and it was probably a stroke—she refused to go to bed—refused to lie down —and stood for 15 hours before the poor old muscles couldn't take any more, and she sank to her knees. I've built a story around the episode and it may get to the stage—but the thing isn't finished yet. Don't be surprised if it never is.

I'll be in New York on May 26th to receive the gold medal for drama from the Institute of Arts and Letters. The gold medal has been given for playwriting only four times before, I believe. Robert Sherwood is the only other living playwright who has received it, now that Eugene O'Neill is gone.[2]

Gilda Oakleaf and I will be married in May, too, as soon as her divorce is final, and we'll go east to live. Where, I don't know. But wish us luck. Best to Dan.

Love
Max

1. Lela had asked about Anderson's current work in preparation for a talk she was to give at a woman's club in Richburg, a town near her home at Belfast, New York.

2. O'Neill, who had died on November 27, 1953, received a Gold Medal from the American Academy and National Institute of Arts and Letters in 1922, and Sherwood received the award in 1941. The other two playwrights so honored were Augustus Thomas (1913) and William Gillette (1931).

192. TO LOTTE LENYA WEILL [1]

[Los Angeles, California]
July 13, 1954

Dear Lenya,

Well, they let me out of the hospital today after that small preliminary operation, and I came home with Gilda, so we can begin to settle down and get ready for the next one. Also I'll do some work which I've been offered (on a picture) to pay for the next one. Life seems to repeat itself in some ways.

I just got a letter from Hesper in the same mail with yours. Poor girl, she does have her personal trials—and she's so secretive about them that she tells nobody but me—at least that's her story. But she'll be all right. She just needs to be straightened out and then find the right man. The right man—as if that weren't like looking for a needle in a field of hay.

About those songs—"The Great Big Sky" sounds like something written for *Sunrise in My Pocket*; at least it isn't mine.[2] As for "The Time of the Cherries" that's a translation from the French of a song which was used by the French resistance during the war and which was to be used in a film Burgess was going to make. It was never used, although Burgess did make a picture about the French Jaques.[3] I wrote the words, which are not a very literal paraphrase, the tune is an old French one. I don't know whether Kurt arranged it or not, but I suppose he did if it's in his hand-writing.

Gilda and I are both glad to have one crisis out of the way—even though we are left with the original one still to meet. I doubt that we'll get east this summer, but I might come by in the fall—or even stay near N.Y. if I have a play to put on. *The Masque of Queens* hasn't found an Elizabeth yet. And I haven't started to work on *The Bad Seed*. But I intend to make a play out of that. Have you read the novel? It's fascinating. —Don't speak of this yet—the rights are still in negotiation, and it's too early to announce.

I'll be happier when I can see you occasionally just to talk things over.

Go well—stay well—[4]
and love—
Max

1. Lotte Lenya, dancer and singer born in Vienna (n.d.), married Kurt Weill in Berlin in 1926 and achieved international recognition as Jenny in the 1928 production of Brecht and Weill's *Die Dreigroschenoper*. With Weill she fled Germany in the early thirties and in 1935 settled in the United States as a neighbor of Anderson. The two families became close friends, and Lenya maintained her career on stage (including *Candle in the Wind* and *Barefoot in Athens*) and in motion pictures. Following Weill's death in 1950 she continued to live at New City and had written to Anderson about two songs found among Weill's papers, asking if the lyrics were Anderson's. Anderson, in Los Angeles, was just out of the hospital following a prostate operation done preliminary to the diaphragmatic hernea operation he would have in New York in February, 1955. A few days after the present letter he began the dramatization of William March's novel *The Bad Seed* and did not undertake a film script.

2. The song is not in the published text of *Sunrise in My Pocket* (1941), a play about Davy Crockett by Edwin Justus Mayer, who had Weill as composer for his Broadway musical *The Firebrand of Florence* in 1945.

3. "Salute to France," a film Burgess Meredith made for the U.S. Army in 1944.

4. A refrain from *Lost in the Stars*.

193. TO VICTOR SAMROCK

[Los Angeles, California]
July 22, 1954

Dear Victor—[1]

Harold Freedman called me this evening to ask about things in general, and in particular about Ralph Levy, and so you may know what this letter's about without reading it. I got to know Levy through doing a t v show with him, and then let him read *Masque of Queens*. He got excited about it, and began to suggest names for the lead and to talk about some necessary re-writing. I am now, under the influence of his enthusiasm and stimulating ideas, planning to bring him in as co-producer and director—*if* he can find the right cast for it and matters work out in the revisions as we hope.

Harold is having breakfast with Roger[2] tomorrow morning. They will go over the question of *The Bad Seed* rights and then Harold will tell Roger that I am taking on Ralph Levy for the *Masque* play. Now, since Levy is almost inexperienced as a director there is a possibility that he won't work out when the play has to get ready for New York. That being the case, there should be some producer or co-producer around who would be strong enough to change directors if that became necessary. I asked Harold if Roger would be able to handle such a situation, and Harold said Roger might not want to take on such a rough assignment, but that his partner, Whitehead, would be quite equal to it.[3] I then suggested that the Producers' Theatre have enough interest in the *Masque* production to give Whitehead a voice in the decisions. He said he would speak to Roger about it.

Levy and I are going to see Rosalind Russell tomorrow afternoon. She may not want to do the play, but Levy is very likely to come up with some suggestion that does work out. Once he persuades a star to come in he may have shot his bolt and have to be replaced, but I doubt it. I'm gambling on his turning in a first-class job the first time. With a little steering he may [be] just the man Broadway has been waiting for.

The plans are tentatively for a November date for rehearsals.

Best to you all in the office.

Max

Reinheimer & Irving Cohn[4] represent Levy, and they'll probably want to talk with you and Roger about his compensation. He says he'll take the minimum, whatever that is.[5]

1. Anderson had read William March's novel *The Bad Seed* (1954) and begun to outline his dramatization of it. He had also completed *The Masque of Queens*, and Ralph Levy, a television director in Hollywood ("The Burns and Allen Show," "The Jack Benny Show," and several "Playhouse 90" productions) without previous experience on Broadway, wanted to direct it.

2. Roger L. Stevens.

3. Robert Whitehead, Stevens's partner in the producing organization Whitehead-Stevens Productions. In 1953 Stevens had made an arrangement whereby the Playwrights' Company and Whitehead-Stevens could coproduce plays, and in such cases the producer was to be known as the Producers' Theatre, Inc.

4. Howard E. Reinheimer, New York attorney specializing in legal matters relating to people in the arts; and Cohn, a Hollywood theatrical agent.

5. Not finding an actress for Elizabeth, Anderson postponed *The Masque of Queens* and devoted his time to *The Bad Seed*. *The Masque of Queens* was not produced or published (see *Catalogue*, pp. 73–74).

194. TO VICTOR SAMROCK

[Los Angeles, California]
August 23, 1954

Dear Victor—[1]

As I have just told you in a wire I spent an hour & a half with Ralph Levy today, and at the end of it he resigned from directing *The Bad Seed* and we shook hands in parting. There really was a conflict of schedules—though he knows so little about the theatre that he was unaware that you can't have a commitment to do 3 t.v. shows in California in October and still be free to direct a show that may open any time in Sept. or October, in N.Y. I did my best to make this clear, but he still thinks he was somehow misled. Now I do hope we find a good director, in New York. Please keep me informed about whatever comes up.

John says it wouldn't be much use coming to the east at Labor Day time, as nearly all are out of town then, so I shall probably not try to get a reservation till after the early Sept. rush. There will have to be some consultations on the phone, no doubt. Maybe we'll know more about the possible directors.

Meanwhile, as you know, Harold F. made the arrangements with the Wm March estate, and it gets half the royalties. As for the half that I get, I want it to be split in two—in other words my wife & I want to split the royalties 50–50.[2] Her name was Gilda Oakleaf before we were married—and that was her stage name in the '30's,—so she could receive them under that name.[3]

You might call Harold and ask him if he can draw the collaboration agreement—he may have done it before.

Best to you all
Max

1. After postponement of *The Masque of Queens*, Ralph Levy had wanted to direct *The Bad Seed*, a job eventually done by Reginald Denham.
2. For tax purposes.
3. Gilda had acted in a number of plays, among them Robert Turney's *Daughters of Atreus* (1936), Leopold Atlas's *But For the Grace of God* (1937), Ian Hay's *Bachelor Born* (1938), and, at the Pasadena Playhouse during its Midsummer Drama Festival in 1940, Sir James Barrie's *A Kiss for Cinderella*.

195. TO JOHN F. WHARTON

January 22, 1955

Dear John—

The next time we have a meeting I wish we could bring up the matter of paying Lenya for the stock which Kurt owned in the Playwrights' Company.[1] As you know, he paid $3,000 for the stock he acquired when he came in, and since his death we have taken in members who must have paid similarly for their places on the board.[2] It seems to me that Lenya should not take a loss on this. The stock still exists and is just as useful and necessary as it was when Kurt bought it.

Harold tells me he is coming close to a picture sale.[3] In that case I should soon be able to pay my long-standing debt to the company, and we should all feel a little less financial pressure than we've been accustomed to. Anyway we don't need to be stingy with an old friend.

As ever

Max

1. Lotte Lenya, widow of Kurt Weill, who had died in 1950.
2. Roger L. Stevens and Robert Anderson.
3. Of *The Bad Seed* to Warner Brothers Pictures, which released the motion picture in 1956.

196. TO ELMER RICE

March 8, 1955

Dear Elmer—[1]

"ORDEAL BY FIRE" is an impressive play, beautifully written, absorbing, and about as ambitious as any playwright could attempt. It puts the Book of Job into modern terms, and in doing so questions every value on which modern life is built. It seems to say that a man who has everything that constitutes success, and then suddenly loses it all, may find that life still tastes sweet and is worth living when he is reduced to base, unflattered existence, if he faces things as they are left, makes the necessary compromises, and makes himself as useful as he can.

It is not a popular theme. It has some excellent comic lines but no real comic relief, and remains as serious basically as the Old Testament original. It would need great playing in any case, but to be a success probably needs spectacular casting.

As to specific suggestions, I have a few, confined to the last scene. Olga, the servant, seems to be a Hollywood cushion, and completely out of place in a play that is saying anything really drastic. Also there should be something for Vera to do when she returns. The left-over champagne is in the same category as Olga. Personally I wouldn't touch it at such a time. The surgeon should not again attempt a speech—certainly should not read from the lush Nelson letter. Whatever is said by the others should be sparse and real and indicate that what they have found in torture and loss is not great wisdom but only the realization that life had spoiled them—that all men must bear torture and loss and yet keep on—and that they can do it, too, now that they must.

Max

1. Rice wrote *Ordeal by Fire* (also entitled *As The Sparks Fly Upward*) during 1954 following his divorce from actress Betty Field and the failure of *The Winner* in early 1954. *Ordeal by Fire* was suggested by the Book of Job, Rice says in *Minority Report*, and reflected his obsession with "the situation of a man who suddenly discovers that his house is founded upon quicksand and not, as he believed, on a rock" (pp. 440–41).

197. TO VAN WYCK BROOKS

141 Downes Avenue
Stamford, Connecticut
January 8, 1956

Dear Brooks—1

(Which seems much less formal than Van Wyck) Maybe we will meet oftener than we used for I've bought a house at the above address and left New City behind me. Your letter followed me and came here yesterday. I will of course write a tribute for Sherwood, whom I miss more than I'll say—and you won't mind if I use part of the words I wrote to be read by Lunt at the funeral. And I'll read them myself, since I expect to be there.2

I don't regret staying alive, but it is increasingly tough to say goodbye to such old and steady friends just when you and they are beginning to learn what an age we could have made of it if we'd been able to use just a little more gold—

Yours
Maxwell A.

1. Anderson was to be inducted into the American Academy of Arts and Letters on May 23, 1956, and Brooks had asked him to write a memorial for Robert Sherwood and read it at the ceremony. Sherwood, who nominated Anderson for membership in the academy, had died on November 14, 1955, and Anderson's eulogy of him had been read at the funeral by Alfred Lunt. Brooks, at the time secretary of the academy, lived at Bridgewater, Connecticut.

2. At the induction ceremony on May 23 Anderson read the memorial poem "Robert E. Sherwood," which recounts their association from the twenties onward (printed in Wharton, *Life Among the Playwrights*, pp. 232–35).

198. TO VAN WYCK BROOKS

141 Downes Avenue
Stamford, Connecticut
February 19, 1956

Dear Van Wyck—[1]

If I were to present Conrad Aiken's name to the academy for membership would you second the proposal? I note that five "proposers" are needed. I have found much of Aiken's work moving, delicate and amazingly musical.[2]

Yours
Maxwell Anderson

1. Anderson had long admired Conrad Aiken (1889–1973) and as early as 1921 had praised him as having "the most notable gift among poets writing English in this generation," an estimate based on the subtle music of Aiken's versification ("Conrad Aiken and the Minor Mode," *Measure* 3 [May, 1921]: 25–26).

2. Anderson nominated Aiken, and he was elected to the American Academy of Arts and Letters in December, 1956.

199. TO LELA CHAMBERS

141 Downes Avenue
Stamford, Connecticut
March 26, 1956

Dear Lela—[1]

Your outline of our lives was most interesting to me—probably more interesting to me than it would be to anyone else. My first impression is that the three of us—Ethel, you and I—would be needed to really remember what went on, for Ethel's memory is fantastically good, and mine is fallible.

When it comes to adding to the recollections and giving them a sort of editorial scrutiny I come up against a strange quirk in my own psyche—I have always fought shy of writing down anything about myself. Not from reluctance to reveal what happened, but because autobiography is not the kind of work that interests me, yet it does take time. If I sat down to make a list of my memories that were worth recalling it would be a major effort, and one that would keep m[e] from thinking about that next play that's always in my mind. So far as I'm concerned I've never written a play good enough to be remembered and I still have hopes of writing one. At least I'm not willing to give up the few creative days I have left to any other purpose.

Perhaps too I'm a little sensitive on the score of perhaps estimating myself too highly. It's my conviction that I haven't ma[d]e a high enough mark on the sands of time, or the eternal beach, to be worthy of long remembering. If I were to write, even to assist you, a list of the little happenings that come back to me, I should feel that I was making myself a little ridiculous. What have I done that I should be held up to future generations—or to this?

If you weren't a well-beloved sister I wouldn't write this bit of truth to you out of my insides. I don't think I've ever said it to anybody except Gilda, and she doesn't understand it. But I do sincerely feel that way, and to you and Dan I can say so.

The spring does come on slowly here—the nights continue cold and the snow lingers on. I'm trying to pull myself together and pounce on a new play if I can plan it to my satisfaction.[2] If I can't I'll try another pot-boiler like *Bad Seed* or another picture.

Gilda & the childer are well.[3] We'd certainly like to have you—one or both—come to see us. It will soon I hope be warm enough for swimming. Yesterday there were seven clam diggers in front of our house—

Love to you both—
Max

1. She had sent him a sketch of their immediate family that she had done in preparation for an Anderson family history.
2. *Madonna and Child*.
3. Laurel and Craig, Gilda's "childer" by a previous marriage.

200. TO THE PLAYWRIGHTS' COMPANY

[April, 1956]

To the Members of the Playwrights' Co.

As you know the company has changed a great deal in the last few years. It is no longer an organization of playwrights but a general producing company. This change has been for the better, I think, for the company, but it has put the playwright members in a rather untenable position.

We have become a general producing company, producing plays which the playwright members don't choose, don't finance, don't control and often don't like. My name shouldn't be on the office stationery. I have no part in the business except a nominal one.

I have listened, several times, to Elmer's analysis of how a member playwright is penalized for belonging—and I'm inclined to agree with him. Outside playwrights can present their plays to many managers. We can't because it's assumed that when our home company has turned a script down it's not worth producing—which is not always true.[1] As we all know a play makes the rounds of many offices in search of an enthusiastic producer, and doesn't get on till it finds one. Our right to production amounts in practice to nothing, for no playwright wants to be produced by a reluctant manager. It's better to let the play rot than to go on half-heartedly.

It may be that, because it broke with this tradition, and because playwrights are not naturally fitted to be producers, the Playwrights' Company was not a good idea from the beginning. However we did put on some good plays and we had a lot of fun together. If play production should go back into business hands, and I think probably it should, then the playwrights who are now in the Playwrights' Co. should be free once again to go looking for new sponsors for each new play.

Personally, I don't feel responsible for the acts of the company, and feel that I'd rather my name were not on its flag. Perhaps the only way to remove it is to resign. I'll miss having a home office, and miss my friends here, but I can't afford to let things ride the way they are. It's misleading to the public and it's costly to me. I'm trying to pay off an old income tax debt, and what I invested in our original company would help if somebody wants to buy my stock.

Maxwell Anderson

1. Anderson had had the experience with two recent plays, *Devil's Hornpipe* in 1953 and *Richard and Anne* in 1955. For *Richard and Anne*, unproduced and unpublished, see *Catalogue*, pp. 75–76.

201. TO JOHN F. WHARTON

141 Downes Avenue
Stamford, Connecticut
April 18, 1956

Dear John—[1]

After thinking it over I would like to put my Playwrights' Co. stock in Gilda's name. If there are papers to be prepared could you do that for me?

And thanks again for the explanations.

Yours
Max

1. The day before the present letter Anderson had lunched with Wharton to discuss his resignation from the Playwrights' Company (see no. 200). Wharton had urged Anderson not to resign, emphasizing the long-run financial advantages of remaining

with the company, particularly the likelihood that company stock would increase in value over the next few years (Wharton to Anderson, April 14, 1956; JFW).

202. TO ELMER RICE

141 Downes Avenue
Stamford, Connecticut
April 20, 1956

Dear Elmer—[1]

For some reason or reasons which I can't pin down your play seems not to be improved by rewriting. I say this with some regret, knowing that it means a great deal to you, and wishing very earnestly that it could be the play to win all the prizes.

Reading through it I got the effect of being taken through a dazzling display of verbal fireworks, but I was not warmed or stirred by it, and was not moved by the ending. As I say, I don't know why, but the people don't seem real or sympathetic. No hope is held out, nothing but a sort of inhuman facing up to the facts as we know them.

Maybe the theatre isn't up to that kind of statement. Maybe I'm not. As I've grown older I've been conscious of losing illusions, and conscious too that the loss made me less capable of writing salable plays. Maybe it's impossible to make a logical statement of the human position dramatic. If we've lost everything, or everything is worthless, what have we got to lose? The rewriting does, I think, make the story clearer and the motives more believable. But it has also removed a lot of the agony that was present in the first version.

Or so it seems to me. I've never been able to rewrite much. I hear of these playwrights who go over and over scripts, re-working, and emerging with final brilliant versions, but in my case either the first draft looks good or it never will be any good.

If you want to put *Ordeal by Fire* on I think you should. But personally I wouldn't set my hopes high. People don't want to listen to dusty answers. I wish I could say something more cheerful.[2]

Yours—
Max

1. Rice had revised *Ordeal By Fire*, which in an earlier draft Anderson had liked (see no. 196).

2. Rice did not produce or publish the play.

203. TO ENID BAGNOLD [1]

> 141 Downes Avenue
> Stamford, Connecticut
> April 27, 1956

Dear Miss Bagnold—

Douglas Moore forwarded a copy of your letter (to him) to me, and I take pleasure in answering your question "Is it allowed to know?"

I don't know whether or not it's allowed, but my wife and I had such an enchanted time at "The Chalk Garden" that we couldn't think of any other candidate for the award. When MacLeish[2] asked me to get together with Marc Connelly and Thornton Wilder to choose a candidate your name and the delightful dialogue of the play came to mind and nobody else was proposed.

It would be pleasant to meet you (your work I've known as long as it's been known over here) but I understand your feeling about flying. Instead of making a chore out of it, please take the time to dream out another play, and put it on here. You're good for us.

> Sincerely
> Maxwell Anderson

1. Miss Bagnold (b. 1889), English novelist (*Serena Blandish*, 1924, adapted for the stage by S. N. Behrman, 1929; *National Velvet*, 1935) and playwright, was currently represented on Broadway by her play *The Chalk Garden*, which had opened for a long run on October 26, 1955. For the play she was to receive an Award of Merit from the American Academy of Arts and Letters, and concerning the award and whether she needed to attend the ceremony she had written to Douglas Moore, composer, professor at Columbia, and member of the academy. Moore forwarded the letter to Anderson, who had been on the committee that selected Miss Bagnold's play for the award.

2. Archibald MacLeish, at the time president of the academy (1953–56).

204. TO ENID BAGNOLD

141 Downes Avenue
Stamford, Connecticut
May 14, 1956

Dear Enid Bagnold—

Your letter came fluttering across the salt water like a bit of yourself. My wife was so enchanted by it and by the play and by the award to you that she hoped no word of mine had encouraged you to stay comfortably at home—then she said, "But I know what you'd do in a similar case. You'd skip the ceremony, especially if you had an idea for a new one."

I find it so difficult to make rules for myself that I certainly can't make them for others. It does seem unnecessary to fly six thousand miles to receive a salvo of admiration when you're going to get it anyway and much more comfortably in your own livingroom. Yet so often the unnecessary trip or the acquaintance you tried to avoid turns out to be the key to your best future.

In all truth I don't want to influence you. I've written some stodgy literary adjectives to go along with the medal. They won't sound any better near at hand. "The Chalk Garden" speaks more ably for itself than I can speak about it. However, it would give me great personal pleasure just to meet you and talk with you, even briefly, and if you come that will be possible.[1]

By the way, Harold has been my agent a long while. I think I met him in 1922.[2]

Summer came to Connecticut yesterday with no intervening spring. You'll find New York in flower if you come. But of course you'll leave the Sussex buds behind. Everybody would be happy to see you, and it makes me happy to know that you're in the world and have an idea for a new planting.[3]

Yours,
Maxwell Anderson

1. Miss Bagnold did not attend the ceremony on May 23, 1956, at which Anderson made the presentation of her award. (For Anderson's speech, see *Catalogue*, p. 99.) With the thousand dollars that accompanied the award Miss Bagnold "built the little canal that crosses my garden" (*Enid Bagnold's Autobiography*, 1969, p. 235).

2. Harold Freedman, Anderson's agent, was also Miss Bagnold's American agent and he arranged the production of *The Chalk Garden* by Irene Mayer Selznick.

3. *The Last Joke*, produced in London on September 23, 1960.

205. TO ELMER RICE

[Stamford, Connecticut]
September 19, 1956

Dear Elmer—[1]

I'm sorry you didn't hear my muttered warning against reading *Madonna* at the last meeting. It's obvious that I had nothing to say and took overlong saying it. I doubt that it's worth revising, for there's still nothing on my mind.

My personal troubles have a way of snow-balling and compounding with physical troubles that would discourage me completely only I can't afford to die yet. The income tax people are holding a vast and growing claim over my head and seem inclined to hold it there the rest of my life, but it would fall on my estate automatically in the event of my death. This lends death a new terror, as somebody said in another connection.[2]

Anyway thanks for your note, which I agree with, and I'll try to make a play out of something that doesn't require me to have any convictions.

Yours
Max

1. At a recent meeting of the Playwrights' Company, Anderson had given the other members his new play *Madonna and Child*, a humorous satire on romantic love. Rice did not like the play and the company rejected it.
2. *Hamlet*, III, i.

206. TO VICTOR SAMROCK

[Stamford, Connecticut]
[October 9, 1956]

Dear Victor—[1]

The Sin of Pat M is in a tradition so well known since *Juno and the Paycock* that I've grown weary of the whole subject. An ancient, irritable, blasphemous, dying but loveable Irishman says his last ten thousand words and goes to his own place. The hell with him.[2]

Molly's play is a clever and smoothly written go at a topical subject which would have been timely in the year when Gadge recanted publicly and named names. It might even have drawn an audience then. Today I think it doesn't have a chance—though I agree with the attitude—or did at the time when it was pertinent to the discussion. We've moved enough since then so that the temper of the argument has cooled and, according to Brownell,[3] the reds are (within the U.S.A.) dwindling and less confident.[4]

Yours

Max

1. Samrock had sent Anderson two plays to consider for production by the Playwrights' Company. *The Sin of Pat Muldoon*, which Anderson compares to a Sean O'Casey play, was by John McLiam (b. 1920), Canadian actor and playwright (who began his acting career in a production of *Winterset* in San Francisco in 1946).

2. *The Sin of Pat Muldoon*, McLiam's only play, was not produced by the Playwrights' Company, but Richard Adler and Roger Stevens produced it in March, 1957. The second play, *The Egghead* by Molly Kazan (1906–63), was suggested by the appearance of her husband Elia Kazan (Gadge) before the House Committee on Un-American Activities in 1952, when he told of belonging to the Communist party in the mid-thirties and identified other members.

3. Herbert Brownell, U.S. attorney general (1953–57).

4. *The Egghead* was not produced by the Playwrights' Company, but Hope Abelson produced it in October, 1957.

207. TO THE EDITOR, *New York Times*

[Stamford, Connecticut]

October 19, 1956

Dear Sir,[1]

It can't matter very much to anybody that I'm not supporting Bill Mauldin for Congress, but since your New City correspondent took the trouble to say, in your October 18th issue, that I was among Mauldin's New City boosters, perhaps you won't mind printing my statement that I am not. In fact, I have seldom agreed with Bill in political matters, and back in 1952 when he was highly vocal on one side of South Mountain Road in his support of Adlai Stevenson I was just as definitely for Gen. Eisenhower, though perhaps not so voluble, on the other. I shall vote for Eisenhower again, and continue generally Republican. Moreover, I couldn't vote for Bill, even if I wanted to change parties, for I no longer live in Rockland County, and my vote will be cast in Connecticut. Bill, of course, knows this, though Emma Harrison (your correspondent) did not. I hope she was better informed in other details of her story.[2]

Yours,
Maxwell Anderson

1. In 1956 Bill Mauldin, World War II cartoonist (*Up Front*, 1945), ran unsuccessfully as the Democratic candidate for Congress in New York's 28th Congressional District, which included New City, and *New York Times* correspondent Emma Harrison reported on the race in an article that listed Anderson among Mauldin's New City supporters ("Mrs. St. George and Bill Mauldin Offer Contrast in 28th," *New York Times*, October 18, 1956, p. 26, cols. 1–2).

2. The *Times* acknowledged its error, October 23, 1956, p. 22, col. 5.

208. TO JOHN F. WHARTON

141 Downes Avenue
Stamford, Connecticut
April 21, 1957

Dear John—[1]

Congratulations on your new partner. And thanks sincerely for your letter which helps me make up my mind about the play. What I was trying to do was to telescope the beginnings of the Roman Empire into a mystery-history, but it was evidently an impossible task, for it doesn't sell itself any way, any where, and probably should be used as fill in some thruway project.

I'm thinking of another one now—they're fun to write whether or not they go on.[2]

Yours
Max

1. Members of the Playwrights' Company had read *The Golden Six*, which focuses on the Roman Emperor Claudius (19 B.C.–A.D. 54). Wharton, remembering earlier plagiarism suits, had asked whether the play was indebted to Robert Graves's historical

novel *I, Claudius* (1934) and had also said that he thought the play would not interest a modern audience. On the day before the present letter newspapers announced that Adlai E. Stevenson, following his defeat by Dwight D. Eisenhower in the 1956 presidential election, had joined Wharton's law firm as a senior partner in its newly created Chicago branch.

2. Anderson wrote no more history plays.

209. TO JOHN F. WHARTON

[Stamford, Connecticut]
April 22, 1957

Dear John—[1]

I forgot to answer your question about *I, Claudius*. The matter is academic at present, I think, but this is the situation. There is very little indeed in Graves' book that isn't also in *Tacitus* and *Suetonius*.[2] I took care to avoid any fact or fancy that didn't have a basis in the histories. I was quite willing to share royalties with Graves if I found his book contained anything I needed, but it didn't so I forgot about him.

Maybe he did have an influence on me though. His book is very dull, and that may have infected the play—[3]

Yours

Max

1. In no. 208 Anderson had failed to answer Wharton's question whether *The Golden Six* was indebted to *I, Claudius*.

2. Tacitus (c. 56–117 A.D.), Roman historian whose *Annales* covers the period from Augustus to the death of Nero, including Claudius's reign (41–54 A.D.). Suetonius (c. 69–160 A.D.), Roman historian whose *Lives of the Caesars* covers the period from Julius to Domitian. Suetonius is largely a chronicler, but Tacitus is an interpretive historian whose sympathy for the freer institutions of the Republic colors his treatment of the empire, and his sympathy corresponds with the theme of *The Golden Six*.

3. In May, 1958, *The Golden Six* was produced at Boston University, and on October 26, 1958, it opened for a short run in New York. It has not been published (see *Catalogue*, pp. 69–70), but an acting script is available from Dramatist Play Service.

210. TO MABEL DRISCOLL BAILEY [1]

141 Downes Avenue
Stamford, Connecticut
October 7, 1957

Dear Miss Bailey—

I want to thank you for devoting so much clearheaded thinking to my plays. At the moment they hardly seem worth it—but I was always too bored with rehearsals and too busy writing the next one to look back at the jangle of writing I've left behind me, so perhaps I'm not a good judge. I hope not.

Anyway I'm grateful.

Only now that it's done you'd better go on to someone who's in fashion. Time, as you know, has a wallet at his back wherein he puts alms for oblivion. [2]

As for me, I'm putting on a new play this season if we can find a cast. It's an adaptation of "The Day the Money Stopped." [3] One way to make a living.

Sincerely
Maxwell Anderson

1. Dr. Bailey (b. 1904), in the English Department of Eureka College, had sent Anderson a copy of her recently published book *Maxwell Anderson: The Playwright As Prophet.*
2. *Troilus and Cressida*, III, iii.
3. Novel (1957) by Brendan Gill. The adaptation opened for a brief run on February 20, 1958, and has not been published (see *Catalogue*, p. 68).

211. TO PAUL GREEN

141 Downes Avenue
Stamford, Connecticut
August 13, 1958

Dear Paul— [1]

That was a pleasant note to get, one that should help me go ahead with this bit of work I'm trying to do at the moment. Rewriting a play as usual, looking toward production. [2] It was especially good to hear from you. I have a high regard for your brain and your method of work and your intuition.

And, as you know, the best reward of all is a word of praise from a contemporary you respect. I don't know whether that essay is good at all. It's my custom never to look back—it might lead to regret or gloating—equally to be avoided. But if you liked it that much it was worth doing—and you put me in good spirits and a working mood. Thank you, Paul, and all good fortune to you![3]

Max

1. Green had told Anderson that he had just reread "The Essence of Tragedy" and found it an inspiration. He called it one of the best discussions of the nature of tragedy since Schiller and Goethe, and said he hoped Anderson would go back to the essay and expand it (Green to Anderson, August 4, 1958; T).

2. *Madonna and Child*, which Anderson had written in 1956 and put aside.

3. *Madonna and Child*, which Anderson was revising at his death, has not been produced or published. For the play see *Catalogue*, pp. 71–73; and Laurence G. Avery, "Maxwell Anderson: A Changing Attitude Toward Love," *Modern Drama* 10 (December 1967): 241–48.

212. TO THE UNIVERSITY OF NORTH DAKOTA [1]

141 Downes Avenue
Stamford, Connecticut
November 3, 1958

Dear UND:

You are celebrating your seventy-fifth anniversary this year—and that reminds me of something. I entered the University of North Dakota in the fall of 1908. It's just fifty years (plus a month or two) since I first walked among the little cluster of buildings on the prairie which was then the UND. This is not important to anybody but myself, but I shall celebrate it because it's now a half a century since I was first exposed to higher education on that bare and wind-swept campus at the end of a trolley line.

The buildings were brick and most of them new. The trees, save for a few along the coulee, were saplings, too slender to cast a shade or could name every building that stood there then, from Sayre Hall, on the outer fringe, where I lived, to the gymnasium and the railroad tracks, where everything ended. Around, on every side, was treeless prairie. Grand Forks was two miles away.

And now a word about myself and how I arrived at Sayre Hall. I was the son of an itinerant Baptist minister—we moved about once a year, as I remember it—and had picked up a scrambled education in many small towns in Pennsylvania, Ohio, and Iowa. It happened that I graduated from high school in Jamestown, North Dakota, and one of my classmates, Garth Howland, urged me to continue my education at a university. The university he had in mind was the nearest—the UND at Grand Forks. Since I knew nothing about universities and had no plans for the future, I went along. My finances were non-existent. I planned to work my way through.

As for my preparation, I had been an indifferent student. The only thing I had a smattering of was English literature. Before I finished the eighth grade I had discovered and read most of the well-known novelists, Dickens, Stevenson, Scott, Dumas, Cooper, and a vast sampling of others. In high school I discovered poetry—first Keats, then Shelley and Shakespeare—these in drugstore shelves and in libraries—and then all the major names from Tennyson, Browning and Swinburne on into the past. This caused a major revolution in my life and my thinking. Reading poetry was an overwhelming experience. With me it became a consuming vice. And having got so deep in, I took another step—I began to write poetry. This, however, I did in secret. In the Middle West in the years when I attended high school, the arts were not encouraged. The people around me were immersed in three activities—farming, banking, and trade. Religion and religious thought were accepted as minor necessities by the minister. If you wrote music or poetry you hid it. You didn't want to be jeered at by the other boys in school.

But this changed suddenly and dramatically when I arrived at the university. For the first time in my life I found myself among people who thought the life of the mind was more important than banking, and who respected any attempt to conquer an art form. Professor Gottfried Hult, who taught me Greek, also wrote poetry, and sometimes sold it. Professor Vernon Squires, who was Dean of the English Department, made me proud that I was able to quote and tried to write in verse. I found there was a place in society even for an odd duck like me! This is perhaps the most important cultural influence a university can have. In a world given over so largely to getting, using, and keeping property, it maintains a retreat for those who are more interested in the creation of beauty or the discovery of truth than in making a profit. Mind you, I am not opposed to the making of profits. If nobody saved, if nobody bargained, if nobody made profits, there would be no time and no money for the creation of beauty or the discovery of truth. But a balance must be maintained between the crafts and the arts, and the university does its best to maintain it. Anyway, the UND did it for me. If I hadn't gone to the university, I might have been an unhappy and mediocre banker, farmer, or store-keeper. I'd have gone no farther.

By my own standards I have not gone very far or achieved very much, but as a farmer or banker I'd have been a most unhappy man—and so I write this note of grateful appreciation to my alma mater, thanking it for being there when I needed it so badly, and for supplying hope to the current crop of youngsters as they come to it from the windy plains.

I have been looking through an old copy of the *Dacotah*, which I edited in 1911, and have been studying the young, keen, beautiful faces of the girls and the young men who were my classmates and friends fifty years ago. There are so many of them I can't mention them all, and they are so scattered by time and distance that I'm not sure what few of them are still alive, but to those who recall the years 1908 to 1911, I'd like to send greetings and affection. I wish I could be with you. Since I can't be, I'll remember you as you were then. And, still looking at the young faces in the old book, I want to thank each of you for being there then and for being the kind of person you were when the world and the university and you and I were so young.[2]

1. The University of North Dakota, founded in February 1883, held its Seventy-Fifth Anniversary Convocation and Faculty Conference on November 6, 7, and 8, 1958. Anderson, graduate of the university in 1911, was invited to speak on the first day's program, on "The Cultural Influence of the University," and to receive an honorary degree. Prevented by sickness from making the trip, he sent the present letter instead, entitling it "Love Letter to a University."

2. "Love Letter to a University" was published in the *North Dakota Quarterly* 38 (Winter, 1970): 89–90.

APPENDIXES

APPENDIX I

The chronology of Anderson's life that precedes the letters cites each of his works, published and unpublished alike. The previously unpublished documents relating to his career as a dramatist are given here.

No.	Date	Title	Nature and Location of Original
1	April, 1936	Acceptance Speech for the Drama Critics' Circle Award to *Winterset*	Typescript; Anderson Collection, Humanities Research Center, University of Texas.
2	March, 1937	Acceptance Speech for the Drama Critics' Circle Award to *High Tor*	Typescript; Anderson Collection, Humanities Research Center, University of Texas.
3	May, 1943	*The Eve of St. Mark*, Act II, scene 4	Typescript; Playwrights' Company Collection, Wisconsin Center for Film and Theater Research, University of Wisconsin.
4	January, 1950	Acceptance Speech for the Brotherhood Award to *Lost in the Stars* from the National Conference of Christians and Jews	Typescript; Anderson Collection, Humanities Research Center, University of Texas.
5	May 10, 1956	Anderson Memoir	Typescript; Oral History Collection, Columbia University.

1. ACCEPTANCE SPEECH FOR THE DRAMA CRITICS' CIRCLE AWARD TO *Winterset*

[The New York Drama Critics' Circle, created out of dissatisfaction with the Pulitzer awards in the drama, was organized in October, 1935, and included seventeen drama critics of the New York area, with Brooks Atkinson of the *Times* as its first president. Dissatisfaction with the Pulitzer award resulted in part from its seemingly narrow grounds, for Pulitzer assumed a civilizing purpose for the drama and had stipulated that his award should go to the original American play "which shall best represent the educational value and power of the stage in raising the standard of good morals, good taste and good manners." But disagreement with the grounds of the award was fanned into open discontent by the method of choosing the Pulitzer recipient, a method in which the nomination of a play jury could be set aside by the Pulitzer committee in favor of some other play. Several such instances had occurred, most recently in 1934 when the jury had recommended *Mary of Scotland* but the committee had awarded the prize to Sidney Kingsley's *Men in White*, and this arbitrariness on the part of the committee seemed to deprive the Pulitzer award of significance as an indication of merit in American plays. Consequently, when the prize in 1935 went to Zoë Akin's *The Old Maid*, the Drama Critics' Circle came into being for the purpose, stated in its original constitution, of "fostering and rewarding . . . merit in the American theatre, and the awarding of a prize, to be known as the Drama Critics' Prize, for the best new play by an American playwright produced in New York during the theatrical season."

The first Drama Critics' Circle Award, represented by a silver plaque designed by Henry Varnum Poor, went to *Winterset*. The award dinner was held at the Algonquin Hotel on April 5, 1936, and the ceremony was carried nationwide over NBC radio. The citation accompanying the award stated that: "The Circle's decision is based on the conviction that in *Winterset* the author accomplished the notably difficult task of interpreting a valid and challenging contemporary theme dealing with the pursuit of human justice in terms of unusual poetic force, realizing a drama of rich meaning and combining high literary distinction with compelling theatrical effect." Following presentation of the award, Anderson read the present acceptance speech.]

This is an unusual occasion. For one thing seventeen critics are present in this room with one playwright and they are not tearing the playwright limb from limb. For another a playwright has received so much praise from his critics in the course of an evening that he hesitates whether to say modestly that *Winterset* was *not* the best play of the year, or to admit that with such a preponderance of critical authority in its favor it probably was.

Surely if a playwright were ever justified in tossing his cap on the horns of the moon it would be when a group of critics get together to award him a prize. At the risk of seeming self-satisfied I must say that I have long believed there is but one jury competent to pass a verdict on current productions in our theatre. Except for the theatre critics of New York no body of men in the country is qualified by training, education and professional experience to render judgment on a season's plays. I am, I assure you seriously, much more interested in that aspect of this ceremony than in the fact that the first award goes to *Winterset*.

Anybody with the requisite cash can offer a prize for excellence in the theatre, but in order to encourage excellence it is necessary to know it when it appears, and a knowledge of what is excellent is more difficult to obtain than cash. I have never been greatly impressed with the Pulitzer prize for the best play of the year because the final authority for its presentation rests with a committee which is aware only dimly and at second hand of most of what occurs in the theatres of Broadway. It follows that in so far as the Pulitzer prize has had any influence on our theatre it has been a confusing and misleading influence, an encouragement to mediocrity, a gift passed out to a lucky winner by authorities who possess in this field neither standards nor information. But neither ignorance nor lack of standards can be charged against the Critics' Circle. The Critics know very definitely what they are for and why they are for it, and whatever their faults of judgment may be, they *earn* their knowledge of the plays offered during any year, by an undeviating attention to what can be seen and heard from the aisle seats of Manhattan playhouses, an attention which amounts on some occasions to sheer martyrdom. I have, in my time, contributed to that martyrdom, and learned by stinging comments in the next day's papers that the boys knew what they were about. I have had both praise and blame in stimulating quantities, and have learned—perhaps unequally—from both.

And I am not sorry that in the balloting on the Critics' award for this year there should have been some dissenting votes.[1] As Saint Joan observes nightly this Spring in 45th Street: "Woe unto me when all men praise me."[2] I am aware that *Winterset* is far from a perfect play. It's an experiment, an attempt to twist raw, modern reality to the shape and meaning of poetry. That it succeeded so far as it did with its audiences, and that it won so many friends, is due as much to superlative direction, setting and acting as to anything I contributed. Still, I like it better than any other play I've had my name on. Even a playwright's reach should exceed his grasp occasionally, and fools who rush in where wise men fear to tread will sometimes find themselves in the vanguard of wisdom.

1. *Winterset* had received fourteen votes among the critics, the three remaining votes going to Robert Sherwood's *Idiot's Delight*.
2. Bernard Shaw's *Saint Joan*, then running in Katharine Cornell's production.

2. ACCEPTANCE SPEECH FOR THE DRAMA CRITICS' AWARD TO *High Tor*

[The second Drama Critics' Circle Award went to *High Tor*, and the award dinner was held at the Algonquin Hotel on April 1, 1937. The citation accompanying the award, read by Burns Mantle of the *New York Daily News*, stated that: "In its decision, the Circle celebrates the advent of the first distinguished fantasy by an American in many years. Imaginative and as comic as it is poetic in both spirit and expression, *High Tor* is a singular accomplishment, giving rare grace to this theatrical season in New York." Following presentation of the award, Anderson read the acceptance speech.]

Thank you, Mr. Mantle. Speaking for the old firm of McClintic, Anderson, Meredith and Mielziner,[1] I thank the Critics' Circle for the plaque and the honor that comes with it, and, in the same breath, warn you that though this is the evening of April Fool's Day, we do not intend to give it back. We shall keep it because God knows we shall in all probability never see its like again. Success in the theatre is a chancy and vanishing affair. To win this prize once calls for a complex combination of lucky throws and lucky efforts which nobody could hope to repeat. To win it twice, as we have, is only possible because anything is possible, however unlikely. In other words we are lucky dogs, and this is our day.

This is said quite without humility, for I am not a humble man, but I have learned some simple facts about the theatre, the first of them being that the better you think you are the harder the floor will seem to you when you hit it, as you surely will. The second is that of all the workers in the theatre the playwright is most in need of a durable and resilient physique. The mind and body of a playwright who is to live long should be composed entirely of vulcanized rubber, his outer integument should be chain mail on horsehide, and he must thrive on a diet of cold steel and poison. Time after time, even with this equipment, he will find himself stuck with knives from every direction, like the cork in a hardware window, and the only reason he doesn't die when, on these occasions, he drinks cyanide in his lonely retreat, is because he is used to cyanide and has been drinking it for years.

This is not all, of course. A playwright must be insanely certain of himself and also quite sanely critical of all he does. He should be straight Irish by descent, because the Irish write the best English. He should also be pure Scotch, if possible, because the Scotch write even better English than the Irish. He must function as a sincere high priest at the inner altar of the theatre, and at the same time as the beguiling prostitute in the porticos of his temple. He must be born with a sensitive soul that is somehow accompanied by a complete incapacity to feel pain. Otherwise he will go mad, or die young and go to Hollywood.

But of all these qualifications, necessary as they may seem, only one is central. The others are protective armor or protective coloring; his priest-hood, his belief in what he is doing, his belief in the theatre and its destiny, are the essentials to significance. Not that significance is necessary for success. There are playwrights who don't mean a thing beyond midnight and never intended to. There are playwrights who try hard to mean something and don't, and of these I may be one for all I know, for many have seemed to think so. But if a civilization has any meaning at all that meaning will be found concentrated in its arts, and the theatre is our national art. I have tried to add to its meaning, and you tell me I succeeded with HIGH TOR, as I failed, in your eyes, with others.

And, as I stand here, plucking the knives from my gutta percha heart, trying to conceal the gaping wounds in my horse-hide and chain mail, I begin to feel my appetite for cyanide returning and am almost persuaded that I may some time write another play. Again, in the name of the firm, I thank you.

1. Guthrie McClintic had produced and directed, Burgess Meredith had taken the lead in, and Jo Mielziner had designed sets for both *Winterset* and *High Tor*.

3. *The Eve of St. Mark*, A C T I I , S C E N E 4

[*The Eve of St. Mark* was one of Anderson's more extensively produced plays. The Playwrights' Company produced it in New York on October 7, 1942, where it had a long run. During 1942 and 1943 it also had over a hundred amateur productions throughout the country under the auspices of the National Theatre Conference, and played as well at numerous military bases. In 1943 it was also produced by the U.S. Army in London. The present scene was written for the London production and does not appear in the published texts of the play.

The London production ran at the Scala Theatre, provided by the British government, opening on July 4, 1943, and playing into December. Admission was free to Allied service personnel and civilians accompanying them. Cast members came from the U.S. Army and the American Red Cross, and the production was directed by Russell Lane of the Red Cross, formerly a member of the theater department at the University of Wisconsin. This scene, which Anderson wrote in London in May during rehearsals, took the place of two scenes in the printed texts of the play—Act II, scenes 4 and 5.]

Janet's bedroom. As the lights come up Janet is seen asleep in her bed.

QUIZZ: (unseen) Janet.

JANET: (asleep) Yes, —yes.

QUIZZ: (still unseen) Janet.

JANET: (opening her eyes) Quizz—no, it—couldn't be—Quizz. (she closes her eyes) For a moment I thought—Oh, Quizz, darling—if I could only, only hear your voice—just a word— (there is silence)

QUIZZ: Janet.

JANET: (her eyes opening again) It was Quizz. It was. I heard him. He spoke to me. (she sits up) Quizz, where are you?

QUIZZ: Janet, darling. Can you hear me?

JANET: Yes, I do hear you. Oh, darling, I do hear. Where are you?

QUIZZ: Sweet, I try to reach out to you sometimes, across all that salt water— and all those hours—and I never know whether you hear me or not. But I have to try to tell you—

JANET: What is it you try to say, dear? Because I'm always listening. I'm always here listening.

QUIZZ: I guess I just want to say I love you. And—and—

JANET: Yes.

QUIZZ: And if I don't come back—

JANET: Please, please, sweet—you must come back to me—

QUIZZ: If—I don't come back—

JANET: I won't think of that—

QUIZZ: If I don't come—back—it won't be because I didn't want to—because that's all I want—all I ever want in this world—
JANET: It's all I ever ask for.
QUIZZ: But if I don't—will you understand?
JANET: Dear, what do you mean?
QUIZZ: That I had to stay. That I had to. There was nothing else to do.
JANET: If you don't come home, I'll want to die.
QUIZZ: A man has to give more than is asked of him Janet—more than he's ever commanded to do. I think you're there now, in your bed—where I've never lain—and it seems I'd give all heaven and all earth, and all men ever had, to put my arms round you once. So if I don't come home—do you hear me now?
JANET: Yes.
QUIZZ: Remember how much I love you.
JANET: Yes, darling.
QUIZZ: Janet, I heard your voice. I heard you speaking to me. —It'll be all right. It's all right now. That was what I needed. Just your voice. And so God keep you. God keep you. (His voice fades)
JANET: Quizz darling. (a silence) No, no there's nothing. There's nothing— and I'm here alone.
CURTAIN

4. ACCEPTANCE SPEECH FOR THE BROTHERHOOD AWARD TO *Lost in the Stars* FROM THE NATIONAL CONFERENCE OF CHRISTIANS AND JEWS

[Following an introduction by Louis Nizer, who quoted from several Anderson plays on the imperative nature of freedom and justice, Anderson delivered the speech at a luncheon held by the conference at the Waldorf Astoria Hotel on February 2, 1950.]

I want to thank you and your officers heartily for this citation. I don't deserve it, but a fellow isn't offered a thing like this every day, and I'd better take it when I can get it. And I want to say that your organization is the only one I know that is trying to find a cure for the most terrifying disease of our time—the disease of racial hate. Racial antagonisms have existed as long as races have existed, and they have caused explosions and disasters, but two new factors have emerged in our century that transform this ancient condition into an immediate crisis—modern means of communication, which make us all next-door neighbors, and modern weapons, which will shortly make it possible for one man to wipe out a nation.

Let me emphasize at the beginning that I am not an optimist nor a utopian. I am not at all sure that men are not going to destroy themselves in an attempt to destroy each other. I am not at all sure that men are capable of understanding the danger they are in and changing their ways. Competition among nations, races and individuals is just as natural as life itself. Life grew out of that rivalry—grew out of a bloody, brutal and unending struggle for existence—and the struggle still goes on under the fine words of all peace compacts. We are one and all engaged in this battle to survive, and only a blind man can look on at our world and its activities without realizing that this is so. Moreover, the rapid communication of modern times has brought men closer together not only in understanding, but also in enmity. Russia was no problem to us a hundred years ago. We were no problem to Russia. The papers tell us every day how that has changed. The peoples of China and India are not at present in competition with us, but when they have learned to use modern tools they will be. And competition, when it gets really acute, takes the form of war.

That is one horn of the human dilemma. We are competitive animals. We came up out of the mud that way; we are that way. The other horn of our dilemma is that we can no longer afford to be that way.

We can't afford it because men are beginning to get their hands on the powers that used to be possessed by the gods of Olympus. What those powers will turn out to be nobody at present knows, for there are no reliable prophets, including me, but we can be pretty sure that with the start they have men will soon be able to do anything they can imagine. This might include travelling with the speed of light, operating space ships throughout the planetary system, and producing plenty and scarcity at will. But you can be sure that the first things we make with those new god-like skills will be weapons. Some great power will capture the moon and hold it as a military base. Another will very likely and very soon set an artificial satellite revolving about our planet and be able to drop hydrogen bombs from it to targets on the earth, aiming them with astronomical accuracy. And lest these prognostications sound fantastic let me assure you that the scientists and the war departments of every great nation are studying plans for exactly these projects.

So long as weapons of war were comparatively inefficient men could afford to hate each other and whole nations could try to blow out each other's brains. There were always survivors. But when we begin to use hydrogen bombs it's possible that the survivors will be few or none. There is one hope for us in all this, however. It's this: If men have got to the point where they can achieve anything they can imagine, maybe they will begin to imagine the most difficult thing of all, a way to get along without wars. It's discouraging to reflect, though, that even if we hit on a solution, it takes only one to make a quarrel, and nothing we think or say will influence Russia.

Now with this grisly introduction over let me get down to a personal narrative. About two years ago my wife and I returned from Europe on the Mauretania.[1] After we got settled in our cabin we looked at the passenger list and discovered that we knew two or three people on board. Among those we'd met before were Dr. and Mrs. Everett Clinchy[2] and Mr. and Mrs. Oscar Hammerstein. Oscar I think I had seen only once. Dr. Clinchy had come once to see us. But we all got fairly well acquainted on this voyage, played chess together, and discussed the darkening prospects of the human race. We were not, any of us, historians, scientists, or experts of any kind. We were just concerned, as all of you are, about what may happen to us and to all men if world wars continue to break out in this century of slackening controls, diminishing faith and weapons that grow more deadly by geometric leaps and bounds. Beyond our trouble with Russia we saw the possibility of a race war between East and West gathering in the sky, and little chance of the West winning it. Before we separated Dr. Clinchy asked if it would be possible to get a group of theatre people together to talk these matters over in New York.

Well, we agreed, and Oscar took the responsibility for calling several meetings of playwrights and directors and producers to consider what the theatre might do to lead men toward some kind of amicable adjustment that would avoid these recurrent and expanding disasters we've so far lived through. Some of the theatre folk who attended these meetings were Oscar Hammerstein, Howard Lindsay, Russel Crouse, Kurt Weill, Robert Sherwood, Elmer Rice, Howard Dietz,[3] and Elia Kazan.

One of our meetings was notable for the presence of Arnold Toynbee, the historian, whose *A Study of History* is the most complete and erudite of all the attempts to set down a record of men and civilizations on this planet.[4] Naturally Dr. Toynbee did most of the talking this time, because we insisted on it. Most of all we insisted on pinning him down to what he thought the theatre could say that might help at this moment in history. Dr. Toynbee was very definite in his advice. "There is nothing that can save us except brotherhood," he said. "Brotherhood, amity, tolerance, understanding— understanding that crosses all the boundaries—this is the great need." He didn't know, of course, how effectively this could be said in a play, nor whether enough people would ever listen to influence the series of crises that looms ahead of us. And none of us present had any idea of how brotherhood and understanding could be taught from the stage. People who go to the theatre would rather not be taught anything if they can avoid it. They go to see a play, not to hear a sermon. In short, we weren't at all sure that anything had come of our meetings and discussions. One rather irreverent playwright said he thought the only result from our talks would be that Dr. Toynbee would write a play. Anyway, no immediate project resulted.

However, the Andersons and the Hammersteins did meet several times that same winter, and on one occasion when we had dinner at their home Dorothy Hammerstein gave me her copy of *Cry, The Beloved Country* to read,[5] saying that she had tried to get Oscar to do something with it for the stage but he wasn't sure it could be dramatized. I read it, and I wasn't sure either, but I knew I had to try, for this was a true, moving and honest story and its subject fitted exactly into the scheme for a musical tragedy which Kurt Weill and I had hoped for some years to be able to write. It wasn't till after Kurt and I had gone to work on the outline, however, that we realized that this was the very play that Dr. Clinchy had been asking for—a play about mutual tolerance and understanding that refuses to recognize any barriers between neighbor and neighbor. The origin of a play is always obscure, even to the writer of it, but I begin to see now that Dr. Clinchy had more influence on Kurt and me than we knew, or than he knew. *Lost in the Stars* would probably not be on Broadway, or wouldn't be there as it is, if Everett Clinchy had not prodded and counselled and cried for help in the attempt which your Conference is making to urge brotherhood on men before it's too late. *Lost in the Stars* is definitely your play, the one Dr. Clinchy was asking for. Dr. Clinchy is a modest man, and he'd never claim this for himself, but he must have realized it when he saw the action unfold on the stage.

As I said at the beginning, I don't know how much good it can do, or even whether it's possible for all of us together, with the greatest good will attainable, to avert or influence the calamities which the very nature of humanity seems to let us in for. The Communist dictatorships seem impenetrable and malignant. But if there is anything that can help it is the concept of the brotherhood of man, a concept still and not a reality, but possible because we have been able to imagine it. If we can think it, sooner or later we can do it. The only question is, how soon?

1. Returning from a trip to Greece, Anderson boarded the *Mauretania* at Southampton on December 9 and arrived in New York on December 15, 1947.

2. Everett Ross Clinchy, Presbyterian minister, was president of the National Conference of Christians and Jews from its formation in 1928 until his retirement in 1958.

3. Librettist for numerous stage and screen musicals including *Dear Sir* (1924), *The Band Wagon* (1931), and *Sadie Thompson* (1944).

4. Toynbee, on leave from the University of London, toured the U.S. extensively, 1947–50, and held visiting lectureships at Bryn Mawr, Princeton, and Columbia.

5. According to Anderson's diary, Mrs. Hammerstein gave him Paton's novel on March 1, 1948, having talked about it enthusiastically during their crossing to New York the previous December.

5. ANDERSON MEMOIR

[The memoir is taken from a 34-page typescript in the Oral History Collection at Columbia University, and the typescript transcribes a tape recorded interview with Anderson conducted by Louis M. Starr of the Oral History Office. The interview took place at Anderson's home in Stamford, Connecticut, on May 10, 1956.

Since the typescript was taken from a tape, and since Anderson, though given an opportunity to do so, did not proofread the typescript, it required emendation in ways not justified with the letters and other documents in this edition, where a written text was the authoritative source. The spelling of proper names in the typescript required the greatest amount of alteration. In the case of names with variant spellings the typist, listening to the tape, frequently chose the wrong variant. For example, the typescript gives Anderson's grandmother Stephenson as Stevenson, Herbert Croly as Croley, and Philip Littell as Lyttel. In other cases the typist could not understand Anderson's pronunciation on the tape and, for example, typed Polland for Paulin and Horton for Wharton. This edition gives proper names in their correct form and silently departs from the typescript when it is in error.

This edition also silently corrects other kinds of mistakes in the typescript. These include obvious typographical errors, incorrect wording of titles and inconsistency in the underlining (italicizing) and quoting of titles. Titles are given in their correct form, following the usual practice of italicizing the titles of longer works and placing within quotation marks the titles of shorter ones. Furthermore, the typescript contains a few errors of elementary fact. In the eighth paragraph, for instance, the typescript reads: "My father and mother were named Anderson and Sutton." Anderson's mother was not a Sutton, but his paternal grandmother was; and the context of the paragraph indicates that it is his grandparents who are under discussion. The sentence in this edition thus reads: "My father's father and mother were named Anderson and Sutton." Much farther along in the typescript appears the statement that "*Outside Looking In* was taken from *The God of the Lightning*, by Jim Tully." *Gods of the Lightning* is of course an Anderson play, and the Tully book on which *Outside Looking In* was based is *Beggars of Life*. In the edition, therefore, the sentence says that "*Outside Looking In* was taken from *Beggars of Life* by Jim Tully." Since the tape recording of the interview no longer exists, it is impossible to determine whether it was Anderson or the typist who made the sort of factual mistake illustrated here. In any case, such errors would have been corrected had the typescript received a proofreading, and this edition attempts to avoid confusion by making the corrections.

This edition occasionally departs from the typescript in punctuation as well. The punctuation there is the typist's and does not conform to Anderson's characteristic pointing. But generally it maintains the clarity of the discourse and also reflects the rhythm of the speaking voice. This edition departs from the punctuation of the typescript only in the interest of clarity, and changes are confined largely to the deletion or addition of commas.

Finally, it will be helpful to remember that the memoir, being the product of an interview, consists of the answers to a series of questions without the questions themselves. One result of that fact is, at certain points, a rapid jumping from one topic to another. At such points the missing questions provided the transitions. Another result is an occasional vagueness of referent, where the referent was provided by the missing question. On such occasions, if the vagueness is more than momentary, the edition provides the referent within square brackets.]

I was born in Atlantic, Pennsylvania, December, 1888. My father at that time was working on the farm there. It was a farm, where I was born. It was my grandmother's farm—my mother's mother's farm. My father later became a railroad fireman, and studied in the evening, and got himself ready to be a Baptist minister. I remember him preaching in his first pastorate. I was three years old. He gave up farming, gave up the railroad, and became a minister. As I remember it, the first year was in Richmond Center, which I think was in Ohio, Western Pennsylvania, somewhere. He got $250 a year and donations, and the parsonage. We lived on that. The donations included, of course, potatoes and apples and other vegetables. It was a railroad community.

Then we went from one small town to another, all during my youth. Brothers and sisters accumulated as we went along. There were eight—four girls and four boys. The last child, Lawrence, was born after I left home, and we never all got together under the same roof. I was the second child. The oldest was a girl. The first child, Ethel, was a girl, and the third child, Lela, was a girl. So I played with those two sisters most of the time, and they were closest to me.

As for my schooling during that time, all our schooling we picked up in the public schools as we went from one little town to another. On the way I remember going through McKeesport, which was larger than most places, and I went to the second or third grade there. Then there was a time when we were in Harrisburg. I remember the pickings were rather thin in Harrisburg, and I went and stayed on my grandmother's farm while the rest of the family stayed there.

My father went from one pastorate to another. We were migratory, peripatetic. Then we got to Iowa. Before I got to high school I was in Iowa, I remember—in Algoona, Iowa, and then New Hampton, Iowa, where we stayed longer than anywhere else. I went to high school all but the last year in New Hampton. Then we went to Jamestown, North Dakota. I finished high school there and took off for the University of North Dakota. Yes, the schooling was very ragged. I can't remember much about adjusting to new communities. It was the way we lived. I don't know how much it bothered me.

My mother? I think one of her main occupations was packing up and following my father, who usually went ahead to hold down the pulpit. I think one of my occupations was nailing up boxes, because all the moving in those days was done via the freight cars, so we had to pack all the furniture.

Every summer, from the time I was able to work until I went to the university and even afterward, I worked on a farm. I used to get $25 or $30 a month on the farm. These were in Iowa and North Dakota. In Iowa it was usually corn and pigs and cows. In North Dakota it was wheat and thrashing. And there was always a garden. We always kept a cow and sometimes a team of horses which I took care of at home. My father was very proud of having the best team in town, usually.

I didn't like farm work especially. In fact, I never found any physical labor that I liked very much, but I was able to do it. My father, as I remember it, was an expert woodsman. He could handle a double-bladed axe very well. He'd been out in the Michigan woods as a lumberman. That was before he was married. He'd also been in Kansas. He was born near Atlantic—he was born at Geneva, Pennsylvania, not far away. On both sides we seemed to be mostly Scotch. I'm Scotch and Irish.

My mother's father and mother were named Stephenson and Stewart. My father's father and mother were named Anderson and Sutton. Sutton, I think, is English.

Who was I closest to, as to parents? I don't know. I don't think I played any favorites. I had a favorite grandmother. She was a widow. I never saw

Grandfather Stephenson, but he was evidently an elderly fellow when he married her. He had many, many sons, so there were a lot of half-brothers. My mother had one full sister, and I knew her well and I knew her mother very well. She was always the grandma to whom we went in the summer, to spend the summer vacations.

My childhood was like all childhoods. It was somewhat happy, somewhat unhappy. It's very difficult to say, looking back. I couldn't be at a loss for companions because of moving—our house was always full. There were always plenty of children around.

My father and my mother too had bought so many books that the whole family spent a lot of time reading. What they hadn't bought, we bought. I remember my father had a set of Dickens and practically all the English poets, and we got familiar with them very early. The novels of Dickens seem like one big novel to me now. I get the characters all mixed up—I've read them all so many times, as a child. No, that wasn't the reading I liked most. I went out on my own, I remember, and bought *Treasure Island* and *Kidnapped* and *The Adventures of Sherlock Holmes. A Study in Scarlet* was the first of those that I saw.[1] I read Cooper. In fact, the reading went on so constantly that it seems to have been our only occupation. Yes, it was the influence of both parents.

My father was rather a stern father. He had to be, there were so many of us. He was an excellent speaker. He was hail-fellow-well-met and was liked everywhere. I think his eloquence oppressed us a little, because he wasn't so eloquent at home, and perhaps we rather resented the salesmanship that went into his evangelism. We went to church every Sunday, and to Sunday School and to prayer meetings and to young people's meetings, whenever they were. Church was a pretty constant factor, and we got to know the Bible well by just listening.

I don't think I was very good at games in school. My eyes were bad, and I was never able to hit the ball when we played baseball. I was not very much interested anyway. I can remember being interested in the broad jump, which I was only fairly good at. I remember taking a fourth in the high jump in high school, which was rather a low record. There weren't any school newspapers, and the study of the drama was confined to Shakespeare, as far as I know, until I got to the University, and there I was too busy earning my way through and studying to do anything of that sort [acting].

When I finished high school, I had a friend named Garth Howland who lived not far away and who graduated from high school when I did, and he was going to the University of North Dakota and persuaded me to go. It hadn't occurred to me, what I would do. I just went along with him. Having got there, I found that this was the life I enjoyed. I went through the University in three years, partly by the device of taking examinations in courses that I was already up in. I found that I knew enough English literature so that I could pass all the courses that they gave in English literature.

I think that wouldn't be allowed now. The University hadn't made a rule yet, you see, that you had to put the time in. If you were able to pass the examinations, they gave you the credit. The professor who was responsible for giving me the examinations was Professor Squires who was a very good friend of mine.[2] Another good friend at the University was Professor Hult, who taught Greek. Although I studied Greek under him and liked him best of any of the professors, I think, I never did learn much Greek. I got to know a good deal about Greek philosophy and the philosophers—or I got a working knowledge of them. I don't think I ever knew much about them before.

I earned my way through the first year by doing odd jobs and waiting on tables and so forth. The second year I got a job on the Grand Forks *Herald*. Grand Forks is the nearest town to the University. I was what they called a telegraph editor on that paper. What it really amounted to was that I was the copy desk. I wrote headlines and edited the stuff that came in over the wires for the paper. I went to work in the evening and it kept me up pretty late. However, it got me through the University. I worked at night and during the day I slept in classes.

The newspaper work was just routine—a matter of editing the copy that came in. However, I learned the job of writing headlines, and was able to make a living at that later when I needed it.

Yes, I was the entire copy desk. There was no other copy desk. There were two reporters and there was the editor. There was a fellow who wrote a column, and myself. That was the whole staff. This was about 1908, '9, '10. They did have linotype in the composing room, but I was seldom out there. Earlier than that, when I was in high school, I was the printer's devil on a paper, as I was going through high school in New Hampton. I learned how to set type with a stick, so I knew that end of it. I never set type very fast, but I could set it. The work I did on the newspaper really didn't get me anywhere, except it got me through the University.

As soon as I finished the University, I got married and took a job as principal of the high school in Minnewaukan, North Dakota. I may have been highly recommended and got the principal job that way—it wasn't a very big high school nor a very big town, but I spent two years there. Then we saved enough money out of our small salary to go with our first child to California. That was in 1913 or 1914.

That next year in California my wife and I both went to Stanford University. I took an M.A., and earned my way part of the time by being janitor in a country school, and part of the time by being an instructor in the English Department. I was taking the M.A. in English.

After I got it, I got a job in San Francisco teaching English in the Polytechnic High School. Flügel at Stanford was influential. He taught Chaucer. I studied Middle English under him. So was Henry David Gray, who taught the modern drama,[3] and Professor Carruth was Head of the English Department. Professor Alden wrote a book on Shakespeare which is very good. Raymond McDonald Alden—you've heard of him, perhaps? I never studied with him. The man I met out there that I've since spent a lot of time with was Frank Hill—Frank Ernest Hill. I wrote editorials with him on the *Globe*. On the *Globe* there were four of us youngsters writing editorials together—Frank Hill, Bruce Bliven, Robert Duffus and I.[4] Duffus is now, I think, writing editorials on the *Times*. Hill has been with the Rockefeller people for a long time, hasn't he, in Adult Education? Bruce Bliven has had a long career as chief editorial writer one place or another.

I met Hill at Stanford, and Duffus I met through Hill, I guess. There was a group of young fellows who were writing poetry and writing other things, too. Hill was a member of that. He got me into it, and I met Duffus there. Duffus and I became fast friends and took long walks together over the Coastal Range there, near San Francisco. Then later on Duffus and I were working on the *Globe* in New York. It was through Duffus that I got my first job in the newspaper business, as a matter of fact. After I finished teaching three years in Polytechnic High School, I went down to Whittier College as the Head of the English Department. I was let out of Whittier because I didn't want to sit on the platform during Chapel. I didn't enjoy prayers. They didn't like that, so I left.

I took a job writing editorials on the *Bulletin* in San Francisco, where Duffus was writing editorials. Well, just about this time—I forget what happened—I think the *Bulletin* was sold, and became the *Call-Bulletin*. I think so. Anyway, Duffus went over to write on another paper, and I lost my job somehow or other. I think I got the flu. That was the time of the big flu epidemic. And by the time I'd recovered, there was no job there. It was during the war.

So I went over to the *Chronicle* and got a job on their copy-desk which I was able to handle because I'd had experience with that in Grand Forks. I hadn't been there very long before I got a letter from New York offering me a job on a New York magazine, the *New Republic*. I'd never been in New York and I didn't know anybody there. I had written some poems and an article for the *New Republic*, which was the new magazine; it was *the* thing then. And the editors asked me to come East and join the staff, which I did. I was able to come East because I was able to borrow some money from a neighbor, which I didn't pay back altogether until *What Price Glory* came on later on.

Bruce Bliven wasn't on the *New Republic* at that stage—that was much later. Croly was there. I knew him. Croly and Francis Hackett and Alvin Johnson and Phil Littell and Lippmann were all on the *New Republic* then.[5] I stayed there only a few months—six months, I think it was—and then went on to write editorials for the *Globe*, where Duffus had come East to write editorials at that time. Duffus and Hill and Bliven were there at that time.

Then after a while a strange thing happened. I got a mysterious phone call from somebody asking if I'd come and have lunch with him. I did. And this man revealed that he was an emissary from somebody on the *World*. He said they'd been reading all the editorials on the *Globe* and checking on the ones they liked best. It turned out that their spies had discovered that I had written the majority of the ones they liked, so they asked me to come over and write editorials for the *World*. After some soul-searching, I did this. It entailed giving up those friendships and the association I had with the *Globe*. The *Globe* was a pleasant paper to work for. Old man Wright was there. He was our editor, and he was quite an acute old fellow. It was he who had assembled this gang of young editorial writers, and took his own life in his hands doing it, I guess. But we turned out a fairly good editorial page for him.[6]

Then on the *World* I found myself working with much older men, mostly— people who had been there for a long while. After a while their ranks began to thin and they were reinforced by people like Charlie Merz[7] and Walter Lippmann. Heaton was the one I knew best—Heaton and Paulin—do you know Paulin? They were in the offices next to me. He was a friendly white-bearded genial man, a very able fellow—a traditionalist.[8]

I think more quoting of Pulitzer was done by Don Seitz than anybody else.[9] Did you know Don Seitz? He used to quote Pulitzer all the time. Well, I was there the better part of three years, and while I was there I wrote a play in verse. I'd been trying all this time to write verse, write poetry, and I occasionally sold some poetry, but I never made much money at it. I came to realize that I wasn't going to be a success as a poet, although I was really putting most of my essential industry on it. I wrote a play in verse, without any thought of production because I didn't know anything about the theatre. But Stallings showed it to Deems Taylor, who had a friend in the theatre named Brock Pemberton, and Pemberton put the play on. It was called *White Desert*.[10]

Having got a taste of the theatre that way, there was no stopping me, and I wrote another play right away with George Abbott. We wrote it in four days. I met George Abbott because he was in *White Desert*. He was one of the leading actors. That play lasted a couple of weeks. It was a poetic tragedy, and didn't deserve to last that long. Oh yes, I felt that way about it at the time. I didn't know why anybody produced it. No, Stallings didn't work with me on it. I'd known Deems Taylor around the office—he was the music critic.

Then I wrote this play with George Abbott, which was later put on, and I took a thousand dollars to take my name off it and sell it to somebody else. That's the first thousand-dollars I got in one lump.[11]

Then I went to Stallings, who'd been telling stories about the war at lunch. He was the literary editor at that time. I told him I thought there was a play in some of the things he'd been saying, and he belittled that because he was writing a musical at the time with Herman Mankiewicz, about the war.[12] But he said, "Go ahead and see what you can do with it."

So I worked out a story for a play, and wrote the first two acts, and showed them to him. I told him I needed an act in another scene, in a dugout, and I couldn't write the dialogue for that because I'd never had the experience. I told him what was supposed to happen. He read those first two acts, and rattled off the dugout scene in one afternoon. I wrote the last act—it was a four act play at that time—and did some revising on both scripts, and when I got through with it, it was *What Price Glory*, which was put on the next fall by Hopkins.[13]

I named it, but I think I named it out of Stallings' conversation. He'd been raving about what was going on—this fellow who came in out of the battle storming about what was going on out there and how horrible it was for everybody. "What price glory, now?" he called. So this I thought was a good name.

On the *World* the chief editorial writer was Frank Cobb, and every editorial writer went in to see him in the morning, and Frank assigned subjects. We'd all read the paper before we came in, and if we had a favorite subject, we spoke of it. Cobb told me very frankly that he was hoping when I came in that I could take over the editorship. I said there was very little hope for that because I didn't think I wanted to write about politics. This showed up more and more during my session on the *World*, until finally I was writing all the decorative editorials, about the flowers, the human interest things. I wasn't worrying about politics.

Cobb was a very able man, and he was of course an old time journalist. He spent a lot of time in Detroit, I think. He used words like machine-gun bullets. He shot them at you. Or, he shot them at the readers.[14]

The most forceful man in the office was Swope. He's still rather forceful, I think. When he came into the room, you didn't hear anybody else. He was executive editor. No, he didn't confer with Cobb. Cobb ran his part of the business pretty much as he pleased. Pulitzer was there—Ralph Pulitzer was there—and he was very quiet and didn't take much obvious part in directing things.[15]

I think Swope managed the news gathering and general policy of the paper. But editorially it was Frank Cobb's.

Aside from Heaton and L. R. E. Paulin—it's hard to describe these men, such a long way off, their different characteristics. One remembers odds and ends of episodes and incidents. I can't say that anything especially struck me about Paulin. He brought me from time to time old volumes of verse that he'd picked up in the book-shops. I remember him coming back from a vacation on the beach one day and saying he was astonished that he had knocked a man down. He'd never had occasion to do it before. Somebody had annoyed him, and he, for very good reason, had knocked the man down by hitting him under the chin, and he fell over. Paulin was not a young man. He was very proud of that.

The morale in the office was very different from that at the *Globe*. On the *Globe*, Wright, of course, was a fellow of fifty or more, but all the fellows writing editorials were youngsters. There was a feeling of fun and hilarity about it all. The editorials were a small chore, easily done, quickly finished. We all expected to be going places.

On the *World*, they were all older men. They'd all earned their reputations, and they didn't expect to have careers coming up. Their careers were more or less finished. And aside from Stallings, they were all like that, around those upper floors. Then Deems Taylor came in. He was one of the younger fellows. I knew Woollcott. Let's see, was Woollcott there? I knew Alexander Woollcott very well, but I'm not sure when he came in.[16] Of course, I knew F. P. A. too. He was running "The Conning Tower," and he was quite often in the lunchroom at the hour when we were there. I remember meeting him because of the way it happened. I'd known the name Franklin Adams, and I'd known the initials F. P. A. When somebody introduced him to me, I said, "My God!"

And he said, "Thank you."[17]

There was a lunchroom in the tower, just below the *World* editorial offices. Merz came on shortly before I left. When they decided that I was really no good as an editor, that I never would shape up as an editor, they had to get somebody in. They got Lippmann at first, and then they saw that Lippmann wasn't going to stay with them. They got Merz. They thought he would stay.

I'd known Lippmann pretty well on the *New Republic*. The *New Republic* would have been an exciting place for me to work if I'd known more about it. I'd never been in New York. I knew nothing about national politics and practically nothing about international politics. I'd been in the West or the Midwest all my life, and the war was practically unknown to me. I got only what one gets from reading the newspapers in the West. I didn't know the New York newspapers. I had a lot of homework to catch up on before I could know what they were talking about.

Croly and I always had lunch together every day. We had a big business table with a lazy susan, and we sat there with the guests and talked things over. They were all much more knowledgeable than I was, because I was really a newcomer. Croly was very serious. The only thing I remember about Croly later—because it had a personal application to myself—was some time before his death, maybe about 1930 or so (I forget what year he died) I saw him somewhere at a party, and he told me that he had gone to see *Outside Looking In* five times. I said, "Why did you do that?"

He said, "I liked it."

Lippmann was sure of himself in every company, I think. He was quiet, but it was usually the quiet of a man who was very sure he knew what he was about. He was on even terms with anybody.

I don't remember what guests we had.

I came to the *New Republic* somewhat as I went to the *World*, at Alvin Johnson's invitation, and Johnson was hoping that I would write about political matters and take some interest in political subjects. He told me, he warned me at the beginning that if I didn't do that, there was no real future in it. He said, "If you persist in being interested in books and literary matters, you can ride yourself right up a tree and get nowhere." Which I did. I wasn't interested in politics.

I stayed on the *World* until *What Price Glory* was a success, and that day I quit. As soon as it was a success, I felt, "Now I can be on my own." So I haven't gone to work in an office since. It was obvious that it was going to be successful by the next day; as soon as the reviews came out, it was a success, and then I resigned.

By the way, you spoke of Paulin. Paulin said to me, "Now, the thing to do—you've got a success here—the thing to do is put that money away and forget it. You'll probably never have another success. Put that money away, and keep on as a journalist."

But I didn't listen.

I don't think I was very important to the *World*. They may have been rather relieved. You know, when you get a birds and flowers editor, you can usually dispense with him.

I haven't seen Allan Nevins, to my memory, since I bought that house. I knew him on the *Globe*. We used to meet then for lunch, and Frank Hill was a mutual friend. I went to Staten Island to visit them a couple of times.[18]

I knew the people on the evening side of the *World*. I didn't know them well, but I knew them—Paulin and Claude Bowers.[19] It was utterly just a way to make a living, from my point of view.

I hadn't tinkered much with being a playwright as a lifework until *White Desert*, which I told you about. That was an experiment. Then I tried another play, as I told you—after *White Desert*, Abbott and I wrote a play very fast. Then immediately afterward, Stallings and I worked on *What Price Glory*.

The play Abbott and I did was put on, with Abbott in the leading part. It was called—it was originally called *The Feud*. They gave it another name and put it on. I can't remember what it was.

Abbott was a very good actor and a very nice fellow—and clever. I was somewhat astonished to find that here was a man in the theatre who didn't drink, didn't smoke, who saved his money and bought stocks, and was very careful. I guess he's saved money every since. He's been a very good workman in the theatre, an excellent director. That play didn't go well—not at all. But it didn't impede me even slightly.

I can't remember, but it seems to me I was (as I once said in a line that I put in my book of verse that I published) "intoxicated with a great lack of birthdays."[20]

As to getting *What Price Glory* into production—well, the playwright always watches rehearsals, and both Stallings and I went to rehearsals and worked on what needed to be done, but actually there was very little changed. Hopkins did all the casting, all the rehearsing. We didn't know much about the theatre, either Stallings or I, so Hopkins did it all, and it came out perfectly. He was an excellent director. But he made no obvious effort. You never heard him speak to an actor. You never saw him make any suggestions or heard him make any suggestions. Things just happened, but they happened smoothly and perfectly.

After that I paid back the money that I borrowed to come East in 1918, and I bought a couple of farms in western New York. On one of them my father and mother lived until their death. My father had been going from one pastorate to another, just as usual. I bought a farm in Rockland County before *What Price Glory*, when I was still just working on the *World*. I moved out there. It was in 1922. Of course, as soon as *What Price Glory* was a success, I started remodelling the house. It was an old farmhouse. I commuted from there every day.

I remember seeing a cartoon one time in the *New Yorker* of a couple walking to the public library in New York with notebook in hand, searching for the spot on which *What Price Glory* was written. Now it was actually true that I did a lot of the writing on *What Price Glory* in the public library, because the reading room was nice and quiet, and it was a good place to go and write. I did this evenings.

An editorial writer's life is not an arduous one. You don't have any fixed hours, usually. If you get away early, you can go home. I had plenty of time for writing. There must have been a lot of that going on among my colleagues.

The next year Stallings and I put on two plays, and I put on a venture which I didn't write with him, which I took from a book. *Outside Looking In* was taken from *Beggars of Life* by Jim Tully, and *The Buccaneer* was taken from a book on Morgan,[21] and *First Flight* was a story we made up about the young Jackson. *First Flight* and *The Buccaneer* both failed. *Outside Looking In* had quite a long run downtown, and then moved uptown and didn't last very long there.

Do you remember the Greenwich Village Theater, the Sheridan? That's where it was, downtown. That's where it ran. I wrote two of those with Stallings, and *Outside Looking In* I wrote alone, from Jim Tully's book. That was 1925.

The next play I turned out was *Saturday's Children*, which was my own, and that was a success.

Stallings went to Hollywood and sort of master-minded a lot of pictures. He was a very good idea man, with an extraordinary vocabulary, and a wide range of interests, a lot of knowledge. He seems to have been able to construct a play very well. He did one of his own. He adapted a book as a play, *A Farewell to Arms*. Of course that was Hemingway's novel, but it was Laurence's adaptation. It didn't go. I think he did a musical, but I've forgotten the name of it. I didn't see much of him after he went to Hollywood. Oh, he did *The Big Parade*. That was what took him to Hollywood first. That was right after *What Price Glory*. And he'd written a novel which had some other name, but it was made into *The Big Parade*. That was an enormous success.[22]

I went out to Hollywood myself. I went to the dogs for a handout, several times. I put on a couple of plays, after *Saturday's Children*. *Gypsy* and *Gods of the Lightning* were both failures. Then I went to California and worked on the pictures to make a living, for a while. I did *All Quiet on the Western Front*, and meanwhile I wrote *Elizabeth the Queen*, while I was in Hollywood, and came back with it. That was the success of the month. Lytton Strachey's book inspired that.[23]

I don't know as there was an inspiration for *Saturday's Children*. I thought it was a good idea for a play, that was all. I remember thinking at one time that probably I'd got my idea from Ibsen's *Love's Comedy*. Looking back over it, *Love's Comedy* seems to be a play about the fact that marriage ends romance, and I was using the same idea in *Saturday's Children*. They tried marriage and didn't like it, and went back to romance.

My experience in Hollywood was routine. I did *All Quiet* with

Milestone, Lewis Milestone, and he was a very good workman, and all I had to do was write the dialogue. He took care of the rest of it. With Milestone, the material wasn't changed very much. This was Milestone's first dialogue picture, and he was inexperienced enough so that he was inclined to leave things alone, except for the pictures. He left the dialogue alone. I think George Abbott came in and did some rewriting after I left, to fit in with what they wanted, but nothing of major importance. I never went around the studio much—I wasn't expected to. You mean to work? Oh no, I didn't watch the shooting of it. I worked at home. I rented a house on the water, and worked there. In fact, Milestone used to come down there and work with me. But after the shooting started, I didn't see it or go near it.

Later on, I went over to work for a while at Metro. They were trying to work out a story for Gilbert, John Gilbert, who had never been in a talking picture and they wanted to put him in one.[24] They got Stallings and me together to do that for him, write some things. He never did it—never got it finished—but I was there for a while, and while I was there, Milestone wanted a new ending, wanted some new lines for the end of *All Quiet*. And he was some little distance away. I drove down to where he was, at La Jolla I think, wrote the few lines he wanted, and came back. That's all I saw of the shooting of the picture. No, I didn't go to see it. I never did see it.

All Quiet was in '29. *Elizabeth the Queen* went on in '30, and my life since then has been a succession of plays, one after another.

The organization of the Playwrights' Company was more or less accidental. I had gone to a meeting of the Dramatists' Guild, and as I remember it, Bob Sherwood was the president at that time. We'd had a rather tough session. This was in 1937. There were usually a few Communist-inclined members who kicked up a rumpus, and Sherwood always tried to have a number of people on hand so we could out vote them. We got together afterwards, Sherwood and Elmer Rice and I. We were having a drink or coffee or something of that sort. And one of us proposed that we produce our own plays.

Well, we each thought it was a good idea, and later on we got in touch with Sam Behrman and Sidney Howard, and the five of us decided to organize. One of us must have got in touch with a lawyer, John Wharton, and one of our meetings was held with him. We all liked him so much that we decided to take him in as a fellow member. So we did organize, with the six of us, John Wharton and the five playwrights, to produce our own plays.

I don't know if this was the first time this had been done.

The Company has been a very happy center. I think we've all enjoyed having it and going to it. It's a good thing for fellow craftsmen to talk things over occasionally, even if you don't talk shop. You at least feel that there are people engaged in the same line of business in the world. I don't think I ever did talk shop much with any of them, but when we got together to put on a play, the comments that came from the others on a play of mine were always stimulating and likely to be much more helpful than they would be coming from a producer. Oh yes, after they looked at the script and while we were in rehearsal, they would be very helpful, suggesting changes, cuts—whatever goes on in rehearsals. I'm never quite sure what it is. It's kind of a madhouse. I would attend their rehearsals too—not always. Usually if a man's putting on a play, he likes to keep it private most of the time. He'll have the director and himself there. Then occasionally, when he wants help, he'll call on the other playwrights to come in and give him advice. It wouldn't do any good anyway to stay there all the time and watch. You'd get calloused and wouldn't know what to say.

The capital pooling was rather small, because what it amounted to was that each one of us put in $10,000. You couldn't produce a play for that amount now. There's been such a big change in the cost of producing and running a play. When I started out, I remember Hopkins telling me that it cost him about $10,000 to put on *What Price Glory*. It made a profit of about $10,000 a week, so he had $10,000 to do what he pleased with. He said there was practically no income tax. He could therefore put on several plays and not miss the money, even if they were flops. It didn't bother him to put on plays. He could always capitalize them. Nowadays the income tax is such that you can put on a play for perhaps $85,000 or $100,000. It may make a profit of $5000 or $2500 a week. You don't save a great deal of it because if there's any profit it goes into the income tax.

The Playwrights' Company always seeks outside backing. It doesn't always have to, but it always does. It's just a way of doing business. If you get outside backers, they put up all the money and get half the profits. That means you can't lose on any production, because you get half the profits for nothing, half the profits for your producing. If you produced it yourself, you could lose.

I don't remember much about the writing of *Winterset*.

The Playwrights' Company was formed in '38.

How can one tell about the writing of a play? It's a matter of putting words on paper.

I can remember one thing about that [the writing of *Winterset*]. A friend of mine who was a lawyer in Boston, a fellow by the name of Montgomery with whom I went to the University of North Dakota, told me that I shouldn't think so badly of the fellow who condemned Sacco and Vanzetti. He said the poor old fellow, the judge, was just about out of his mind. He went around asking one man after another, "What was wrong about that? They were guilty. They were obviously guilty. I had to do this and this and this—legally I was in a box. I had to do it. They were—the evidence was such that I really couldn't do anything else."

Montgomery said, "The old fellow really deserves your sympathy."

That really gave me the idea for the judge, and then for the rest of it.[25]

I don't think I ever wrote a masterpiece. I'm still hoping to write a good one.

As to which were the best that I've done, well, I'll go along with the crowd. Whenever they think it's a good play, I'll say, "All right, if you think so."

The critics do determine the life or death of a play. They do. But I have to
go along with them too, because they are able to do that. I don't think I want
to go into that subject. I wouldn't be able to make up my mind now if some
have flopped because of the critics. It's true, I don't read their reviews of my
plays. Somebody always reads them. They always tell you. But if you avoid
reading them, then you don't come in contact with the actual words. The
feeling about the play is the important thing. What they actually say about it
can cut pretty deep, if you let the words hit you. But if I don't read them, then
they don't bother me so much. No, I don't read them even if they're
good—that wouldn't be fair. Oh yes, I read the reviews of other plays. But I
don't go to first nights. That can be too painful. If it's not painful for me, it's
painful for some friend of mine.

Such things as relationships with one's colleagues in the Company are
awfully difficult to sum up offhand, without preparation, in a few words. I
can say that I've enjoyed tremendously the company of some of the
playwrights I've known. I think Robert Sherwood was probably the wittiest
and most amiable, all around the best friend I've known among the
playwrights. I'm not sure when I met him. I met him when he was, I think,
reviewing movies, and after I'd written *What Price Glory*—before he wrote
The Road to Rome. He told me anyway that he started writing plays after he
saw *What Price Glory*. He got the idea he might write plays.[26]

I had a very good time whenever I've met S. N. Behrman, who was one of
the liveliest, wittiest people who ever lived. He's very quiet. He doesn't go out,
and he doesn't go in for society at all, but he certainly has a fast-moving mind.
Elmer Rice is also someone with a very high I.Q. and flashing wit and tongue.
I see him at Playwrights' meetings now. We meet irregularly, every two weeks
or so. It's all shop talk, really. We have a play opening tonight, but I'm not
going to it. It was one I didn't pick out.[27]

We have a business manager named Roger Stevens, now, who occasionally puts on plays that he likes. I don't think any of us cared very much for this
one. People come to us with scripts—that often happens. I don't go to the
theater very often. I've got so it's quite a chore. Of course, I went in to see *The
Chalk Garden* and I thought that was fantastically good, beautiful dialogue. I
thought *My Fair Lady* was an excellent musical, probably the perfect musical,
largely because of Shaw. It's a beautiful job of writing. It's done with odds
and ends of phrases. It's all oblique.[28]

Tennessee Williams' work I don't understand very well. No use posing
about it, I just don't understand it. I don't know what he's talking about most
of the time. I think he's a little like the song writers who write songs for
youngsters, for teen-agers to sing and have a good time with, and I can't tell
what they're enjoying. That happens to everybody, probably.[29]

I have the play, *The Bad Seed*, which is still on the road. As long as that's
bringing me an income, I don't have to worry too much. As soon as that
slacks down, I'll try to put another play on. It's not that economic pressure is
helpful, but if you make more than a certain amount every year, you might

just as well give it to the government, because they take it anyway.

As to the future of the American theater—as Eisenhower keeps saying, "I have no crystal ball." Anything can happen. The movies are on their way out, probably. They seem to be taking second place to television. But what I remember feeling about them was that since they were based on a mechanical invention, it was always possible for another mechanical invention to come along and take their place, which is what is happening, I think.

I've taken some money from television, but no interest in it. I have written two or three little things for television. I adapted *High Tor*. These were all just potboiling jobs.

I suppose it's pure prejudice on my part—prejudice in favor of the theater we all learned about through our literary histories. Pictures and television, with their mechanical devices, don't seem to have the same effect on me that the theater has. Maybe they do, on young people, people who are born to this age.

It's true, I got into the theater through my interest in poetry. Before I began writing plays, I had gone to a few plays in New York, but very few. My contact with the theater was mainly through the plays I'd read.

In North Dakota, Grand Forks was visited very rarely by touring troups. Nazimova came there in *A Doll's House*. That's one of the first plays I saw. *The Servant in the House*, by Charles Rann Kennedy, wasn't it? In San Francisco I saw Forbes-Robertson, not in *Hamlet*. He played *The Passing of the Third Floor Back*. But these are pretty sketchy things. I saw Sarah Bernhardt in San Francisco, in that last tour she did in this country, when she did a little scene from Rostand, I guess.[30] Those things wouldn't have jogged me into the theater, certainly. I think the thing that got me into the theater, unquestionably, was Deems Taylor showing that play to Brock Pemberton, and then putting it on.

Elizabeth the Queen was the first play that was a success that was written in verse—it was written partly in verse. *Mary of Scotland* was in verse. *Winterset* was the first modern play in verse that was a success. I don't account for my plays in verse being successes when the form is not much used now. The plays in verse that have succeeded have been pretty few, the modern plays, and obviously the society we live in doesn't look for the kind of speech on the stage that calls for it. If you give it to them, you have to trick them or force it down their throats—make them listen by some other device. Because the music of words is a very small part of what people are listening for now. The prose that Enid Bagnold writes in *The Chalk Garden* is beautiful, elliptical, full of flashing images, and has a lot of qualities that could have gone into the making of verse, but I think if she had made it into verse, she would have had more trouble getting people to listen to it.

I don't know whether you've followed what I've done lately or not. *The Bad Seed* is in prose. That was just an adaptation of a novel. I wrote a play about Socrates that was in prose. It naturally would be, because Plato is in prose. I wrote a play about Henry the Eighth and his Anne—that was in a sort of ragged verse that you couldn't call blank verse, and partly in prose. I think my verse has been disintegrating under the pressure—the pressure of public opinion. They don't want it.

You look back on the days of Scott and Byron, when a poem could be a best seller. Some of Scott's poems, early poems, were best sellers, and some of Byron's were best sellers. Then the period of the Romantics came in, and Scott was a best seller in prose. Keats and Shelley, when they were attempting their long flights, were writing for a market that really existed, and they might have hit it. They didn't just know [how to write verse (?)].

There isn't that now. There's just the bare possibility that something will slip through and become a best seller in spite of being a poem, but very little chance that there'll be a poem sold every year, or a poem on the best seller list every year. There used to be.

My verse is disintegrating into prose, under the pressure of the public. They'd rather listen to prose. T. S. Eliot has written some plays in verse, or what looks like verse on the page, but when you come to analyze it, it turns out to be prose, spaced.

1. *A Study in Scarlet* (1887), earliest of the Sherlock Holmes stories, is not one of those in *The Adventures of Sherlock Holmes* (1892).

2. Vernon P. Squires (1866–1930) taught English at the University of North Dakota from 1897 until his death.

3. Ewald Flügel (1863–1914), prolific Chaucer scholar, joined the Stanford English faculty in 1892 and remained until his death. Henry David Gray (1873–1958) joined the Stanford English faculty in 1905 and remained until retirement in 1939. He published studies of Elizabethan drama and of Emerson and also wrote plays, two of which received New York productions, *Gallops* in 1906 and *The Best People* in 1924.

4. All four attended Stanford and belonged to the group of aspiring writers that met monthly at the home of Henry David Gray. Duffus (1888–1972), who became an editorial writer on the *New York Times*(1937–62), recounts his friendship with Anderson in Palo Alto and San Francisco in *The Tower of Jewels* (1961). Bliven (b. 1889), who finished his career with the *New Republic* (1923–55), describes his association with Anderson on the *Globe* in *Five Million Words Later* (1970). Hill has an article in the *Flügel Memorial Volume* (Stanford Unviversity Press, 1916) that is of interest because of his close association with Anderson, an article entitled "A New Emotional Effect in Tragedy," pp. 166–78.

5. Herbert David Croly (1869–1930) was founding editor of the *New Republic* in 1914 and remained its editor until his death. Hackett (1883– 1962) associated with Anderson on the *New Republic* and then on the *New York World*, later brought an unsuccessful plagiarism suit against him in connection with *Anne of the Thousand Days* (see no. 166). Johnson (b. 1874), on the editorial board of the *New Republic* from 1917 until 1923, had been professor of economics at Stanford since 1911, and it was he who invited Anderson to join the *New Republic* staff, an event he recounts in *Pioneer's Progress* (1952). Philip Littell (1868–1943), whose play *Septimus* had a New York production in 1909, was book review editor of the *New Republic*. Walter Lippmann (1889–1974) remained with the *New Republic* until he joined the editorial staff of the *New York World* in 1921, the same year Anderson joined the *World*.

6. Henry John Wright(1866–1935), born in Glasgow, came to the United States in the eighties, joined the *New York Globe and Commercial Advertiser* in 1897, and edited it until it was sold in 1923.

7. Charles Merz (b. 1893) left the *New Republic* to become associate editor of the

World in 1924, remained with the paper until its demise in 1931, then went to the *New York Times*.

8. John L. Heaton (1860–1935) joined the *World* as associate editor in 1889 and remained with the paper until 1931. His books include *The Story of a Page* (1913) and *Cobb of THE WORLD* (1924), to which Anderson in collaboration with Laurence Stallings contributed "On the Eve of War: A Recollection," an account of a Frank Cobb interview with Woodrow Wilson. L. R. E. Paulin (1864–1952) came to the *World* in 1904, from the *San Francisco Chronicle*, and remained with the paper until 1931 as an editorial writer on international affairs.

9. Don Carlos Seitz (1862–1935), with the *World* from 1895 until 1926, wrote historical and political novels and *Joseph Pulitzer: His Life and Letters* (1924). Joseph Pulitzer owned the *World* from 1883 until his death in 1911.

10. Laurence Stallings (1894–1968) was book review editor on the *World*, and Taylor (1885–1966) was the paper's music critic. Pemberton (1885–1950) was known as a producer of unconventional plays with artistic merit on the basis of such productions as Pirandello's *Six Characters in Search of an Author* in 1922.

11. Abbott (b. 1887), actor who also wrote, directed, and produced a number of plays, had the part of Sverre Peterson in *White Desert*, and the play on which he collaborated with Anderson was at first entitled *The Feud*. During rehearsals of *White Desert* (September–October, 1923), Anderson suggested that they collaborate on a play based on the Hatfield-McCoy feud. After *White Desert* closed, the two of them went to Boone, N.C., to work on *The Feud* (probably in November, 1923). Abbott was to have the lead in Hatcher Hughes's *Hell-Bent Fer Heaven*, and the producer, wishing him to have an authentic accent, paid his expenses to Boone so he could listen to the dialect in the region of the play. Abbott paid Anderson's expenses, and the two of them worked on *The Feud* each day. Early in 1924, while Anderson was at work on *What Price Glory*, Abbott interested the producer John Golden in *The Feud*, and Golden secured a new collaborator, Winchell Smith. Golden paid Anderson for his rights in the play, and Abbott and Smith changed the title to *A Holy Terror*. But "neither Winchell nor I was the right author for this idea," Abbott said in "*Mister Abbott*." "We made it into a show, a melodrama, whereas its only hope was to be treated in a more important way—to delve deeply into the causes of feuds and hatreds, and their footlessness" (p. 113). *A Holy Terror* opened on September 28, 1925, with Abbott in the lead, and ran for thirty-two performances.

12. Herman Jacob Mankiewicz (1897–1953), primarily a film script writer (with Orson Wells he wrote *Citizen Kane*, 1941), collaborated on a number of plays, but apparently his musical with Stallings about the war was not produced.

13. For a description of the drafts of *What Price Glory*, see *Catalogue*, pp. 10–12. Arthur Hopkins (1878–1950), a notable producer from the second decade of the century into the forties—*Anna Christi* (1921), *The Hairy Ape* (1922), *The Petrified Forest* (1934), *The Magnificent Yankee* (1946)—discusses the production of *What Price Glory* in *To A Lonely Boy* (1937) and calls it "the most gratifying production I have made" (p. 241).

14. Frank Irving Cobb(1869–1923) came from the *Detroit Evening News* in 1904 to head the *World*'s editorial staff and retained that position until his death. An adviser to President Wilson, he played a primary role in transforming the *World* into perhaps the most prominent and respected American newspaper of the teens and twenties. His editorials and speeches are collected in Heaton's *Cobb of THE WORLD*.

15. Herbert Bayard Swope (1882–1958) became a reporter for the *World* in 1909 and was its executive editor from 1920 until 1929. Ralph Pulitzer (1879–1939) inherited the *World* at his father's death in 1911 and sold it in 1931.

16. Woollcott was not on the *World* during Anderson's tenure. Anderson resigned from the paper in September, 1924, after the success of *What Price Glory*, and Woollcott joined the *World* as drama critic in the fall of 1925, a position he held until 1928. But it had been Woollcott who showed the script of *What Price Glory* to Arthur Hopkins (*To A Lonely Boy*, pp. 235–36).

17. Franklin P. Adams (1881–1960), whose column "The Conning Tower" was a feature of the famous page-opposite-the-editorial-page on the *World* (the page that carried signed articles such as book reviews, drama criticism, and social commentary), always signed the column with his initials. It consisted of verse, usually satirical, and a personal diary modeled on Pepys; pieces from the column were collected as *The Diary of Our Own Samuel Pepys* (2 vols., 1935).

18. Allan Nevins (1890–1971), journalist and historian, founded the Oral History Research Office at Columbia in 1948; it was because of his friendship with Nevins that Anderson, who did not usually grant interviews, granted the present one. Among his many books is a three-volume study of the life and times of *Ford* (1954, 1957, 1963) done in collaboration with Frank E. Hill.

19. Claude G. Bowers (1879–1958), later U.S. envoy to Spain and ambassador to Chile, was an editorial writer on the *World* from 1923 until 1931.

20. "Shadow of Youth," *You Who Have Dreams*, p. 66.

21. No definite source for *The Buccaneer* has come to light. The classic account of Sir Henry Morgan's life (1635?–1688) is by one of his men, John Esquemeling, *Bucaniers of America* (London, 1684), a book that was reissued in 1924.

22. Stallings's dramatization of *A Farewell to Arms* ran for twenty-four performances after opening on September 22, 1930. In 1925 he had gone to Hollywood for the filming of *The Big Parade*, a picture based on his story of the same title and his novel, *Plumes* (1924). He wrote the book and lyrics for two operettas, *Deep River* (1926) and *Rainbow* (1928).

23. Lytton Strachey, *Elizabeth and Essex: A Tragic History* (London, 1928).

24. Gilbert (1895–1956), silent film star, who had the lead in *The Big Parade* (1925).

25. Robert H. Montgomery (b. 1889) had received an A.B. from the University of North Dakota in 1909, a law degree from Harvard Law School in 1912, and since then has practiced law in Boston. For his view of the case, see his *Sacco-Vanzetti: The Murder and the Myth* (1960). Judge Webster Thayer presided at the trial.

26. Sherwood began reviewing films in 1920, for *Life*, and continued to do so (sporadically after 1924, when he became editor of *Life*) until his dismissal from the magazine in 1928. His *Road to Rome* was produced in 1927.

27. Leslie Stevens, *The Lovers*.

28. Enid Bagnold's *The Chalk Garden* had opened on October 10, 1955; *My Fair Lady*, Alan Jay Lerner and Frederick Lowe's adaptation of Shaw's *Pygmalion*, had opened on March 15, 1956.

29. Williams's most recent play, *Cat on a Hot Tin Roof*, had been produced by the Playwrights' Company on March 24, 1955.

30. Sir Arthur Forbes-Robertson (1853–1937), famous for his Hamlet, also toured extensively as the Stranger in Jerome K. Jerome's popular *The Passing of the Third Floor Back* (1908). Sarah Bernhardt's last tour of the United States came in 1917 and included Edmond Rostand's *L'Aiglon* (1900).

APPENDIX II

THREE GENERATIONS OF MAXWELL ANDERSON'S FAMILY

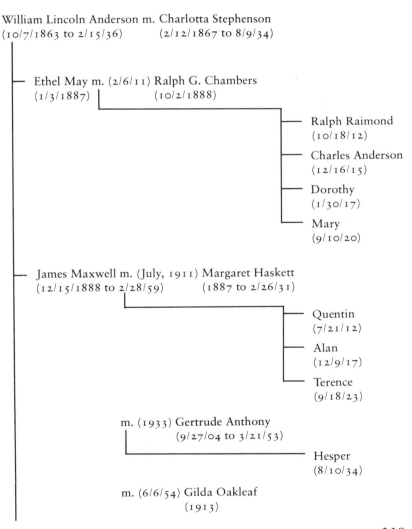

William Lincoln Anderson m. Charlotta Stephenson
(10/7/1863 to 2/15/36)   (2/12/1867 to 8/9/34)

Ethel May m. (2/6/11) Ralph G. Chambers
(1/3/1887)   (10/2/1888)

Ralph Raimond
(10/18/12)

Charles Anderson
(12/16/15)

Dorothy
(1/30/17)

Mary
(9/10/20)

James Maxwell m. (July, 1911) Margaret Haskett
(12/15/1888 to 2/28/59)   (1887 to 2/26/31)

Quentin
(7/21/12)

Alan
(12/9/17)

Terence
(9/18/23)

m. (1933) Gertrude Anthony
(9/27/04 to 3/21/53)

Hesper
(8/10/34)

m. (6/6/54) Gilda Oakleaf
(1913)

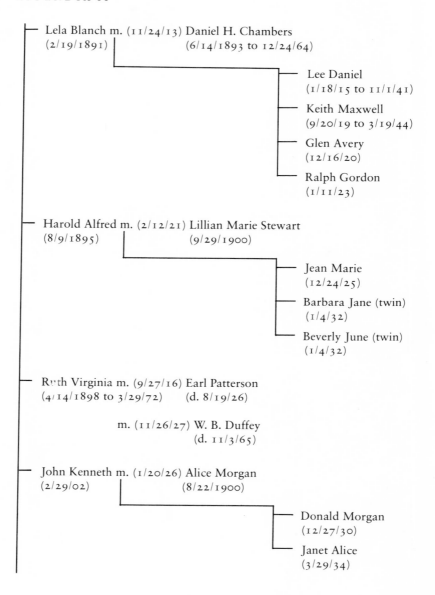

Lela Blanch m. (11/24/13) Daniel H. Chambers
(2/19/1891)   (6/14/1893 to 12/24/64)

Lee Daniel
(1/18/15 to 11/1/41)

Keith Maxwell
(9/20/19 to 3/19/44)

Glen Avery
(12/16/20)

Ralph Gordon
(1/11/23)

Harold Alfred m. (2/12/21) Lillian Marie Stewart
(8/9/1895)   (9/29/1900)

Jean Marie
(12/24/25)

Barbara Jane (twin)
(1/4/32)

Beverly June (twin)
(1/4/32)

Ruth Virginia m. (9/27/16) Earl Patterson
(4/14/1898 to 3/29/72)   (d. 8/19/26)

m. (11/26/27) W. B. Duffey
(d. 11/3/65)

John Kenneth m. (1/20/26) Alice Morgan
(2/29/02)   (8/22/1900)

Donald Morgan
(12/27/30)

Janet Alice
(3/29/34)

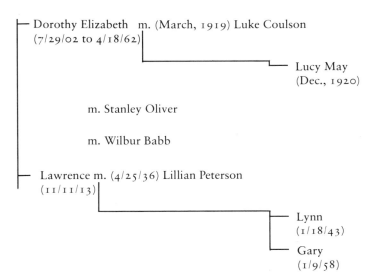

Dorothy Elizabeth   m. (March, 1919) Luke Coulson
(7/29/02 to 4/18/62)

Lucy May
(Dec., 1920)

m. Stanley Oliver

m. Wilbur Babb

Lawrence m. (4/25/36) Lillian Peterson
(11/11/13)

Lynn
(1/18/43)

Gary
(1/9/58)

APPENDIX III

PRINCIPAL CORRESPONDENTS

GERTRUDE ANTHONY ANDERSON

Anderson's first wife, Margaret Haskett, died in February, 1931, and in the fall of 1933 he married Gertrude Anthony. Gertrude, known to the family and friends as Mab, was born in 1904 and had come to New York as an actress in the twenties, where she married Charles Maynard. She and Anderson met in 1930, when she had a small part in *Elizabeth the Queen*, and he secured another small part for her in *Night Over Taos* in 1932. Following their marriage she largely gave up her acting career and spent her time at their home on South Mountain Road, where their daughter Hesper was born in August, 1934. Anderson had few occasions to correspond with Mab, since they were usually together, but war conditions prevented her from going with him to London and North Africa in 1943. His several long letters to her at that time provide a daily account of his activities on the edge of the war and also reveal his devotion to her and loneliness in her absence. She was devoted to him as well but was not entirely satisfied with her life and in the late forties experienced frequent periods of depression, induced perhaps by a feeling of isolation in the farmlike surroundings of their home, worry over their huge income tax debts, and a sense of purposelessness occasioned by the abandonment of her acting career. In 1951, to help meet the tax debt, she took a job as producer with a television series, and in July of 1952 Anderson discovered that she was also having an affair. He left home, returned briefly when her television job fell through, then in November went to Los Angeles, where he was in March, 1953, when she committed suicide at their home. Though her last years were troubled, Mab was a vivacious and capable person, and during the thirties and early forties she and Anderson were unusually happy together. Her infidelity and suicide were a shattering experience for him, and he regained a sense of emotional well-being only after his marriage in May, 1954, to Gilda Oakleaf and their establishment of a home in Stamford, Connecticut.

MARGERY BAILEY

Margery Bailey, born in Santa Cruz in 1891 and a friend of Anderson during their student days at Stanford University, renewed the acquaintance in 1936 when she organized the Dramatists' Alliance at Stanford. She had been at Stanford (B.A., 1914; M.A. in English, 1916; instructor in English until

1920) throughout Anderson's California years and was one of a group of aspiring poets and writers in the San Francisco area that included Anderson, Frank Hill, Robert Duffus, and Bruce Bliven. Earning a Ph.D. at Yale in 1926, she returned to the Stanford English faculty and quickly became an inspirational teacher of Shakespeare. She also began numerous projects to encourage live drama on the West Coast, one of which was the Dramatists' Alliance. The alliance, which she directed until her retirement in 1956, grew out of a summer course in play production in 1935 and consisted of a national competition for original plays and production of the winning scripts. She launched the annual competitions in 1936, for plays in verse, and named the award for that kind of play the Maxwell Anderson Award. As she planned the first year's competition, she opened the correspondence with Anderson; though embarrassed at having the award named for himself, he assisted her for several years with encouragement, advice, money, and the reading of scripts. To her, an old friend who shared his lifelong interest in verse drama and in breaking the hold of Broadway on new play production in America, he wrote some of his more relaxed and revealing letters. Her letters to him (Anderson Collection, Humanities Research Center, University of Texas) show an altogether charming personality—vigorous, insightful, humorous, and warmly sympathetic. She died in June, 1963, while preparing to direct a play at the Shakespearean Festival at Ashland, Oregon, a festival she helped to organize in the late twenties.

LELA ANDERSON CHAMBERS

Anderson's second sister, Lela, born in February, 1891, was just over a year younger than him and with their older sister Ethel (born in 1887) was his chief companion as a child. Lela married Daniel H. Chambers in 1913, while Anderson was at Stanford, and lived in Wisconsin until the mid-twenties, when she moved with her family to a farm that Anderson helped them buy near Hinsdale in southwestern New York. Thereafter she maintained close contact with Anderson through visits and letters (most of which she has kept), and her family figured importantly in *The Eve of St. Mark*, which is dedicated to her oldest son, Lee, who was killed in an army training accident in 1941. Lela wrote a few plays herself during the thirties and later collected much material for an Anderson family history. She always had a sympathetic interest in her brother's career and was proud of his achievements. Because of their mutual affection and many shared experiences, Anderson wrote Lela some of his more spontaneous and personal letters. She retains fond memories of him and is patient and generous with those who seek her out on his behalf.

MEMBERS OF THE PLAYWRIGHTS' COMPANY

The Playwrights' Company grew out of discussions between Anderson, Robert Sherwood, and Elmer Rice that began in November, 1937. The three, discovering a shared interest in producing their own plays, decided to form a company for that purpose and soon involved S. H. Behrman and Sidney Howard in their plans. The five then enlisted John F. Wharton, a lawyer whose legal and financial expertise made up for their own inexperience in business operations, and Wharton secured William Fields (1899–1961) as press representative and Victor Samrock (b. 1907) as business manager of the company. Announcements of the company's organization appeared on March 8, 1938.

During its first season, 1938–39, the company produced plays by four of its five playwriting members: Sherwood's *Abe Lincoln in Illinois* (October 15, 1938), Anderson's *Knickerbocker Holiday* (October 19, 1938), Rice's *American Landscape* (December 2, 1938), and Behrman's *No Time for Comedy* (April 17, 1939). Thereafter it averaged about four productions a season through its final season of 1959–60, but it never again had its full complement of playwrights as envisioned by the founders. Howard died in 1939 without producing a play through the company. Sherwood spent the first half of the decade of the forties in Washington devoting full time to his work in Roosevelt's administration. And Behrman resigned from the company in 1946. In the same year Kurt Weill joined the company after several collaborations with its members, but he died in 1950. Roger L. Stevens joined the company in 1951 to handle the major business of its productions. And in 1953 Robert Anderson became a member following the company's production of *Tea and Sympathy*. But Sherwood's death in 1955 and Anderson's early in 1959 left the company with only two playwriting members, Rice and Robert Anderson. Rice, the only remaining playwright from the original group, resigned shortly after Anderson's death, and the company remained in operation through the 1959–60 season only to produce Robert Anderson's *Silent Night, Lonely Night*.

The original group of playwrights organized the company hoping to increase their profits but primarily to gain artistic control over the production of their plays. Anderson was further attracted to the group by his friendship with its other members and its promise of providing a stable and sympathetic center for him in the theater. The name he first suggested for the company, the Playwrights' Guild, indicates his conception of it as a group of skilled craftsmen working together cooperatively for their mutual benefit. His expectations were not disappointed. A high sense of camaraderie developed among the members, and each gave serious attention to the plays of the others, criticizing them during the writing and offering suggestions and moral support during production. Anderson was strongly attached to the company into the early fifties and produced more plays with it than did any other playwright (thirteen), largely sustaining the company through the forties. Thereafter, however, his enthusiasm for the company waned. During its early existence the company had produced plays only by its members, and each playwright thus felt a strong sense of involvement in all of the company's activity. But by 1950 rising production costs and declining output from its playwrights placed the company in financial peril and forced on it a change of policy. It became a general producing organization, actively soliciting scripts from playwrights outside the company, and Stevens was brought in to pursue the more aggressive production policy. His skillful management helped to sustain the company financially through the fifties. But the change in policy and depletions in the ranks of its playwriting members (culminating with Sherwood's death) undermined Anderson's sense of involvement with the company. He remained a member until his death and continued to produce his plays through the company. But during his last years he did not derive the satisfactions from it that had bound him to the Playwrights' Company during its earlier years.

John F. Wharton, the only member of the Playwrights' Company throughout its existence, has provided an inside account of its members and activities in his *Life Among the Playwrights* (1975). And Kay I. Johnson has investigated the significance of the company in American social history in her *Playwrights as Patriots: A History of the Playwrights' Producing Company* (Ph.D. dissertation, University of Wisconsin, 1974).

Robert E. Sherwood (1896–1955)

Following combat duty in World War I Sherwood pursued a varied career, beginning as a journalist and film critic in the early twenties, devoting himself mainly to the theater only during the late twenties and thirties, holding several high governmental positions in Roosevelt's administration during World War II, then attempting unsuccessfully to return to playwriting after the war and publishing the highly acclaimed history *Roosevelt and Hopkins* (1948). Sherwood said the success of *What Price Glory*, the tumultuous response it generated and the money it made, caused him to decide to take up playwriting, and his first play was *The Road to Rome* in 1927. He and Anderson met about that time and became close associates in the thirties in the Dramatists' Guild, of which Sherwood was secretary in 1935 and president in 1937. It was following a Guild meeting that the two of them and Rice, over drinks, began the discussions that led to the Playwrights' Company. After formation of the company they met regularly, usually every two or three weeks, and Anderson attributed the wit and good humor of their sessions largely to Sherwood's presence. Sherwood, who had achieved prominence with *Petrified Forest* (1935) and *Idiot's Delight* (1936), produced four plays through the Playwrights' Company, *Abe Lincoln in Illinois* and *There Shall Be No Night* (1940), each of which received a Pulitzer Prize, and *The Rugged Path* (1945) and *Small War on Murray Hill* (posthumously, 1957). He spent the war years mainly in Washington as a speech writer for Roosevelt, and it was through his influence as director of the Overseas Branch of the Office of War Information that Anderson obtained permission to visit London and North Africa in 1943. Sherwood also nominated Anderson for the Gold Medal he received from the American Academy and National Institute of Arts and Letters in 1954, during the emotionally desperate period following Mab's suicide. Anderson said that Sherwood was his closest friend in the Playwrights' Company, and after Sherwood's death in November,

1955, Anderson read a memorial poem before the American Academy that voiced his great sense of personal loss.

Elmer Rice (1892–1967)

Trained as a lawyer, Rice achieved immediate success with his first play, *On Trial*, in 1914 and went on to write over fifty plays by the time of his death. Some of these he directed as well, beginning with *Street Scene* in 1929, and several he did in collaboration, including the musical version of *Street Scene* in 1947, for which Kurt Weill composed the score. After *The Adding Machine* in 1923 Rice was among the more prominent American playwrights, and in 1925 he played a conspicuous part in reorganizing the Dramatists' Guild in such a way that it gave real protection to the rights and interests of playwrights. For a time in 1935–36 he was head of the New York Region of the Federal Theater Project, for which he devised the Living Newspaper plays, and for a good part of his career he served on the board of the American Civil Liberties Union. Except for their common opposition to fascism, Rice and Anderson were usually on opposite sides of the fence in political sympathies, with Rice demurring at the satire on the New Deal in *Knickerbocker Holiday* and differing with Anderson's view that communist infiltrations posed a threat to the United States in the decade following World War II. They nevertheless worked together congenially in the Playwrights' Company, and one of Anderson's more detailed and sympathetic critiques of a member's script was the one he sent to Rice concerning *American Landscape* (no. 66). Rice produced ten plays through the Playwrights' Company, more than anyone else except Anderson, including *Flight to the West* (1940), *A New Life* (1943), *Dream Girl* (1945), and *Cue for Passion* (1958).

Sidney Howard (1891–1939)

Howard, raised in California, came to New York following service in France during World War I and had his first major success with *They Knew What They Wanted* in 1924. Thereafter he had a play almost every season, including *Lucky Sam McCarver* (1925), *The Late Christopher Bean* (1932), and *Yellow Jack* (1934). He had nearly finished his last play, *Madam, Will You Walk?*, when he was killed in a tractor accident on his Massachusetts farm in August, 1939. Anderson and Howard had met late in 1925, after Howard put a note in the *World* praising *Outside Looking In* and *You Who Have Dreams*, and Howard was an eager participant in the Playwrights' Company, having tried to form such a company himself earlier in the thirties. His critique of the first draft of *Key Largo*, because of its thoroughness, called forth one of Anderson's most detailed letters about revisions in his plays (no. 79). Following Howard's death the Playwrights' Company attempted to produce *Madam, Will You Walk?*, with Sherwood taking the job of revising the script. When he met opposition from Howard's widow, Anderson tried to persuade her to allow Sherwood a free hand, and his praise of the play in his letters to her (nos. 82 and 86) was not merely diplomatic. Though the production was cancelled before its New York opening, Anderson thought the play was one of the best any of the company had written. In Howard's memory the Playwrights' Company established an award for younger playwrights, and the first Sidney Howard Memorial Award went to Robert Ardrey in 1940 for *Thunder Rock*.

S. N. Behrman (1893–1973)

Behrman, after several collaborations, had his first success with *The Second Man* in 1927, and during the thirties came to be known for witty drawingroom comedies such as *Biography* (1932), *Rain From Heaven* (1934), and *End of Summer* (1936). The approach of World War II caused him to doubt the justification of his kind of comedy, a doubt he dramatized in his first play with the Playwrights' Company, *No Time For Comedy*, but Anderson thought him the most accomplished comic author in the American theater. Something of the fun among the members is suggested by Anderson's mock attack on him during Behrman's campaign for the ceremonial presidency of the Playwrights' Company (no. 128). But Behrman was dissatisfied in the company, the dissatisfaction stemming from opposition to his wish to have an outside producer for his plays, a wish in which Anderson supported him (no. 141), and he resigned in June, 1946. After *No Time For Comedy* he produced three plays through the Playwrights' Company, *The Talley Method* (1941), *The Pirate* (1942), and after his resignation *The Cold Wind and the Warm* (1958). His last substantial play, *But For Whom Charlie*, was produced in 1964 by the Lincoln Center Repertory Company during its inaugural season.

John F. Wharton (b. 1894)

Wharton, who pursued an active law practice from the twenties onward and also interested himself extensively in the business of the theater, especially in the problem-filled system of merchandising tickets, became the hub of the Playwrights' Company. Sherwood knew him and early in their discussions suggested to the other playwrights that they contact Wharton about the legal aspects of a producing organization. According to Anderson, they were so impressed with his knowledge, common sense, and geniality that they soon asked Wharton to become a full partner, and it was Wharton who drafted the basic agreement of the Playwrights' Company and then announced the company's formation in March, 1938. Thereafter he oversaw business operations of the company and served as a contact point for the playwrights, who were often widely dispersed. Anderson corresponded extensively with Wharton, keeping him posted on the progress of his plays, and relied on Wharton's judgment in financial and legal matters. He changed the name of the central character in *Journey to Jerusalem* when Wharton called attention to a New York law prohibiting the depiction of deity on the stage. Wharton defended him successfully in the plagiarism suit that arose over *Anne of the Thousand Days*. And twice, when financial pressure made Anderson consider resigning from the company, he decided not to resign after talking with Wharton. Wharton usually participated in the discussions of member plays, sometimes introduced plays by outsiders for consideration by the company, and once attempted a play of his own, a courtroom drama that was not produced. But his major writing consisted of his thoughtful books, *This Road to Recovery* (1933), *Earning a Living* (1945; rev. ed., 1961), and *The Explorations of George Burton* (1951). His *Life Among the Playwrights* is based on the voluminous records of the company, including his own extensive correspondence with its other members.

Kurt Weill (1900–1950), Roger L. Stevens (b. 1910), Robert Anderson (b. 1917)

For various reasons Anderson had little correspondence with the three later members of the Playwrights' Company. Weill, born in Germany and a musical collaborator with Brecht in the twenties, came to the United States to escape the Nazis during the thirties and thereafter made his home on South Mountain Road as a neighbor and close friend of Anderson. He composed the score for a number of Broadway musicals, most prominently his two collaborations with Anderson, *Knickerbocker Holiday* and *Lost in the Stars*, and at his death in April, 1950, they were at work on *Raft on the River*, a musical adaptation of *The Adventures of Huckleberry Finn* that Anderson did not subsequently produce. Weill was a member of the Playwrights' Company only briefly (1946–50), and he and Anderson, living so close together, had few occasions to correspond (none of Anderson's letters to Weill survive, though a small group of Weill's letters is in the Anderson Collection, Humanities Research Center, University of Texas). Anderson frequently expressed his admiration for Weill as a person and composer, as in the published memorials following Weill's death and the preface to *Knickerbocker Holiday*, where Anderson said that for the play Weill had composed the best score in the history of the American theater.

Roger L. Stevens joined the Playwrights' Company in April 1951, when the company abandoned its earlier policy of producing only member plays and became a general producing organization. Anderson's letters to Stevens repeat the reports he wrote to others on the progress of his own plays or on his reactions to plays by nonmembers. Stevens, chairman of the finance committee of the Democratic party in 1956, continued as an active producer after the demise of the Playwrights' Company and in 1964 became special assistant to President Johnson on the arts. The next year he was made chairman of both the National Council for the Arts and the National Endowment for the Arts, and presently he is chairman of the John F. Kennedy Center for the Performing Arts.

Robert Anderson joined the Playwrights' Company in 1953, when the company produced *Tea and Sympathy*, his first Broadway production. None of Anderson's letters to Robert Anderson (they were not related) have come to light, though Robert Anderson wrote some spirited critiques of Anderson's last plays as they were being considered by the company. The Playwrights' Company produced a second Robert Anderson play in 1954, *All Summer Long*, then had as its last production his *Silent Night, Lonely Night* (1959). His plays since the demise of the company include *The Days Between* (1965), *You Know I Can't Hear You When the Water's Running* (1967), *I Never Sang For My Father* (1968), and *Solitaire—Double Solitaire* (1971).

APPENDIX IV

[Letters in the list are identified in a way designed to make them easily accessible. In columns one and three of the list information that does not appear on the letters is placed within square brackets. In column four the codes used to signify type and location of the letters are the codes used with letters included in this edition. The fourth column also indicates the length of each letter by stating its number of pages when it is more than one page long.]

Date	Recipient	Place of Composition	Type and Location of Original
1921			
[July, 1921]	William Stanley Braithwaite	[New York City]	Als; H
[Summer, 1921]	Harold Monro	[New York City]	ALs; LC
1922			
[Fall, 1922]	William Stanley Braithwaite	[New York City]	ALs; H
October 6 [1922]	William Stanley Braithwaite	[New York City]	ALs; H
1924			
[December 21, 1924]	Lela Chambers	[New York City]	ALs; LAC
1925			
[March 6, 1925]	Lela Chambers	New York City	ALs; LAC
[Summer, 1925]	Mr. M'Kaig	New City	ALS; PTA
September 21 [1925]	Guthrie McClintic	New City	ALs; NL
[September, 1925]	William Stanley Braithwaite	New City	ALs; H
[November 18, 1925]	Lela Chambers	New City	ALs; LAC

330

Date	Recipient	Place of Composition	Type and Location of Original
1927			
January 17 [1927]	Lela Chambers	[New City]	ALs; LAC
February 1 [1927]	Lela and Dan Chambers	New City	ALs; 2 pp.; LAC
April 1 [1927]	Lela Chambers	[New City]	ALs;LAC
1928			
[May 29, 1928]	Lela Chambers	[New City]	ALs; LAC
September 4	Lela Chambers	New York City	ALs; LAC
1930			
January 10	Theresa Helburn	Hollywood	TLs; Y
January 26	Theresa Helburn	Hollywood	TLs; Y
July 17 [1930]	Lynn Riggs	New City	ALs; Y (Barrett H. Clark Collection
November 21	Theresa Helburn	New York City	ALs; Y
1932			
January 28	Barrett H. Clark		ALs; Y
January 31	Melvin Ruder	New City	C; T
[March 28, 1932]	Barrett H. Clark		ALs; Y
April 26	Barrett H. Clark	Hollywood	TLs; Y
July 18	Barrett H. Clark	New City	ALs; Y
[Late Summer, 1932]	Gertrude Anthony (Anderson)	[New City]	ALs; T
August 22	Barrett H. Clark	New City	ALs; Y
[Fall, 1932]	Gertrude Anthony (Anderson	[New City]	ALs; T
1933			
April 25 [1933]	Barrett H. Clark		ALs; Y
May 16	George Middleton	Santa Monica	TLs; LC
[Summer, 1933]	Gertrude Anthony (Anderson)	[Los Angeles]	ALs; T
[Late July, 1933]	Gertrude Anthony (Anderson)	[New City]	ALs; T
[Late Summer, 1933]	Gertrude Anthony (Anderson)	[New City]	ALs; T
[Late Summer, 1933]	Gertrude Anthony (Anderson)	[New City]	ALs; T
[Fall, 1933]	Gertrude Anderson	[New City]	ALs; T
[September 10, 1933]	Lela Chambers	[New City]	ALs; LAC

Date	Recipient	Place of Composition	Type and Location of Original
November 21	Barrett H. Clark		TLs; Y
[December 14, 1933]	Lela Chambers	[New York City]	ALs; LAC
1934			
[March 6, 1934]	Lela Chambers	[New York City]	ALs; LAC
March 7	George Middleton	New York City	TLs; LC
March 20	William A. Slade	[New York City]	C; T
March 20	Hazel M. Musselman	New York City	C; T
1935			
April 20	Katharine Cornell	New City	C; T
May 31	Waldemar Juers	New York City	C; T
July 9	Ruth Anderson Duffey	Hinsdale	ALs; 2 pp.; LAC
August 31	Cecil Madden	New City	Tel; T
1936			
January 14	Harold Anderson	New City	ALs; HA
July 2 [1936]	Lela Chambers	New City	ALs; LAC
July 7	Margery Bailey		ALs; S
1937			
March 13	Lawrence Anderson	Naples (Fla.)	C; T
July 3	Arthur L. Thayer	New City	C; T
[July, 1937]	Fred B. Millett		ALs; Y
September 2	Selden		C; T
September 4	Lela Chambers	New City	ALs; LAC
[September 15, 1937]	Lela Chambers	Buffalo	ALs; 2 pp.; LAC
October 25	Peggy Wood		C; T
1938			
March 8	John F. Wharton	New City	TLs; JFW
March 15	John F. Wharton	New City	ALs; JFW
[May, 1938]	John F. Wharton	[New City]	ALs; JFW
July 15	S. N. Behrman		Tel; W
July	S. N. Behrman		Tel; W
November 1	Louis Azrael	New City	C; T
November 10	Georgia S. Fink	New City	C; T
November 10	Longmans, Green	New City	C; T
November 10	John B. Opdycke	New City	C; T

Date	Recipient	Place of Composition	Type and Location of Original
November 10	Lela Chambers	New City	TLs; LAC
November 10	Lizzie A. Wharton	New City	C; T
November 12	Frank Anderson	New City	C; T
November 17	Katharine Cornell		Tel; W
November 18	Sculley Bradley	New City	C; T
November 18	Barrett H. Clark	New City	TLs; Y
December 31	Justine van Gundy	New City	C; T
	Robert Sherwood		Tel; W
1939			
January 31	Melvin Ruder	New City	C; T
January 31	Kenneth Anderson	New City	C; T
February 18	Manuel E. Kopelman	New City	C; T
June 1	Victor Samrock	Hollywood	Tel; W
June 5	John F. Wharton	Santa Monica	Tel; JFW
June 6	Sidney Howard	Santa Monica	Tel; JFW
June 7	John F. Wharton	Malibu	TLs; JFW
June 9	Victor Samrock	Santa Monica	Tel; W
June 13	Charles Vanda	Malibu	C; T
June 13	William Fields	Malibu	C; T
June 24	Victor Samrock	Santa Monica	Tel; W
June 30	Collier Young	Malibu	C; T
July 1	Arthur Train	Malibu	C; T
July	Victor Samrock		ALs; W
August 24	Victor Samrock	Santa Monica	Tel; W
September 16	Paul Muni	New York City	Tel; W
October 11	Alvin Johnson	New City	C; T
[Fall, 1939]	Fiorello H. La Guardia	[New City]	AL; 2 pp.; T
November 13	Kate Clugston	New City	C; T
December 13	Harold Anderson		ALs; 2 pp.; HA
1940			
February 5	Harold Anderson		ALs; HA
March 10	Archer Milton Huntington		ALs; SY
May 1	Stanley Young	New City	C; T
May 5	Harold Anderson	New City	ALs; 2 pp.; HA
[May 14, 1940]	Lela Chambers	[New City]	ALs; LAC
[June, 1940]	Archer Milton Huntington	[New City]	ALs; SY

Date	Recipient	Place of Composition	Type and Location of Original
[June 8, 1940]	Lela Chambers	[New City]	ALs; LAC
July 5	John M. Jeffrey	New City	C; T
July 19	Rev. C. O. Pederson	New City	C; T
July 30	Burns Mantle		C; T
July 30	Kenneth Anderson		Tel; W
July 31	Ralph Theadore	New York City	Tel; W
August 12	Clarkstown Zoning Board	New City	C; 2 pp.; T
September 3	Stanley Young	New City	C; T
September 8	Helen Hayes	New City	C; T
September 19	Archer Milton Huntington	New City	ALs; SY
October 12	Archer Milton Huntington	New City	TLs; SY
October 15	Ethel and Ralph Chambers	New City	C; T
October 26	Homer Fickett	New City	C; T
[November/ December, 1940]	Victor Samrock	[New City]	ALs; W
	Homer Fickett	New City	ALs; T
1941			
January 8	Paul Ferguson	New City	C; T
January 8	James Boyd	New City	C; T
January 14	S. N. Behrman	[New City]	Tel; W
January 20	Albert J. Kahn	New City	C; T
February 6	Louis J. Hexter	New City	C; T
February 6	Archer Milton Huntington	New City	C; T
February 27	Douglas Fairbanks	New York City	Tel; W
March 5	Frank Anderson	New City	C; T
March 5	Charles Pelton	New City	C; T
March 5	Robert Whitehand	New City	C; T
March 5	John F. Wharton	New City	C; T
April 15	Harry Woodburn Chase	New York City	Tel; W
April 19	Harry Woodburn Chase	New York City	Tel; W
April 21	Victor Samrock	New City	ALs; W
April 25	Helen Hayes	[New York City]	Tel; W
April 30	Helen Hayes	[New York City]	Tel; W

Date	Recipient	Place of Composition	Type and Location of Original
May 5	E. Bernard	New City	C; T
May 9	E. Bernard	New City	C; T
May 21	Helen Hayes	New York City	Tel; W
May 21	Lawrence Langner	[New York City]	Tel; W
May 29	Raymond Rubicam		Tel; W
June 4	Archer Milton Huntington	New City	TLs; SY
June 15	Elmer Rice		C; W
June 18	Raymond Rubicam	New York City	Tel; W
July 1	Robert Sherwood	New City	TLs; W
July 17	Margery Bailey	New City	TLs; S
August 16	Warren Munsell	New City	C; T
[August 22, 1941]	Dan and Lela Chambers	Nyack	ALs; LAC
1942			
January 12	Eunice Tietjens	New City	TLs; NL
February 28	Viola Paradise	New City	C; T
March 14	Lee Norvelle	[New York City]	ALs; LN
May 15	Lucy Mitchell		ALs; W
June 22	Information Please	New City	TL; W
July 6	Henry F. Pringle		C; T
July 6	Gen. Irving J. Phillipson		C; T
July 7	Gen. Irving J. Phillipson		C; W
July 7	Gen. Alexander D. Surles		C; W
July 8	Robert Sherwood	[New York City]	ALs*; W
July 12	Lucy Mitchell		ALs; W
July 28	Anatole Litvak		C; W
[September 11, 1942]	Lela Chambers	[New City]	ALs; LAC
September 12	Victor Samrock	New York City	Tel; W
[September 23, 1942]	Lela Chambers	Boston	ALs; LAC
October 15	Russel Crouse		C; T
October 31	Dan and Lela Chambers	[New City]	ALs; 2 pp.; LAC
November 4	Dan Chambers	[New City]	ALs; LAC

Date	Recipient	Place of Composition	Type and Location of Original
November 27	John Halliday	New York City	Tel; W
	Victor Samrock		ALs; W
1943			
January 5	Lela Chambers	[New City]	ALs; LAC
[January 12, 1943]	Lela Chambers	[New City]	ALs; LAC
February 17	Robert Sherwood		C; T
[February, 1943]	Robert B. Greenberger	[New York City]	AL; W
[March, 1943]	Victor Samrock	[New York City]	ALs; W
March 3	Terence Anderson	New York City	Tel; W
March 22	American Field Service		C; W
March 22	Nicholas Murray Butler		C; W
April 17	Gertrude Anderson	[London]	Tel; W
May 27	Gertrude Anderson	Scotland	P; T
July 9	Manning Whiley	New York City	Tel; W
July 19	Manning Whiley	New York City	Tel; W
July 19	Dwight Wiman	New York City	Tel; W
July 19	Russell Lane	New City	Tel; W
August 6	Harold Anderson	New City	ALs; 2 pp.; HA
[August, 1943]	Lucy Mitchell	[New York City]	ALs; W
September 7	Kurt and Lenya Weill	New York City	Tel; W
October 27 [1943]	Lela and Dan Chambers	[New City]	ALs; LAC
November 13	Elizabeth Wheeler Manwaring	[New York City]	ALs; WC
November 22	Russell Blauvelt	New City	C; T
November 22	*Rockland County Journal-News*	New City	C; W
	Gabriel Pascal	New City	Tel; T
December 15	J. P. Kenney	New York City	Tel; W
1944			
February 19	A. Eldon Winkler		C; W
February 25	Lawrence Langner	New City	TLs; Y
April 3	Katharine White	New City	C; T
April 18 [1944]	Lela Chambers	[New City]	ALs; LAC
April 18	Barrett H. Clark	[New City]	ALs; Y

Date	Recipient	Place of Composition	Type and Location of Original
April 27	Theresa Helburn		ALs; Y
June 2	Lela Chambers	[New City]	ALs; LAC
[Early Summer, 1944]	unspecified		TLs; W
July 7	Lela Chambers	[New City]	ALs; LAC
September 29	Terence Anderson	New York City	Tel; W
October 1	Lela and Dan Chambers	[New City]	ALs; LAC
October 12	Mrs. Willis Fisher	New York City	Tel; W
[Early November, 1944]	unspecified		C; T
December 27	Terence Anderson	New York City	Tel; W
1945			
February 6	Gertrude Anderson	New York City	Tel; W
February 13	unspecified		TL; W
February 20	Harold Anderson	Hollywood	ALs; 2 pp.; HA
March 24	Harold Anderson	[Hollywood]	ALs; HA
April 30	John F. Wharton	Los Angeles	ALs; W
May 8	Lela Chambers	Los Angeles	ALs; 2 pp.; LAC
May 15	Victor Samrock	Los Angeles	Tel; W
1946			
February 27	*Truckline Cafe* Company	[New York City]	ALs; 2 pp.; W
March 19	George Freedley		ALs; NYP
June 20	Peter Lindstrom	New York City	C; T
July 9	Walter Wanger	[New City]	C; W
July 25	John F. Wharton	[New City]	C; T
July 30	Barrett H. Clark		ALs; Y
August 21	Mrs. Frank E. Lindsay	[New York City]	AL; 2 pp.; W
August 26	Alexander Sandor Ince	[New City]	C; W
August 26	Arthur S. Lyons	[New City]	C; W
September 13	Terence Anderson	New York City	Tel; W
September 17	Lewis Milestone		C; W
September 17	Walter Wanger		C; W
September 18	Terence Anderson	[New York City]	Tel; W
October 23	Walter F. Doyle		C; W

Date	Recipient	Place of Composition	Type and Location of Original
October	William Herndon	[New City]	ALi; T
December 11	Stanley Reid	New City	C; T
December 11	Louise M. Sillcox	New City	C; T
1947			
[January, 1947]	Walter F. Doyle		ALi; W
January 10	Barbara Manton		C; W
January 18	Harold Anderson		ALs; 2 pp.; HA
February 1	Gertrude Anderson	New City	TLs; T
February 17	Archer Milton Huntington	[New York City]	TLs; SY
March 6	Margaret Mayorga		C; T
March 14	John F. Wharton	[New City]	TLs; JFW
March 20	Gus Lobrano		C; W
March 28	Victor Fleming	[New City]	C; T
March 28	Walter Wanger	[New City]	C; T
[Early April, 1947]	Victor Fleming		ALs*; T
[Early April, 1947]	Walter Wanger		AL; T
April	Elizabeth Lawrence	New City	ALi; T
May 7	Victor Samrock	Los Angeles	ALs; 2 pp.; W
May 8	Victor Samrock	Los Angeles	ALs; W
May 19	Victor Samrock	Los Angelse	ALs; 2 pp.; W
May 21	Victor Samrock	Los Angeles	Tel; W
May 26	Victor Samrock	Hollywood	ALs; 2 pp.; W
May 30	Victor Samrock	[Hollywood]	ALs; W
June 15	Harold Anderson	Hollywood	ALs; HA
August 7	Harold Anderson	[Hollywood]	ALs; HA
August 21	Dinsmore Alter	New City	C; T
September 29	John F. Wharton		C; 2 pp.; T
November 10	Lucy Mitchell	Athens (Greece)	Tel; W
1948			
January 7	Walter Wanger	[New City]	C; T
February 28	Editor, New York Times	New City	C; T
May 3	Dwight Griswold	New City	C; T

Date	Recipient	Place of Composition	Type and Location of Original
1949			
March 19	Archer Milton Huntington	New City	TLs; SY
April 7	Editor, *New York Times*		*Times*, April 10, sec. 4, p. 10, col. 6
April 14	Archer Milton Huntington	[New York City]	ALs: SY
1950			
March 22	Fred Ahlert	[New City]	C; W
March 22	H. J. Jelinek	[New City]	C; W
March 22	William Koppleman	[New City]	C; W
March 22	Albert Sirmay	[New City]	C; W
May 24	Theresa Helburn	New City	TLs; Y
June 15	Archer Milton Huntington	New City	TLs; SY
August 4	Lawrence Langner	[New City]	TLs; Y
August 4	Theodore Kritas	New City	C; T
August 4	Theresa Helburn	[New City]	TLs; Y
August 5	Ellen Violett	New City	C; T
August 15	Brooks Atkinson	New City	ALs; NYP
1951			
April 21	Elmer Rice		ALs; TR
May 14	John F. Wharton	[New York City]	ALs; JFW
June 30	John F. Wharton	New City	ALs; JFW
August 21	Rex Harrison	[New York City]	Tel; W
September 25	Archer Milton Huntington	[New York City]	ALs; SY
September 25	Leland Hayward		ALs; NYP
November 30	John T. Chapman	[New City]	C; W
November 30	William Yandell Elliott	[New City]	C; W
1952			
January 31	Roger L. Stevens	Los Angeles	Tel; W
October 7	John F. Wharton		ALs; JFW
1953			
June 15	Roger L. Stevens	Agoura	ALs; W

Date	Recipient	Place of Composition	Type and Location of Original
June 15	Victor Samrock	Agoura	ALs; W
June 22	John F. Wharton	Agoura	TLs; W
July 22	Victor Samrock	Los Angeles	Als; W
August 15	Victor Samrock	[Los Angeles]	ALs; W
August 29	Victor Samrock	Los Angeles	ALs; W
September 18	Victor Samrock	[Los Angeles]	ALs; 2pp.; W
October 18	Harold Anderson	Los Angeles	ALs; HA
November 5	Harold Anderson	[Los Angeles]	ALs; HA
November 21	John F. Wharton	Los Angeles	TC; 2 pp.;W
	Victor Samrock		ALs; W
1954			
January 27	John F. Wharton	Los Angeles	ALs; JFW
March 14	John F. Wharton	[Los Angeles]	ALs; JFW
March 17	John F. Wharton	[Los Angeles]	ALs; JFW
March 20	Lillian Anderson	[Los Angeles]	ALs; HA
August 14	Victor Samrock	[Los Angeles]	ALs; 2 pp.; W
August 16	John F. Wharton	[Los Angeles]	ALs; 2 pp.; JFW
[October, 1954]	Lee Petrasek	[New York City]	ALs; B
November [5]	Lela Chambers	[New York City]	ALs; LAC
December 1	Lela Chambers	Baltimore	ALs; 2 pp.; LAC
December 14	Theresa Helburn		ALs; Y
1955			
October 29	John F. Wharton	[New York City]	ALs; JFW
December 15	Harold and Lillian Anderson	Stamford	ALs; HA
1956			
February 13	Lela and Dan Chambers	Stamford	ALs; 2 pp.; LAC
February 27	Van Wyck Brooks	Stamford	ALs; P
March 4	John F. Wharton	[New York City]	ALs; 2 pp.; JFW
March 5	Roger L. Stevens	Stamford	ALs; W
April 11	John F. Wharton	Stamford	TC; W

Date	Recipient	Place of Composition	Type and Location of Original
April 23	John F. Wharton	[Stamford]	ALs; JFW
May 7	Harold Anderson	Stamford	ALs; 2 pp.; HA
October 9	Victor Samrock	[Stamford]	ALs; W
[1956]	Alfred Hitchcock	[Stamford]	ALs*; T
1957			
March 27	Donald Gallup	Stamford	ALs; 2pp; Y
[April] 1	Lela Chambers	Stamford	ALs; LAC
April 26	William Fields	Stamford	ALs; NYP
April 26	Donald Gallup	Stamford	ALs; Y
April 27	Donald Gallup	Stamford	ALs; Y
May 1	Donald Gallup	Stamford	ALs; Y
May 10	Walter Alford	Stamford	ALs; NYP
May 17	Victor Samrock	Stamford	ALs; W
May 17	Walter Alford	Stamford	ALs; NYP
June 6	Donald Gallup	Stamford	ALs; Y
June 6	Lela Chambers	Stamford	ALs; 2pp; LAC
September 7	Avery Chambers	[Stamford]	ALs; AC
September 11	Edward H. Davis	[Stamford]	ALs; W
September 19	John F. Wharton	Stamford	ALs; 2 pp.; JFW
1958			
February 28	Lela Chambers	Stamford	ALs; LAC
July 16	Lela Chambers	Stamford	ALs; 2 pp.; LAC
November 7	Lela Chambers	Stamford	ALs; LAC
Undated			
	Gertrude Anderson	[New City]	ALs; T
	Gertrude Anderson		ALs; T
	Gertrude Anderson		ALs; T
	Gertrude Anderson	Pittsburgh	ALs; T
	S. N. Behrman		ALs; SNB
	S. N. Behrman		ALs; SNB
	Mrs. Brown	New York City	ALs; PTA
	Richard H. Cordell	New York City	ALs; I
	Archer Milton Huntington	New York City	Tel; SY
	Miss Kanser	New City	ALs*; T

Date	Recipient	Place of Composition	Type and Location of Original
	Benjamin Kornzweig	New York City	ALs; NYP
	David Lingwell		ALs*; T
	Alfred Lunt		ALs*; T
	Alfred Lunt	New York City	Tel; W
	Guthrie McClintic	New York City	ALs; W
	Lewis Milestone	Sea Island	ALs*; T
	Lucy Mitchell		ALs; W
	Nick		ALs*; W
	Elmer Rice		ALs; TR
	Rowan		AL; T
	Victor Samrock		ALs; W
	Selective Service Board	New York City	ALi; T
	Robert F. Wagner	New York City	ALs*; W

INDEX

INDEX

138, 141, 144 (n. 3), 199–200; need control by writers, 205–6, 207–8; writing for, 311; prospect of, 315
Moses, John, 37
Mrs. Warren's Profession (Shaw), 247
Mumford, Lewis, 112 (no. 99, n. 1), 115 (no. 101, n. 1)
Muni, Paul, 81, 82 (n. 1*), 83, 88, 89, 99, 333
Munsell, Warren, 335
Munsey, Frank Andrew, 14
Murray, Amy, 18 (no. 15, n. 2)
Murrow, Edward R., 162, 165 (n. 5)
Muses' Darling, The (Norman), 235, 238 (n. 6)
Music: MA's interest in, 4
Musselman, Hazel M., 332
My Fair Lady (Lerner and Lowe), 314
My Own Story (Older): MA's interest in, 6
Myron Selznick, Inc., 33 (n. 1)

N
National Conference of Christians and Jews: gives Brotherhood Award to Lost in the Stars, 298–301
National theater, 122–24
National Theatre Conference, 81 (n. 1); and The Eve of St. Mark, 122–25, 297
Nazis, 81; and communists in war on civilization, 110
Negroes: outlines play about, 84–86; visits in army, 128; tragedy of, in America, 221
"Nets to Catch the Wind," xxxviii
Never Steal Anything Small, 263 (n. 4)
Nevins, Allan, 5 (n. 3), 310, 318 (n. 18)
New Deal, 98 (n. 2); opposition to, 90–91
New Era in American Poetry, The (Untermeyer), 12 (n. 1)
Newman, Robert, 79, 80 (no. 70, n. 1*)
New Musical Resources (Cowell), 4 (n. 1)
New Republic, xxxvi, xxxvii, 13, 14, 15, 18, 29, 306, 316 (n. 5); MA's experience on, 9, 309
New Theatre, The, 54
New Voices: An Introduction to Contemporary Poetry (Wilkinson), 5 (nn. 1, 2)
New Yorker, 187, 206, 214 (n. 1), 215
New York Globe and Commercial Advertiser, xxxvii, 13, 14 (n. 2), 18 (n. 2), 29, 305, 306, 308, 310
New York Herald Tribune, 218, 220 (n. 1), 223, 240, 259
"New York's Theatre," xl
New York Sun, 14, 22 (no. 20, n. 2)

New York Times, 240, 259, 284, 285 (no. 207, nn. 1, 2), 338, 339
New York World, xxxviii, xli, 20, 22 (no. 20, n. 2), 29, 238 (n. 1), 239, 306, 307, 310, 317 (nn. 9, 14, 15), 318 (n. 17); MA's time on, 308–9
Nicoll, Allardyce, 43; on Winterset, xvii; on Mary of Scotland, 43 (n. 2)
Night Over Taos, xliv, 36, 39, 40, 41 (n. 10), 49 (n. 1); textual problem in, 36 (no. 33, n. 2); Gertrude Anderson in, 322
"1908–1935 (For F. H. Koch)," xlvii
Nizer, Louis, 298
Nock, Albert Jay, 15 (n. 1)
"Noon in a Wood," xxxix
North Carolina, University of, 30 (n. 4), 128 (n. 1), 165 (n. 8)
North Dakota, University of, 29, 30 (n. 4), 304–5; awards MA honorary doctorate, lxx; student days at, 3, 78 (n. 1), 288–90
Northwestern University, 94 (no. 85, n. 1)
Norvelle, Lee: and The Eve of St. Mark, 122, 124*, 335
"Notes for a New Play," lvi
"Notes on a Dream," lxix
"Notes on Socrates," lxvi
No Time for Comedy (Behrman), 324
Novels, 222; loss of interest in, 195
November Hereabout (Murray): MA writes preface to, li
"Now Could I Trace the Passages Through Air," xlii
Noyes, Alfred, 12

O
Odets, Clifford, 54 (n. 1)
Oedipus the King: MA sees, lviii
Off Broadway, lx, 213 (n. 2), 232 (n. 1); MA on, 242
"Off Broadway": read at Rutgers, 115; textual history of, 116 (n. 2)
Office of War Information, 121 (n. 1), 129 (n. 1)
O'Hara, John, 116 (n. 2)
Older, Fremont, 6*
Old Maid, The (Akins), 294
Ondine (Giraudoux), 267, 268 (n. 3)
"One Future for American Poetry," xxxvii
O'Neil, George, 17
O'Neill, Eugene, 269
"On the Eve of War: A Recollection," xl, 317 (n. 8)
Opdycke, John B., 332
"Open Letter to Writers of Verse, An," xxxviii

THE AUTHOR

Laurence G. Avery, a Baylor graduate with an M.A. degree from the University of Michigan and a Ph.D. degree from the University of Texas, is associate professor of English at The University of North Carolina at Chapel Hill. He compiled *A Catalogue of the Maxwell Anderson Collection*, a bibliographical guide to Anderson's career.

THE BOOK

Text set in Photocomposition Sabon
Composition by The University of North Carolina Press

Printed on sixty-pound Olde Style by S. D. Warren Company, Boston, Massachusetts

Binding cloth by Holliston Mills, Inc., Norwood, Massachusetts

Printing and binding by Vail-Ballou Press, Inc., Binghamton, New York

Designed by Joyce Kachergis

Published by The University of North Carolina Press